D0646226

The End of the European Era
1890 to the Present

THE NORTON HISTORY OF MODERN EUROPE

General Editor: FELIX GILBERT, Institute for Advanced Study

The Foundations of Early Modern Europe, 1460–1559

EUGENE F. RICE, JR.

The Age of Religious Wars, 1559–1689

RICHARD S. DUNN

Kings and Philosophers, 1689–1789

LEONARD KRIEGER

The Age of Revolution and Reaction, 1789–1850

CHARLES BREUNIG

The Age of Nationalism and Reform, 1850–1890

NORMAN RICH

The End of the European Era, 1890 to the Present

FELIX GILBERT

The End of the European Era
1890 to the Present

FELIX GILBERT
Institute for Advanced Study

W · W · NORTON & COMPANY · INC · NEW YORK

FIRST EDITION

SBN 393 05413 6 (Cloth Edition)

SBN 393 09933 4 (Paper Edition)

Library of Congress Catalog Card No. 74–95536

ALL RIGHTS RESERVED
Published simultaneously in Canada
by George J. McLeod Limited, Toronto

Cartography by Harold K. Faye

PRINTED IN THE UNITED STATES OF AMERICA
1 2 3 4 5 6 7 8 9 0

Contents

Illustrations

Maps

Introduction

WHAT FOLLOWS IS the story of the twentieth century. In the terminology of historical science, this is "contemporary history." But this term immediately raises questions and doubts, because it often has been asserted that contemporary history cannot be considered a serious scholarly undertaking. The traditional argument against the pursuit of contemporary history is that nearness of the events in time makes access to vital documents impossible for the historian; the archives are still closed to him. Another argument bears particularly upon the history of the twentieth century: developments have come so fast, the geographical limits of history have been extended so widely, the problems of the various areas of history—political, economic, social, intellectual—have become so complex that, until the dust has settled and much monographic work has been done, no one can have sufficient control over the material to give a comprehensive account of the present century.

It would be a declaration of bankruptcy on the part of historical scholarship if the work of the historian stopped short of the most burning issues of the day. And there are good reasons why the objections against the writing of contemporary history should be rejected. The arguments take much too limited a view of the historian's work. Even if contemporary history cannot be written strictly according to the methods which are applied to the history of earlier centuries, this does not mean that contemporary history is not a scholarly undertaking; it means only that contemporary history has aims and methods of its own.

There is no lack of source material. The twentieth century has been an increasingly democratic age; political actions have been preceded by public debate or at least subjected to public scrutiny. It is possible to reconstruct, partly on the basis of newspapers and parliamentary debates, not only what happened but also why it happened. Moreover, since the two world wars, the archives of the foreign offices of some of the European powers and, in some cases, of all the government agencies have been opened. War-crime trials have brought many further official documents to light. Although the inaccessibility of eastern European, and particularly of Russian, archives remains a serious gap, no historian has ever possessed complete knowledge of all the relevant documents. In writing twentieth-century history the historian is in danger of suffocating in material rather than of being handicapped by scarcity.

The overabundance of material; the disappearance of clear boundaries among geographical regions; the great variety of political, social, technical, and ideological factors which enter into a decision—these indeed are difficulties in the writing of contemporary history. But they are not insuperable, though they do show that, in writing contemporary history, an historian cannot do everything; he must keep possibilities and limitations clearly in mind.

The following presentation of European twentieth-century history does not depict European life in all its aspects. Its primary aim is to make crowded and confused events comprehensible by organizing them clearly around the predominant trends of political change, with developments in other spheres taken up only insofar as they encroach upon or illuminate political events. For the period before the First World War the conflicts which industrialization and competition had produced in all the great European powers and the relation of these internal tensions to foreign policy become the focus of the narrative. For the interwar period the decline of European hegemony over the world, the attempts to restore some measure of European influence, and the failure of these attempts are central themes. For the period after the Second World War the transformation of political life under the impact of scientific discoveries and technological advances has emerged as the crucial issue; this is a transformation which placed the conduct of politics in the European countries in a new setting and which went far to erase the boundaries between Europe and the rest of the world. It sealed the end of the European era.

CHAPTER 1

The New Industrial Society

ONE AFTERNOON early in the twentieth century a member of the British aristocracy, a great landowner, stood with one of his guests on the terrace extending along the back of his large country house. In the valley at their feet lay farms, cottages, a railway, a colliery, and streets densely teeming with workingmen. Beyond the valley, a hill with another large country house at its top was visible. Pointing to this house the host said to his guest, "You see there is no one between us and them."

Eccentric as this gentleman may have been, his remark does express the feelings of people of his social standing and wealth at the beginning of the twentieth century. A great distance separated the upper classes from the working population. Social and economic differences and distinctions had always existed in European society, but in earlier centuries noble and peasant, wealthy patrician and small tradesman, ruler and ruled, rich and poor lived in a community which was an integrated whole. Economic inequality and dependence were complemented and mitigated by personal bonds. Servants knew their masters and the masters knew the men working for them.

However, since the end of the eighteenth century, industrialization and the growth of population had been steadily reducing the personal element in the relationship between the owning classes and their dependents, between employers and employees. The Industrial Revolution, which started in Great Britain and France, penetrated in the second part of the nineteenth century into central, southern, and eastern Europe. Competition accelerated industrialization. Most city dwellers became industrial workers living in quarters distant from the elegant and older parts of the cities. The big city was both an accompaniment and a result of industrialization. Without railroads, steamboats, and streetcars, without innovations in the building industry, without street lighting by gas and then by electricity, the assembling and maintenance of masses in cities would have been impossible. Industrialization made the distance which separated the possessing classes

1

from the proletariat more noticeable. Hotels became palaces; the rich could indulge in exotic foods and flowers brought by railroads from distant areas; their motorcars appeared on the roads; their private yachts cruised the Mediterranean and the North Sea.

At the end of the nineteenth century many people believed that the future would see a complete polarization of society. A small number of individuals would possess all wealth, while everyone else would become steadily more impoverished and more dependent. The assumption of an inevitable schism in society—a few wealthy men on the one hand and a mass of oppressed, poor people on the other—was the basic tenet of socialist theory. This view of the future was shared by many thoughtful observers. Pope Leo XIII spoke of the danger of such a polarization in the encyclical *Rerum novarum*, the first encyclical devoted to the problems of industrial society.

Actually, the fear that society would become polarized was exaggerated. Not all the members of the ruling group were immensely wealthy, and the concentration of wealth in the hands of a few was not proceeding as quickly as many around the turn of the century believed or feared. A large segment of society was neither very rich nor very poor. Although small independent entrepreneurs faced increasing difficulties in maintaining their ventures, members of the middle classes could make a satisfactory living as white-collar workers, as officials, or in the professions. But while the dividing line between the wealthy upper classes and the middle classes remained fluid, the distance between these groups and the fast-expanding industrial proletariat was wide and unbridgeable. Railroads had at least three classes, and sometimes four. The wealthiest people might travel first class, or even in their own private railroad cars, while their maids and valets traveled second class. But the well-to-do would never travel third class, and even the waiting rooms of the first and second classes were strictly separated from those of the third class; every contact was to be avoided. No less important than the divisions and conflicts between nations was this separation of the working classes from the other groups of society. Therefore, in order to understand what happened in Europe in the twentieth century, we must give close attention to its social divisions and class structure.

THE RULING GROUP IN EUROPE

Around the turn of the century the prevalent form of government in Europe was the monarchy. There were only two republics: France and Switzerland. The degree to which monarchical rulers possessed concrete political power varied. But whether or not they had sufficient power to exert real influence on state policy, the monarchs were justified in considering themselves the most important persons on the European political stage. In

A royal jamboree. *Among those present are King Edward VII of Great Britain (seated left) and standing behind him, the German Emperor William II. The Spanish King Alfonso XIII has his arm on the shoulder of the future King George V of Great Britain.*

each country the monarch was the apex of society, and the status of both individuals and groups was dependent on their relationship to the throne. Among themselves, royalty formed a kind of gigantic family which seemed to tie European society together into one great unit.

Members of ruling dynasties could marry only members of other ruling dynasties, unless they were willing to relinquish all their rights and status. At the beginning of the twentieth century even the members of the British royal family, who with the ruling monarch's permission might marry commoners, were for the most part married to members of princely families. Religion somewhat separated the dynasties into two groups. Almost all of the Catholic princes were related to the Habsburgs and the Bourbons. The Protestant ruling families, into which the Eastern Orthodox rulers, particularly the Russian tsars, also liked to marry, were tied together through the numerous small German dynasties, which provided marriageable princes and princesses for almost any contingency. In the nineteenth century the remarkable fertility of the admirable couple Victoria and Albert had bound the Protestant rulers still more tightly together. Thus the British king, Edward VII, was the uncle both of the German emperor, William II, and of the wife of the Russian tsar, Nicholas II. The birthdays, weddings, and funerals of monarchs were not only state occasions but also family reunions. It was natural that at the wedding of the daughter of William II in 1912 the tsar and tsarina of Russia and the king and queen of England would come to Berlin, and that almost all of Europe's rulers would be present at the funeral of Queen Victoria in 1901 and of her son Edward VII in 1910.

After the death of Queen Victoria the oldest ruling monarch in Europe was the Emperor Francis Joseph of Austria-Hungary, born in 1830, who had

The funeral procession of Queen Victoria. *King Edward VII leads the entourage, followed by the German Emperor William II.*

ascended the throne in 1848. He was venerated as a kind of patriarch by all the rulers and his seventieth birthday in 1900, his eightieth in 1910, and the sixtieth jubilee of his reign in 1908 were all occasions for royal meetings. Visits among cousins were frequent. The German emperor often met with the tsar. Edward VII, in order to lose weight and to remain in shape for the gastronomic feats which he loved, regularly visited the spa of Marienbad, and when he passed through Germany on his way, it would have been impolite for him not to arrange a meeting with his nephew, William II, though there was little love between them. On their travels the monarchs were accompanied by high officials, and unavoidably, political subjects were discussed. Most of all, this network of princely relations and connections gave the monarchs a feeling of solidarity against the common danger of revolution, although, as the First World War would show, this feeling of standing together against a common danger did not guarantee peace.

The monarchs were also the leaders of the society in their respective countries. In holding court they reinforced a traditional hierarchy and determined its order by giving titles and decorations and by receiving or excluding people according to the standards of the crown. That the

monarchy fulfilled the function of guaranteeing the existence of an established order was the view not only of its adherents but of the enemies of the existing system, the advocates of revolution, as well. For them the monarchs were an important target. Although attacks on the lives of the princely heads of state were fewer than in the 1870's and 1880's the monarchs were still on the firing line in the first two decades of the twentieth century. In 1900, King Humbert of Italy was assassinated. In 1906, at the wedding of the king of Spain, an assassination attempt was made which had many victims although the king and his bride escaped. In 1908 the king of Portugal and his oldest son were killed. In June, 1914, a Serbian nationalist killed the heir to the Habsburg throne, the Archduke Francis Ferdinand. This assassination precipitated the outbreak of the First World War.

The existence of a monarchy presupposed the existence of a ruling group closely connected with the throne. In the eighteenth century the princes of continental Europe had become absolute by gaining direct control of the armed forces and by allying themselves with the landowning nobility. This alliance of the monarchs with the army and the landed aristocracy lasted into the twentieth century. Although by that time an elected parliament had become an influential factor in politics, the arbiter of social status remained the court, with its officialdom of ministers, chamberlains, masters of ceremonies—all nobles and mostly descendants of the oldest families. The monarchs kept up their special closeness to the army by insisting on a voice in the promotion of officers. Moreover, the monarchs stood in particularly intimate relation to certain regiments—the guard regiments. These were stationed in or near the capital, and in them the heirs of the throne and other princes received their military education. The officers of these regiments, almost exclusively the sons of aristocratic families, were among the few who were on familiar terms with members of the royal families. Thus in the monarchy a landed aristocracy with military values and a military code of honor continued to set the social standard.

The eminence of a landed aristocracy, which had been justified by the economic and political conditions of previous centuries, seemed an anomaly in the twentieth century, when industry and commerce became dominating factors in economic life. The heads of the large banks, the owners and managers of the great industrial enterprises, were the creators of the prosperity and power of a nation. But even in those countries in which industrialization was most advanced, agriculture still retained an important place in the economy. To be sure, it was losing ground to industry and commerce. Despite a steady population increase, the number of people in agriculture remained stable. Nevertheless—with the exception of Great Britain—in northern and western Europe about 50 per cent of the population still followed agricultural pursuits during the first decades of the

The assassination attempt on King Alfonso. *The bomb had been thrown at the wedding procession of the Spanish king on May 31, 1906.*

twentieth century. And in the Balkans and in eastern Europe this figure was around 70 per cent. Moreover, in many parts of Europe the possessor of a large landed estate was still very wealthy. Although the Dohnas, an old noble family with vast estates in East Prussia, were not as rich as the Krupps, the great armament manufacturers of the Ruhr, they were still among the richest families of Germany. The estates of the Esterházy and Károlyi families in Hungary yielded incomes which permitted them to indulge themselves in every luxury resort of Europe. The fabulous wealth of the Russian aristocracy came from agriculture. A Prince Yussupoff even as a teen-ager traveled in his special train through Europe. Moreover, many of the aristocrats had lands on which coal, the most precious raw material of that time, was discovered and mined. Lord Derby, of the Stanley family, in England, the princes Pless and Henckel-Donnersmarck in Germany, the Hohenlohes in Bohemia were landowners and industrialists at the same time. Moreover, in France, Italy, and Germany the cultivation of vineyards and the installation of breweries yielded the owners of landed estates an income often equal to that of the great bankers and captains of industry.

There remained differences, however, between the industrial and agricultural sectors of European society, and these differences were most clearly reflected in the bourgeois advocacy of free trade and the aristocratic demand for tariffs. Moreover, the less well-situated members of the nobility looked with envy and disdain on the increasing wealth of the bourgeoisie. The owners of smaller industrial enterprises usually retained many of the antiaristocratic views of the early nineteenth century, when the bourgeoisie had been struggling against the Old Regime. Yet, between the upper strata of the landed aristocracy and the wealthiest members of the industrial and commercial society there were many links; and gradually these two elements came to be joined together in a single ruling group. The monarchs furthered this process by receiving the important personages of the commercial and industrial world at court and giving them titles, ennobling such bankers and industrialists as the Rothschilds, the Sassoons, and Ernest Cassel in Great Britain, the Krupps and the Siemenses in Germany, the Rothschilds and the Gutmanns in Austria, the Franchettis in Italy. The manner and the extent of the amalgamation into the ruling classes of these two—the old landed aristocracy and the new leaders of the commercial and industrial world—varied in the different European countries. But generally the business class became closely tied to the policies of their governments. Authoritarian concepts and aristocratic mores and interests pervaded the thinking and the aims of the owners and managers of industry. And the dominance among them of this point of view hardened the tensions and conflicts within an industrial society.

A preindustrial, antimodern element persisted in the European society of the early twentieth century. The code of honor of the nobility—its duels, its concern for rank and for gentlemanly behavior—the social preeminence of the military profession, and the prestige of the life of leisure, along with a certain contempt for moneymaking activities, were characteristic of the period. Symbolic was the importance of the horse in this society. It would be reasonable to assume that in a technical and industrial age the horse, previously important for agriculture, transport, and war, would become obsolete. But horse racing remained the most elegant sport, and its great events were honored by the presence of royalty. Establishing a stable of race horses was the surest way for a wealthy man to advance into the upper strata of society. Admission to membership in the jockey clubs, founded for the promotion of horse racing, was a sign of having entered the Upper Ten Thousand, as the ruling group was called. In the armies the guard-cavalry regiments were the most elegant: the blue-and-red tunics and the helmets with drooping horsehair plumes of the English Royal Horse Guards, the black caps with death's-heads and the fur-trimmed jackets of the Prussian "black" hussars, the light-blue coats and the golden froggings of the Austrian imperial chasseurs—these were the uniforms of the cream of the European armies. In all Europe, cavalry regiments were maintained in a strength hardly compatible with the changes in warfare which the technical age required and strategic thinkers envisaged. Soon after the First World War had started, the uselessness of these trappings became obvious. Colorful uniforms were replaced by drab gray; horses bred and trained for the cavalry were left behind and cavalrymen had to fight as foot soldiers.

THE WORKERS

In previous centuries a number of social groups—household servants, serfs and half-free peasants, craftsmen, artisans—had formed the economically weakest class of society, but at the end of the nineteenth century the lowest stratum was made up of the industrial workers—the proletariat. The manpower required by industry had to be housed in the cities near the factories. Whereas few effects of industrialization could be seen in the countryside in the years before the First World War, immense changes took place in urban life. The population of most of the existing cities increased and new urban centers developed. In Great Britain and France, where the Industrial Revolution had started more than a hundred years earlier, the rate of urban growth began to slow down by the end of the nineteenth century. Nevertheless, Greater London grew from five million inhabitants in 1880 to seven million in 1914; Paris, from two million to almost three million. Cities in those countries which entered the industrial age in the fifty years before the First World War grew even more strikingly. Berlin, with about 500,000 inhabitants in 1866, had more than two million in 1914. Barcelona and Milan, the industrial capitals of Spain and Italy, both surpassed the half-million figure by 1914. Most significant was the rise in population and the growth of urban settlements in the great coal- and iron-mining districts. In northern France, Lille doubled its population between 1850 and 1914. In 1914 Lille had 200,000 inhabitants and the population in neighboring cities so increased that northeastern France began to form one megalopolis. The same phenomenon could be observed in Germany in the Ruhr area, where Essen, Gelsenkirchen, Bochum, and Mülheim began to run into each other, and in the coal-mining districts of upper Silesia around Kattowitz. Russia entered the industrialization race last. But the urban development was rapid. In 1863 Russia had only three cities with more than 100,000 inhabitants. Forty years later there were more than fifteen. Around the coal and iron-ore mines of the Donetz Basin and in the oil areas of the Caucasus densely populated districts were formed.

In Great Britain people continued to live in small one-family houses, but numerous families were herded into houses which had been built for one family, and became slums. In other countries workers were housed in large apartment buildings four to six floors high, each floor containing five or six apartments. Built side by side with no intervening space, centered around small dark courtyards, these buildings had no gardens, no green areas, and even the streets were treeless.

Factories were generally tall structures without adequate air and light. Working conditions usually improved after the first cruel years of the beginning of industrialization. But even at best sanitary conditions in the

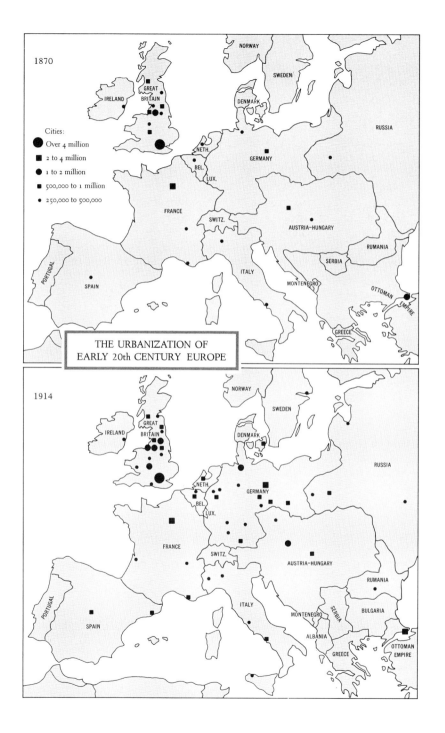

1870

NORWAY

SWEDEN

IRELAND

GREAT
BRITAIN

DENMARK

RUSSIA

NETH.

BEL.

LUX.

GERMANY

Cities:

Over 4 million

2 to 4 million

1 to 2 million

500,000 to 1 million

250,000 to 500,000

FRANCE

SWITZ.

AUSTRIA–HUNGARY

RUMANIA

SERBIA

PORTUGAL

SPAIN

ITALY

MONTENEGRO

OTTOMAN
EMPIRE

GREECE

THE URBANIZATION OF
EARLY 20th CENTURY EUROPE

1914

NORWAY

SWEDEN

IRELAND

GREAT
BRITAIN

DENMARK

RUSSIA

NETH.

BEL.

LUX.

GERMANY

FRANCE

SWITZ.

AUSTRIA–HUNGARY

RUMANIA

PORTUGAL

SPAIN

ITALY

MONTENEGRO

SERBIA

BULGARIA

ALBANIA

OTTOMAN
EMPIRE

GREECE

factories were appalling and little was done to ensure the safety of the workers from occupational hazards. Safety precautions, particularly in the coal mines, were disastrously unsatisfactory. In Russia, Italy, and Spain there were no laws against the employment of children or women, nor were their working conditions different from those for adult men. Economic crises, frequent dismissal of workers, and a considerable rate of unemployment were regarded as unavoidable. There was no provision for these recurring periods of hardship, and wages were so low that the workers were unable to accumulate savings to fall back on. In the oil fields of the Caucasus, workers like young Iosif Vissarionovich Dzhugashvili, who later would take the name of Stalin, were imprisoned in barracks for eight hours during the night and worked during the day supervised by armed police. The young Aneurin Bevan, after the Second World War one of the inspiring leaders of the British Labor party, grew up in the misery of a Welsh coal-mining village. One of his brothers was killed in what Bevan was always to regard as an avoidable mine accident, and his mother died of starvation. A picture of life in a worker's house, of the desperate struggles of mothers for food for their children, of the lack of medical care, of the men's escape into drunkenness, of the recruitment of teen-agers for work in the mines is given by D. H. Lawrence in his novel *Sons and Lovers* (1913). This British writer, with his message of a free life, grew up amidst the collieries of a midland mining village.

People living under such conditions were naturally inclined to regard with hostility the world which permitted such misery. Realizing their economic and social weakness, many workers placed their hope in organizing themselves and formed trade unions in the expectation that unified action would improve their common lot. In the 1890's the trade-union movement began to make great strides, and by 1905 the British unions, which had developed earlier than those on the Continent, had more than three million members; in Germany one and a half million workers were unionized; and in France, one million. These figures sound impressive; actually not even 25 per cent of the adult industrial workers in these countries belonged to unions. Nevertheless, the trade unions benefited the entire working population because employers gradually were forced to provide better conditions if they wanted to keep their workers.

The main activities of the trade unions were directed toward improving the material situation of the workers by collective bargaining, by granting financial assistance to strikers when negotiations failed, by collecting benefit funds with which the unemployed, the sick, and the aged could be supported. But unions also attempted to equip the workers for the struggle for social betterment. They organized training schools, they set up educational courses, they arranged holiday excursions. They made the lives of the workers more meaningful, liberating them from a sense of helpless isolation.

It was soon noticed that the trade unions exerted considerable influence on the minds of the workers. Ministers and priests became aware of the extent to which these organizations were successfully competing with the churches. Many Catholics, among them the bishop of Mainz, Wilhelm von Ketteler, in Germany, and Albert de Mun in France, realized that if the Church was to maintain any influence among the broad masses, it would have to introduce an active social program. In his encyclical *Rerum novarum* (1891), Pope Leo XIII expressed approval of the attempts to form Christian trade unions. Although the Catholic trade unions never were as powerful as the "free" trade unions, they became a significant political and social factor in Germany and Austria.

Yet the existence of trade unions was by no means secure. They had to fight for recognition, which they achieved only slowly and gradually: in Great Britain between 1870 and 1876, in France in 1884, in Germany after 1890. In some countries only local trade unions or trade unions for particular industrial activities were permitted. In Russia trade unions remained illegal until 1906. Few countries recognized the right of collective bargaining. Strikes and picketing were frequently prohibited. Since the activities by which the trade unions tried to improve the lot of their members met with only limited success, many workers came to feel that a real improvement of their situation required a change in the entire political system: action in the economic sphere had to be complemented by action in the political sphere. Many trade-union leaders shared this view and took a leading role in political movements that attempted to organize the workers for revolution.

The last quarter of the nineteenth century saw the formation in almost all European countries of political parties which called themselves socialist or social democratic. These parties shared the main tenets of the political creed which Karl Marx (1818–1883) had formulated. Before the First World War the most powerful socialist party was the German Social Democratic party. Its program, named after Erfurt, the town where it was adopted in 1891, was written with the cooperation of the aged Friedrich Engels (1820–1895), Marx's friend and collaborator. The Erfurt Program, which became the model for the programs of all the European socialist parties, was based on a few clear and simple tenets. Fundamental was the Marxist assumption that every society consisted of classes determined by economic interests, and every political struggle was actually a struggle between different economic classes. Thus, no improvement of the economic situation of the workers could be expected without a political revolution in which the workers would wrest power from the capitalist ruling group. Then the means of production would fall into the hands of the proletariat; private property would be replaced by common possession of all goods; and the results of labor could be distributed to the benefit of all. Everyone would receive according to his needs.

"Dangerous Enemies of Society." *This picture was taken in 1910 at the Annual Congress of the German Social Democratic Party. The man sitting in the center is Karl Liebknecht, one of the prominent Socialists, who in 1918 became leader of the most radical wing and was assassinated in 1919.*

These developments were presented not as a desirable utopia but as the sequence of events which scientific investigation showed to be necessary and inevitable. Marxists believed that under capitalism wealth was becoming increasingly concentrated among fewer and fewer people, and therefore more and more people were being pushed down into the proletariat. Consequently, because fewer people would have the means to buy goods and to stimulate the economy, the economic crises which were considered to be inherent in the capitalist system would become progressively more frequent and severe. However, the Marxists urged the workers not to stand idly by waiting for the final crisis and the collapse of capitalism. The capitalists would defend themselves by force, so the workers had to strive for a position from which they could seize power. They were to work for a democratization of political life in capitalist society in order to undermine the existing state and to defeat the last stand of capitalism. Since capitalism dominated the world, its overthrow presupposed an international revolution. In 1889 the socialist parties of all countries therefore formed an alliance, called the International, and representatives from these parties met regularly. Although the decisions of the International were recommendations only and not binding on the individual socialist parties, the International did create the impression of a great supranational force working toward a single goal.

The socialist doctrine had obvious attractions for the workers who lived as outsiders in prewar society. But the doctrine had inner contradictions. If society had to be entirely transformed, was it meaningful to work for its democratization? If the collapse of capitalism was historically inevitable, what were the reasons for forming political parties and for undertaking a political struggle? These contradictions became the more puzzling because the actual political and economic situation in the prewar years did not develop according to the Marxian scheme. Economic crises did not become more frequent or more serious. Indeed, no serious economic crisis arose between 1890 and 1914. And although a number of economic recessions occurred, in general there was an upward trend in the standard of living on the Continent. By 1900 the wages of skilled workers were almost double those of unskilled workers, and the skilled workers were able to accumulate some reserves.

The growth of socialist parties and of trade unions led to the creation of large bureaucratic apparatuses. They employed numerous officers; they acquired publishing houses and newspapers; some of their leaders were elected to parliaments. Consequently, many party and trade-union officers became more interested in keeping their organizations alive than in risking their existence by political action. Some socialists suggested that evolution rather than revolution was the way to socialism. Since the workers would slowly become a majority, it might be possible, they thought, to achieve the transition to socialism gradually, by a democratic process. The originator of this theory was a German socialist, Eduard Bernstein (1850–1932), who had been impressed by improvements in the situation of the working classes in Great Britain during the nineteenth century. Revisionism, as the movement was called, was particularly influential in Great Britain and Germany, countries with highly developed industrial systems, where the workers received some of the benefits of economic progress. In Spain, France, and Russia, where industrialization was still in its infancy, and where the governments looked with disfavor upon demands of the workers which might retard the process of industrialization, socialists rejected the entire doctrine of Revisionism. In the meetings of the International, the views of the Revisionists were debated, but they never became official socialist doctrine. The demand for revolution was maintained.

THE MIDDLE CLASSES

"Middle classes" is a useful but tricky term. In European society a large number of people belonged neither to the upper strata nor to the proletariat, and for the characterization of this group "middle classes" seems literally correct and appropriate. But it is difficult to find common concerns and common aims among those who were neither noble nor workers. In

The middle classes reveling at the beach in the first summer of the twentieth century.

preindustrial Europe this segment of society had usually possessed a considerable degree of economic independence. Engaging in commerce or in the trades, the merchants, artisans, and shop owners had recognized their common economic bond and frequently had shared a common political outlook. But the homogeneity of the middle classes was shattered by industrialization. Industrialization favored concentration and bigness in economic life; it became increasingly difficult for the middle classes to maintain a moderate degree of economic independence. Some shop owners and artisans, of course, succeeded in adjusting to the times; they developed their trade or business into a small factory or chain stores. Over some shops, particularly those of a wine merchant or a butcher or a greengrocer, signs still proclaimed ownership in the same family extending over several centuries, but such cases became increasingly rare. In most countries the small family-owned business sooner or later was changed into a joint-stock company or absorbed by the larger companies working in the same field. The directors or managers of large factories and banks had higher incomes than the owners of small enterprises struggling to remain independent. Thus the economic basis of the middle classes was thoroughly changed. The independent small entrepreneur disappeared or was pushed down to the lower levels of the economic scale. The leaders of the great industrial and commercial enterprises could no longer be regarded as members of the middle classes; they had become part of the ruling group. Even the salaried managers and directors just below the top business leaders were highly paid, and a wide gap separated them from their employees, the white-collar workers.

Because of the white-collar workers, the middle group of society remained numerically strong, and its ranks have steadily increased in the course of the twentieth century. White-collar workers were in demand not only in commerce and industry but in the modern industrial state, which needed the services of an expanding bureaucracy. As the population grew, more and more post-office and railroad employees, police officers, administrators, and civil servants were required. Similarly, the need rose for members of the so-called free professions—doctors, lawyers, teachers. Increased demand made these professions so attractive and rewarding that they quickly became overcrowded. As supply outraced demand, wide differences in financial position appeared within the professional groups. The great corporation and criminal lawyers and the renowned medical specialists had very high incomes; many lawyers and doctors, however, had to scrape by on meager earnings.

Thus, the middle group in society was composed of people of different callings and of greatly varying economic status. Some were wealthy or at least well off; others had not much more than a minimum subsistence. Some could still consider themselves independent, but most were employees whose opportunities were closely tied to changes in the economic situation. To them the uncertainties of economic life made dependence a concrete reality.

The members of the middle group varied in more than their economic status, however; they also lacked a common intellectual bond. Their divergent interests created great differences in outlook and education. Until far into the nineteenth century men engaging in economic activities had not needed higher education; the universities had served to train the relatively limited number of doctors, lawyers, ministers, teachers, and civil servants. But because industrial society required highly trained specialists— economists, engineers, chemists—the content of higher education underwent a change. Secondary schools introduced programs concentrating on natural science and modern languages; in the universities emphasis began to shift away from a general education in arts and letters, toward scientific training and technical instruction; technical colleges were founded which, like the universities, received the right to grant higher degrees. Philosophers and historians no longer dominated the universities as they had in the early and middle decades of the nineteenth century. The most prominent and admired figures were the great scientific discoverers—men like Helmholtz, Pasteur, Lister.

Because of the instruction provided in the natural sciences, in economics, and technology, university training and a university degree were of the greatest practical use to the members of the middle classes. The wealthy upper group of the leaders of industrial and commercial life was small and entry into their circle was difficult, but it was not impossible. The best, almost the only, means for economic and social advancement was the possession of special knowledge and techniques. And these could only be acquired at a university or technical college. Middle-class parents were naturally eager to give their sons these educational opportunities, but only the relatively affluent could afford the preparatory schools and universities. Despite the value of the university degree the number of those who enjoyed a higher education remained small; statistics from the year 1913 show that in the various countries of Europe before the First World War the number of university students among each ten thousand of the population ranged between seven and eleven.

Disparity of economic status, interests, and education resulted in divergent political aims. In the eighteenth and the first half of the nineteenth century the members of the middle classes were united in their struggle for a legal and constitutional order which would end the economic and political privileges of the nobility, give protection against arbitrary rule by the monarch, and permit the people some influence in the government. As the nineteenth century wore on, members of the middle classes for the most part continued to believe that the status and rights of the individual had to be protected by law, that no legal order was secure unless it was embedded in a fundamental law or constitution, and that the best guarantee of the maintenance of the constitution was the existence of an elected parliament with some control over the government. In the 1890's the condemnation of Captain Alfred Dreyfus in France in secret military-court proceedings, and in the following decade the execution of the anarchist Francisco Ferrer in Spain without sufficient proof of his participation in revolutionary activities, aroused an excitement all over the western world that reflected the tenacity of such ideas.

Openly and consciously few members of the middle classes doubted the validity of a basically liberal outlook. But, leaders of big business, independent entrepreneurs, dependent employees, small shopkeepers, officials, men of the free professions held differing views on such fundamental questions as the right of the state to intervene in economic affairs, the need for protection of the economically weak and helpless, and the desirability of extending parliamentary powers. What at the beginning of the nineteenth century had been a unified liberal movement at the end of the century started to fragment in most countries, and a number of new liberal parties were formed—some of them tending more to the right, others more to the left. These political divisions not only weakened liberalism as a political force but also opened the door to the acceptance of notions and policies which undermined the tenets of the faith which the older middle-class generation had held.

All the political parties representing the interests of the middle class felt themselves to be sharply separated from the socialists. The socialist attack on private property united the various nonsocialist groups—disparate in their status or interests though they might be—in self-defense; hostility against the proletariat was a common trait of the rest of capitalist society—of the bourgeoisie. Nowhere was this hostility greater than among those of the bourgeoisie whose economic situation was precarious. The more the members of the middle class lost their economic independence, the more they were inclined to stress their superiority over the working man. Thus the door was opened for the acceptance of ideas which were in stark contradiction to the original liberal belief in the equality and dignity of all men.

Thinking in terms of racial differences began to gain importance in this period. Racism often took the form of anti-Semitism, and indeed anti-Semitism, not as the social attitude of individuals but as a political movement, gained a certain mass appeal in these years. Racism also underlay the acceptance of the notion that birth or race made one segment of society superior to others; this view rationalized the exclusion of large groups—like the workers—from the right to participate in government. Differences in social status were believed to follow from natural selection, from having "better blood"; the existence of a ruling group, of an elite, in every society was not an accident, but a natural necessity.

Doubts were voiced as to whether the masses could be trusted and whether full democracy, in which every citizen had the same vote and the majority ruled, was the best form of government. Movements for extending the franchise slowed down; and there was little inclination to limit the powers of the upper houses of parliaments, whose members generally gained their seats either by heredity or by weighted elections in which the wealthier classes preserved control. The march of democracy seemed to falter.

The most striking break with liberal tenets occurred in the economic realm. Originally the middle classes had wanted to keep the government out of this sphere, but in the latter part of the nineteenth century their attitude changed. One of the links which brought government and industry together was the armament industry. Commissions for the production of guns or the building of warships were eagerly sought by heavy industry. Armament. manufacturers wanted steady orders from their own governments. Hence, steel and coal industrialists often became allied with those elements of society which were wedded to the expansion of the military. Moreover, the great armament concerns—Krupp in Germany, Schneider-Creusot in France, Skoda in Austria—were anxious to sell their goods all over the world. They frequently needed government support because they were unable to expand their businesses without protection against foreign competitors. In the last quarter of the nineteenth century most states hesitantly and gradually turned away from free trade and introduced protective tariffs. Customs walls rose, closing nations off from their neighbors.

As a result of these developments, nationalism acquired a new explosive and aggresive character. In the first half of the nineteenth century the expression of nationalism and the demands for national unification were part of a broad liberal political program; it was assumed that, united by their belief in the same human values, the various national states would harmoniously live together as one great family. But with the weakening of the faith in liberalism and democratization, nationalism served to emphasize what was unique and different in each nation rather than what was common to them and bound them together.

By the turn of the century nationalism had become a divisive force, and racism was a factor not only in domestic, but also in foreign policy. The idea of Europe as a community lost its appeal. If nations looked for outside support they considered as their "natural" allies those of the same "race." The views on the nature and importance of racial differences had no scientific basis; they were a myth, built of crude observations and prejudices. Still, they had a significant political influence. Frenchmen and Italians advocated closer ties between their countries because they were "Latin sisters," the only true heirs of the classical tradition. Germans, Englishmen, and Americans felt themselves to belong together because they came from the same "superior" Teutonic stock. Cecil Rhodes (1853–1902) left in his will a fund for endowing scholarships for Germans and Americans at Oxford in order to establish closer relations among the elite of the three "Germanic" nations. In this period the "pan" movements flourished; they aimed at establishing cooperation among "all" people of the same race, wherever they might live. At the congresses of these "pan" movements, vehement protests against the oppression of racial brethren by foreign governments were issued and the various states were urged to undertake policies which would unite all the members of the same race in a great federation. The statesmen of the day were less impressed by the concept of "natural" allies than the masses, and the practical effects of the "pan" movements should not be overestimated, but some of them did work as strong pressure groups. Pan-Slavism, for example, forced the Russian government into an aggressive foreign policy.

The situation was paradoxical. Europe dominated the world more than ever before or ever after. But the forces which held European society together had become increasingly tenuous. The mass of the working population had no part in the government and believed in an internationalism encompassing the whole world and extinguishing all national boundaries. At the other end of the social hierarchy, royalty and aristocracy still formed a supranational element united by personal relationships and a common style of life. But the most important constituents in the social life of the period, the industrial and commercial groups, became more and more closely tied to the national state and placed their hopes on its strength and on its support in the competition against others. Thus, industrialization increased rather than diminished tensions among the great powers.

FOREIGN AFFAIRS

In all the countries of Europe diplomacy was by tradition an aristocratic profession. Even in France, where after the establishment of the republic the aristocracy refrained from participation in the government or in politics, members of the nobility continued to pursue diplomatic careers. Because diplomats were accredited to the head of the state and closely connected with the court, there was justification for the aristocratic monopoly in diplomacy. Furthermore, diplomacy was an expensive career and could be afforded only by those belonging to the wealthiest stratum of the nobility. Usually diplomats—as members of the landowning classes—were more closely connected with the agrarian part of economic life than with the industrial and commercial sectors.

Tradition, therefore, was a powerful force in the practice and the assumptions of European diplomacy before 1914. The world of states was regarded as a hierarchy with seven great powers at its summit: Great Britain, France, Italy, Spain, Germany, Austria-Hungary, and Russia. The highest rank in the diplomatic profession was that of ambassador, and this title was reserved for those diplomats of great powers who served at the courts of other great powers. In its forms and ceremonials, in its ideas and assumptions, diplomacy remained wedded to the traditions of former centuries. Most of the diplomats who advanced to high positions in the period before the First World War had received their training under the great masters of nineteenth-century diplomacy: Bismarck in Germany, Gorchakov in Russia, Disraeli in Great Britain, Cavour in Italy, and Andrássy in Austria-Hungary. Diplomats in the early twentieth century held firmly to the ideas which had dominated diplomatic thinking in the two previous centuries: balance of power and *raison d'état*. They believed in a "concert of Europe," which really meant that the smaller nations were coerced into carrying out what the great powers had agreed upon among themselves. Without openly acknowledging it, the great powers still assumed the right of intervention propounded a century earlier by Prince Metternich. They did not subscribe to the principle of national self-determination, for it threatened to lead to a disturbance of the balance of power.

But the traditional concepts no longer corresponded to the situation which had developed in industrialized Europe. The states which were numbered among the great powers were in truth very unequal in strength. For instance, Spain, which had rightly enjoyed the distinction of being a great power up to the end of the eighteenth century, had become an almost negligible element in the balance of power by the beginning of the twentieth century. For at this time the political strength of a state was dependent on the extent of its industrialization.

The intimate relationship between industrial development and political

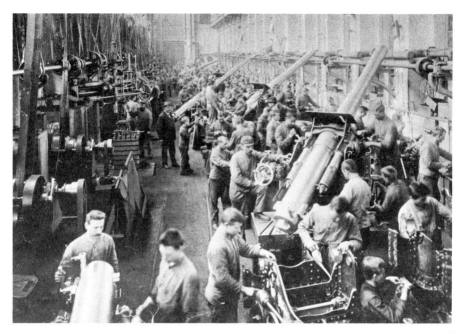

The Krupp gun factory in Essen in 1904.

strength was particularly evident in the military sphere. The processes which Alfred Nobel had invented for the development of explosives were applied to small caliber weapons, particularly machine guns, and to new models of heavy long-range artillery. On the sea ironclad ships replaced the older wooden vessels and increased in strength, size, and mobility. The new armaments could be produced on a sizable scale only in a country which had developed a modern industrial apparatus and possessed or could obtain the necessary raw materials. Moreover, speed in the mobilization of mass armies, on which military success was believed to depend, could be achieved only if there existed a well-developed railroad system. The military establishment thus became an integral part of industrial society and encroached upon the freedom of action of the diplomats in a way of which they seem to have been almost unaware.

The distinction between mobilization and war became increasingly difficult in the industrial age. Whereas in the preindustrial age a country could mobilize its troops, march them to the frontier, and stop them there, now mobilization and war became almost identical. For the mobilization and the deployment of mass armies a timetable had to be established well in advance, and once the military plans had been worked out, last-minute modifications could not be made without leading to chaos. In the crisis of 1914 almost all the European states were bound to military plans worked out many years before and to the arrangements with other powers which had been set up by their military staffs. But no country had coordinated its diplomatic strategy and its military planning. Political leaders were shocked to discover how restricted their freedom of action was. They all seemed to have believed that, as in earlier times, mobilization and military action could be turned on and off at a moment's notice.

Diplomacy was also modified and limited by the pressures of popular interest in the making and conduct of foreign policy. As illiteracy was steadily reduced, and in some countries almost entirely eliminated, newspapers gained in circulation and in influence. Both newspapers and the newer forms of communication—telegraph, telephone, photography—bridged distances and gave events in foreign and distant lands concreteness and immediacy. The popular media often placed special emphasis on the exploits of men of their audience's own nation. People followed breathlessly the expeditions into darkest Africa, full of pride if their own countrymen made new discoveries; the attempts to reach the North and South Poles became competitions of nation against nation. In the race to the North Pole the Americans Peary and Cook were pitted against the Norwegian Amundsen, and Amundsen made the race to the South Pole against the British explorer Scott. Scott's notes, found after his death in the Antarctic, give an affecting picture of the suffering and heroism involved in these enterprises in which scientific curiosity, romanticism, and national pride were strangely combined. Seeing the flag of his own nation implanted in the polar snow or flying among the palm trees of an island in the South Seas filled the common man with pride. The prestige of one's country became a popular concern, and diplomacy could not remain aloof from this national competitiveness. Even those diplomats who did not share these sentiments were aware that they could not ignore them. In the quest for national prestige, diplomats became anxious to achieve resounding successes without regard for the lasting hostility which temporary triumphs might arouse.

The popular concern with international affairs was effectively used by economic interest groups to exert pressure on the direction of foreign policy. By means of newspapers and other communications media they aroused public attention to their causes and created active propaganda lobbies. Thus industrialists and naval officers might unite to found a naval league; others might create organizations for colonial propaganda. Manufacturers and landowners might form societies to promote their particular interests and obtain popular backing. Neither political parties nor governments were able to keep free from such influences and entanglements.

The most popular cry was for overseas expansion. Every great European state wanted to become a "world power." At the beginning of the twentieth century, this phrase dazzled even cool and critical minds. The demand that one's nation should become a world power reflected simultaneously the heated climate of national competitiveness and the pressures of industrial and commercial interests. Bound by the idea of their race's superiority, European diplomats in their forays into the non-European world sought success and prestige rather than concrete advantages. Their lack of feeling for their limitations induced a ruthlessness which often led to crises and military clashes. The international scene was kept in continuous tension.

IMPERIALISM

The European preoccupation with world politics in the decades before the outbreak of the First World War made this period the "Age of Imperialism." In the literal sense "imperialism" meant that the policies of the great powers were directed toward the creation of overseas empires, but the term usually contained the further suggestion that these policies were determined by an economic motive: the intention of acquiring control over the sources of raw materials for industrial development and over new markets for the sale of finished products.

The economic aspect of imperialism has been most strikingly presented by Lenin in his famous pamphlet *Imperialism, the Highest Stage of Capitalism.* According to Lenin, the industrial and financial forces in each country were united in one large combine and the few men at its head determined the foreign policy of their nation. After the undiscovered and unexplored areas of the world had been divided among the great powers, a period of world wars was inevitable because the states would clash with one another in their efforts to increase their markets and stave off economic crises at home. It is true that the concerns of big business played an important role in the foreign policy of this period. But Lenin's picture of the foreign offices of the great powers serving as the tools of large private companies was exaggerated. He used ideas which the British political scientist H. J. A. Hobson (1858–1940) had developed, and he gave them a sharply Marxist turn. As an analysis of the situation in Germany, from which Lenin took almost all his examples, his thesis might have been somewhat justified. But even with regard to Germany his picture was oversimplified.

If foreign policy often followed the lead of industrialists and bankers, sometimes the relationship was the reverse. A government might ask businessmen to make investments in a foreign country to supply a pretext for the presentation of political demands. Moreover, the financiers of the various European nations did not always compete against one another. Frequently, as in their loans to Russia, Turkey, and Persia, they cooperated in order to distribute the risks. And such cooperation was sometimes achieved against the will of the irrespective governments.

Contrary to widespread belief, imperialism did not always lead to the creation of overseas empires by colonization. The economic expansion of

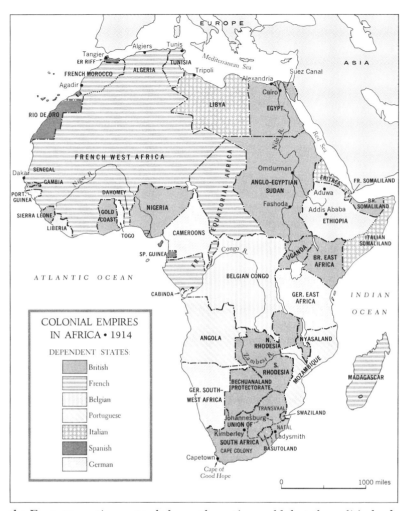

COLONIAL EMPIRES
IN AFRICA • 1914

DEPENDENT STATES:

- British
- French
- Belgian
- Portuguese
- Italian
- Spanish
- German

the European nations extended over the entire world, but the political rule of these powers was limited to only a small part of it. British and German investments in Latin America were large and formed a sizable part of their overall investments. Yet neither the British nor the Germans attempted to transform their economic influence into direct political control in this area. Economic domination did frequently result in *de facto* political dependence while *de jure* the autonomy of the economically inferior power was maintained. Turkey remained a sovereign state; it was sometimes even counted among the great powers. But actually, as a result of German investments, notably the supplying of capital for the building of the Baghdad Railway, Turkey became a German satellite. The degree to which the nations of the non-European world were dependent on the great European powers varied widely.

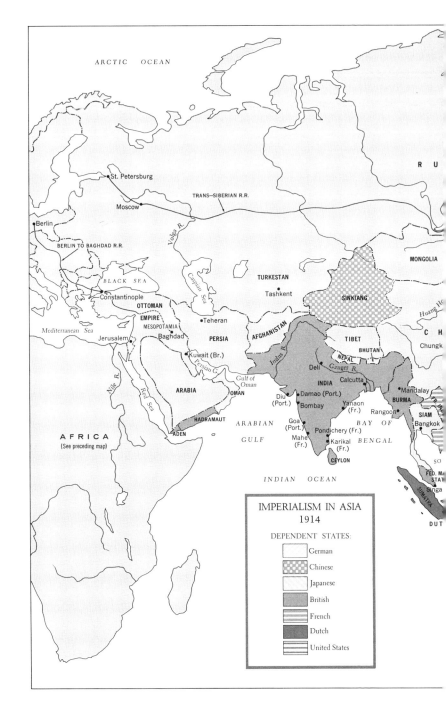

ARCTIC OCEAN

R U

•St. Petersburg

TRANS–SIBERIAN R.R.

•Moscow

MONGOLIA

•Berlin

BERLIN TO BAGHDAD R.R.

Volga R.

SINKIANG

Huang H

BLACK SEA

Caspian Sea

TURKESTAN

•Tashkent

C H

•Constantinople

OTTOMAN

EMPIRE

MESOPOTAMIA

AFGHANISTAN

TIBET

Chungk

Mediterranean Sea

Jerusalem

•Baghdad

•Teheran

PERSIA

BHUTAN

Indus R.

NEPAL

Ganges R.

•Kuwait (Br.)

Deli

Calcutta

Persian G.

•Mandalay

Nile R.

Red Sea

ARABIA

Gulf of
Oman

OMAN

Diu
(Port.)

•Damao (Port.)

•Bombay

INDIA

Yanaon
(Fr.)

BURMA

Rangoon

HADRAMAUT

ARABIAN

Goa
(Port.)

SIAM

Bangkok

AFRICA
(See preceding map)

•ADEN

GULF

Mahe
(Fr.)

Pondichery (Fr.)

BAY OF

Karikal
(Fr.)

BENGAL

SO

CEYLON

FED. M.
STA

INDIAN OCEAN

Singa

SUMATRA

DUT

IMPERIALISM IN ASIA
1914

DEPENDENT STATES:

	German
	Chinese
	Japanese
	British
	French
	Dutch
	United States

ARCTIC OCEAN

SIBERIA

ALASKA

BERING

SEA

NS–SIBERIAN R.R.

SEA OF
OKHOTSK

SAKHALIN I.

ALEUTIAN ISLANDS (U.S.)

MANCHURIA

Amur R.

Vladivostok

KURIL ISLANDS (Jap.)

Port Arthur
(Jap.)

Mukden

KOREA

SEA OF
JAPAN

PACIFIC

ng

Weihaiwei
(Br.)

TSUSHIMA

JAPAN

Tokyo

Kiaochou
(Ger.)

Shimoniseki

A

ngtze R.

EAST
CHINA
SEA

MIDWAY IS.
(U.S.)

ao
t.)

BONIN IS.
(Jap.)

OCEAN

HAWAIIAN ISLANDS (U.S.)

FORMOSA

Hong Kong (Br.)

g-chou-wan
(Fr.)

NA SEA

WAKE (U.S.)

MARIANA IS.
(Ger.)

PHILIPPINE
ISLANDS

GUAM
(U.S.)

CAROLINE ISLANDS
(Ger.)

MARSHALL IS.
(Ger.)

EI BR. NORTH
BORNEO

Davao

PELEW IS.
(Ger.)

WAK

GILBERT IS.
(Br.)

NEO

CELEBES

KAISER
WILHELMS
LAND

BISMARCK
ARCHIPELAGO
(Ger.)

EAST   INDIES

NEW
GUINEA

TIMOR
(Port.)

PAPUA

SOLOMON
ISLANDS
(Br.)

ELLICE IS.
(Br.)

SAMOA

(Ger.) (U.S.)

NEW
HEBRIDES
(Br.-Fr.)

FIJI IS.
(Br.)

AUSTRALIA

NEW
CALEDONIA
(Fr.)

NEW
ZEALAND

Nevertheless, the possession of colonies was regarded as the outward mark of a world power. Colonial ambitions centered on two areas: Africa and the Far East. By the beginning of the 1890's a large part of the African continent had been colonized; only Ethiopia, the Boer republics, and Morocco—states that had long histories of independence—remained sovereign. The ambitions of the European powers focused on these independent territories. The Italians, in a vain effort to become an important colonial power, attempted to conquer Ethiopia. The British set out to create a contiguous stretch of colonial dependencies from Cairo in the north to the Cape of Good Hope in the south. But this undertaking brought them into conflict with the French, who wanted to extend their territory in North Africa eastward to the Red Sea. And finally, at the turn of the century, the plans of the British led them into a war with the Boer republics.

In the Far East colonial expansion took place in two areas: the islands of the South Pacific, and China. The South Pacific islands stirred the interest of quite a number of powers after 1874, when the British started the competition by annexing the Fiji Islands. Great Britain saw the need to protect Australia and New Zealand against the possibility of a foreign power establishing itself nearby. The French and the Dutch were eager to extend their colonial empires in the South Pacific. The United States was conscious of the strategic importance of islands in this area for securing American access to the Asian continent; and the Germans, convinced that as latecomers they were handicapped, tried to grab whatever they could. But because of the clashing ambitions of so many powers, each was slow and cautious in proceeding to outright annexations. New Guinea, for which Australia and Germany competed, was divided between the Germans, the Dutch, and the British in 1885. The Germans then proceeded to annex the Marshall Islands and the Solomons. The British established a protectorate over the Gilbert and Ellice Islands, and together with the French, ruled the New Hebrides. The issue of the control of this Pacific area became critical when Spanish colonial power collapsed as a result of the Spanish-American War of 1898. As victor in this war the United States gained the Philippines, but a wrangle set in about the smaller islands which had belonged to Spain. The crises arising from this struggle for the remnants of the Spanish empire proved to be a storm in a teacup and ended with a peaceful division of the spoils among the rival powers. The United States acquired Wake Island; the Samoas were shared by Germany and the United States; the British took over some of the Solomon Islands from Germany, which as compensation received the Marianas and the Carolines.

Of incomparably greater importance was China. This gigantic empire, ruled according to traditional and obsolete forms, was almost defenseless. Whether China would come under foreign domination and which of the powers would control it were critical issues in these decades. In the treatment of the Chinese question European diplomacy showed its worst aspects: brutality, inconsistency, and shortsightedness. All of the powers involved asserted that their aim was to preserve the integrity of China and to provide the opportunity for trade with China to all states—that is, to maintain an "open-door" policy, to use a term introduced by the American secretary of state, John Hay. If accompanied by support for modern reforms in China, such a policy might in the long run have brought greater advantages than attempts by individual powers to secure exclusive control of parts of China for themselves. However, none of the states could resist the temptation of occupying Chinese ports when the opportunity offered itself. "The various powers cast upon us looks of tiger-like voracity, hustling each other in their endeavors to be the first to seize upon our innermost territories." Thus did a secret edict of the imperial Chinese government in November, 1899, describe the behavior of the white powers. The result was that all Chinese movements for reform and modernization assumed a decidedly antiforeign, nationalist character. A violent expression of this Chinese nationalism was the Boxer Rebellion of 1900; the European military intervention, which saved the encircled legations in Peking, defeated the Boxers, and forced the Chinese government to pay an indemnity, only pushed antiforeign feeling underground.

The struggle in the Far East for influence in China had peculiar features. Whereas the Russian government had no interest in the division of Africa, it regarded the Far East, and particularly China, as an eventual area for Russian colonial expansion. Moreover, two non-European powers, Japan and the United States, were vitally concerned. China had come into the forefront of the considerations of the European powers because, after a resounding victory over China in the war of 1894–1895, the Japanese had obtained in the peace treaty of Shimonoseki territorial cessions which made their nation supremely powerful in China. Russia, France, and Germany intervened in favor of China, and Japan looked for support to Great Britain, the one great naval power which had refused to back up China. These tensions and conflicts came to a head ten years later, in 1905, in the Russo-Japanese War, which resulted in the first defeat of a major European nation by a non-European state. Thus the struggle for China revealed that the great powers of Europe could no longer freely dispose of the rest of the globe. Here was a portent of times to come.

Nevertheless, though the struggles for control and colonies in Africa and the Far East did have the effect of sowing distrust, creating tensions, and maintaining an atmosphere of rivalry and hostility among the European states, the characterization of the entire age as an "Age of Imperialism" is somewhat misleading. The crucial conflicts among the European powers arose from issues within Europe.

CHAPTER 2

The Great Powers, 1890-1914

GENERALIZATIONS in history are dangerous.When closely examined, historical events and developments almost invariably reveal aspects which are individual and unique. For a true picture of the past, a grasp of the general pattern of development must be combined with an understanding of the individual features which in each country modified the pattern and gave to each nation's history its particular shape. Thus, after a broad survey of the factors determining the course of European history at the beginning of the twentieth century, we now turn our attention to the developments in the individual European nations.

THE PARLIAMENTARY GOVERNMENTS

Great Britain

Of the great powers Great Britain had advanced furthest in democratic evolution and in industrialization. Having made progress while preserving continuity, Britain gave the impression of remarkable political and social stability. The "miracle of its constitution"—the British two-party system, British parliamentarism—seemed to offer an example of how the problems and tensions of the twentieth century could be overcome.

Yet at the close of the nineteenth century even in Britain one epoch seemed to come to an end and a new one to begin. Queen Victoria died in 1901. A famous cartoon by Max Beerbohm illustrates the difference between Victoria and her heir, King Edward VII (ruled 1901–1910). No more striking contrast can be imagined than that between the strict and dignified queen and her flamboyant son. Edward indulged in all the pleasures of a gilded society. He was devoted to beautiful women and good food. In his youth he gambled; in later years he played bridge from afternoon until late at night during his weekend visits to the country houses of the British rich. He had a stable of race horses, and he was also a motorist. When he died, the *Illustrated London News* praised him for his

King Edward VII as advocate of the motorcar.

support of the motorcar industry: "When public opposition was at its height, when the outlook was dark indeed for the industry, when rumors and signs portended repressive legislation, His Majesty's accepted patronage of the then Automobile Club of Great Britain and Ireland—by which it became the Royal Automobile Club—came in the very nick of time." Together with his wife, Queen Alexandra, one of the great beauties of the age, the king was the recognized social leader of an ostentatiously opulent and luxurious society.

The sudden change from the dignified and aloof court of Victoria to the pleasure-loving and indulgent court of Edward VII had the effect not of impairing the position of the monarchy, but of strengthening it. During Victoria's reign the bourgeoisie through hard work—slowly and steadily—had transformed Great Britain into the leading industrial country of the world. By the turn of the century this work was done and its fruits could be enjoyed. Edward was the perfect representative of this stage of British economic development, and he was extremely popular.

With the wisdom of hindsight it is easy to see that the British economic position in the first decade of the twentieth century was not as brilliant as it appeared. In the last quarter of the nineteenth century the tempo of British economic development had slowed down. If there was no absolute decline, certainly growth decelerated. Between 1885 and 1913 the rate of increase in Britain's industrial production was 2.11 per cent, while Germany's increased by 4.5 per cent and that of the United States by 5.2 per cent. The actual output of steel, iron, and coal, the chief sources of Britain's strength as an industrial and commercial power, was still very high. But Great Britain was no longer the leading producer of these goods. By 1906 it had been overtaken by the United States in the production of steel, iron, and coal and by Germany in the production of steel. Similarly, in the development of innovations connected with electricity, the motorcar, and chemicals Britain lagged behind Germany and the United States. Besides, these two countries possessed more modern industrial equipment than Great Britain. Other aspects of economic life were more favorable. In the shipping industry, in textile production, and as a center of trade, Britain remained the leading power. Above all, during its period of economic growth, Britain had made immense investments in foreign countries, which now paid off and generated new investment possibilities. Thus, it was the world's greatest capital market. Its banks enjoyed enormous prestige. The gold standard and the pound were almost synonymous. But Britain did not produce as much as it imported, although the receipts from its foreign investments concealed this deficit in the balance of trade. The basis for the economic difficulties which it had to face after the First World War, and still more threateningly after the Second World War, had already been laid.

The golden glimmer of the Edwardian era was an evening glow, but few were aware of this. To most people, London was the capital of the world in the decades before the First World War, the embodiment of a luxurious style of life unequaled since the Roman Empire. The harmoniousness of the ruling group confirmed this impression of stable prosperity. Conflicts between the attitudes of a feudal and authoritarian military class and that of a bourgeois society did not exist in Great Britain. The British people had successfully fought against the standing army which they viewed as an instrument of princely absolutism and their insular position made conscription unnecessary. Moreover, the economic basis of a military caste—agriculture—had been almost eliminated. If in the first half of the nineteenth century the repeal of the corn laws and the establishment of free trade had signified the victory of the industrial and commercial classes over agricultural interests, this development was completed by the agricultural crisis of the 1880's. In a country unprotected by tariffs, competition against grain imported from Russia or America became impossible; the cultivation of grain was virtually abandoned and the soil was used for grazing, dairyfarming, or fruitfarming. But the landowners remained wealthy. Many found that their soil was rich in coal; industrial settlements sprang up on their land, and they drew large incomes from rents. Landowners frequently became involved in industrial and financial activities. The amalgamation of the rising classes of businessmen with the old aristocratic ruling group represented no problem in Britain: "While business men were becoming peers, peers were becoming business men, so that when the new rich reached the Upper House they found themselves on familiar ground."[1]

[1] Élie Halévy, A History of the English People, Epilogue, trans. by E. I. Watkin, Vol. II (London, 1934), p. 306.

THE POLITICS OF THE RULING CLASS

Politics mirrored this homogeneity of the ruling class. Although strife between the Unionists, as the Conservatives were officially named, and the Liberals was quite vehement, the social composition of the leadership in each of the parties was very much alike. After William Gladstone's resignation in 1894 and the short-lived Liberal government under Lord Rosebery, the Conservatives held power for ten years, from 1895 to 1905: until 1902 the marquis of Salisbury (1830–1903) was prime minister; from 1902 to 1905 Salisbury's nephew Arthur Balfour (1848–1930). In both parties, descendants of the aristocratic families who had ruled Britain in previous centuries continued to be prominent. Salisbury and Balfour were Cecils; Greys and Ponsonbys were to be found on the councils of the Liberals. The leadership of both parties included aristocrats with industrial and financial connections, like the Liberal Rosebery, who was married to a Rothschild, and the Conservative earl of Derby, who had large coal-mine holdings. In both parties, businessmen played significant roles. Conservative and Liberal politicians enjoyed the same strictly classical education. Attendance at one of the great public schools—Eton, Harrow, Rugby—followed by Oxford or Cambridge was the usual background for a political career and almost a requirement for it; prominence in the debating society of one of the two universities marked a young man for political success. In this period, Oxford's Balliol College was the breeding ground of statesmen. Its master, Benjamin Jowett, the translator of Plato, attracted the most brilliant minds to his college and infused them with the idea that public service was the duty of the social elite.

Leaders of both parties were also knit together by strong common intellectual interests. Among the Liberals, John Morley (1838–1923) was an eminent literary historian; Richard Burdon Haldane (1856–1928) a distinguished student of German philosophy. The philosopher among the Conservatives was Arthur Balfour, who as a young man wrote the stimulating *Defence of Philosophical Doubt*. Balfour is the most puzzling and fascinating figure among Britain's statemen of the early twentieth century. Although he never became prime minister again after 1905, he remained influential in the inner councils of the Conservative party. His mind was open to all that was new and modern in the social, literary, and artistic scene, and politics was only one of his many interests. He considered politics a game rather than an avocation and kept aloof from the enthusiasms and nationalist passions of the masses. Skeptical, ironical, and languidly elegant, he never lost the instincts of a member of the ruling class.

The British ruling class had no doubt of the nation's right to rule over other peoples, to maintain the empire, and to continue imperial expansion despite the increasing competition of other states. The most important leaders of both parties were conscious imperialists. The Conservative government of Salisbury used the occasion of Queen Victoria's Diamond

Arthur James Balfour. *States-man, philosopher, and Magister Elegantiarum.*

Jubilee in 1897 to glorify Britain's world-spanning empire. But Liberals like Rosebery and Haldane were equally enthusiastic advocates of Britain's imperial role. Conservatives might be more concerned with maintaining their nation as the world's foremost power, while Liberals might emphasize its mission of guiding the colonial peoples to self-government and the other blessings of British society, but leaders of both parties were firmly resolved not to be content with what Britain possessed and to compete actively for the African and Asian lands which were up for grabs.

This was the time when the visionary dream of a British empire in Africa reaching from the Cape to Cairo made its impact on British policy. The first consequence was a serious clash between the British and the French. Seeking to enlarge their African holdings, the French had organized two expeditions, one starting from Ethiopia in the east and moving west, the other moving from Lake Chad to the east. They were to meet in the upper Nile Valley and there establish the French claim to this area, the possession of which would link French Somaliland in the east with the French colonies of Algeria and Senegal in the west. This empire would cut straight across the continuous territory stretching from the Cape to Cairo which was sought by the British. Hence they quickly decided on countermeasures.

They ordered General Herbert Kitchener (1850–1916) to move up the Nile into the Sudan, which, since the defeat of General Gordon in 1885, had remained in the control of the Mahdi. In 1898 the army of the Mahdi was overcome in two battles, at the Atbara River (April 8) and at Omdurman (September 2), and "the whole mass of the dervishes dissolved into fragments and into particles and streamed away into the fantastic mirages of the desert," according to a description of the battle of Omdurman by a participant, the young sublieutenant Winston Churchill. Kitchener moved quickly ahead along the upper Nile, for the French expedition under Colonel Jean Baptiste Marchand, coming from the west, had reached Fashoda, in the southeastern Sudan, and had planted a French flag there on July 10, 1898. With a few of his troops Kitchener sailed up the Nile, arriving at Fashoda on September 18. He asked Marchand to withdraw; Marchand refused. Kitchener and Marchand conferred and agreed to await the decision of their home governments; then they drank whiskey and soda together. Public opinion in Great Britain was so enraged by the French audacity in placing obstacles in the path of the British imperial plans that even if the government had wanted to make concessions it could not have done so. The French were faced with the alternative of going to war against Great Britain or giving in. On November 3 the French government decided to surrender and ordered the unconditional evacuation of Fashoda.

THE LABOR MOVEMENT AND SOCIAL REFORM

The Diamond Jubilee of Queen Victoria in 1897 and Omdurman and Fashoda in 1898 represented the apex of British imperial power. Nevertheless, the coherence of society, the grasp of the ruling classes over the mass of the nation, was less firm and secure than one might have expected as a result of the unbroken success of British policy in the nineteenth century. Although Great Britain had passed the worst hardships and sufferings which accompanied industrialization in its early stages, misery among the masses of the working population was still great. The sacrifice of agriculture to industry, accelerated by a severe agricultural crisis in the 1880's, had forced small farmers and farm hands to migrate to the cities, thus increasing the number of unskilled workers. Housing conditions in the great industrial centers were bad. In the East End of London, families of eight or ten people often lived in one room.

From the middle of the 1890's to the outbreak of the First World War no severe economic crisis occurred in Great Britain. But wages, which had been steadily rising until the turn of the century, then began to stagnate—while prices increased. Moreover, the shadow of unemployment hovered perpetually over the industrial workers. At the end of their lives they were almost unavoidably dependent on charity and the very insufficient provisions of the Poor Law. The trade unions, which supplied almost the only protection the workers had, were handicapped by their limited financial means, and their rights were not clearly determined. Hence, a new, more militant spirit arose in the trade unions: the conviction grew that a change of the economic system to provide "collective ownership and control over production, distribution and exchange"[2] was necessary and that to effect this change labor had to enter the political arena as an independent force. The driving personality in the new movement was James Keir Hardie (1856–1915), a Scottish miner and trade-union organizer. Whereas previously trade-union men elected to Parliament had joined the Liberals, Keir Hardie and his friends had succeeded by 1900 in persuading the trade unions to finance and to support at the forthcoming elections a slate of candidates who would represent the interests of the workers in Parliament. The Labor party, then called the Labor Representation Committee, had come into life.

This development was helped by a movement among middle-class British intellectuals whose social consciences were deeply stirred by the contrast between the wealth of the ruling group and the misery of the workers. Calling themselves Fabians after the Roman dictator Fabius, whom they admired because he had waited patiently for the right moment but then had struck hard, the influential members of this movement were rather disparate. Among them were reform-minded radicals like Annie Besant, successful literary figures like the novelist H. G. Wells, and George Bernard Shaw, at that time not yet a dramatist, but a music and literary critic, and scholars like the political scientist Graham Wallas. But the guiding spirit was that of a husband and wife whose closeness of aims is well testified by the fact that they are usually named together as "the Webbs." Sidney Webb (1859–1947) began as a civil servant, but soon decided to devote himself to the problems of industrial society. Beatrice Webb (1858–1943) was a woman of great beauty from a socially prominent family, and had a sensitive social conscience. Under her husband's influence, her somewhat sporadic welfare activities became more serious and systematic.

The Webbs' house served as a kind of headquarters for intellectuals concerned with social questions. The Fabians began by publishing a series of studies on the problems of modern industrial life. The Webb's *History of Trade Unionism* (1897) is a classic. One of the Webb's most lasting achievements was the founding of the London School of Economics, later a division of the University of London, which has been particularly devoted to the investigation of political and social problems in the modern world. The Fabians believed that the march of modern society was irrevocably set toward greater democratization. But democratization could be complete

2 From the program issued at the foundation of the Independent Labor Party in Bradford in 1893.

only if it was economic as well as political. And economic democratization meant socialization: the public authorities—local, regional, or central— were to have the right to organize basic industries and to determine how capital income would be used. Fabianism was socialism, but not Marxism. It did not presuppose a revolution which would give all power to one class, the proletariat, and it did not advocate the end of the national state. The socialist transformation of society was to be brought about democratically, by the will of the people. The Fabians felt that their goals were in accordance with the British political tradition, constituting the natural destination toward which their nation's political life had been moving since the beginning of the nineteenth century.

For a while the Fabians tried to convince the leaders of the existing po- litical parties that they ought to adopt the Fabian program. Sidney Webb, who disapproved of spending money on clothes or jewels, permitted Beatrice (to her inner delight) to buy a new dress if doing so might help make one of the socially prominent political leaders more willing to listen to the ex- position of Fabian ideas. But when both Conservative and Liberal leaders proved unresponsive, some of the Fabians turned to the idea of establishing a third party, which would realize socialism in Britain. They joined forces with Keir Hardie's Labor Representation Committee, and their ideas soon began to dominate the young Labor party; the combination of intellectuals and trade unionists has remained a characteristic of the British Labor party. When in the 1920's the Labor party came to power, several of the Fabians received high government positions. So prominent had some of their leaders become that on the occasion of their fiftieth anniversary in 1933, George Bernard Shaw, the principal speaker, began by saying, "Ladies and Gentle- men," but then, looking to his right and left on the podium, where the early members of the Fabian movement were seated, he quickly added, "Oh, I see I have to say My Lords, Ladies and Gentlemen."

Both the Conservatives and the Liberals were aware that the founding of an independent Labor party was a threat to the two-party system. They recognized that they had to make a greater effort to satisfy the demands of the laboring classes. Ever since Disraeli had coined the slogan "Tory Democracy," a wing of the Conservative party had placed emphasis on social reform. This movement received new impetus when in 1886 Joseph Chamberlain (1836–1914), with a group of followers, broke with Gladstone and the Liberals and joined the Conservatives. Chamberlain, coming from industrial Birmingham, had made a name for himself as an advocate of radical reforms. As lord mayor of Birmingham he had introduced "munici- pal socialism"; he had improved public services and made them less expensive by placing streetcars, street lighting, and public utilities under the administration of the city government. Chamberlain had also modernized party politics by creating wards with party organizers who would get the masses to the polls. For a politician of this outlook "Conservative" seemed hardly the right label, and following his alliance with the Conservatives they were officially named "Unionists."

A similar tendency toward social reform could be observed in the Liberal party. Nonconformists and radicals had always formed a strong element in this party. Such Liberals felt that leaders like Rosebery and the imperialists did not represent the true Liberal tradition, and many thought they ought to oppose the imperial expansionism which oppressed other peoples. They believed that the Liberal party ought to concentrate on domestic problems and work toward the solution of the Irish question by seeking to obtain for Ireland its own government and parliament: home rule. The members of this group were sometimes called Little Englanders because of their doubts about the value of the empire. Their most respected leader, Sir Henry Campbell-Bannerman (1836–1908), had held high government office under Gladstone and was regarded as Gladstone's authentic heir, the man who would continue his reform policy. Among this group a new leader arose in a young lawyer and brilliant orator from Wales, David Lloyd George (1863–1945), whose political passion was fired by the misery which he saw among the Welsh mine workers.

IMPERIALISM VERSUS DOMESTIC REFORM

The tensions between the imperialists and the domestic reformers were sharpened by Britain's conflict with the Boer republics in South Africa. In Salisbury's government Joseph Chamberlain had become secretary for the colonies. Partly because he saw little chance to move his Conservative colleagues toward social reform, and partly because of the demands of his office, Chamberlain turned his great energies to the realization of an empire extending from the Cape to Cairo. French ambitions for the upper Nile Valley had been thwarted at Fashoda, but Transvaal and the Orange Free State, the independent Boer republics in southern Africa, still remained a barrier to these plans. A conflict between these independent states and Great Britain seemed unavoidable; its outbreak was accelerated by the discovery of gold in the Transvaal. The Boers feared that the immigrants streaming to the Transvaal in search of quick riches would soon outnumber them, limiting Boer political influence, and—since most of the immigrants (known as Uitlanders) were British—that they might decide to make the Boer republics part of the British empire. There is no doubt that Cecil Rhodes, the dominating figure in the British Cape Colony, aimed at an absorption of the Boer republics by the empire. He believed that the unrest created by the tension between Boers and Uitlanders might provide the opportune moment. In 1896 he organized an invasion by a small force of 470 men under the leadership of a Dr. Jameson, an adventurer. The expectation was that the march of this force into the interior of

An incident of the Boer War. *An armored train destroyed by the Boers.*

the Transvaal would give the signal for a rebellion in Johannesburg by the Uitlander against the Boers. But no such upheaval occurred; Jameson and his men were quickly defeated and surrendered to the Boers. Rhodes's responsibility for the raid was incontestable and he was forced to resign as prime minister of the Cape Colony. But the much-discussed question was whether Chamberlain, the British colonial secretary, had previous knowledge of the raid. The British government immediately declined all responsibility for the raid and a committee of the House of Commons gave Chamberlain a clean bill of health. But doubts about Chamberlain's role were never entirely removed and recent investigations have revealed that he knew much more about what was planned than he admitted at the time.

People outside England had no doubt that the Jameson Raid was a British defeat. The German emperor, William II, sent a telegram to the president of the Transvaal republic, Paul Krüger, congratulating him upon his success "in restoring peace and in maintaining the independence of the country against attacks from without." This message, which rubbed salt in Britain's wounds, may have been unwise politically, but in giving vent to his indignation about British ruthlessness, William expressed the feelings not only of the German nation but of all the European continent. The Jameson Raid and the telegram of the German emperor made war between the Boers and Great Britain almost certain. To the British, conquest of the Boer republics had become a matter of prestige. On the other hand, the raid confirmed the Boers in their fear of the influence of the immigrants, while at the same time the public acknowledgement of the Boers' right to independence encouraged them to resist the British. Hence, they continued their discriminatory policy against the Uitlanders, while the British took up the cause of these new immigrants and insisted that they should receive the right to vote. When negotiations proved fruitless, Britain sent troop reinforcements to the Cape Colony; and on the demand of the Boers for withdrawal of these troops, the British cut off all discussion. In October, 1899, war broke out between the Boer republics (Transvaal and the Orange Free State) on the one hand and the British on the other.

The Boer War followed a pattern common to many colonial wars. The resistance of the indigenous forces proved to be more effective than had been expected, and initially the British had severe losses. But when the full force of the British was brought into play, the difference in strength proved decisive. Where the Boer War differed from most other colonial engagements was in the severity of the reverses suffered by the invading British forces, which were first repulsed, then encircled at Ladysmith and Kimberley and there besieged. They were relieved only at the end of February, 1900, after large reinforcements from England had arrived and a change in command had taken place. The British offensive ended with the conquest and annexation of the Transvaal in September, 1900. But military action continued for another year and a half. The Boers engaged in guerilla warfare, and Kitchener, the British commander, proceeded against them ruthlessly, burning the farms of Boer guerillas and interning the women and children of Boer soldiers in specially constructed camps. Finally, on May 31, 1902, a peace treaty was signed in which the Boers acknowledged British sovereignty.

The Boer War was a terrible shock to the British people. Since the colonial army was not sufficiently large, troops had to be sent from England; 350,000 men were needed to subdue 60,000 Boers. In England families grew increasingly anxious over the fate of relatives and friends whose lives had been unexpectedly endangered by a colonial war. Moreover, all over Europe there was an outburst of fury against Great Britain. This sudden revelation of their unpopularity was a great surprise to the British, and although the European governments did not take any common action against them, they began to fear that their country might be confronted by a combination of all the continental powers. Thereafter British foreign policy gradually began to veer away from "splendid isolation" and into an acceptance of cooperation with other states. The Boer War had shown the obsoleteness and clumsiness of British military organization, and raised serious doubts about the aims of British policy and the efficiency of British political processes.

Was the imperial expansion worth the loss of life and the expenditure of money exacted by the Boer War? At first, the opponents of the policy which had led to war were shouted down and socially boycotted. But as the conflict dragged on, the politicians who had resisted the wave of imperialist enthusiasm—men like Campbell-Bannerman and Lloyd George—gained in political stature. They found increasing support for their arguments that attention should be focused upon domestic problems. Events confirmed the view that internal tensions were reaching a dangerous state. The newly militant trade unions had encountered fierce resistance by employers, and had retaliated with local strikes against the employment of "free," or nonunion, labor. The tenseness of this situation was aggravated by the Taff Vale decision (1901), which asserted that a trade union was financially liable for damage caused by all strikes in which its members took part. Indignation among the working population was immense because the decision underlined the precarious position of the trade unions and the helplessness of the working classes. The government also lost popularity as a result of the measures it instituted for reform in education. The need for such reform was generally recognized. Great Britain had only a limited number of elementary schools maintained by the state, that is, by the counties and towns. More than half of the children of England and Wales received their elementary education at voluntary schools which were unable to maintain reasonable standards. The Education Act of 1902 placed all these schools under county and town control so that they were forced to adhere to recognized standards; if necessary they would receive financial support from local taxes. The measure undoubtedly represented a great improvement in English education. But because it implied that tax money would be used to support Anglican and Roman Catholic schools, it aroused the vehement opposition of an important segment of the British population, the nonconformists.

THE TRIUMPH OF THE LIBERAL PARTY

The final cause for the end of ten years of Conservative rule was a split among the Conservatives themselves. Joseph Chamberlain had not abandoned his original radicalism when he turned from internal reforms to imperial expansion. On the contrary, he regarded a resolute imperial policy as a means for improving the lot of the masses. He believed that his country's continued economic prosperity depended on the expansion of opportunities to emigrate to the colonies. He advocated protective tariffs which would limit foreign competition in the British market, and by giving preferences to the British colonies, would tie the empire together as a great economic unit. To promote these aims Chamberlain organized the Tariff Reform League, and to devote himself to this campaign he left the government. In Prime Minister Balfour's view, British public opinion was not ready to accept protective tariffs. In a country dependent on the importation of agricultural goods the first result of protection would be an increase in the price of food, which would place another burden on the masses. Split over the tariff question, the Conservatives seemed to lack an economic policy, while the Liberals adhered to the hallowed tradition of free trade. Unable to control his own party, Balfour resigned in December, 1905, and the Liberals took over. Campbell-Bannerman became prime minister, not without the displeasure of the imperialist elements in his own party. But he reconciled them by giving them strong representation in the cabinet. Sir Edward Grey (1862–1933) became foreign secretary; Herbert Asquith (1852–1928), chancellor of the exchequer; and Haldane, secretary of state for war. The radical wing of the reformers was also well represented. Lloyd George became president of the Board of Trade, and John Burns (1858–1943), president of the Local Government Board. The new government was an incongruous mixture of imperialists and social reformers. But at this time Great Britain was still prosperous enough to attempt simultaneously to maintain a powerful position in foreign affairs and to undertake reforms at home. In the elections of January, 1906, the Liberals gained a sweeping victory, but it was a sign of the times that the new Labor party gained twenty-nine seats. Ten years of Liberal rule followed the Conservative defeat of 1906; it would be a decade of wide-ranging reforms.

Actually, in the eight years of Liberal rule before 1914, two periods must be distinguished. In the first years of the Liberal government, legislation was somewhat cautious and tentative; the government was mainly concerned with revising those measures of the preceding Conservative governments which had aroused the greatest resentment and with improving those aspects of the administration which were inefficient or defective. The Liberal government contributed to the healing of the wounds of the Boer War by giving self-government to the Transvaal. A Trade Disputes Act legalized peaceful picketing and relieved trade unions from liability for damages caused by their members—thereby annulling the Taff Vale decision—and Haldane carried through an army reform which fully proved itself in the First World War. The army was divided into two parts, an expeditionary force ready for immediate action on the Continent, and a territorial force into which were merged traditional organizations such as the volunteers and the yeomanry; moreover, Haldane created a general staff after the Prussian example. Like most successful military reforms his measures also resulted in financial economies.

The first years of Liberal rule yielded meager results, partly because many measures which the government advocated—among them a change in the Education Act which would have removed the objections of the nonconformists—were rejected by the House of Lords, which was controlled by the Conservatives. Moreover, Asquith, the chancellor of the exchequer, pursued a traditional line in his financial policy and was disinclined to finance social experiments. This situation changed in 1908 when Asquith succeeded Campbell-Bannerman as prime minister and entrusted the office of chancellor of the exchequer to Lloyd George in order to reconcile the radical wing of the Liberal party with the leadership of an imperialist. These changes ushered in a new period of energetic legislation. Lloyd George resolutely used the power of the purse for social reform. The most important feature was the National Insurance Act (1911), patterned after the social legis-

Radicals of the Edwardian era. *Lloyd George and Churchill on the way to the House of Commons on Budget Day, 1910.*

lation which Bismarck had sponsored in Germany. Contributions made on a compulsory basis by workers, employers, and the state were to provide payments to workers in case of sickness and unemployment. Social reforms were to be paid for by means of a revised system of taxation which placed the chief burden for the expenses of the new programs on the wealthy classes. Thus Lloyd George's first budget, that of 1909, represented a radical departure. He raised the death duties, made a sharp distinction between earned and unearned income, and introduced a supertax to be levied on the possessors of large incomes. He also increased the taxes on tobacco and liquor.

In present day terms, Lloyd George's proposals were moderate. The payments given to workers in case of sickness or disability were low, and the small unemployment benefits were granted for only a limited period, a maximum of fifteen weeks in any one year. On the other hand the supertax started only on a yearly income of over £5,000 (which might be compared to an income today of more than $100,000) and the general income tax for unearned income and for earned income above £2,000 was raised only from one shilling to one shilling two pence in the pound. Nevertheless, on a very small scale Lloyd George's budget incorporated all the essential features of the future British welfare state; in the benefits provided and in the methods of financing them the government of present-day Britain continues the policy initiated by Lloyd George in 1909.

Lloyd George emphasized the novel character of his budget by introducing it with a four-hour speech. Opposition formed at once. The Conservatives were particularly upset by a suggestion which later proved to be impractical and was abandoned—the taxing of increases in land value. Since much of the wealth of the British landowners came from estates having mineral resources like coal, this tax was regarded as a direct attack on the position of the propertied classes.

The Conservatives fought the budget vigorously, and when it reached the House of Lords it was rejected. Since the Liberals had been constantly balked in their legislative proposals by the House of Lords, they were deeply aroused by this further frustration of their plans, particularly since tradition had established that the handling of finance bills was primarily a function of the House of Commons. The rejection of the budget by the House of Lords was regarded as a breach of the constitution.

As a next step the Liberal government introduced the Parliament Bill, designed to eliminate the House of Lords as a partner equal to the House of Commons in the law-making process. If it passed, the House of Lords would be able only to delay legislation, not to veto it absolutely. The great problem which faced the Liberal government was how to persuade the House of Lords to agree to its own diminution of power. This matter now began to overshadow the budget conflict.

The Liberals were not unhappy about this course of events. After the somewhat unspectacular results of their first years of rule, their electoral chances were insecure, and they hoped that an issue of consequence would help them to retain the support of the electorate. Lloyd George aimed at transforming the parliamentary controversies into a great constitutional conflict which could be represented as a fight of the people against the lords. In a number of speeches, and with great oratorical force, he castigated the unequal distribution of wealth in England due to "the fraud of the few and the folly of the many." Lloyd George was happily seconded by Winston Churchill, who in 1904, had moved from the Conservatives to the Liberals and in 1908 had been made president of the Board of Trade in the Liberal government. But the Conservatives fought back with equal vehemence, characterizing the Liberal proposal as a subversive attack on the entire English tradition. The fight over the Parliament Bill took on aspects of a class conflict and brought a bitterness and animosity previously unknown into the modern English political scene. The struggle lasted for over two years and ended only after two dissolutions of the House of Commons, new elections, and the threat that the government would create enough Liberal peers to get the proposal through the House of Lords. The final vote, on August 10, 1911, took place with immense excitement because the outcome seemed quite uncertain; the bill was passed only after thirty-seven Conservatives and thirteen bishops decided not to abstain and cast their votes with the government.

THE WANING OF CONFIDENCE

Edward VII died on May 6, 1910, in the midst of the struggle over the Parliament Bill. With his death, British life seemed to lose some of its splendor. His son and successor, King George V (ruled 1910–1936), was a much less glamorous figure; in a sense his somberness corresponded to the dark and threatening atmosphere which prevailed in Great Britain in the two or three years before the outbreak of the First World War. It is difficult to judge whether the fight over the Parliament Bill had heightened political tensions or whether the bitterness of this struggle was a reflection of a change in the political climate. The fact is that the end of the parliamentary struggle was followed by conflicts outside parliament. The victory of the Liberals might have been expected to strengthen confidence in progress by democratic means, but instead the long uncertainties about the outcome seem to have shaken the British people's faith in the efficiency of traditional parliamentary methods. Many became convinced that they would be heard and receive their due only if they used other means, perhaps even violent ones. For example, the advocates of female suffrage, the suffragettes, believed that the ruling males would give up their monopoly over political power only if forced to do so. Therefore, they pursued a policy of violent disruptions. They broke windows in shops and clubs and slashed pictures in the National Gallery; at the Epsom Derby one suffragette threw herself in front of the favorite, the king's horse, ending not only the chances of the horse, but also her own life.

Contempt for legally established authorities and procedures became evident also in the negotiations about the most ticklish issue of British policy, the Irish question. Home rule for Ireland was part of the program of the Liberal party and the Liberals were bound to fulfill this promise because, since the elections of 1910, they had no clear majority in the House of Commons and were dependent for their majority on the vote of the Irish nationalists. The Irish steadfastly supported the government in the constitutional crisis because they were aware that until the power of the House of Lords was limited, no home-rule bill would ever become law. But now they wanted to receive what they believed they had earned. Accordingly, a Home Rule Bill was drafted by the government in 1912. As in the past, home rule aroused passionate opposition. The center of this opposition, of course, was Northern Ireland (Ulster) which was Protestant and where preparations were made to fight against integration with the south which was Catholic. A less expected and more astounding sign of political extremism was the fact that the people of Ulster received clear encourage-

A violent protest. *The suffragette Emily Davison throwing herself in front of the king's horse at the Derby on June 4, 1913. At this time, action photographs were rare and usually obtained only by chance.*

ment for revolt from the leaders of the Conservatives. One of them, Sir Edward Carson, openly advocated armed resistance in Ulster if home rule should become law. Moreover, encouraged by Carson and the Conservatives, army officers, most of them Conservative and many of them descended from the Protestant Irish, demanded a government pledge that they would not be asked to coerce Ulster; otherwise they preferred to resign rather than follow orders to go to Ireland; the government seemed faced with mutiny. Only the outbreak of the First World War prevented a test of the resolve and power of the government to carry through its Irish policy.

A further expression of failing confidence in the possibility of obtaining reform through parliamentary action was the wave of strikes which rocked Great Britain between 1911 and 1913. They reflected serious weaknesses in the nation's economic structure. The period from 1911 to the outbreak of the First World War was characterized by economic prosperity. Unemployment represented no serious problem. Yet prices had been rising much more quickly than wages, and in those industries, notably coal mining, which were faced by serious foreign competition, wages had not risen at all. The workers were all the more dissatisfied because the chance of achieving results by political action seemed to be fading rather than improving.

The success of the Labor party in the elections of 1906 had not been repeated in subsequent elections. The party's parliamentary prospects had been further weakened by a court decision which prevented trade unions from levying political contributions. Disillusionment about the efficacy of the pressure exerted by their party led elements of the labor movement to look favorably upon other recipes for the ills of their economic situation. They became attracted by the idea, which reached Britain from the Continent, particularly from France, that "direct action"—strikes—was the appropriate weapon for workers seeking to improve their situation. Thus, economic and political motives lay behind a number of strikes in 1911 and 1912. The most notable were a seamen's strike, a general railway strike, a strike of the coal miners, and a strike of the dockers. Most of them were accompanied by violence, looting, and sabotage of the machinery in the factories. Frequently troops had to be used, since the police were not able to keep order. Some of the strikes were ended quickly by concessions on the part of the employers. The miners' strike resulted in the introduction of the Miners' Minimum Wage Act, which was a tacit admission by the government of the hardships faced by the mine workers. But some of the strikes simply collapsed, partly because the wage lag began to be made up and partly because the public, tired of economic unrest, began to turn sharply against the trade unions. In the debate accompanying these social tensions and conflicts the statistics of a contemporary best-seller were frequently quoted: in Great Britain, it was stated, 38,000,000 people had hardly more than half of the national income, whereas 1,250,000 "rich" had more than a third. Even if these figures were rough and somewhat exaggerated, the social unrest of these years confirmed that a deep cleavage existed in Great Britain. It was yet to be proved whether the British political system could meet the new demands placed upon it.

France

During the decade before the First World War France was the most democratic of the powers on the continent. France, too, had a parliamentary system. The head of the state, the president, had little power and the executive arm of the government, led by a prime minister, was dependent on the confidence of elected representatives—the Senate and the Chamber of Deputies. In a formal sense, France was even more democratic than Great Britain, for the French upper house, the Senate, was elected, whereas in Britain membership in the upper house was hereditary. However, the voting system by which French senators were chosen favored rural districts and the well-to-do, so the Senate functioned as a conservative counterweight to the more liberal Chamber of Deputies.

In contrast to the British system, French political life was not characterized by the dominance of a two-party system. The French parliament was composed of a large number of small parties; every government was a coalition, and governments changed frequently. In the twenty-four years between 1890 and 1914 there were forty-three governments and twenty-six prime ministers. Yet these statistics are deceptive; stability was greater than the figures imply. The multiplicity of French political parties was not a reflection of irreconcilable internal tensions. The French population was socially quite homogeneous. France was a country of small businessmen and farmers. Industrial enterprises were generally limited in size and frequently family owned. Until the First World War, more than half of the entire population was occupied in agriculture, which accounted even in 1890 for more than a third of the national income. The multifariousness of the political groupings was chiefly a reflection of tiny differences in economic interests and of variations stemming from local and regional particularities. Politicians moved easily from one party to the other. The center of the political spectrum formed the basis of almost all governments. A number of the same politicians were to be found in almost every cabinet, although they were usually assigned different ministries each time a change in government took place. The various governments differed mainly in whether the center ruled with support of the left or with support of the right.

Ironically, the strength of the center in French politics was an indication that France was lagging in the industrial race. France had entered the industrial age almost simultaneously with Great Britain. But after the spurt given by the French Revolution and Napoleon, the rate of industrial growth slowed down in the nineteenth century and France trailed far behind the United States and Germany. By its accumulated wealth the nation remained a great financial power. However, the French were inclined to invest their capital not in industrial enterprises, but—more cautiously— in public loans. In the market for government loans French banks played a particularly great role. The heavy industries were mainly centered in the northwest, where there were rich coal mines and a textile industry, and in Lorraine, which had valuable iron-ore deposits. Thus the problems arising from modern industrialization were concentrated in relatively small areas and aroused little interest in the rest of the country. Health and safety precautions in industrial enterprises, particularly in the mines, were unsatisfactory. Collective bargaining was forbidden, and trade-union activities were restricted.

France had an active Socialist party, but it was small and many of its deputies could not have been elected without support from the rural population. Thus the Socialists, despite theoretical radicalism, were inclined to be conciliatory in practice. Since the workers could not expect much from parliamentary action, theories which recommended direct action and emphasized the efficacy of purely economic weapons—such as strikes— were appealing. As the propagandist of the myth that the general strike was the proper instrument for the overthrow of capitalism, Georges Sorel became an influential figure among radical intellectuals through his book entitled *Reflections on Violence* (1908). His views increased the appeal of syndicalism, a revolutionary doctrine which preached direct action with the goal of building a new society through the cooperation of the trade unions of individual factories. Syndicalism was popular among workers in France and spread from there to Italy and Spain. Among the workers of these countries it was a serious competitor to Marxian socialism.

THE CONFLICT BETWEEN THE REPUBLICAN REGIME AND MONARCHIST TRADITIONS

Because the progress of industrialization in France was slow, political life was not dominated by social conflicts. The main divisions were ideological: they concerned issues which the French Revolution had raised. It has been said that after the French Revolution there were two Frances, an aristocratic monarchical France and a republican France. Defeat in the Franco-Prussian War had strengthened the feeling of malaise about the unavoidable decline of the deeply divided nation. The republic, which had been born in the times of the heroic resistance at the end of the Franco-Prussian War, was now beset by scandals and corruption and appeared unable to give an impulse to a regeneration of power. The enemies of the republican and revolutionary tradition felt justified in their conviction that the democratic form of the French government was the reason for the decline of their nation's power and that what France needed was a more authoritarian regime. Moreover, the enemies of the republic were firmly entrenched in two institutions: the army and the Church.

In the last decade of the nineteenth century a crucial event brought about an open confrontation of the two Frances. The impact of the Dreyfus Affair on French thinking was so profound that it took decades to digest and absorb it. This is strikingly indicated by the role which the Affair played in the work of the great French novelists of the twentieth century. Roger Martin Du Gard inserted in his novel *Jean Barois* an almost stenographic report of some of the high points of the Affair. In *Remembrance of Things Past* by Marcel Proust the Affair serves to question the values of the brilliant society which the novel pictures. Anatole France in his *Penguin Island* pictured the Affair as an example of the eternal struggle between reason and human weakness.

The importance of the events beginning in 1894 became clear only slowly. On October 15, 1894, Alfred Dreyfus (1859–1935), a captain in the French general staff, was placed under arrest for high treason. After some weeks Dreyfus was found guilty at a secret military trial, and a few days later, on January 5, 1895, he was sentenced in a solemn ceremony in the

The Dreyfus Affair. *Above: Dreyfus leaving the court building after his trial.*

Right: Le Bordereau. This famous document, on which the Dreyfus Affair turned, was given to the German military attaché.

courtyard of the general-staff building; he was deprived of his rank, his sword was broken, and he was sent for life to Devil's Island, in French Guiana. The trial had been full of legal irregularities. The main proof used against Dreyfus was a small piece of blue paper, which became famous as the *bordereau.* It had been found by a cleaning woman in the wastepaper basket of the German military attaché; it contained information about the French army; and handwriting experts maintained that it had been written by Dreyfus.

A republican and a Jew, Dreyfus had been an outsider among the aristocratic and Catholic officers of the French general staff; his fellow officers were easily convinced, therefore, that if a traitor was among them, it could only be Dreyfus. He belonged to a wealthy Alsatian family, which made every effort to obtain a new trial. A few journalists and lawyers who opposed the military caste were active on Dreyfus' behalf. But for a long while no one could make headway.

In 1896 the counterespionage section of the French general staff received a new chief, Colonel Georges Picquart, who must be considered the true hero of the Dreyfus Affair. Picquart noticed that the removal of Dreyfus had not ended the leakage of military secrets. He also became aware that the handwriting of the *bordereau* was much more similar to that of Walsin Esterhazy, another member of the general staff, than to that of Dreyfus. Moreover, Esterhazy was in continuous financial difficulties. But when Picquart insisted on proceedings against Esterhazy, nobody in the general staff was willing to listen to him and he was transferred from Paris to Algiers. Before leaving Paris he confidentially informed a few people, among them the vice president of the Senate, Scheurer-Kestner, of his suspicions about Esterhazy. Now a number of influential voices joined the campaign for Dreyfus. In addition to Scheurer-Kestner, there were Georges Clemenceau (1841–1929), a journalist and politician; Anatole France; and others. Still, this was not a popular cause. The Socialist leader Jean Jaurès (1859–1914) was for a long time doubtful of Dreyfus' innocence, and when he finally became convinced that a miscarriage of justice had occurred, and was ready to take up the fight, he met reluctance and hesitation in his own party. The Socialist leaders doubted that their adherents, the workers, would perceive a connection between their own interests and the cause of a wealthy Jewish officer.

It is hard to say what would have happened if the army leaders had not got rattled and overplayed their hand. In order to quell once and for all the agitation for Dreyfus, they ordered a trial of Esterhazy, and he was acquitted. Picquart, one of the witnesses against Esterhazy, was arrested and imprisoned. This arbitrary procedure provoked one of the great political documents of modern times—*J'accuse* (1898). In this open letter addressed to the president of the republic, Émile Zola (1840–1902) stated the case against the army leaders briefly and concisely, singling out the responsible officers by name and devoting to each of them a single paragraph beginning *J'accuse.* The publication led to proceedings against Zola, and rightly expecting that he would be condemned, he fled to England, where he continued the fight. Zola's intervention represented the turning point in the Dreyfus Affair. Immense public interest had been aroused, and every step taken in the proceedings was carefully scrutinized. It emerged that in order to strengthen the case against Dreyfus, documents had been falsified. Colonel Hubert Henry who had done this falsification, committed suicide; Esterhazy fled to England. Under these circumstances the highest court of appeal on June 3, 1899, set aside the previous condemnation of Dreyfus and ordered a new trial. But the military were unwilling to accept the humiliation of the rehabilitation of Dreyfus. It was widely assumed that the officers were preparing a *coup d'état* to overthrow the republican regime.

This threat against the existing regime made all the adherents of the republic realize that they had to act and to act quickly. For the first time in European history Socialists declared their willingness to support a bourgeois government. On June 22, 1899, René Waldeck-Rousseau, a member of a well-known family that was both republican and Catholic, and a man who had proved himself an able administrator in previous governments, formed a coalition government reaching from the right of center to the left, with the suppressor of the Paris Commune of 1871, Gaston de Galliffet, as minister of war and the left-wing Socialist Alexandre Millerand (1859–1943) as minister of commerce. When the new trial culminated in a grotesque verdict which confirmed Dreyfus' guilt while conceding him "extenuating circumstances," the Waldeck-Rousseau government was strong enough to pardon him.

In the course of the Affair the personal fate of Dreyfus became relatively insignificant. When Dreyfus accepted pardon from the Waldeck-Rousseau government, Charles Péguy, a young French writer, wrote: "We would have died for Dreyfus. Dreyfus did not die for Dreyfus."[3] In Péguy's opinion Dreyfus was no Dreyfusard; he should have continued to insist on his full rehabilitation because the fight had involved irreconcilable principles and ought therefore to have ended with the full victory of the right principles over the wrong ones—of the republican over the authoritarian ideas.

THE EMERGENCE OF A NEW IDEOLOGY ON THE RIGHT

The obstinacy of the anti-Dreyfusards, which appeared to be stupid, if not downright criminal, becomes more comprehensible when the Affair is seen as a struggle for principles. The most influential advocate of a monarchical revival in France was Charles Maurras (1868–1952), who fought for his idea in a number of brilliantly written essays and articles, notably his *Enquête sur la monarchie* (1900). But Maurras' concept of monarchy had little to do with the institution as it had existed in France. In his view monarchy, army, and church were necessary because they formed and maintained discipline and order. Discipline and order were the conditions of national strength. National power and vitality depended on the completeness with which the individual was willing to identify and subordinate himself to the national organization of which he was part. Against the revolutionary doctrines of individual rights, Maurras set the idea of a hierarchically organized society. Therefore to him the question of Dreyfus' actual guilt or innocence was unimportant. The individual had to be sacrificed if his rehabilitation would damage the prestige of institutions— like the army—which were essential for the life of the nation. Similar views were championed by another great figure of that period, Maurice Barrès. He placed particular emphasis on the idea that every nation was a racial unit and that those of other races have no rights as citizens. One of Barrès' novels bears the characteristic title *Les Déracinés* (1897). Gifted as these

---

[3] Charles Péguy, "Notre Jeunesse," in *Oeuvres en prose 1909–1914* (Paris, 1957), p. 541.

The chief editors of the *Action Française*. *Charles Maurras and Leon Daudet, and some of their collaborators shown together in 1917. The* Action Française *was a newspaper that promulgated the ideas of the French nationalist right.*

writers were, they must be counted among the intellectual ancestors of all the antiliberal and antidemocratic movements of the twentieth century. Their intense nationalism and racism, their attacks against Jews as an alien internationally minded force, their praise of discipline and military values, their contempt for law and right in favor of strength and vitality contained the germs of Fascist philosophy.

The Dreyfus Affair gave to the republic and to the republicans a prestige which they had never possessed before. High courage had been necessary to defend Dreyfus, for the Affair had aroused violent emotions. If Zola had not fled to England he might have been assassinated. Scheurer-Kestner was beaten in the streets; Dreyfus' lawyer was shot at; stones were thrown at windows in the houses of Dreyfus supporters; and the police were very slow in protecting the Dreyfusards. But after the Affair was over, the individuals who had risked their careers and their lives for the sake of justice were highly esteemed. In the following decades most of those who played a leading role in French politics were men who had first attracted public attention as defenders of Dreyfus: Clemenceau, Briand, Millerand, Viviani, Caillaux, Blum.

As a result of the Dreyfus Affair the political right acquired an ideology; the left received a new sense of direction, becoming aware that the aims of the French Revolution had not been realized, that the social problems inherent in the rise of industrial society involved new tasks to which the structure of government must be adapted. It was characteristic that the history of the French Revolution, previously a rather neglected field of study, now became a topic of scholarly interest. Indicative was the establishment of a chair for the history of the French Revolution at the Sorbonne.

THE CONSOLIDATION OF THE REPUBLIC

Obviously, progress toward a more democratic society could be achieved only if those institutions which had shown themselves open enemies of the government and obstructed its policy were deprived of power. The chief target was the army, which was now brought under civilian control: promotions to the rank of general in the army were taken out of the hands of a military council and placed in those of the minister of war, a civilian. He was inclined to favor those officers whom he considered to be reliable republicans. But while this measure did eliminate the danger of an antirepublican military coup, it also had the effect of splitting the officer corps into monarchist and republican groups. Moreover, the influence of political considerations did not always bring the most capable generals into the forefront; for instance, the selection of Maurice Gamelin (1872–1958), an officer popular among republican politicians but of moderate military gifts, as commander in chief at the beginning of the Second World War demonstrates the disadvantages of these political appointments.

The other force which had shown itself openly hostile to the republic was the Church, and the attempts at curbing its influence became the crucial issue in French politics in the first decade of the twentieth century. The problem had two aspects. One was the legal relationship between the Roman Catholic Church and the state; this was regulated by Napoleon's Concordat, according to which members of the secular clergy were paid by the state, and bishops were appointed by the Church from a list of names approved by the government. Another problem arose from the leading role which the Church had in education. A large number of French schools were controlled by Roman Catholic religious orders, which provided most of the teaching personnel. Even before the Dreyfus Affair the government had undertaken to build additional state schools and to increase their attractiveness by offering free primary education. The religious orders, however, continued to control a great many schools. After the Dreyfus Affair the government decided on a policy of reducing the number and influence of these schools. The means which the government used was a more rigid interpretation of the law regulating the existence of associations. Religious orders were declared to be associations; to exist legally, they had to obtain authorization, which required a legislative act. In 1902 Waldeck-Rousseau, whose policy had been to limit the influence of the Church on education, but who had not been anxious to eliminate all Catholic schools, resigned and was succeeded by Émile Combes (1835–1921), a fanatic anti-Catholic. Combes decided to refuse authorization to most of the religious orders. They had no choice but to leave France. The measures against the orders were vehemently denounced by the Church and the entire Catholic clergy, and provoked widespread demonstrations against the government all over France. The possibilities of a compromise between the anti-Catholic political powers and the Church began to disappear. In 1904 a law was passed that prohibited all teaching by religious orders. The relations between France and the Vatican were broken off and the Concordat was terminated. Diplomatic relations between France and the Holy See were restored only after the First World War, and then the religious orders were permitted to return.

The outcome of this conflict was the separation of church and state in 1906. The state guaranteed freedom of conscience but refused to pay the clergy. In France, where for centuries the Catholic Church and the state had been closely linked, this break between the two was revolutionary. Certain practical issues kept tensions alive until the First World War. The most difficult problem concerned the ownership of Church buildings. The state claimed them, but was willing to give them to private societies organized for this purpose, which might lease them to the Church. The Church, however, maintained that it must have the right of ownership. Because of the pressure of the Church, the private societies were not formed, and the state closed Church buildings, a step that resulted in excited demonstrations, with the police guarding Church doors. On Sundays Catholic worshipers knelt outside the closed churches, on the steps and in the streets, stopping all traffic.

Only slowly and gradually were compromises reached. In the long run, however, the situation created by the separation of Church and state did no serious damage to the Church. French Catholicism survived, and the hostility between Church and state died down. A man like Aristide Briand, who had guided the law of separation through the Chamber of Deputies and had been denounced by Catholics as an irresponsible revolutionary, would become in later years a leader respected by all groups.

The educational policy of the government could not be confined to eliminating the influence of the Church. The vacuum had to be filled, and the importance of infusing education with republican ideals was apparent. New schools had to be created; more teachers had to be trained, and they had to be guided by new educational ideas. The center from which the government's educational philosophy spread was the École Normale Supérieure, which prepared the future professors of high schools and universities. It provided an anticlerical, secular education, inspired by a belief in human rights and scientific progress. Whether taught directly at the École Normale Supérieure or by professors trained there, school teachers became the protagonists of the spirit of the Third Republic. Many novels describe the situation in the villages where the aristocratic landowner and the priest represented the Old Regime, while the mayor and the school teacher embodied the spirit of the French Revolution.

THE RISE OF NEW TENSIONS

The governments that carried through the rehabilitation of Dreyfus and the separation of church and state—those of Waldeck-Rousseau and Combes—were left-center coalitions, and their measures were prepared by the *cartel des gauches*, a committee including representatives of all the center and leftist parties. After limiting the political role of the army and the Church, the government had to determine to what extent it would undertake social reform in favor of the masses of the people, particularly the workers. On this question the *cartel des gauches* broke up; this was a demonstration of the validity of the old proverb that "Frenchmen wear their hearts on the left and their pocketbooks on the right." Some improvements in the situation of the workers were made, such as the setting of minimum standards for safety and hygiene in factories and mines, but in the crucial issues of modern industrialization—social security, the legalization of collective bargaining—little was done; France was far behind Great Britain and Germany. The failure to harvest concrete advantages from their support of the left during and after the Dreyfus Affair created dissatisfaction among the workers and increased their susceptibility to revolutionary appeals. The trade unions encouraged soldiers to mutiny. From 1906 on, there were frequent strikes, some of which had significant political consequences. In 1906 a mining disaster for which the workers held the mine owners responsible led to a strike in which, to the indignation of the Socialists and other radicals of the left, Prime Minister Clemenceau ordered troops to protect the strikebreakers. A strike of the postal workers resulted in the adoption of a law forbidding state employees to strike. And this law was regarded as a further demonstration that the power of the state was being brutally used against the masses. In 1911 the government defeated a strike of railway workers by ordering mobilization; the workers were forced to run the railroads under military command. These events weakened the political center: indignation over the government's lack of zeal for social reform and over its support for antilabor forces strengthened the left. Fear arising from the radicalization of the workers and resentment aroused by labor unrest helped the right to recover from its defeat in the Dreyfus Affair.

In the years immediately before the outbreak of the First World War the political struggle in France developed into a fight between right and left. Among the many issues over which they clashed, the most important were a modernization of the taxation system, particularly the institution of a progressive income tax, and an extension of conscription from two to three years. The left wanted an income tax which would fall mainly on the well-to-do

Jean Jaurès. *The French Socialist leader speaking in 1913 against the law requiring three-year military service.*

classes and might pay for social legislation, and was unwilling to see more money go for military expenses, of which its members disapproved in any case. But the tax reform failed, while the prolongation of military service was adopted. The main opponents in these struggles were Joseph Caillaux (1863–1944), a wealthy financier of progressive outlook, and Raymond Poincaré (1860–1934), a lawyer from Lorraine. The trend toward the right was indicated also by the election of Poincaré to the presidency of the republic in January, 1913. Yet, as the elections to the Chamber in the following spring showed, a countertrend soon set in, and the further course of French policy seemed undecided when war broke out in 1914.

FOREIGN POLICY

In the decade before the outbreak of the war, left and right were beginning also to differ about foreign policy. In the years of the Dreyfus Affair and the struggle over the separation of church and state the conduct of foreign policy had been almost independent of the domestic party struggles. From 1898 to 1905 the foreign ministry had been held by one man—Théophile Delcassé (1852–1923)—and France had a number of extremely capable ambassadors who remained at the same post for unusually long periods—Paul Cambon in London for over twenty years (1898–1920), Camille Barrère in Rome for more than twenty-five (1897–1924). Foreign policy was not subjected to pressure from economic interest groups because France was almost self-sufficient, at least more self-sufficient than any other industrial nation. This situation made for the ready acceptance of the protective tariffs which the agricultural interests desired. From 1892, when a new tariff was adopted, France was a highly protected country. Undoubtedly as a result of this protection, French agricultural prices were above those in the world market and agriculture remained highly profitable. France's export trade was not much affected by the adoption of a protective tariff because the exports were primarily luxury goods—wine, leatherware, textiles—and their sales suffered little from countermeasures by other countries.

France had already aquired an extended colonial empire and there was no pronounced economic interest in further colonial expansion. Although France did participate in the imperialist race of the 1890's, it quickly abandoned this policy after the setback at Fashoda. France retained, however, a serious concern in the countries on the North African shore across the Mediterranean: Tunisia and Morocco. This interest was political and strategic rather than economic, because in case of war the control of these countries by another power might make the transport of troops from Algeria to France impossible, and might even open France to an attack from the south. In the interest of securing domination in this area the French were willing to abandon other colonial claims. They conceded to the British their rights in Egypt and recognized the Italian demands on Tripoli. In compensation Great Britain and Italy acknowledged France's predominant interest in Morocco. Since neither of these states had claims on Morocco their concrete gains from these agreements were greater than those of France. But the ties with Great Britain and Italy gave France increased weight in Europe. This was the chief aim of French foreign policy: the nation was to become again a factor to be reckoned with in Europe. In the pursuit of this policy, financial strength was a precious asset. By means of loans France was able to establish close ties with Russia. French firms invested widely in Russian private industry, particularly in mining and metallurgy. Indeed, one third of all foreign investments in nongovernmental enterprises in Russia were of French origin. But the French banks also took up a substantial proportion of Russian government loans. At the time of the outbreak of the First World War almost half of the loans which the Russian government issued were held by foreigners and the French people held 80 per cent of this amount.

Thus France had again become powerful in European politics, a situation disadvantageous to Germany, which since the war of 1870–1871 had attempted to keep France isolated. Indicative of the tension between the two states is the fact that between 1871 and the outbreak of the First World War no official visit between French and German statesmen ever took place. Whether the maintenance of such a rigidly hostile posture was unavoidable, or whether after France had reasserted its position in Europe some gradual lessening of the tension could have been effected remains an open question. There were French financial circles interested in economic cooperation with Germany. Left-wing groups would have liked the government to spend less on defense and more on social reform. Moreover, the French Socialists were pacifists and their leader, Jean Jaurès, gave eloquent voice to their ideals. Yet, there was deep emotional resistance to any attempt at reconciliation with Germany. Throughout this period, on the Place de la Concorde in Paris, where each large French city was represented by a statue, the statue of Strasbourg remained veiled in black. The French did not envisage a war to reconquer Alsace-Lorraine, but there was strong feeling that as long as Germany held Alsace-Lorraine, cooperation between the two States was impossible. French foreign policy, it was felt, ought to hold the line against Germany. And this indeed remained the prevailing tendency of that policy.

The Mediterranean Powers

The constitutional arrangements in Spain and Italy were externally very similar to those of Great Britain. But below the surface the differences were great. In Spain and Italy the kings could exert some influence of their own by means of the army, commanded by generals conservative in outlook and bound by deep loyalty to the crown. Moreover, the political systems of Spain and Italy, despite two-chamber parliaments and the dependence of the governments on securing votes of confidence from these chambers, were actually pseudoparliamentary. The parliamentary form served to disguise the rule of a relatively small social group; the majority of the people were powerless, and in both countries the Church was a powerful force resisting change.

In both Italy and Spain the middle classes, the chief protagonists of liberalism, formed only a small section of the population; in Spain Catalonia almost alone possessed a middle class. Both countries were predominantly agricultural, and the rural areas, dominated and controlled by the owners of large landed estates, retained a feudal aspect. There were a few highly industrialized regions: in Italy, around Turin and Milan; in Spain, Barcelona and wide stretches of Catalonia around it in the northeast, Andalusia with its coal and zinc mines in the south, and the rich, foreign-owned copper mines of Riotinto in the southwest. Even in these districts industrial development was still embryonic, however, and the workers were subjected to all the hardships of the beginnings of industrialization. Wages were so low that not only the father of a family but the wife and the children had to work. Treated with ruthlessness and forming a small minority, the workers were receptive to ideas of revolutionary change, and this radical activism is indicated by the fact that a high proportion— almost one third of them—were members of labor organizations. Those who were organized were divided among various movements. Marxism, anarchism, and syndicalism all had adherents, and the radicalism of the workers was frequently expressed in violence. The rest of Europe regarded Italy and Spain as unstable and threatened by revolution.

SPAIN

In Spain the rule of a small group—great landowners allied to a few wealthy industrialists—behind a parliamentary façade had been secured by agreements made in the 1870's between the Conservative leader Antonio Canovas and the Liberal leader Mateo Sagasta. They arranged that each party would constitute a government for a number of years and then hand it over to the other party, which would arrange new elections. It was a foregone conclusion that these elections would produce the desired majority for the party in power. Suffrage was limited to the propertied classes, and in the rural areas the *cacique*, a government official, determined who should vote and how to vote. By the end of the century, discontent with the system was increasing. A group of young writers, known as the Generation of 1898, was particularly vocal in advocating political and social reforms. In an article which soon became famous one of the leaders of this group, Miguel de Unamuno (1864–1936), made a distinction between the political nation and the real nation, stating that the real nation was entirely unrepresented in politics.

Dissatisfaction increased with the defeat suffered by Spain in the Spanish-American War and the resultant loss of Cuba and the Philippines. In addition to being a national humiliation, the defeat created serious economic problems. Officials, military officers, priests, entire religious orders, had to be settled and reestablished after their return to Spain. Moreover, Cuba and the Philippines had absorbed a certain part of Spain's industrial production. Faced with a rising wave of discontent, the ruling group began to feel insecure. In both parties, the Liberals and the Conservatives, the feeling grew that revolution could be avoided only if broader groups of the population were drawn more closely to the state. A competition for the masses set in between the two parties, and the tacit understanding which had secured the tenures of successive Conservative and Liberal governments broke down. Among the Conservatives, the leader of a group urging an energetic policy of renovation and social reform was Antonio Maura (1853–1925), who was prime minister in 1903–1904 and returned to that office in 1907. But because Maura was not willing to observe any longer the agreed rules of the political game, unrest set in and a revolutionary outbreak, triggered by protests against the conscription of young workers for a campaign in Morocco, occurred in Barcelona.

During the so-called Tragic Week of Barcelona, in July, 1909, the masses seized the city, and their long-endured suppression and sufferings exploded in acts of violence. Twenty-two churches were destroyed and thirty-four convents burned to the ground. After the revolt had been defeated by military forces, the government carried out a number of executions; that of Francisco Ferrer, a well-known intellectual anarchist, aroused wide indignation because valid proofs of his role in the uprising were lacking. The entire revolt was a spontaneous outbreak of dissatisfaction rather than a well-planned conspiracy. The actions of the masses as well as the reaction of the government strongly revealed the violence underlying Spanish political life.

Moreover, the Tragic Week of Barcelona disclosed the two basic difficulties militating against effective opposition to the established order in Spain. One was the unavoidable connection of all reform movements with anticlericalism. As in France—and what had happened in France was highly influential in Spain—the extension of the state school system and restriction of the influence of the teaching orders became the most essential demand of the reformers. The anticlericalism of the intellectuals in the urban centers reinforced the bond between the Church and the conservative landowners, but the Church had strong supporters also among the masses, for the clergy and the numerous religious orders were frequently the refuge of the sons and daughters of the poor.

At the same time, reformers were handicapped by the fact that the most industrialized part of the country, and hence the center of liberal and progressive movements, was Catalonia, with its capital Barcelona. With some justification the Catalans were suspected by the rest of Spain of separatist tendencies, and for this reason the revolt of July, 1909, did not spread beyond Barcelona. It was difficult to organize a unified opposition on a national basis. Thus the regime was able to survive. Maura, the Conservative prime minister, was overthrown soon after the Tragic Week of Barcelona because his plans for social reform were believed to have seduced the revolutionaries to action. The Liberal leader, Jose Canalejas, who made an attempt to carry out an anticlerical program with the help of all the forces of the left, was assassinated in 1912. With the wisdom of hindsight it is not difficult to see that the alternatives in Spain were dictatorship and revolution.

ITALY

The loss of Cuba and the Philippines exemplified Spain's decline as an imperial power. If it was still counted among the great powers this status had its basis in tradition rather than in the nation's actual strength. In contrast, Italy was a newcomer among the great powers and the recent struggles, through which unification had been achieved, left Italian political life strongly tinged with nationalism, which now manifested itself in the urge to demonstrate that Italy could be rightly counted among the great powers.

The Italian social structure showed the same sharp contrasts as that of Spain. In the south were large landed estates owned by an old nobility which was allied with the Church. Little industry existed in the south, and the percentage of the people going to school or receiving some technical training was smaller than in the rest of Italy. In the north, industry extended over a wider area than in Spain. Italy's performance as an industrial and military power was limited by the fact that its resources of pig iron and steel were insignificant, but with the help of waterpower a modern textile industry had been developed. Northern Italy had a large working population and a prosperous middle class. The nation's social stresses were increased by the great fecundity of the peasants of the south. For them the only possibility was immigration either to the industrial districts of the north, where the steady influx of unskilled workers held down wages and nourished revolutionary radicalism, or to foreign countries. National unification had primarily been the work of the middle classes in northern and central Italy, and after unification had been achieved the contrast between the firmly entrenched feudal nobility in the south and the revolutionary proletariat in the north stifled further liberal advances.

The outstanding figure among Italian statesmen in the last decades of the nineteenth century was Francesco Crispi (1819–1901), one of the heroes of the *Risorgimento* period. Crispi decided to turn Italian energies to colonial expansion, a policy that corresponded with Italy's ambition to be a great power. Many Italians still lived under the rule of the Habsburg empire in South Tyrol, Gorizia, and Istria. Crispi, however, wanted to turn Italian nationalist ambitions away from these areas because he was anxious to avoid a clash with Austria-Hungary and its ally, Germany; the only support for Italy in an anti-Austrian policy could come from France, and such an alliance would be inferior in strength to the German-Austrian combination. Moreover, Italian colonial expansion might overcome the feeling that Italian policy had reached a dead end. Crispi decided to enter the race with the other great powers for the control of African areas which had not yet been subjected to European rule; because Italy had a small colonial possession along the Red Sea, he wanted to extend its rule in the area to neighboring Ethiopia. A first Italian advance from the Red Sea toward Ethiopia had suffered a setback at Dogali (1887). But then the Italians helped Menelik (1844–1913), one of the tribal chiefs, to make good his claim to the imperial throne. In return, so Crispi claimed, Menelik had recognized an Italian protectorate over Ethiopia. But neither Menelik nor the other Ethiopian tribal chiefs acknowledged this claim and there were frequent military encounters between Italian troops and local Ethiopian forces along the frontier between Eritrea and Ethiopia. In 1896, against the better judgment of his military advisers, Crispi ordered the advance into Ethiopia of the troops stationed in Eritrea. Crispi miscalculated his opponent's military strength. The Ethiopians were good warriors; they had received some training from French officers and had been equipped with guns by the French. At Aduwa, in difficult mountainous terrain, the Italian army of 20,000 men—half of them Italians, half of them natives—encountered a well-directed force of about 100,000 Ethiopians. The Italians were completely defeated; about 6,000 were killed, 2,000 wounded, and 2,000 taken prisoner. When the news of the defeat reached Rome, the Crispi government resigned amid immense public demonstrations demanding the immediate end of the African adventure. Crispi's successor, Antonio Rudinì (1839–1908), made peace with Menelik immediately, thus recognizing the independence of Ethiopia. Italy's status among the European states plunged. Instead of solidifying Italian national unity, the attempt to become a world power had only increased discontent, and the Ethiopian adventure was followed by years of unrest.

Moreover, the protective tariffs adopted by France had provoked Italian countermeasures and the ensuing tariff war diminished Italian exports and impeded industrial expansion by cutting off loans from French banks. Unemployment rose in the industrial areas, and in May, 1898, bread riots broke out in Milan, barricades were erected in the streets, and order was restored only after some fighting and a declaration of martial law. A general, Luigi Pelloux (1839–1924), became prime minister. He ruled by royal decree and tried to establish a military dictatorship. He was defeated in the elections of 1900, and a month later King Humbert, who had appointed Pelloux and had supported his dictatorial policy, was assassinated.

Thereafter, the situation quieted. An important reason for the improvement was a gradual upward trend in the economic situation. Moreover, the radical left had overplayed its hand. Railway strikes in 1902 and a general strike in 1904 aroused widespread indignation. They appeared inspired by political motives rather than by economic hardships, and were viewed as an attempt at revolution. In consequence, all the moderate forces drew more closely together; the threat of revolution even led to a softening of the hostility between the Italian state and Roman Catholicism. Previously no Roman Catholic was supposed to participate in Italian political life, but Pope Pius X now permitted Catholics to enter the party struggle because the safety of the social order was threatened. In the elections of October, 1904, the radical left suffered harsh defeat. Moreover, in 1903 an unusually clever parliamentary tactician, Giovanni Giolitti (1842–1928), became prime minister. His consummate political skill assured a remarkable degree of political stability. Between the turn of the century and the beginning of the war Giolitti was prime minister three times—from 1903 to 1905, from 1906 to 1909, from 1911 to 1914. And even when out of office he remained the dominant figure in the Italian political scene. His main concern was the modernization of Italian economic life, and this meant industrialization. In this policy Giolitti had success. In the twenty years before the outbreak of the First World War industry in the national production increased its share from 20 to 25 per cent. Most important was the development of the silk industry, and favored by protective tariffs, some heavy industry began to develop.

For Giolitti industrialization also meant democratization. He inaugurated numerous measures of social reform. Trade unions were legalized and collective bargaining was promoted. Minimal standards for hygienic conditions in factories were laid down and working conditions for women and children were improved. The railroads, previously privately owned, were taken over by the state and in consequence both the situation of the railroad workers and the functioning of the transportation system improved. By such means Giolitti tried to provide the government with a broader democratic basis; he was anxious to draw the Socialists into collaboration with the government. The Italian Socialists were split into a revolutionary and a reformist wing and Giolitti aimed at strengthening the reformist group. The climax of Giolitti's democratization policy was, in 1912, an electoral reform which raised the number of voters from 3.5 to 8 million and made universal suffrage of males over thirty years old a reality. Only illiterates who had done no military service were denied the right to vote.

But his regime had its less progressive, dark side. His fundamental aim might have been the strengthening of democracy, but in the handling of the parliamentary machinery he was cynical and opportunistic. To the disgust of his liberal supporters, he accepted the support of the Catholics when this seemed to promise electoral success, and he permitted the south to remain in a state which made a sham out of parliamentarism and democracy. He made no serious attempt to institute agrarian reform in the south, to dissolve the great *latifundia* and provide land for the numerous peasants living there in abject poverty. Instead, the opponents of change—the great landowners and the Church—were left in control of the south. Giolitti even made some concession to Church interests by facilitating religious education in those localities where the parents demanded it. This meant that in practice the schools in the south were in the hands of the priests, who were themselves only half educated, and the masses there remained superstitiously pious and illiterate. The illiteracy rate in some areas was more than 90 per cent.

Giolitti's surrender of the south to vested interests had sinister consequences. The people remained bitterly poor. If possible they emigrated. More than half a million Italians, out of a population of about thirty million, left the country in 1910. Those who remained could not be employed in work which demanded even a minimum of skill; nor did they have the money to buy industrial goods. The internal market, and the entire industrial development of Italy, was retarded by the south. Giolitti had reasons for ignoring this problem; in return for being left in control in their areas, the southern deputies—representing the conservative land-owning group—supported his proposals for economic reforms in the industrial north. But because the south remained underdeveloped Giolitti's policy of forcing the industrial development of the north had only limited results.

For what went on in Italian parliamentary life in the times of Giolitti's domination, the Italians used the word *trasformismo*, after the political maneuver by which a deputy to parliament—even if he did not belong to the parties which composed the government—voted in favor of a govern-ment proposal and in return obtained special advantages for the district he represented. Thus the government ruled with fluctuating majorities. Ideals and principles became a façade behind which the deputies bargained for political and material advantages. This debasement of liberal and demo-cratic values and principles kept alive discontent with the existing system. The most devastating attack against Giolitti's regime was launched by a young Italian historian, Gaetano Salvemini. In a pamphlet character-istically entitled *Il ministro della mala vita* ("The Minister for Misery") he formulated the program which Italian liberalism ought to adopt: partition of the *latifundia*, spread of secular education, honest elections.

Thus, the means which Giolitti employed worked against the goal which he wanted to reach: a secure democratic basis for the regime. Contempt for democracy and parliamentarism and demands for a change of system became widespread on the left and on the right. In the Socialist party the reformist wing had the upper hand only for a brief period. In general the radical wing, which had anarchist tendencies and argued for revolutionary actions, strikes, and sabotage, set the tone, and at the party congress of 1912 the radicals gained control. One of their leaders, Benito Mussolini, became editor of the *Avanti*, the official paper of the Socialist party.

Because Giolitti's support on the left was insecure, he was willing to make concessions to the right. Diplomatic preparation for the war against Turkey for the conquest of Tripoli, which began in 1911, had been going on since the end of the nineteenth century; Giolitti's decision to embark on this enterprise at this particular time was meant to take the wind out of the sails of the nationalists on the right. They ascribed the defeats of Dogali and Aduwa to the lack of heroism inherent in democratic government, and nationalism became imbued with hostility toward parliamentarism and democracy. These resentments and aspirations found expression in a nation-alistic political movement organized by Enrico Corradini, which had a powerful spokesman in Gabriele D'Annunzio, Italy's most famous writer; he proclaimed the need for one great man to rule the country, and found many adherents among the younger generation.

Giolitti's expectations proved incorrect; the conquest of Tripoli increased the appeal of antiparliamentary nationalism instead of weakening it. The elections in 1913, based on the new law establishing universal suffrage, demonstrated the strength of radicalism on the left and on the right. It cannot be claimed that Giolitti's system resulted in the firm establishment of parliamentary democracy in Italy in 1914.

THE AUTHORITARIAN GOVERNMENTS

To what extent Great Britain, France, Spain, and Italy were democracies can be disputed, but in all of them parliaments existed which decided on the composition of the government. This was not the case in Germany, Austria-Hungary, or Russia, in the sense that their governments were not dependent on parliaments. Russia at the beginning of the twentieth century was an autocracy; the system of government in the various parts of the Habsburg monarchy varied; the German empire had a constitution, the rights of the citizens in Germany were legally secured, and elected representatives had a part, although not a decisive one, in the government. However, because the power of the parliaments insofar as they existed was limited, the rulers of these three countries—Nicholas II, Francis Joseph, William II—were highly influential in determining policy.

Germany

The authoritarian system of the German empire was primarily a product of its historical development in the preceding century. Because the unification of Germany had been accomplished by Prussia, the political structure of the German Reich bore a Prussian pattern.

Prussia had successfully withstood the middle-class revolution of the nineteenth century. Its constitution was highly authoritarian; the army was outside civilian control, under direct command of the king, and the Prussian parliament was elected by a method which guaranteed control to the great landowners from east of the Elbe, the *Junkers*.

The Prussian monarch and the Prussian leaders did not want to see their system of government submerged in a wider Reich. Hence, the German empire became not a unitary state but a federal state composed of twenty-five individual states. With the exception of three free cities, the rulers of these states were princes; the government of each of these states appointed a delegate to a federal council, the Bundesrat, which met in Berlin under the chairmanship of the delegate appointed by the Prussian king, who regularly designated the Prussian prime minister for this post. It was as president of this federation of princes that the king of Prussia held the title of German emperor. Since the number of votes which each state possessed within the council was determined by its geographical extent and

A military review in Berlin in 1900. *The street is Berlin's chief avenue, "Unter den Linden," and the building in the background is the University.*

the size of its population, the Bundesrat was dominated by Prussia.

The leaders of Prussian policy at the time of German unification had to take into account, however, that the chief resistance to unification had come from the princely rulers of the German states and the groups bound to them through interest or loyalty. The chief protagonists of unification had been the masses of the people, particularly the middle class. Thus, in order to check separatist tendencies which might come into the foreground in the Bundesrat, a parliament—the Reichstag—was created, with members elected on the basis of a most progressive voting system: universal suffrage of all males above twenty-five years of age.

Legislation for the Reich had to be passed by both the Bundesrat and the Reichstag. The areas over which the Reich could decide and legislate were strictly limited: foreign affairs, naval affairs, the mail and the telegraph, customs, colonies. And it had the right to establish common standards for the administration of justice and military affairs, although the armies remained under the control of the rulers of the individual states and were placed under a unified command only in wartime. The Reich was to receive a certain percentage of the taxes raised by the states, and it had the right to levy indirect taxes.

Although the tasks of the Reich were limited, they were extended enough to require governmental agencies, and the manner in which the federal administration was organized reinforced the dominating position of Prussia.

The control and supervision of the federal administration was entrusted to the chairman of the Bundesrat, who was expected to explain and to defend new legislation in the Reichstag. Since this chairman was always the Prussian prime minister, he combined in his person two functions. As head of the federal administration he had the title of chancellor—*Reichskanzler*—and had under him a number of high officials, "secretaries," who administered the various areas under federal control: foreign affairs, naval affairs, colonies, and so on. As Prussian prime minister he directed Prussian policy and presided over the Prussian cabinet, composed of "ministers": of the interior, of war, of education, of finance, and so on. This arrangement gave the chancellor a remarkable amount of independence. He was appointed by the Prussian king and could be removed neither by the Bundesrat nor by the Reichstag. Despite the strength of his position, the chancellor could more easily prevent a new departure in politics than initiate one. He could frustrate measures of which he disapproved by playing against each other the Reich and Prussia, the Bundesrat and the Reichstag. But he had to maneuver carefully to move these different forces in the same direction. Thus, the complicated political structure of the Reich led to strange contradictions. It made it possible for Prussia to take the leading role without having to give up its system of government and its autonomy. But in providing guarantees against meddling in Prussian affairs, the constitution of the Reich also secured the other German states against interference in their systems of government. Hence, within the German empire great political diversity existed. In contrast to the conservative north, the southern German states—Bavaria, Württemberg, Baden—were liberal, even democratic, and they had parliamentary governments. The majority of the German population was Protestant but the Catholic minority was very considerable; in 1900 there were 35 million Protestants and 20 million Roman Catholics in Germany. Some of the German states were prevailingly Protestant; in others Catholicism had an important political influence.

The complex constitution doubtless required of the Reich's leaders great art in balancing the divergent forces which constituted the German empire. The unified Reich was Bismarck's creation and its constitution had been tailored to his forceful but prudent personality. He was also favored by the fact that in the first decade after unification, an equilibrium of social forces still existed: the conflict between the interests of agriculture and industry was still muted. But toward the close of the nineteenth century the conditions for a successful functioning of the German constitution began to disappear: Bismark was dismissed in 1890, and at the end of the century there was a rapid and striking change in the German social structure which upset the delicate balance of social forces. The extent of the changes in Germany between 1870 and 1914 can best be illustrated by a few statistics. The population increased from 41 million to 65 million; whereas in 1870 more than half of the population had been employed in agriculture, by 1914 this proportion had been reduced to less than a third. Germany had become a highly industrialized and commercial country.

At the outbreak of the First World War, Germany's merchant marine was the second largest in the world, surpassed only by that of Great Britain. By then, too, Germany was the third largest coal-producing power—behind the United States and only slightly behind Great Britain. Germany produced considerably more pig iron and steel than any other European power, Great Britain included, and almost half as much as the United States. Germany's rich mineral resources favored the development of an armament industry. Krupp, the leading German armament manufacturer, together with Skoda in Austria and the French firm of Schneider-Creusot, dominated the armament market of the world. The electrical and chemical industries also flourished. Some of the German dyestuffs and pharmaceuticals enjoyed a kind of monopoly on the world market. In contrast to the United States and the British empire, Germany produced much more than could be consumed on the domestic market. Between 1887 and 1912 the value of German exports increased 185 per cent. Germany's rise as an industrial world power thus involved a rapid penetration into foreign markets; until 1880 it had traded almost exclusively with other European countries; thereafter Germany began to exchange goods increasingly with other continents.

The mineral resources on which industrial development was based could be found in almost every part of the nation. Most important was the Ruhr, where coal and iron were available. In the southwest, in the areas ceded by France in 1871, were iron and potash; in the east, Upper Silesia was rich in coal; and in central Germany, lignite deposits served the electrical and chemical industries. Thus the impact of industrialization was felt over all the country. Since industrial development in Germany started later than in Great Britain and in France, large capital investments were needed to facilitate competition with the more advanced nations. Such quantities of capital could be provided only by banks, not by the industrial entrepreneurs themselves or by private financiers. In German economic development banking and industrial enterprises became closely interconnected. This alliance promoted the formation of big companies possessing greater efficiency than smaller ones that produced the same goods. In some fields the large enterprises achieved a monopoly; in others a few big industrial companies banded together in cartel agreements that enabled them to fix prices and delimit markets. The members of a cartel could establish high price levels at home to maintain profits while they attempted to conquer foreign markets by "dumping" goods there at low prices. For this reason the German government not only permitted monopolies and cartels but even gave legal protection to cartel agreements;

violators could be brought to court and punished.

Small and middle-sized economic enterprises did not entirely disappear from German economic life, but in Germany there was some truth in the picture, given by Lenin in his treatise on *Imperialism, the Highest Stage of Capitalism*, of the domination of a nation's economic life by a small group of financiers and industrialists.

The rapid development of Germany into a great economic power, and the accompanying rise in wealth in almost all groups of the population, had a dangerously intoxicating effect on the German upper and middle classes. Most of them succumbed to the fatal fascination of the idea of becoming a "world power": Germany ought to have a navy; it ought to have colonies; German passenger ships had to be the largest and fastest. German bankers and industrialists were convinced that wherever they found the opportunity for economic penetration—in Turkey, in China, or anywhere else—they ought to make use of it, regardless of the claims, rights, or interests of other nations. Since Germany was a latecomer on the world scene, they felt, it had to be pushy to gain its due "place in the sun," as William II characterized his realm's political ambitions.

Nevertheless, industrial development in Germany did not progress without conflicts. Wherever industrial and agrarian interests clashed, the *Junkers* were able to put up strong resistance for they dominated the political system of Germany's most powerful state. Moreover, the transition to industrialization was unavoidably accompanied by social tensions, and the gap between entrepreneur and workers was widened by the resentment which Bismarck's repressive antisocialist laws had created. After these laws had lapsed, and as a consequence of the rapid progress of industrialization, the socialists made great strides. The Social Democrats increased their number of deputies in the Reichstag from 35 in 1890 to 110 in 1911 and became the strongest political party. Although by then the Social Democratic party and the allied trade unions had become big bureaucracies inclined to move slowly and cautiously, the Marxian view of the need for a revolution remained dominant among the workers, especially since the government continued to proceed vigorously against all subversive agitation and propaganda.

After 1890 instability was further increased by the fact that the role which the constitution assigned to the emperor, but which actually had been filled by Bismarck, had fallen to a monarch who wanted to rule, but lacked the qualities necessary for doing so.

THE EMPIRE UNDER WILLIAM II

In the public mind, particularly in those countries which fought against Germany in the First World War, William II (ruled 1888–1919) is usually pictured as the prototype of the warlord—imperious, brutal, barbarian.

Indeed, William did like to appear in full military panoply, preferably in the uniform of an officer of the cuirassier guards, in silvery, shining mail and a helmet crowned by a golden eagle. He talked to his ministers and to his people as an officer talks to his soldiers, giving them orders and commands. William felt himself the heir and successor of the absolutist Hohenzollern kings of the eighteenth century. He believed that his power came from God and considered himself, as he said in one of his bombastic speeches, "an instrument of God." Most of all, he felt obliged to maintain the Prussian military tradition. He was hardly aware that the army was no longer an army of mercenaries, the personal property of the monarch, but was now based on general conscription. Addressing a Berlin regiment about the socialist opposition, he told the soldiers that they would have to shoot their fathers and mothers if he ordered them to do so. Because he disapproved of modern dances he forbade all men in uniform to dance the tango, when it became popular in 1913. Since the inner organization of the army, and the appointment of officers, were entirely outside of civilian control, William had some legal justification for believing he could demand absolute obedience.

Nevertheless, he wanted to be more than the preserver of an absolutist tradition. He wanted to be a modern monarch who would lead Germany into a new era of history. He surrounded himself not only with members of the Prussian aristocracy but also with industrialists and bankers. Albert Ballin, the leading spirit of the largest German shipping line, was his friend. Rhenish industrialists such as the Stumms and the Krupps were his favorites. Although in his youth William had participated in meetings of an anti-Semitic group, he was later inclined to favor wealthy Jews and to grant them titles, to the great disgust of the Prussian aristocracy. He was fascinated by discoveries in the natural sciences and delighted in bestowing decorations on outstanding scientists, and occasionally nobilitating them. He preached enthusiastically the need for making Germany a world power. William was a zealous reader of Mahan and accepted his view that sea power was the crucial factor in the struggle of nations and the competition for empire.

This combination of Prussian authoritarianism with faith in technological progress and capitalist expansion corresponded to the inclinations of the German bourgeoisie. In the earlier years of his reign William II was extremely popular. There is some justification for the brilliant satire of the German middle-class mind in Heinrich Mann's novel *The Patrioteer* (1918), in which the hero, a bourgeois parvenu, is depicted as modeling his life in every detail according to that of his ideal, the emperor.

But William II also had many opponents, and their number increased over the years. His adversaries and critics were to be found not only among the socialists, who condemned the entire regime, but also among those who

William II, left, with Admiral von Tirpitz, center, and Admiral von Holzendorf, in 1910.

knew him best. Some considered him to be the gravedigger of the German monarchy. They were aware of his superficiality; his various intellectual and aesthetic enthusiasms were short-lived and he was incapable of sustained effort and serious work. Nervous and restless, he traveled continually from one place to another and expected to be constantly entertained. And these entertainments were not very refined. Quite a public scandal developed when one of his chamberlains, elderly and fat, died of a heart attack while dancing before him in the costume of a ballet girl. Most of all, despite his martial appearance and powerful gestures, William II was weak, easily influenced by men with stronger wills, especially when they presented their ideas in amusing and flattering forms. A kind of Byzantine atmosphere permeated the court. Military men, industrialists, bankers, and courtiers could sway the emperor. In the first decade of his reign William's great favorite was Count Philipp Eulenburg (1847–1921); his homosexual inclinations, which were unknown to the emperor, led to a scandal that severely damaged the prestige of the court. In later years a powerful influence was the secretary of the navy, Admiral Alfred von Tirpitz (1849–1930), who kept alive William's interest in the building of a great navy.

Although he failed to provide unifying direction to the nation, William II was unwilling to concede to his chancellors that decisive influence which Bismarck had possessed. Each chancellor had to struggle against military, naval, and personal influences, and the course of German policy became erratic.

Of Bismarck's successors, the first, Count Leo von Caprivi (chancellor from 1890 to 1894) was a military man; the others were civil servants. Prince Chlodwig von Hohenlohe, (from 1894 to 1900) had been the administrative head of Alsace-Lorraine; Bernhard von Bülow (from 1900 to 1909) came from the diplomatic corps; Theobald von Bethmann-Hollweg (from 1909 to 1917) from the Prussian administration. The appointment of civil servants to high positions of political leadership emphasized the independence of the government from parliamentary influence. But as we have seen, although the role of the Reichstag was limited, its approval of new legislation and taxation was necessary. The Social Democrats, as opponents of the entire system, always voted against the government, which therefore had to seek support from the parties to the right of the socialists. And these were of greatly varying political shadings. The Conservatives spoke chiefly for the agrarian interests, while the Center party included members of every stratum of society since its unifying bond was religion: Roman Catholicism. The bourgeois world was represented by two groups: the National Liberals, who championed the interests of heavy industry; and the Progressives, supported by small entrepreneurs and white-collar workers, and retaining the nineteenth-century ideal of a liberal and democratic Germany.

Cooperation among parties of such varied interests was difficult to achieve, and German domestic policy remained singularly weak in creative legislation. Laws which could be justified by an appeal to nationalism had the best chance to find support among all the nonsocialist parties. The most significant legislation was a finance bill, accepted in 1913, which, in order to permit an increase in the strength of the army, instituted a capital levy that could be raised directly by the federal government. Previously the federal government had been limited to indirect taxes and contributions from the individual states. Measures and laws which had been introduced under Bismarck were perfected. One general law code for the whole of Germany was established. The social-insurance system was extended to additional groups and payments to the elderly and invalids were increased. Working hours for women and children were strictly limited. Although politically Germany remained authoritarian, its administration was efficient and was concerned with the well-being of the citizens.

For the passage of any legislation the government always had to have the vote of both the Conservatives and the National Liberals. In addition, the backing of either the Center party or the Progressives was needed for a majority. This support could usually be bought by some concessions to the particular interests of one party or the other. In particular, the Center party was willing to vote with the government in return for obtaining positions for Catholics in the administration.

The crucial aim was to achieve an alliance between the Conservatives and the National Liberals, that is, between agricultural and industrial interests. On one hand this was an economic problem. There was the conflict between the landowner's demand for protective tariffs against American and Russian grain and the industrialist's desire for low food prices which would allow low wages and facilitate competition on the world market. At the beginning of the reign of William II, under Bismarck's

William II with
Chancellor von
Bethmann - Hollweg
in 1910.

successor, Caprivi, agricultural tariffs were lowered in the interest of industrial expansion. But the *Junkers* forced Caprivi's fall and the government changed its course and embarked on a policy of agricultural protection, buying the agreement of the National Liberals by concessions to industrial interests. Thus the rise in agricultural tariffs in 1899 was complementary to the acceptance of a law initiating the building of a fleet of battleships. A large navy provided heavy industry with a continuous flow of government orders, and in the eyes of the leaders of heavy industry this advantage outweighed the disadvantages of protective tariffs; in compensation for obtaining protective tariffs the Conservatives gave up their opposition to a large fleet. The origin of the naval program has to be ascribed to William II's envious admiration of Great Britain and to the influence of Admiral von Tirpitz on the emperor. But it was continuously pursued because it cemented the alliance between agricultural and industrial interests.

This alliance between industry and agriculture also presented a social problem. The Prussian *Junkers* were reluctant to admit members of the bourgeoisie into the ruling group. As in Great Britain, however, there were many points of contact among the wealthiest groups of society, and William II's favorable attitude toward members of the rich bourgeoisie was politically significant in creating bridges between them and the old aristocracy. But in Germany the agricultural and feudal forces continued to dominate the ruling group because German economic development needed government support and the Prussian *Junker* was firmly entrenched in the government. The adjustment of the sons of the bourgeoisie to the feudal and militaristic values of the Prussian nobility was promoted by the control which the government exerted over education. But the crucial factor was the institution of the reserve officer. Service in the army as a reserve officer was an admission ticket to society and to government positions. A commission in the officer corps of a regiment was like membership in a club. Those who were officers would accept only those who shared their standards of behavior. Thus, in Germany aristocratic values were not replaced by bourgeois values; instead, the German high bourgeoisie became feudalized.

However, it should not be assumed that Germany was a totalitarian state. The government was not despotic. On the contrary, the Germans prided themselves on living in a society which was ruled according to law—in a *Rechtsstaat*. In court proceedings legal forms were strictly observed and the individual could be sure of having his rights carefully protected. There was no censorship. The satirical weekly *Simplicissimus*, which attacked the ruling group and the stereotype of the Prussian lieutenant in a witty but savage way, circulated freely and was widely read. If intellectual life in Berlin and in Prussia was stifled by the narrowness and the conservatism of the outlook of the Prussian ruling group, a livelier and freer intellectual climate could be found in other parts of Germany. The cultural life in Munich, the capital of Bavaria, stood in stark contrast to that of Berlin. Munich was the home of the leading German exponents of Expressionism, and of literary figures like the novelist Thomas Mann and the dramatist Frank Wedekind, who advocated a new, freer morality in his plays. If Berlin was the political capital, Munich was the center of modern movements in German art and literature. Nevertheless, opposition to the prevailing militaristic tendencies was essentially powerless. This was strikingly shown in 1913 when popular demonstrations took place in the Alsatian town of Zabern against the troops stationed there. In an arbitrary extension of their functions the military authorities placed the town under martial law, and all the protests of political moderates did not help. William II even congratulated the responsible officer for his energetic behavior.

The amalgamation of the outlook of the rich industrial and financial bourgeoisie with feudal military traditions had a dangerous effect on foreign policy. In Germany's struggle for a "place in the sun," the accent was very much on power politics. Wherever some acquisition of territory seemed possible—in Africa or China or the Pacific—Germany raised claims, and these widespread claims brought about conflicts of interest with almost all the other major European states. The influence of the Prussian Conservatives made it certain that Germany would remain the strongest military power in Europe. But the building of a first-rank navy, combined with the economic competition arising from Germany's growing industrial strength, complicated German relations with Great Britain, traditionally the strongest naval power. Moreover, in order not to endanger the alliance between

"The Lieutenant the Day before Yesterday, Yesterday and Today," a caricature from *Simplicissimus*. *The caption was presented in slang which is difficult to reproduce in English. The lieutenant says* "Yesterday, gambled at the jockey club, improved my finances; then champagne, nothing but champagne."

agrarian and industrial interests, the government tended to yield to their pressures. Thus, for example, it supported the building of the Baghdad Railway in Turkey by German financial groups, thereby stepping into an area which previously Great Britain and Russia had regarded as exclusively theirs. Because of its ambitious rush into world politics Germany became exposed to pressure from all sides.

The Habsburg Monarchy and the Balkan States

FRANCIS JOSEPH AND THE DISINTEGRATION OF THE HABSBURG EMPIRE

Of the seven great European powers which existed at the turn of the century, Austria-Hungary alone failed to survive the First World War. Even before that conflict, the Habsburg monarchy, including the most different nationalities—Germans, Magyars, Slovaks, Croatians, Czechs, Rumanians, Italians, Poles—was an anachronism. Much of the time, despite feeble and inconsistent attempts at constitutional forms and parliamentarism, it was ruled dictatorially. The anachronistic nature of this monarchy gave to Austria-Hungary, and particularly to the Vienna of the prewar years, a peculiar attraction. Aristocratic and cosmopolitan Vienna seemed to preserve a refined cultural tradition which was disappearing in the rest of Europe. Vienna was the center of the music world, attracting the most famous singers to its opera, and the best orchestra conductors and composers. Johannes Brahms might be seen sitting next to the wife of Johann Strauss; and while Strauss was conducting his waltzes, Brahms wrote on

Mrs. Strauss' fan: "Unfortunately not by Johannes Brahms." The best German actors and actresses performed in the Burgtheater. Vienna was the center of literary trends exploring the complexities of human psychology, and in the coffeehouses the representatives of this modern literary approach—Arthur Schnitzler and Harmann Bahr—might be found talking respectfully to a fragile youth, not yet twenty years old, who had just become famous as the author of a small volume of exquisite poems: Hugo von Hofmannsthal, later to write the libretto of Richard Strauss' *Rosenkavalier* (1911). And there were the elegant Baroque palaces, from which issued carriages drawn by beautiful horses taking their noble and wealthy owners—the Liechtensteins, the Esterházys, the Schwarzenbergs—to Vienna's famous park, the Prater. They all contributed to making the life of the Vienna court the most brilliant in Europe, and because of the scandals in which the wild young Habsburg archdukes became involved, it was also the most romantic.

The embodiment of this anachronism was Emperor Francis Joseph (ruled 1848–1916). In 1900, he had ruled for more than fifty years, and he would go on ruling into the First World War. Having lived through political and personal disasters—having been forced to abandon part of his heritage to Italy, having been pushed out of Germany, having lost his son by suicide and his wife by assassination—he still continued to get up every morning at five to begin the study of the files on his desk and went on to preside over his court, in which the most rigid Spanish etiquette was observed. It is typical of the strength as well as the weakness of this regime that when in June, 1914, Francis Joseph's nephew and presumptive heir, Francis Ferdinand, and his morganatic wife were assassinated at Sarajevo, the emperor's primary reaction was not sorrow about the death of a close relation, but relief that this event would avert the danger that the son of this misalliance might become ruler of Austria-Hungary. "A higher Power has restored the order that I was unhappily unable to maintain" were the words with which he reacted to the news from Sarajevo.

It is not difficult to see why this composite of different nationalities did not survive. Rather, it is difficult to explain why the Habsburg empire continued to exist as long as it did. One reason was that all the great European powers believed that the destruction of this empire would result in a frightening disturbance of the European balance of power. It was feared that if the Habsburg empire collapsed, its Slavic nationals—its Poles, Czechs, Slovaks, Serbs, and Croatians—would turn to Russia thereby allowing it to gain an overwhelmingly strong position in Europe. Moreover, the considerable influence of the Roman Catholic Church was exerted to maintain the Habsburg realm. The frontier between the Roman Catholic and the Eastern Orthodox churches ran through the empire, and the continuing strength of the Roman Catholic Habsburgs seemed

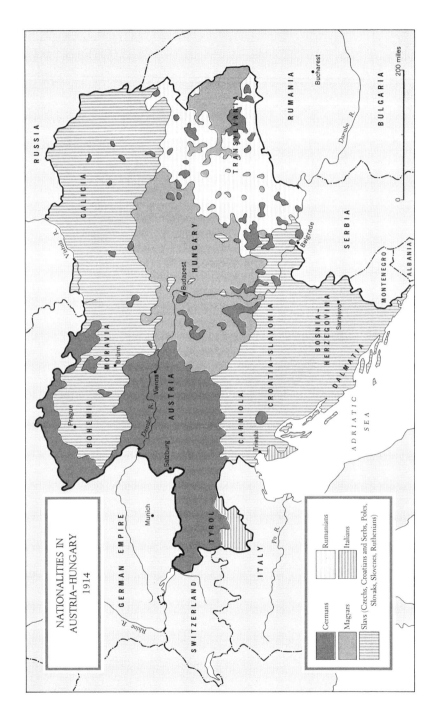

NATIONALITIES IN
AUSTRIA-HUNGARY
1914

Germans

Magyars

Slavs (Czechs, Croatians and Serbs, Poles,
Slovaks, Slovenes, Ruthenians)

Rumanians

Italians

200 miles

RUSSIA

GALICIA

RUMANIA

Bucharest

BULGARIA

Danube R.

Vistula R.

TRANSYLVANIA

HUNGARY

Budapest

Belgrade

SERBIA

MONTENEGRO

ALBANIA

MORAVIA

Brünn

Prague

BOHEMIA

Danube R.

Vienna

AUSTRIA

Salzburg

CROATIA-SLAVONIA

CARNIOLA

Trieste

BOSNIA-HERZEGOVINA

Sarajevo

DALMATIA

ADRIATIC

SEA

GERMAN EMPIRE

Munich

TYROL

SWITZERLAND

Rhine R.

ITALY

Po R.

to the Roman Church a better guarantee for maintaining its position than Slavic states oriented toward the Orthodox tsar.

Furthermore, Austria-Hungary was held together by economic forces. It was a geographic unit; the Danube, which formed the great link between northwestern and southeastern Europe, facilitated an exchange of goods among the regions of the empire. The economy was well balanced. Agricultural production was sufficient to provide food for the areas where natural resources—particularly coal in Bohemia and iron in Styria—stimulated industrial activity.

Despite this development of industry Austria-Hungary remained a predominantly agrarian state. The forms of land ownership forged a further bond within the empire. For the land was in the hands of the nobility. This was particularly true in Hungary, where in 1895, 4,000 landowners—0.16 per cent of all landowners—possessed 33 per cent of the total farming area. Of these, less than 150 owned more than half of this area. The wealthiest among them—the Károlyis and the Esterházys—had immense *latifundia*. On the other hand, there were 1,300,000 peasants with holdings of less than seven acres, hardly enough to squeeze out a livelihood, and in addition the rural population included 2,000,000 farmhands and itinerant farm workers without any land of their own. In other parts of the Habsburg monarchy the social differences were not quite as deep, but the situation was not entirely dissimilar. There were extended *latifundia* also in Galicia and Bohemia. In Bohemia the great landlords were German while the bulk of the population was Czech. Serfdom had ended, but the prosperity of the aristocrats still depended on their keeping the masses of the agricultural population dependent so that they would have to work for the great landowners. Hence the great nobility, fearing economic change, gave firm support to the Habsburg monarchy. The close relationship maintained with the monarchy by the aristocracy from all parts of the empire can be seen in the diverse national origins of the men holding the most important position in the imperial government, that of foreign minister: Count Gustav Siegmund Kálnoky (in office from 1881 to 1895) was a Magyar; Count Goluchowski (1895 to 1906) was a Pole; Baron von Aehrenthal (1906 to 1912) was a Bohemian; Count Berchtold (1912 to 1915) was a German.

Finally, the most effective but also the most dangerous instrument in maintaining the coherence of the empire was the policy of playing one nationality out against the others.

THE DUAL MONARCHY

The Habsburg empire was a Dual Monarchy. In one part—the empire of Austria—the Germans predominated; in the other—Hungary—the Magyars. These two parts had in common only the person of the emperor, foreign policy, customs policy, and the army. But Austria was not purely

German, nor was Hungary purely Magyar, and the maintenance of German or Magyar rule over the subordinate nationalities became more difficult from decade to decade. The widening distribution of printed materials —newspapers and literary works—made the various nationalities conscious of their particular cultural heritage. Industrialization drew many peasants into the cities and gave them economic strength. Social tensions inherent in the general economic changes of this period were heightened by the resistance against German and Magyar rule. In the Austrian part of the empire the most dramatic crisis occurred at the end of the 1890's, when the prime minister, Count Badeni, tried to calm national unrest by a series of decrees which ordered that in districts with a non-German majority, officials had to be able to use two languages: that of the majority group and German. The Germans were vehemently resentful, since these decrees meant the loss of the privileged position which they had held in the civil service because they could be employed all over the country. A nationalist movement proclaiming German racial superiority arose, and staging violent demonstrations, its members threatened to break away from the Habsburgs and join the German empire. Under the pressure of the German agitation, Badeni was dismissed and his language decrees were withdrawn. At this point, government based on the support of the majority of the Austrian parliament ended. After 1897 the prime ministers more and more frequently had recourse to rule by emergency decrees.

In Hungary the crisis came somewhat later. From 1903 to 1905 Hungary had a parliamentary system, but voting was restricted in such a way that the Magyars and the great landowners could be assured of a majority. The fiercely nationalistic Magyars wanted to increase their power in the empire by separating the Hungarian regiments from the rest of the army. They proposed that these regiments have their own insignia; and that the language of military command for them be Hungarian instead of German. When Emperor Francis Joseph rejected these demands, regarding them as direct interference with his powers, the Magyars refused to recognize the government which the emperor had appointed. This Magyar revolt was broken by the threat of the emperor to introduce universal suffrage, which would have destroyed both the Magyar domination and the power of the landowners. The Hungarian leaders realized that they had gone too far. Henceforth, the dominant figure in Hungarian politics, a man who also had an influential voice in the general affairs of the Habsburg empire, was Count Istvàn Tisza (1861–1918); he was a strong defender of Magyar superiority, but he knew that Magyar rule in Hungary was inextricably tied up with the maintenance of the empire as a whole and might suffer from changes or a general upheaval.

The crises in Austria and in Hungary revealed the lack of underlying principles in Habsburg policy. Sometimes the government would seem to favor the non-German or non-Magyar nationalities; sometimes it would rely exclusively on Germans or Magyars; sometimes it would exert power dictatorially; sometimes it played with democratic suggestions. Its only aim was to maintain the *status quo*.

It may be the inherent logic of a fundamentally illogical situation that some of the most energetic leaders in the Habsburg empire turned away from ideas of domestic change and reform and came to believe that the empire could best be maintained by a policy of expansion. Their hope was that the pride aroused by military successes might form a bond among the various nationalities. But Austria-Hungary was without access to an ocean; world politics, sea power, and colonies had no attraction. As in previous centuries, the Balkans were the crucial area for Habsburg foreign policy. Because of the relationship between some of the Balkan nations and the peoples in Austria-Hungary, the nationalism of the Balkan states created unrest and dissatisfaction among the minorities living in the Dual Monarchy; at the same time, the Austrian concern with the Balkans kept alive the tension with Russia, which had its own ambitions in this area.

THE BALKAN STATES AND THE GREAT POWERS

In the early twentieth century, the situation in the Balkans became explosive. The Ottoman Empire still reached far into Europe, straight through to the Adriatic Sea. The Christian Balkan states—Rumania, Bulgaria, Serbia, Montenegro—were anxious to end Turkish rule over European territories, *i.e.* in the Balkans. Greece claimed from Turkey the islands in the Aegean Sea, particularly Crete. But when an insurrection on Crete resulted in war against Turkey in 1896–1897, Greece was saved from complete defeat only by the intervention of the Great Powers. In the northern part of the Balkans, Rumania, Serbia, and the small mountain kingdom of Montenegro possessed full independence. Bulgaria, although autonomous under its own ruler, Prince Ferdinand of the Saxe-Coburg family, was still not fully sovereign, being legally part of the Ottoman Empire. Rumania, especially after its oil fields were discovered, had great wealth, but exhausted most of it in the maintenance of a strong military force. Rumania resented both Russia and Austria-Hungary—Russia because it had annexed Bessarabia, and Austria-Hungary because it possessed Transylvania, which had a large Rumanian population. Thus, Rumanian foreign policy vacillated between Russia and Austria-Hungary.

The main protagonists of nationalist aspirations against the Ottoman Empire were Serbia and Bulgaria. As long as these aspirations were directed toward liberation of the Slavic people in the Ottoman Empire, the rulers of Serbia enjoyed the protection of the Habsburg monarchy. But when, in 1903, the pro-Austrian King Alexander of Serbia, despised because of a foolish marriage, was assassinated by a group of officers, Serbia began to turn to Russia and became hostile to Austria-Hungary. Although both Bulgaria and Serbia were anxious to drive the Turks out of Europe, they were at loggerheads with each other over Macedonia: both supported its aspirations to independence from the Turks, but both planned to annex it, once liberation was achieved. When Serbia turned to Russia, the Austrian government gave support to Bulgaria. The Serbs began to see in Austria-Hungary the main obstacle to their becoming a great national state composed of Croatians, Slovenes, and Serbs—briefly, of all South Slavs. Thus Serbian agitation became increasingly vehement not only for liberation from the Turks but also for the liberation of the South Slavs from Habsburg rule.

In this situation Austrian politicians began to adopt the view that military action might solve all their problems. Some Austrian statesmen—and among them was thought to be Francis Ferdinand, the heir to the throne —seemed to believe that Austria-Hungary might take over the leadership of the South Slavs and add to the Hungarian and German parts of the empire a Yugoslav part. The Dual Monarchy might become a triadic empire. Others, probably with a more realistic appreciation of the possibilities, supposed that a defeat of Serbia might help to cool off the heat of nationalist movements in the Balkans and thereby relieve the pressure from this quarter. The Austrian chief of staff, Franz Conrad von Hötzendorf (1852–1925), favored a preventive war. These men, deeply imbued with the traditions of the Habsburg empire, hoped that by a show of strength the empire would prove the value of its traditional rule as the protagonist of civilization and Christianity against the Turks in the Balkans. As in its entire social structure, so also in its foreign policy, the Habsburg empire— insofar as its leader had any intentions beyond the maintenance of the *status quo*—was still animated by the ideas through which the Habsburgs had become powerful in the eighteenth century.

Russia

Tense and unstable though the situation was in many European countries, the only state in which the tensions led to a full-scale revolution before the First World War was Russia. In its political development Russia was less advanced than any other European nation; at the end of the nineteenth century it was still ruled by an absolute monarch. Moreover, the man who held this formidable power was in character the most insignificant of all the monarchs of his time. The diary of Tsar Nicholas II (ruled 1894–1917), with its monotonous notices about the weather and visits of relations, even on days when the fate of his country and dynasty was being decided, gives the impression that for this monarch the world was confined to the precincts of his palaces. Like other weak and stupid men he clung with a desperate obstinacy to the few ideas with which he had been indoctrinated

Tsar Nicholas II and the tsarina in their coronation robes.

in his youth, and primary among these was the conviction that the absolute power which he had inherited should be left, intact and unlimited, to his son.

Nicholas was easily dominated by stronger personalities who shared this belief. In the first ten years of his reign he was under the influence of the procurator of the Holy Synod, Konstantin Pobedonostsev (1827–1907), who had been his tutor and who in his religious zeal expected that the salvation of Russia would be achieved by shutting the nation off from all liberal Western ideas. In the tsar's later years he was dominated by his wife and the monk Rasputin. The tsarina believed that Rasputin possessed healing powers which could keep her hemophilic son alive. And since Rasputin's grasping and corrupting manners were generally resented and despised, the tsarina felt that he could be kept at court if the tsar remained an autocrat. Thus, it was in the interest of both the tsarina and Rasputin to reinforce the tsar's absolutist notions. But since many ministers opposed Rasputin's political ideas and he was frequently able to force the dismissal of his opponents, Rasputin's presence at the court represented a serious political issue. In rejecting the attacks against Rasputin, the tsar and tsarina convinced themselves that their "friend" was a "holy man," through whom they heard the "voice of the people."

Of course, it was hardly feasible for one man to govern the immense Russian empire in the twentieth century. The real ruler of Russia was a gigantic bureaucracy—slow, clumsy, uncontrolled, and corrupt. If administrators of talent and energy did emerge—as for instance, Count Sergei Witte (1849–1915), who was finance minister between 1892 and 1903, and, after the Revolution of 1905, Peter Stolypin (1863–1911), prime minister between 1906 and 1911—they soon found themselves entangled in bureaucratic intrigues. Furthermore, the tsar became distrustful of the new ideas advocated by such men, and saw in their popularity a threat to his power; thus, neither Witte nor Stolypin enjoyed the full support of the tsar and he was soon anxious to get rid of them. The obvious weakness of an absolutist system in modern times were augmented by the tsar's personal defects.

THE DRIVE TOWARD INDUSTRIALIZATION

The problems which the Russian government faced were staggering. Russia was predominantly agricultural but after the Crimean War it had been realized that the nation would have to develop industries in order to remain a great power. It did possess the natural resources necessary for industrialization: coal and iron in the Donets Basin, oil in the Caucasus, cotton in Turkestan. But the obstacles to industrialization were also formidable. Before 1860 Moscow, St. Petersburg, and Kiev were the only great cities; Russia lacked the social strata which in other countries provided the capital and the skills needed for industrial development. Most of the capital therefore had to come from abroad. In 1900 more than 50 per cent of the capital of Russian industrial companies was foreign; about 90 per cent of the capital invested in mining and over 60 per cent of the capital in metal industries was foreign. The Royal Dutch Oil Company of Henri Deterding led in the exploitation of Caucasian oil; British capital played a major role in the development of the iron industry in the Ukraine.

A requisite for industrial development was the improvement of communications through the construction of a countrywide network of railroads. In the wide steppes of Russia, some of them hardly inhabited or explored, railroad construction was a complicated and difficult task which naturally fell to the state and gave the state a direct share in the development of the iron and coal industries. Thus the government was an important entrepreneur; the capital necessary for its enterprises was derived from loans and they again were largely taken up by foreign banks, particularly the French. Almost 50 per cent of all the interest paid on Russian state loans went out of Russia.

Obtaining the manpower needed for industrialization was difficult. One of the principal motives behind Alexander II's famous emancipation of the serfs in 1861 had been that of making it possible for peasants to emigrate to the urban areas to become industrial workers. But this purpose was partly defeated by details in the emancipation regulations. The former serfs had to pay for the land which had been granted to them. To fulfill this obligation,

A first-class compartment on the Trans-Siberian Railroad.

village committees, *mirs*, were formed; these undertook to make the payments, but they needed men to work the land and were unwilling to permit emigration to the cities. In order to move to the industrial centers the peasants either had to give up all claims to land or had to return for the harvest, spending only part of the year in the cities. Unable to work continuously in industry, they remained unskilled and had to take any job given to them. Their wages were extremely low; in 1880 Russian workers in Moscow received only 25 per cent as much as their British counterparts. The workers were housed in barracks, awakened by bells, marched to the factories, and marched back again after work, and then the gates of the barracks were closed. These conditions created unrest and dissatisfaction; when the workers returned to their villages and families they gave vent to their feelings and spread revolutionary propaganda among the rural population. Moreover, Russia's industrialization suffered from the ills common to the beginnings of industrialization in all countries: the absence of health and safety precautions in the factories, and of limitations on working hours, even for women and children. For instance, in the textile industries workers were expected to work twelve to fifteen hours a day. There was no collective bargaining and no right to strike. In addition, the change in Russian social life brought about by industrialization was deeply upsetting. With the sudden eruption of big cities, industrialization in Russia was not only an economic event but an emotional experience.

Russia was the home of many nationalities. The great masses of the population in the center of the country were Russians, but the situation in the outlying districts was very different. In the west the population was Polish; in the north the Finns had been annexed to Russia only in the early nineteenth century; in the Baltic states German nobles ruled as landowners over Estonians, Latvians, and Lithuanians. The Caucasus was populated by Georgians. Most of these national groups, particularly the Poles and the Finns but also the inhabitants of the Baltic states, had formed part of the European world at the time when Russia was still isolated. Hence they were very different from the Russians in their social structure and their intellectual outlook. They had old medieval towns and a middle class. They had been active in trade and industry; the manufacture of textiles, for example, had been carried on in Poland while Russia was still purely agrarian. They had old universities, and their intellectual life was oriented toward the West. The Poles were Catholics; the Finns and the Balts were Lutherans. Religious differences reinforced the tensions arising from differences of nationality. All these non-Russians, close to the West in their outlook, felt humiliated by the absence of institutions which the West possessed: constitutional government and self-administration. On the other hand, the Russian government feared that the granting of a constitution and of self-administration would increase the centrifugal tendencies in these areas, and was brutal enough to make various attempts at Russification, demanding the use of the Russian language and placing obstacles in the way of all those churches which were not Orthodox. Moreover, the great landowners were favored at the expense of the rest of the population. All of these policies only increased national feeling and social tension.

THE OPPOSITION

The usual outlets for political dissatisfaction, the usual means for testing the strength of opposition, were absent in Russia. Political parties were not permitted. Even associations like trade unions did not exist. A few professional organizations enjoyed approval, but even their meetings were supervised. There was rigorous censorship. Some critical views and plans for change and reform might be inserted in larger theoretical treatises, where they escaped the eyes of the censor, but political literature or even newspapers expressing criticism of the government had to be secretly printed and distributed. Frequently, such publications were the work of exiles and were smuggled over the frontiers.

Switzerland and Great Britain were the chief destinations of Russian political émigrées. *Iskra* ("The Spark"), the main organ of the Russian Social Democratic party, which was an underground organization, was edited and printed in Switzerland. The party's first congress, at Minsk in 1898, had resulted in the arrest of some of the leaders, and the next one, in 1903, was held first in Brussels and then in London; it was attended largely by exiles. One of the chief points of debate of the 1903 congress concerned the organization of the party: whether it should be limited to people who were active revolutionaries or should also admit those who were just sympathizers. Clearly, a small party could be directed and controlled from the outside, whereas a larger organization would be affected by the changing moods in Russia and would be less serviceable as an instrument for conspiratorial activities. The dispute also involved a broader issue. Would the overthrow of absolutism be immediately followed by a social-ist state, or would socialism have to be preceded by a bourgeois liberal regime? The division on this point was the Russian version of the split in European socialism between the orthodox Marxists and the Revisionists.

The advocates of a small revolutionary party were led by Vladimir Ilich Lenin (1870–1924), a young émigré who had escaped from Siberia to Switzerland and had attracted attention by a number of brilliant articles in *Iskra*. In a vote which was of doubtful validity because a number of the principal members of the congress were absent, Lenin's faction won out, and thereafter it called itself the Bolsheviks ("majority group"). Lenin's leadership was soon bitterly attacked, and the control of the party came into the hands of his opponents, the Mensheviks ("minority group"); the Bolsheviks, led by Lenin, essentially became a socialist splinter faction. The policy of the Mensheviks, aiming at closer collaboration with other opposi-tion elements, seemed much more realistic than that of the Bolsheviks be-cause the workers were only a small part of the population. Dissatisfaction was not restricted to them; it was particularly strong among the peasantry. The Social Revolutionaries, who worked chiefly among the rural population, were almost more powerful than the Social Democrats. A successful revolu-tion seemed more likely to come about through collaboration between peasants and workers than through the exclusive efforts of the proletariat on which Lenin wanted to rely.

All these opposition movements worked underground. The threat of punishment, usually exile to Siberia, hung over the heads of everyone involved. Violence was the only effective expression of dissatisfaction with the government. Attempts on the lives of high officials and of members of the ruling dynasty were frequent. To discover prohibited meetings, investi-gate forbidden activities, detect conspiracies, a large police force was a necessity. The police department was one of the most extended and most feared institutions of the Russian bureaucracy. The police were said to have spies in every block of houses. They infiltrated opposition groups, and the revolutionaries countered by offering themselves as spies to the police, in order to find out about police plans. In some cases it seems impossible to establish whether a man was a police spy or a genuine revolutionary. Typical of these enigmatic figures was Azev (1869–1918), an influential mem-ber of the Social Revolutionary party who was deeply involved in orga-nizing the assassination of an uncle of the tsar, Grand Duke Sergius, the governor general of Moscow. Later it was revealed that Azev had been in the service of the police and participated in assassination attempts only in order to gain the full confidence of the revolutionaries.

When Prime Minister Stolypin, who had become unpopular with the reactionaries of the court, was assassinated in 1911, it was widely believed that the police had had some hand in the act. These rumors were characteristic of the atmosphere of suspicion and insecurity which permeated the entire Russian political scene.

Yet, if belonging to the Russian ruling group had dangers, there were also compensations. It has been said that anyone wanting to taste the full sweetness and pleasure of life at the end of the nineteenth century should have lived among the Russian nobility. In Russia at this time land ownership meant great wealth because recent innovations in transportation facilitated the export of Russian wheat to other European countries, and wheat prices were rising. The aristocrats lived in palaces in St. Petersburg and Moscow. During the year they moved from their great city palaces to their estates and to the Crimea; they traveled in private railroad cars to the Riviera, to Paris, and to London. A characteristic expression of the luxury of the Russian nobility was the popularity of the works of Fabergé: miniature sculptures constructed of precious jewels, which the members of the aristocracy found fashionable and amusing to give one another as Easter presents. From all over the world the Russian nobles imported the most famous singers and musicians for private entertainments. Some of them were remarkably sensitive to the current trends in art. Georges Braque and André Derain painted backdrops for the Russian ballet; a wealthy Russian assembled the most complete collection of early paintings by Pablo Picasso; Russian poets experimented in the most advanced literary forms.

If the Russian aristocrats appeared to indulge in senseless luxuries, one reason was that they too suffered from the distrust of the absolutist ruler and his bureaucrats, and were excluded from responsible participation in political life. Thus it should not be assumed that all the members of the Russian nobility were frivolous and unaware of the seriousness of their country's political situation. Tolstoi, with his radical ideas of returning to a life of pristine Christian virtues was one such exception. And Russian aristocrats were active in the *zemstvos*, regional councils established by Alexander II, which represested the nearest approach to local self-administration in Russia. Many tried to work in the *zemstvos* for improvements in the economic situation and attempted to extend the sphere of activities of the *zemstvos*, legally limited to local and charitable tasks, to political matters. But they were always rebuffed by the government.

THE RUSSO-JAPANESE WAR

Resentment about the continued absolutism of the tsars permeated almost all strata of society, and though the opposition groups differed in

Kuropatkin, commander of the Russian forces in the Far East, with Chinese officials in Mukden.

their concrete aims, only a spark was needed to unite them in a general revolutionary explosion. This spark was provided by the Russian defeats in the Russo-Japanese War. The war started on February 8, 1904, with a surprise attack by Japanese torpedo boats against the Russian Far Eastern squadron anchored in the harbor of Port Arthur. But the attack had been preceded by negotiations in which the Japanese had shown their willingness to reach a peaceful solution if the Russians relinquished a Far Eastern policy which would prevent Japanese expansion on the Asian mainland. Responsible Russian statesmen had been inclined to give the Japanese assurances that a penetration into Manchuria and Korea which the Russians had started in the preceding years would remain limited. But a Russo-Japanese understanding was blocked by the tsar. Nicholas II, since his travels in the Far East in his youth, had had vague ideas about making Russia a great naval power by extending its boundaries to the Pacific. These ideas had been fed by William II, who liked to call himself Admiral of the Atlantic and to address the tsar as Admiral of the Pacific. And the tsar listened to military men and financial speculators who urged him to bring all of Korea under Russian control. Probably he was also dazzled by the thought that Russian expansion in the Far East would help silence critics of his absolutist regime.

So the Japanese struck. The defeat of the Russian land forces in the Battle of Mukden was a great surprise. Few had foreseen that a great

Bloody Sunday. *Russian guard troops shooting at the demonstrators marching to the Winter Palace on January 22, 1905.*

European power could succumb to an Asiatic state. With the wisdom of hindsight, one can recognize the reasons for the Japanese victory. The Japanese had been prepared for the war, while the supplying and strengthening of Russian forces in the Far East had been slow and difficult because the trans-Siberian railway had only one track and did not yet extend to the Pacific. Before Russia could bring the full weight of its military forces into play, the Russians agreed to accept the mediation of President Theodore Roosevelt of the United States in arranging a peace with Japan. A treaty with the Japanese was signed on September 5, 1905 in Portsmouth, New Hampshire.

THE REVOLUTION OF 1905

An early conclusion of peace had been forced upon Russia because of upheavals in the interior. The Russo-Japanese War placed an immense strain on the Russian system of transportation, and the provisioning of the great urban centers broke down. Bread prices soared and the wages of the workers proved insufficient. Spontaneous strikes broke out in many places. When on January 22, 1905, a procession of workers approached the Winter Palace of the tsar to submit to him their grievances, the way was blocked by troops, whose commander lost his head and fired on the masses. This Bloody Sunday set in motion the revolution. A general strike was declared in St. Petersburg, and most industrial centers followed suit. The workers combined into unions; the professional organizations which had been allowed a supervised existence now became politically active, electing new leaders and drawing up programs of political reform. The *zemstvos* formulated political demands. The general cry was for the creation of a parliamentary government based on universal suffrage.

Progress toward this goal was achieved in stages. In March the tsar was forced to declare that a consultative assembly would be established. In August he conceded that this assembly would be elected, but he insisted that suffrage would be limited and the power of this assembly, the Duma, would be purely deliberative. Then a new wave of strikes and revolutionary outbreaks occurred; in October, under the pressure of a breakdown of public order, with cities like St. Petersburg and Moscow in the hands of the workers, the tsar made a further concession: the Duma would be elected on the basis of a wide franchise and it would have legislative functions. Civil liberties would be guaranteed. The change in the political system was indicated by the appointment of a prime minister; this office was given to Count Witte. But revolutionary agitation among the workers continued and peasant unrest began to spread. In the southern parts of Russia peasants burned the houses of landowners and occupied the land. Under the threat of this peasant revolt the tsar, on Witte's advice, in December conceded universal and secret suffrage. But this was his last concession. Troops returning from the Far East bolstered the government; the leaders of the workers in St. Petersburg were arrested, and an insurrection of the workers in Moscow was defeated. Boris Pasternak's *Doctor Zhivago* (1957) contains a graphic description of the Cossacks riding down the masses in Moscow in the winter of 1905.

The Revolution of 1905 did not seal the fate of tsarism. It might be called a turning point which did not turn. A constitutional system was introduced. Although universal suffrage was not maintained and the voting structure favored the wealthier classes, large groups of the population were willing to cooperate with the government to make the constitution work. Moreover, the peasants were freed from making further payments for their land, and under Stolypin the dissolution of the *mirs* opened the way to an agricultural development based on private ownership; wealthy peasants— kulaks—began to appear. But the tsar, far from welcoming these developments, obstructed them in every way. In March, 1906, he dismissed Witte, whom he believed to have made unnecessary concessions; Stolypin, who came to office later in 1906, had lost the tsar's favor by the time he was assassinated in 1911. Whenever possible, Nicholas appointed reactionary ministers. He openly bestowed his favor on the most reactionary groups, among them the Black Hundreds, who with the support of the troops embarked on barbaric punitive actions against the peasants. The tsar also encouraged anti-Semitic pogroms. As before, the influence of the crown remained the chief target of all liberal forces.

Actually, the tsar might have utilized the revolution and its consequences to broaden the basis of support for his government. Through the summer of 1905, almost all social groups except for the extreme reactionaries had favored the revolutionary movement. This unified front broke down in the autumn, as agrarian unrest continued and the workers began to fight more openly for a socialist republic. Liberal aristocrats, professional groups, the middle classes—all were by then satisfied with the concessions made by the tsar in the October decree. Revolutionary activity between October and December faltered because it began to lose general support and became restricted to workers and peasants. For a moderately liberal policy the tsar could have counted on the backing of a large segment of society.

Except for the Paris Commune of 1871, previous revolutions had been bourgeois in character. The Russian Revolution of 1905 can be regarded as the first socialist revolution. It showed the immense importance of the general strike as a political weapon. Moreover, it revealed new techniques for effecting a social revolution. For the first time workers' councils, composed of men elected by the workers of the various factories, exerted a directing influence upon events and in certain critical periods functioned as an effective government. The leading spirit of the workers' council in St. Petersburg was a young socialist writer named Leon Trotsky. Like Lenin, he realized that in revolutionary times these workers' councils could serve as the authority which could prevent chaos and at the same time keep power in the hands of the proletariat.

The Russian Revolution of 1905 had a great impact all over Europe. Fear of revolution became tangible in the political atmosphere; governments became more concerned about maintaining their authority and their prestige than they had ever been before. The result was an increase in tensions within the nations of Europe and also a more intensive pursuit of success in foreign policy. And the dangers and opportunities in the international arena were abruptly expanded, for the sudden revelation of Russia's weakness changed the entire European scene.

CHAPTER 3

The End of the Concert and the First World War

THE YEAR 1905 was crucial in the development of European diplomacy. It concluded a period in which—in the Fashoda crisis, the Boer War, the Italian adventure in Ethiopia, the Russo-Japanese War—the degree of control which the European powers would exert over the non-European world, in Africa and in the Far East, had been in dispute; with the events of 1905 the positions of the European nations in Europe and the balance of power among them became the crucial issues. The events of 1905 represent a return to Europe as the center of action, and this is why the conflicts which the partitioning of Africa and Asia evoked could be composed without war among the European powers, whereas the crises in the year 1905 and those which followed resulted in the outbreak of the First World War.

A period of diplomacy dominated by imperialist crises was followed by a period of diplomacy focused upon issues concerning the European balance of power. But it should not be assumed that the period of imperialist expansion was an interlude without importance for what happened later.

THE RIGIDIFICATION OF THE ALLIANCE SYSTEM

By 1905 the entire political atmosphere had become much more tense and heated than it had been in the late nineteenth century. The masses had begun to take an intense interest in foreign policy, and the enterprises and adventures of their conationals in foreign lands and unexplored areas had fired their imagination and their sense of national competitiveness. The conceptions which they had formed of other nations were usually unflattering. The Boer War had created a somewhat contradictory but always unfavorable image of Great Britain: ruthless in its pursuit of worldly treasures on the one hand, and decadent on the other. Perhaps the German emperor seriously believed that Germany wanted nothing but its deserved "place in the sun"; he had certainly convinced many of his subjects that this was the case. But other nations had seen in the German advances into Africa, China, and the South Seas the actions of a spoiled and brutal young man who wanted to grab everything he could lay his hands on. Moreover, the events of these imperialist years had set the policy of some of the great powers into channels from which later there was no escape.

This is particularly true with regard to Germany and Great Britain and their relations with each other.

The principal enterprises of German policy which had a fatal effect on relations with Great Britain were the construction of a powerful navy and the financing and building of the Baghdad Railway. When the building of the German navy began, there was probably little awareness of what its later consequences would be. Because sea power was regarded as essential for effective participation in world politics the navy soon became popular among the German bourgeoisie; in contrast to the predominantly aristocratic officers of the army, naval officers came mainly from bourgeois families. The popular backing for the navy was efficiently promoted by the secretary of the navy, Admiral von Tirpitz, who established a special office which edited pamphlets, helped to organize navy leagues, and arranged meetings where speakers discussed the importance of naval power: this office was the forerunner of all later propaganda ministries. In 1898 the Reichstag had sanctioned a navy bill which was a new departure for Germany in that it proposed not only cruisers which might defend the German coast but also battleships fit for combat on the open sea: the bill provided for the building of eleven battleships and five first-class cruisers by 1905. The German navy envisaged here was still rather small. However, two years later, in 1900, Tirpitz carried through the adoption of a second bill which would expand the building program, calling for the construction of thirty-eight battleships to be completed in twenty years. The anti-British tendency of this second bill was evident. Tirpitz' goal was a fleet of such strength that the British would hesitate to attack Germany.

The German project for a railroad to Baghdad developed from innocuous beginnings into an enterprise with dangerous political consequences. The capital needed and the financial risks involved were so large that the Deutsche Bank, the German financial house interested in the undertaking, obtained concessions for the project from the Turkish government in 1899 almost by default of other competitors. The leaders of the Deutsche Bank tried without success to obtain the cooperation of financiers of other countries for this enterprise. The only serious opponents of the project were the Russians. The French supported the Germans, and the British raised no objections; both Great Britain and France were anxious to bar Russian

The Baghdad Railroad. *German and Turkish officials celebrate the launching of the enterprise.*

expansion in the Near East and to involve Germany in the preservation of Turkey. However, their attitude changed when, almost unavoidably, the construction of the railroad gave Germany economic and then political control in Turkey.

As a result of Germany's striving for world power, German and British interests, which in the past had not confronted each other, began to clash. Just at this time Britain was recognizing the need for moving away from its "splendid isolation." The British had been surprised and worried by their unpopularity, demonstrated in reactions first to the Jameson Raid and then to the Boer War. They wondered whether the formation of an anti-British continental league, of which German and Russian statesmen sometimes spoke in the 1890's, might not really be in the making. Britain's first countermeasure was the treaty with Japan which was directed against Russia. The British also became aware of the advantages for the security of their imperial position which would result from backing by a continental power. To British feelers, particularly those of the colonial secretary, Joseph Chamberlain, Germany gave a very cool reception. The German statesmen in power, especially Chancellor Bernhard von Bülow (1849–1929) and his political adviser Friedrich von Holstein, felt sure that Britain could turn to no other power but Germany which could therefore refuse to be satisfied with an agreement merely delimiting German and British colonial interests, waiting instead until the time was ripe to demand a defensive alliance.

But the British government, having no intention of going that far, turned to France and the result was the Entente Cordiale, concluded on April 8, 1904. Formally, this treaty was an agreement on all the issues concerning colonies that had occasioned disputes between Great Britain and France; the chief points were that France abandoned all its claims in Egypt and Britain recognized that France had a dominating interest in Morocco and promised diplomatic support of French plans for achieving control of Morocco. The marquis of Lansdowne (1845–1927), the British foreign secretary who concluded this agreement, always maintained that the treaty had no aim except that of moderating the tensions which had arisen from colonial conflicts. The Entente Cordiale developed into a close political partnership as a result of the events of the following year—the crisis of 1905.

THE SUCCESSION OF CRISES, 1905–1914

From the German point of view the Entente Cordiale represented a serious loss of prestige; the German statesmen felt that their nation's diplomatic situation had deteriorated and that they must take action to improve it. Accordingly, German policy began to follow two different although not contradictory lines. One was to humiliate France and to show to the French that the Entente Cordiale was without value. The other aim was to reestablish friendly relations with Russia in order to reconstruct the situation which had existed in Bismarck's time, before the abandonment of the Reinsurance Treaty.

The First Moroccan Crisis

The Germans opened their action against France by claiming that the arrangements about Morocco violated German interests. This was just a pretense; German economic activities hardly existed in Morocco, and indeed the German government had found it necessary to exert pressure on the Mannesmann Company, a metallurgical and mining company, to make investments in Morocco so that there could be some substance for the assertions concerning the violation of German interests.

The Moroccan crisis started when William II, on a Mediterranean trip in March, 1905, debarked briefly in Tangier and solemnly declared that the Germans were willing to maintain the independence and integrity of Morocco. German and French claims clearly confronted each other. France regarded Morocco as belonging to the French sphere of interest and planned to absorb the country; the Germans insisted that it was an independent and sovereign state in which all nations should have equal opportunities. From the point of view of international law the French were in a weak position. So they tried to come to some arrangement with Germany, indicating their willingness to make concessions in other colonial areas. The Germans countered by demanding an international conference.

They were not interested in getting advantages to compensate for French rule in Morocco; rather they were concerned with demonstrating French political impotence. They refused to enter into any bilateral negotiations with France, and made it clear that they considered the French foreign minister Théophile Delcassé—whose policy had raised French prestige by establishing close connections first with Russia and then with Great Britain—so hostile to Germany that negotiations with him were purposeless. The situation became increasingly tense. Delcassé insisted that he had a commitment from Great Britain to support France in case of war, but the other French ministers rightly maintained that the close consultation to which Britain had agreed in the Entente Cordiale did not mean that it had any obligation to enter combat on the French side. France without Britain would not be able to hold out against Germany. These questions were thrashed out in a dramatic meeting of the French cabinet. On June 6, 1905, Delcassé resigned.

Germany had achieved a resounding diplomatic triumph. But the Germans did not know what to do with their victory. The French were now willing to agree to an international conference about Morocco but proposed that Germany and France should first work out a settlement between themselves, to be then ratified by the conference. For such a preliminary settlement the French were willing to pay a high price; for a free hand in Morocco they were prepared to make far-reaching concessions to Germany in other colonial disputes. But the German government still refused to enter into bilateral negotiations with France and demanded unconditional acceptance of the convocation of an international conference. This attitude was widely interpreted as a sign that Germany was not content with having shown its superior strength but was driving toward a war against France. Indeed, Count Alfred von Schlieffen (1833–1913), the chief of the German general staff, did want a preventive war, but there are no indications that either Chancellor Bülow or Holstein shared this view. It appears that after they had solemnly declared that the Moroccan problem ought to be submitted to an international conference they found it difficult to withdraw from this position; to make a prior settlement with France would have been to turn the conference into a farce. Furthermore the Germans believed that they would dominate the conference and that France would be unable to offer serious opposition to their demands.

The German statesmen had grounds for optimism; in the summer of 1905, they seemed close to success in their efforts to renew friendship with Russia.

During the war with Japan, Russia felt the need for German support because it feared that Great Britain, Japan's ally, might also enter the war, especially after an incident at Dogger Bank, in the North Sea, in which Russian ships sailing from the Baltic to the Far East had fired erroneously on British trawlers. The tsar and the Russian ruling group were also anxious to move close to Germany because this was the one state from which they expected sympathy and support for their attempts to maintain an authoritarian system. Accordingly, negotiations were begun between Russia and Germany, and in July, 1905, the tsar and William II met at Björkö, on the Baltic coast. Russia, losing to Japan, was then in the midst of revolutionary turmoil, and William II persuaded, almost forced, his dispirited cousin to sign an alliance treaty which, although discussed for months, had never been concluded.

Just when Germany seemed at the high point of power, with Delcassé eliminated and Russia as an ally, things began to go wrong. The Russian statesmen were disgusted with their tsar's weakness in yielding to the German emperor's demands. They began to raise objections to the treaty and to delay its finalization. After the peace treaty with Japan was signed in September, Russia had less need for German support. Moreover, a French loan helped to alleviate Russia's acute financial difficulties and increased the authority of the government. Under these circumstances the Russians had no reason any longer not to give diplomatic support to their French ally in the Moroccan crisis. Moreover, the British had begun to fear that the French might be forced to align themselves with Germany and Russia. The new British foreign secretary, Sir Edward Grey, a Liberal more inclined toward France than toward Germany, encouraged the French by permitting consultations between the French and British military staffs regarding common action in wartime, and promised the French support in the negotiations over Morocco. Thus, although the French in September, 1905, gave in and agreed to an international conference without prior accords with Germany, they could look forward to the conference with confidence.

In January, 1906, when the conference over Morocco convened in the Spanish city of Algeciras, it was not France but Germany that was in an almost isolated position. Characteristic of the polite, subtle, and indirect ways of the diplomacy of this period is the fact that there was no dramatic indictment of German policy. A test vote on a minor question revealed that Russia, France, Great Britain, Italy, even the United States, all sided with France; only Austria-Hungary voted with Germany. This was proof enough: if Germany decided to unleash a war against France it would now be opposed by almost every great power. Chancellor Bülow realized that Germany had to give in. The final agreement was couched in terms which concealed the German defeat. There was confirmation of the independence of Morocco and assurance of an economic open door for other powers. But the police in Morocco were put under the combined authority of France and Spain, and France was given control of the state bank, and thereby the finances, of Morocco. The conference had established that France would be the ruling power in Morocco.

The affair had been primarily a struggle among the European powers for hegemony, and the details of the regulations of the Moroccan situation were less significant than what the conference revealed about the diplomatic constellation in Europe: at Algeciras the powers which would confront one another in the First World War found themselves for the first time grouped in opposing camps.

The Moroccan crisis of 1905–1906 was followed by a chain of further crises and wars—the Bosnian crisis of 1908–1909, a second Moroccan crisis and the Tripolitan War between Italy and Turkey in 1911, the first Balkan War in 1912, the second Balkan War and the Liman von Sanders crisis in 1913—until, in the summer of 1914, tensions exploded into the First World War.

With the renewed concentration of the competition for power in the European continent, the region which in earlier centuries, and particularly in the nineteenth century, had been a chief object of dispute—the Balkans and the Near East—became acutely sensitive once more. In the course of the gradual economic development of this area, which was accomplished largely with the help of foreign capital, the middle classes had become stronger; professional men—lawyers, doctors, teachers—were needed in increasing numbers. Rumanians, Serbs, Greeks, Bulgars, studied in foreign countries, particularly in Germany and France, and absorbed an almost religious faith in nationalism. Contact with the powerful national states of central and western Europe could only increase dissatisfaction with the situation at home, with the subjection of the Balkan peoples to the Ottoman Empire and the Habsburg monarchy. The demand for the elimination of Turkish rule in Europe became more general and more urgent. In earlier times the great powers had always been aware of a last recourse in case the illness of the Sick Man proved fatal—partition. But this means of escape from a clash among the European powers over the spoils of the Ottoman Empire was now barred, for Germany made the maintenance of the Ottoman Empire the cornerstone of its policy. Whereas in Bismarck's time Germany could act as a mediator between the two great powers which bordered the Balkan peninsula—Austria-Hungary and Russia—as they competed for influence over the young nations, now Germany itself had become an interested participant in the affairs of this area. This change in Germany's role constituted a new and dangerous element in the situation.

The Bosnian Crisis

After the humiliation suffered in the war against Japan, the Russian government was eager for a success in foreign policy. The Slavic brethren in the Balkans were popular with the Russian public, and Russian ruling circles believed that a policy favoring independence of the Balkan nations would strengthen the authority of the tsar and weaken the trends toward parliamentarianism and democratic government. Quick action seemed appropriate because in July, 1908, a revolution had taken place in the Ottoman Empire; the tyrannical Sultan Abdul-Hamid II had been forced to abdicate, and the Young Turks, advocates of modernization and parliamentary government, had come to power. Concessions from a Turkey strengthened by reforms would be difficult to obtain. Hence, in September, 1908, the Russian foreign minister, Alexander Izvolski (1856–1919), set out to visit the courts of the European great powers, hoping to obtain their permission to open the Dardanelles to Russian warships, a move which would strengthen Russian influence in Turkey and in the Balkans. Izvolski's first stop was at Buchlau, in Bohemia, where he met the Austrian foreign minister Aehrenthal. The exact nature of the exchange between Izvolski and Aehrenthal has never become entirely clear because the accounts of the two ministers diverge widely. However, there can be little doubt that Aehrenthal promised to raise no objections against the opening of the Dardanelles to Russian warships. As a *quid pro quo,* Izvolski agreed not to oppose Austrian annexation of the Turkish provinces of Bosnia and Herzegovina, which Austria-Hungary had occupied since the Congress of Berlin. Aehrenthal was a clever and ruthless diplomat and Izvolski was not his equal. For while Izvolski continued his round of visits to the European capitals, seeking to work out a general agreement on the opening of the Dardanelles, the Austrian government, on October 6, proclaimed the annexation of Bosnia and Herzogovina. One day earlier, in collusion with Austria, Bulgaria—hitherto under the sovereignty of the sultan—had declared its full independence. The crisis had come about before Izvolski could get agreement from the other great powers, and he had to return to St. Petersburg empty-handed. Austria-Hungary had strengthened its position in the Balkan area without the Russians' receiving any compensation. In order to reassert Russian influence in Balkan affairs, and also driven by passionate hatred of Aehrenthal, Izvolski tried in every way to prevent international recognition of Austria's annexation of Bosnia and Herzegovina. The Turks, under German pressure, accepted the annexation when they were offered financial compensation. The country which was most indignant over the Austrian action was Serbia. Because the peoples of Bosnia and Herzegovina were primarily South Slavs, the Serbs felt that they, not the Austrians, ought to rule these provinces. Thus the crisis dragged on. Encouraged by Russian backing, Serbia made military preparations, and Austria followed suit. Finally, in March, 1909, the German government sent a sharp note to Russia demanding that it abandon its support of Serbia and recognize Austria's annexation of Bosnia and Herzegovina. Still too weak to risk a war against the great European powers, Russia gave in. The crisis was over.

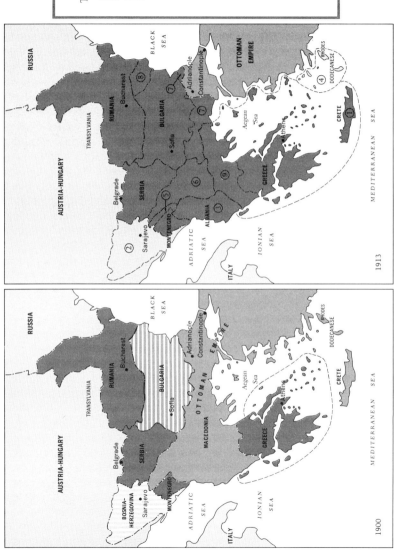

THE RESULTS OF
THE BALKAN WARS

Independent
Balkan states

Ottoman Empire

① To Greece, 1908
② Annexed by Austria–Hungary, 1909
③ New State, 1912
④ To Italy, 1912
⑤ To Montenegro, 1913
⑥ To Serbia, 1913
⑦ To Bulgaria, 1913
⑧ To Rumania, 1913
⑨ To Greece, 1913

1913

RUSSIA

BLACK SEA

OTTOMAN EMPIRE

RHODES

DODECANESE

Bucharest ⑧

RUMANIA

Adrianople
⑦
Constantinople

BULGARIA

⑦

Sofia

TRANSYLVANIA

AUSTRIA-HUNGARY

Aegean Sea

CRETE ①

Athens

Belgrade

SERBIA

⑤

⑥

⑨

GREECE

Sarajevo ②

MONTENEGRO

③
ALBANIA

ADRIATIC SEA

IONIAN SEA

ITALY

MEDITERRANEAN SEA

1900

RUSSIA

BLACK SEA

Bucharest

RUMANIA

Adrianople
Constantinople

BULGARIA

Sofia

OTTOMAN EMPIRE

RHODES

DODECANESE

TRANSYLVANIA

AUSTRIA-HUNGARY

MACEDONIA

Aegean Sea

CRETE

Athens

Belgrade

SERBIA

BOSNIA-HERZEGOVINA

Sarajevo

MONTENEGRO

GREECE

ADRIATIC SEA

IONIAN SEA

ITALY

MEDITERRANEAN SEA

The Bosnian crisis has frequently been considered a rehearsal of the crisis which ended with the outbreak of the First World War. It is indeed true that Germany tried to repeat in 1914 what it had succeeded in doing in 1908–1909. But in 1914 Russia was not willing to back down.

In any case the Bosnian crisis made Germany and Russia direct opponents and ended all ideas of a German-Russian alliance. Germany's reaction was almost automatic; it tried to escape from isolation by moving closer to Great Britain. This shift in policy was connected with a change in the German government. Whereas Chancellor Bülow had been anti-British and chiefly interested in an alliance with Russia, Theobald von Bethmann-Hollweg (1856–1921), who succeeded Bülow in 1909, accepted Russian hostility as inevitable and directed his policy toward cooperation with Great Britain.

The Second Moroccan Crisis

Nevertheless, the German's first important move under the chancellorship of Bethmann-Hollweg could hardly be interpreted as a new departure in their foreign policy. The German government provoked another Moroccan crisis. Although the conference at Algeciras had recognized France's predominant interest in Morocco it had also acknowledged the independence of that state. When internal struggles broke out in Morocco the French intervened and began to take over the entire country. The Germans ostensibly did not want this to happen, at least not without receiving compensation. In order to force the French to negotiate, a German gunboat, on July 1, 1911, anchored in Agadir, a harbor on the Atlantic coast of Morocco. But the French were in a much stronger position than they had been in 1905 at the time of the first Moroccan crisis, when Russia was engaged in the Far East and the Entente Cordiale with Great Britain was still new and untried. The British gave the French strong support, their attitude being particularly evident in a speech, delivered by Lloyd George in Mansion House. He warned that Germany should not forget that Great Britain too had vital interests in Morocco and would not shy away from fighting for them: "National honor is no party question." Although the French government consented to negotiate with the Germans, it was not prepared to yield much; the French were tough, and negotiations dragged on until November. In the agreement which was finally signed, the French gained a free hand in Morocco and the Germans received part of the French Congo connecting the German Cameroons with the Congo River. This was not a brilliant outcome for Germany. The German foreign secretary, Alfred von Kiderlen-Waechter (1852–1912), who was praised by his friends as a second Bismarck and saw himself in this role, rationalized the meager results of his policy by maintaining that the purpose of the entire action had been not to make colonial gains, but to improve relations with France by removing the festering wound of Morocco with one sharp incision of the knife. Also, Germany would now be able to draw closer to Great Britain, which would no longer consider a German-British rapprochement incompatible with the Entente Cordiale. Whatever the actual aims of Kiderlen-Waechter's policy, the impression which the sudden appearance of a German warship in Moroccan waters made on other countries was not that of a country striving for appeasement. On the contrary, both statesmen and the general public chiefly remembered that since 1905 Germany had three times tried to get its way by sudden and brutal action: in Morocco in the summer of 1905; by the ultimatum to Russia in 1909; and finally, at Agadir.

Nevertheless, negotiations between Germany and Great Britain did finally take place. Frightened by the drift toward war which the Agadir crisis had indicated, the British government was also aware that military preparations in response to international tensions would diminish the financial resources available for its program of domestic reform. Hence, the British decided to probe German intentions once more; the secretary of state for war, Haldane, was sent to Berlin. The aim of his mission was to prevent the Germans from carrying out their plan for increased naval construction. Tirpitz had declared that three great battleships (dreadnoughts) would be built instead of the previously announced two. But Haldane did not obtain any modification of German naval plans. Actually, the German chancellor and the German foreign secretary, Bethmann-Hollweg and Kiderlen-Waechter, were willing to slow down the naval program and tried to keep negotiations going even after Haldane left Berlin. But Tirpitz, who entirely dominated William II, was able to prevent any concession. The naval race between Germany and Great Britain was not stopped.

Since 1905 British policies had lost much of their flexibility, and they gave the Germans some reason to distrust British intentions. After the agreement with France in 1904, Britain concluded an agreement with Russia in 1907. Like the Entente Cordiale this concerned colonial questions and settled the most urgent imperialist disputes between the two countries. Persia was divided: the north fell into the Russian sphere of influence, the south into the British sphere, and a neutral zone remained in the middle. Moreover, in the Agadir crisis Britain had not only given diplomatic support to France but agreed to military discussions, which resulted in an understanding between the French and British general staffs that in case of war a British expeditionary force would be sent to France; plans were made concerning transportation, troop-concentration areas, and command organization. While these arrangements did not constitute a definite military alliance and the political commitments between Great Britain and France did not go beyond close consultation, it was clear that the position of the European powers was becoming more rigid. Triple Entente, as the

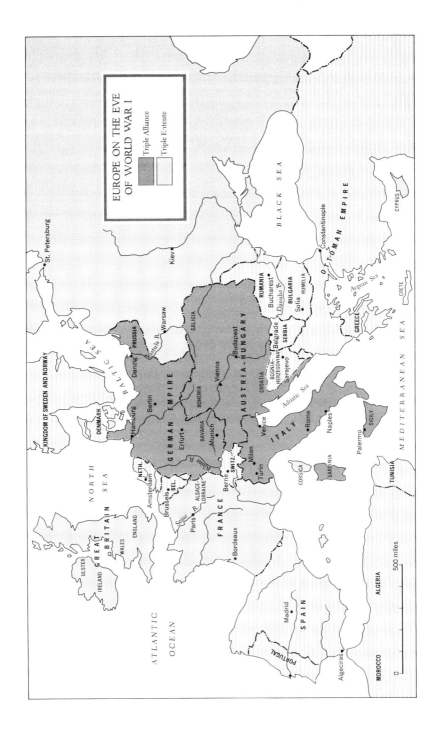

EUROPE ON THE EVE
OF WORLD WAR I

Triple Alliance
Triple Entente

somewhat loose combination of Great Britain, France, and Russia was called, confronted the Triple Alliance of Germany, Austria, and Italy.

War and Crisis in the Balkans

The possibility of avoiding war if tensions continued became increasingly less likely. After the Agadir crisis the focus of tension shifted to the East. From 1912 on the affairs of the Ottoman Empire and the national aspirations of the Balkan nations evoked one crisis after the other. The prelude was the war which began in September, 1911, between Turkey and Italy. All the great powers had recognized that Tripoli was in the Italian sphere of interest; when France finally absorbed Morocco, the Italian government decided to take action and proclaimed the annexation of Tripoli. Turkey answered with a declaration of war against Italy. The Italians won a quick victory, but in the meantime the Tripolitan War triggered action in the Balkans. Serbia and Bulgaria believed that if they did not take action before the end of Turkey's conflict with Italy, they might miss an opportunity for driving the Turks out of Europe. They succeeded in getting the support of Montenegro and Greece, and war against Turkey broke out in October, 1912. The Turkish troops in the Balkans were defeated in a number of battles in which the Bulgarian and Serbian soldiers proved themselves to be excellent warriors.

But a diplomatic settlement was much more difficult to achieve than military victory. There was dissension among the victors about the drawing of the frontiers after the war had assured the end of Turkish rule in Europe. The two areas about which disposition had to be made were Macedonia and Albania.

Bulgaria, Greece, and Serbia all demanded parts of Macedonia, and the claims of Greece and Bulgaria were particularly irreconcilable because both were anxious to control the northern coast of the Aegean Sea. The result was a second Balkan War, in which Greece, Serbia, Rumania, and Turkey rallied against Bulgaria. The outcome of this war determined that only a very small part of Macedonia fell to Bulgaria. Most of it was divided between Serbia and Greece, and the Turks regained Adrianople.

The Serbs were less successful in their demand for Albanian territory which would give them a direct access to the Adriatic Sea. The great powers, meeting with the Balkan nations and Turkey in London, forced Serbia and Montenegro to accept the creation of an independent Albania. Serbia remained cut off from the Adriatic.

In the meetings in London, Russia had backed the claims of Serbia whereas Austria-Hungary advocated those of Bulgaria, and together with Italy, sharply opposed the Serbian demand for access to the Adriatic Sea. To underline the seriousness with which they looked upon the situation, both—Russia and Austria-Hungary—made some military preparations.

Great Britain and Germany cooperated to obtain a peaceful solution of the conflict. Nevertheless, the Balkan wars accumulated new explosive material which the compromise worked out by the great powers in London concealed rather than eliminated. Turkey, in need of military reorganization, called in a German general, Otto Liman von Sanders, but this move evoked violent Russian protests because it appeared to be a further step in the establishment of German control over Turkey. Both Russia and Austria indicated that in the negotiations about the final settlement of the Balkan wars they should have received stronger support from their respective friends, Great Britain and Germany. Consequently, in both Britain and Germany the government leaders felt that their alliances might be endangered if in the next emergency they did not give stronger support to their allies. But the most dangerous consequence of the Balkan wars was that all the resentment of Serbian nationalism was now focused on the Habsburg monarchy. The Serbs had considered the Austrian annexation of Bosnia and Herzegovina in 1908 as a blow to Serbia's aspirations to become the home of all South Slavs. Now in 1913, Austria-Hungary had again been the chief obstacle to Serbia's ambitions and had deprived it of the fruits of victory: access to the Adriatic Sea. To the nationalistic Serbs the Habsburg monarchy was an old evil monster which prevented their nation from becoming a great and powerful state. On June 28, 1914, a young Serbian nationalist, Gavrilo Princip, assassinated the heir of the Habsburg monarchy, the Archduke Francis Ferdinand, and his wife at Sarajevo.

THE OUTBREAK OF THE FIRST WORLD WAR

The events of the five weeks between the assassination of the Archduke Francis Ferdinand and the outbreak of the First World War have been more carefully investigated than almost any others in world history. An endless number of books and articles have reviewed and probed all aspects of the question of responsibility for the outbreak of the war: whether the Serbian government had knowledge of the plans for the assassination of the archduke; whether Germany encouraged Austria-Hungary to take action against Serbia and deliberately instigated a general war in 1914; whether France believed this crisis would be a favorable opportunity for starting a war in order to regain Alsace-Lorraine, and therefore stiffened the attitude of its Russian ally; whether military requirements restricted and eliminated the freedom of decision of the political leaders; and whether British policy was mistaken in not taking a clear stand.

Most of the facts bearing on these questions have been clarified. The responsible leaders of the Serbian government did not know about the plans for the attempt on the life of the archduke. On the other hand, the assassination was the work not of an individual, but of a group of Bosnian

The Murder at Sarajevo. *Archduke Francis Ferdinand on his visit to Bosnia a few hours before his assassination. Right: The police seizing the assassin, Princip.*

and Serbian nationalists who were encouraged and promoted by a Serbian secret society, the Black Hand, in which the chief of the intelligence department of the Serbian general staff was a leading figure. However, when in an ultimatum of July 23, 1914 the Austrian government accused Serbian government officials of being involved in the plot, it had no proof, based its accusation on falsified documents, and did not mention the Black Hand, specifying only individuals and organizations that in truth had nothing to do with the assassination. Thus, the assassination was consciously used by the Austrian government for the purposes of power politics: to remove the threat which Serbia represented to the existence of the Habsburg monarchy. Further proof that this was Austria's intention is the fact that although the Serbian government accepted almost all the demands of the exceedingly harsh and humiliating ultimatum, the Austrian minister in Belgrade, acting on instructions given to him before he had received the Serbian note, declared the Serbian answer unsatisfactory and left Belgrade, making war between the two states inevitable.

However, without the certainty of German backing, the Austrian leaders would not have embarked on the war against Serbia. Actually, Austrian governmental circles were divided in their views on the course to follow; influential men, notably the Hungarian prime minister, Tisza, were opposed to any action which might lead to war. However, the German government urged the Austrians to resolute action against Serbia, and Tisza's hesitations were overcome when he was given proof that Germany desired Austria to proceed against Serbia and had promised support if other powers became involved in the conflict.

The Germans encouraged Austria because they regarded the death of the heir of the Habsburg throne as a danger signal foreshadowing a possible collapse of the Habsburg monarchy, which would leave Germany without allies. The Germans hoped that a successful show of strength against Serbia might revitalize the Habsburg monarchy. Since the assassination of the archduke and his wife had aroused general indignation and widespread sympathy for the Austrian emperor, there seemed to be a chance that the war between Austria and Serbia might remain localized. However, from the outset the Germans were aware that the Austrian action against Serbia ran the risk of a general war in which Russia, France, and Great Britain might be allied against Germany and Austria, and the justifiable indictment against the German leaders might be made that they willingly accepted this risk. Their attitude was the result of a variety of circumstances. A predominant part of the German ruling group was obsessed by the idea that the future belonged to the great world powers and that Germany would become a world power only through a war which would show it to be equal to the strongest and which would gain for the German people and for German economic expansion a broader territorial basis than it possessed. And if war were long delayed, Germany's chances for ascending to the small circle of world powers might be missed forever. Once Russia, with its large population and great mineral resources, became fully developed, it would tower over all its neighbors and Germany's opportunities for development would disappear. From a purely military point of view, too, time seemed to be running against Germany. In a few years Russia's recovery from losses and defeat and France's three-year conscription law would tilt the military balance against Germany. Historical speculations, economic expansionism, military calculations reinforced one another to create a climate in which war became acceptable. Such considerations guided the policy of the German government. Chancellor Bethmann-Hollweg was an earnest and responsible man inclined to pessimism and he was aware that the consequences of a world war were unforeseeable. Yet he encouraged Austria to take action and he gave the Austrian statesmen a free hand, fully conscious of the risk that a great European conflict might result. Bethmann-Hollweg was not simply bowing to the demands of the military who carried such a powerful weight in imperial Germany; he was himself among those who saw the growing Russian power as a threat to Germany's future, and he had an almost fatalistic belief that a world war was coming. In 1914 Germany's chances would be better than in later years. In the last critical days, when the prophesied world war threatened to become reality, Bethmann-Hollweg seems to have become frightened by his own courage and he made some desperate attempts to keep the conflict between Austria and Serbia localized, but in his heart he must have been aware that these efforts were condemned to failure.

If for no other reason, these last attempts could not succeed because the

Austrians had wasted in an almost incredible manner the sympathy which the assassination had aroused. They sent their ultimatum to Serbia only on July 23—after more than three weeks—when the excitement about the murder of the archduke had begun to die down. The reason for the delay was Austrian dilatoriness (*Schlamperei*), although they rationalized these delays by maintaining that the harvest in Hungary had to be gathered in before they could call the men to arms. In the end, there was a further postponement of three days because the French president, Poincaré, was visiting the tsar and the Austrians did not want to present the ultimatum until Poincaré had left Russia, so that the Russian and French governments would not be able to agree immediately upon joint action.

Poincaré and the French prime minister, Viviani, were in St. Petersburg from July 20 to July 23, 1914. It is not known what they said in private to their Russian hosts about the course which ought to be pursued in the approaching crisis between Austria-Hungary and Serbia. The emphasis which in their public declarations the French and Russian statesmen placed on the close bonds uniting the Russian empire and the French republic must have strengthened the Russian will to oppose the Austrian action. And in the following critical week the French ambassador in Russia, Maurice Paléologue (1859–1944), certainly encouraged the Russian government to take a firm line. The Russians were in a better military position than they had been in 1908; their army had been built up and transport had been improved by the development of the railroad system in western Russia. Unquestionably, the Russian rulers, under the pressure of an excited public and of military men eager to avenge the defeat of 1905, felt unable to accept another diplomatic setback, and decided to prevent Austria from encroaching upon Serbian integrity and sovereignty. When, on July 24, they were informed of the contents of the Austrian ultimatum, they decided that if Austria took action against Serbia, they would institute partial mobilization —which meant mobilization of the military districts close to the Austrian border. But on July 30, after Austria had rejected the Serbian answers, had declared war against Serbia, and had mobilized part of its forces, the Russian government persuaded the tsar to declare general mobilization. The reasons for this change of plan were in part technical; the Russian general staff believed that, after a partial mobilization was under way, it would be difficult and slow to organize a general mobilization. It also seems clear, however, that this step must have been necessitated by Russian-French military agreements. The Russians and the French had some general knowledge of the German war plans. They were aware that at the outset most of the German military forces would be concentrated against France and that the possibility of successful French resistance depended on a quick advance of Russian troops into Germany.

After the Russians had ordered a general mobilization on July 30, the military timetables which the various general staffs had worked out began to dominate political action. The Russian mobilization impelled the German military leaders to demand immediate mobilization and to urge full mobilization on Austria. According to the military plans agreed upon by the German and Austrian chiefs of staff, the Austrian armies were to slow down the Russian advances toward Germany while the bulk of the German army, engaged in the attempt to knock France out of the war, would be unable to protect Germany's eastern frontier. With the Russians mobilizing, Austrian general mobilization, which would make possible quick counteraction, was required; but it was also necessary that the German campaign against France be started immediately and ended in time for German troops to be moved from the west to the east before the Austrian resistance against the superior Russian forces broke down. Thus, the German military leaders were anxious to terminate all further diplomatic negotiations so that they could invade France. Neither the monarchs of the three empires— Francis Joseph, Nicholas II, and William II—nor their chief civilian advisers had the courage to resist the military leaders who declared that without mobilization their campaign plans would be ruined and the existence of their nations would be endangered. Germany sent an ultimatum to Russia demanding immediate cessation of military preparations, and when no satisfactory answer had been received, declared war on Russia, on August 1. This move was followed on August 3 by a declaration of war against France, which the Germans justified with the palpably false statement that French forces had violated the German frontier.

The irrevocability of the military timetables condemned to failure the last-minute attempts of Sir Edward Grey, the British foreign secretary, to halt mobilization and convoke a conference. British diplomacy had worked hard to save the peace, but the question has been raised of whether it followed the right tactics. Could peace have been maintained if at an early state of the crisis Grey had declared that Great Britain would back France and Russia in case of war? An early British commitment might have gained time for a conference. Austria might have hesitated to take action against Serbia, and Russia, secure in the promise of British help, might have been less anxious to order general mobilization. Those who defend Grey's attitude argue that an assurance of British support might have had the contrary effect of encouraging Russia and France to assume an aggressive attitude and that such a British declaration would not have restrained Germany from its course because the German leaders expected Britain's entry into the war and discounted its importance, doubting that Britain would be able to act quickly enough to prevent the defeat of France.

Moreover, Grey might have hesitated to make any definite statement on what Britain would do in case of war because he could not be sure whether the British people would follow his lead. British public opinion was split on the issue. Decision was brought about only by the German invasion of Belgium on August 3. Belgium's neutrality had been guaranteed by an international treaty to which Germany was a party, and this violation of international law by Germany convinced both the British government and the British people of the necessity of entering the conflict. War was declared on August 4.

During the critical week before the German violation of Belgian neutrality, the Conservatives had favored the participation of Britain because of its ties with France and its interest in maintaining the balance of power. The Labor party opposed intervention. This view was shared by the radical wing of the Liberal party; thus the Liberals lacked any uniform policy on the issue. The Liberal government, like the Liberal party, was divided; even after the violation of Belgian neutrality two members of the government resigned to demonstrate their opposition to Britain's participation. In the debates and discussions on this issue Sir Edward Grey favored British entry into the war, but maintained that Britain had a free hand and was not obligated to support France and Russia. Formally, he was right, in that a binding political alliance had not been concluded. The agreements between the British and French general staff were purely military. Nevertheless, Grey's contention that Britain was free to choose its course was questionable. On the basis of the conversations between the two general staffs the French could expect the arrival of a British expeditionary force on French soil. No general staff would make such arrangements without informing its government and having its approval. In denying the existence of a commitment to France, Grey either was incredibly naïve about the possibility of separating political and military planning or was bending the truth in order to avoid arousing the resentment of the radicals in his party. The French ambassador in London, Paul Cambon, in demanding a British declaration of war against Germany, said that the British answer to this request would show whether "the word 'honor' will not have to be stricken out of the British vocabulary." Grey himself felt immensely relieved when, after the invasion of Belgium, the cabinet decided to enter the war. Waverers were won over by the argument that Britain's participation had now become a moral necessity.

The European Attitude Toward War in 1914

The First World War revealed the frightfulness of warfare in the industrial age. But the terrible losses in human life and material resources caused by the war have colored and distorted the interpretation of the events of July and August, 1914. The discussion of the origins of the First World War has been dominated by the question of guilt: historical research has been essentially an effort to determine the distribution of guilt among the individuals and nations involved. It should therefore be emphasized that in 1914 war was not considered to be a crime but was regarded as a legitimate though unpleasant and dangerous instrument of politics.

Certainly a few people did have some notion of the changes in warfare brought about by the enormously increased destructiveness of modern weapons. Courageous and farseeing individuals—such as Bertha von Suttner, author of the famous book *Lay Down Your Arms!* (1889)—had tried to arouse the public to the dangers of modern war by organizing pacifist movements. The destructiveness of war had also been underlined by the two International Peace Conferences held in The Hague in 1899 and 1907. But these conferences had been concerned with the limitation of armaments and with the humanizing of war rather than with its abolition. Up to 1914 no attempt had been made to prohibit war itself. Moreover, almost everyone was convinced that because the European economy had become a complex integrated structure, a war could last for only a few weeks or months and would be quickly decided in a few great battles. Nobody in 1914 was able to envisage the possibilities which would become stark reality in the next few years.

If government leaders hesitated to embark on the adventure of military conflict they were not deterred by fear of being stamped as criminals. Rather, after the experiences of the Franco-Prussian War and the Russo-Japanese War they saw lurking behind each war the danger of revolution. They were aware that they might unleash forces which the existing ruling group might be unable to control. The governments of the European nations had another equally weighty reason for refraining from obvious aggression. Their armies were based on conscription of the male population. It seemed difficult, if not impossible, to ask people to abandon civilian life and peaceful occupations when the necessity of war was not obvious. Separated by a deep rift from the bourgeois world, the workers were thought to be unwilling to accept war unless convinced that an attack had been made upon a peaceful country by external enemies.

Thus, in the course of the summer of 1914, all the European governments were eager to appear as the innocent victims of aggression. In the course of the First World War this moralistic element, this insistence on the righteousness of one's own cause, grew steadily in emphasis; increasing hatred of the enemy bolstered internal strength. It helped stiffen the will to resist and minimized social and political friction. The war became a struggle of good against evil which had to be fought through until the enemy was completely destroyed.

The fear in government circles that the lower classes would resist mobilization had been primarily caused by the declaration of the Socialist Second International that the workers ought to respond to a call to arms with a general strike. On July 30, 1914, a nationalist fanatic assassinated Jean Jaurès, the French Socialist leader, because he was expected to pronounce an appeal against the war. But it has now been proved that Jaurès never intended to issue such an appeal. Actually none of the European socialist parties heeded the recommendation of the Second International. Each of them backed the war policy of its government. Not only did opposition fail to materialize, the outbreak of war was greeted with an almost delirious enthusiasm. This astonishing response points to causes of war which went deeper than the calculations and miscalculations of foreign ministers and diplomats.

In most European countries the war seemed like a liberation from an unbearable situation. The feeling that political developments had reached a dead end was widespread among the ruling groups—not only in tsarist Russia and in Austria-Hungary, where the governments were involved in a desperate struggle to maintain outmoded forms of rule, but all over Europe. In Great Britain the reforms of the Liberal government did not mitigate social tensions; labor conflicts and strikes had been particularly vehement in the years immediately before the outbreak of the war. And although an attempt to solve the Irish question could no longer be postponed it endangered the authority of the government. In France politics had again become polarized between right and left, which opposed each other with renewed vehemence. In Italy impatience with the government's cautious policy of industrialization and democratization had stirred up extreme antiparliamentary movements on the right and left. And in Germany the elections to the Reichstag in 1912, from which the Social Democrats emerged as the strongest political party, had demonstrated that the masses could not be reconciled to their lack of political power by orderly administration and measures of social welfare.

The years before the First World War are usually regarded as having been full of sun and light in contrast to the darkness which descended on Europe in 1914. But actually the unrest in the years immediately preceding the outbreak of the war was great. The traditional politics of the ruling groups could not reconcile the alienated segments of society and had not resulted in a broadening of the bases of the existing order. The war was a way out from what had become a deadlock.

In the view of the German sociologist Max Weber rational organization and bureaucratization, which made man a cog in the wheel of a disciplined mass society, was the unavoidable future faced by the modern industrial world; to the people of the middle classes, immured in what was still a rather new phenomenon, the war came as an opportunity to break out of this industrial society. The workers were in an ambiguous situation; they, or at least many of them, were gaining a greater share in a society from which they were alienated. But the revolution which was to make them the masters of the social order seemed far removed, certainly more distant than when the socialist parties had been founded.

In the minds of almost all classes the discontent with the existing social order made the war, with its sudden release from the bonds of daily routine and with its forging of new ties, the harbinger of a highly desirable new social order. Behind the obvious shock and fear there were also hope and expectation—this should not be forgotten in explaining the causes of the catastrophe which resulted in 37.5 million casualties, in the annihilation of nearly an entire male generation, and in the loss of European hegemony over the world.

THE NATURE OF TOTAL WAR

As time has passed since the days of August, 1914, it has become increasingly clear that the outbreak of the First World War meant the end of an age. To be sure, if we consider carefully the developments of the decades preceding the war we can distinguish trends and tendencies which were steering European politics and social life into new waters. But the First World War reinforced these trends and thus accelerated the tempo of change.

It would be a mistake to assume that the new era began only in 1918, with the end of hostilities. The First World War was not just a violent interlude separating the old era from the new. The new age came about during the war years, and what happened between 1914 and 1918 helps to make the period that followed comprehensible.

Most immediately apparent were the changes effected by the conflict itself, by innovations in the techniques and the conduct of the war. When the European powers mobilized in the radiant late-summer days of 1914, the troops marching through the streets to the railroad stations, accompanied by jubilant crowds, offered an impressive and colorful sight. Flowers were strewn before the men who were expected to return triumphant after a few weeks. Flags flew; bands played; and the soldiers went singing into the war. In the first months military action was conducted in a traditional manner. Extended columns of infantry marched along the roads. The cavalry scouted enemy positions; officers led their men to storm a town or village. But after the initial battles in the west the lines became weirdly silent. Soldiers dug themselves into deep trenches fortified by barbed wire; a no-man's-land between the opposing positions was illuminated at night by rockets, intended to reveal any enemy patrols trying to penetrate the lines. The graceful, elegant horses of the cavalry became superfluous. Reconnaissance was most efficient from the air, and sometimes these scouting planes armed with machine guns engaged in air battles. Pilots became the popular war heroes. The infantry soldier, clad in mud-colored gray or khaki, still had his rifle and bayonet but his most valuable weapons were the hand grenade and the machine gun. Before the war was over poison gas was being directed against enemy lines, and tanks moved clumsily over fields and trenches.

War enthusiasm in Germany. *Soldiers on the way to the front in 1914.*

The changes in sea warfare were no less considerable. With one exception—the indecisive meeting of the British and German fleets at Jutland (1916)—no naval battles took place. Warships were used to protect convoys against the attacks of submarines, which became the supreme weapon in the struggle for control of the seas.

These changes indicate that in the twentieth century war was becoming more than the struggle of armed forces: not without reason does the term "total war" appear. To maintain a flow of the weapons which had become decisive, the continuous functioning of a sophisticated industrial complex was required. When the war broke out, only a very few had an inkling of the importance of a steady supply of raw materials and manpower, and it took some time for political and military leaders to be convinced of this fact.

The Home Front

In the question of manpower the crucial problem was to reconcile military and industrial needs. Miners and steelworkers might be perfectly suited for military service, but they possessed the skills and the physical abilities needed in mines and industry. Priorities had to be established. As the war dragged on and casualties became heavy, the tapping of new sources of manpower became a constant concern of the governments. The age limits for military service were extended; and women were employed in jobs previously reserved for men, working in offices and factories, as streetcar conductors and farmhands.

Every industry not immediately serving military ends had to be reduced to a minimum. One reason was the need for conserving manpower; another, the scarcity of raw materials. Before the conflict no European country had been self-sufficient. France, which had been less dependent on imports than other European powers, soon lost this advantageous position because a great part of its most industrialized regions was occupied by the Germans. International trade, through which raw materials had been obtained in peacetime, was interrupted by military action. Moreover, the importation of raw materials represented a drain on the gold reserves of each country because the manufacture of the exports which had brought in foreign currency was no longer possible. Strict control over raw materials—their conservation, collection, and distribution to factories according to military needs—became necessary.

Maintenance of the supply of food was the most burning problem, not only in great industrial countries like Great Britain and Germany which, in peacetime, had relied on imported wheat and other foodstuffs, but also in agrarian countries like Austria and France, where conscription denuded the land of agricultural workers. Moreover, the transportation of food to the urban centers was difficult because the railroads were overtaxed by military needs. All of the governments resorted to rationing, which usually began with bread and meat, then extended to other foodstuffs, and finally included clothes, soap, and so on. Thus, manpower, raw materials, consumer goods, all were placed under government control.

Ministries for directing economic activities were established. Strikes were outlawed, working hours prolonged. Certainly government intervention in economic affairs and government regulation of economic life were more thorough in some countries than in others—more complete in Germany and Great Britain than in Austria-Hungary, Russia, and Italy, with their ineffective bureaucracies. Nevertheless, the subjection of economic activities to government regulation all over Europe represented a radical break with the notion that the economy could function only when free from government intervention. Unquestionably, rationing and government regulations were the only possible means of assuring the existence of all the people. Even so, on the Continent, particularly in Russia, Austria, and Germany, these measures provided hardly a subsistence minimum; people were hungry and easily exhausted, and "black markets," from which the wealthy added to their rations, resulted in a spread of corruption and a decline in morale.

No longer confined to the battlefield, war became total as belligerent activities affected the entire life of the nation. To be sure, airplane construction was not yet advanced enough to permit mass bombing. A few raids by airplanes over enemy cities and a few flights of the big German airship, the Zeppelin, over the English east coast and London were more effective in inspiring terror than in inflicting serious damage. But they were signs of the form of wars to come.

The chief instrument used to throttle the economic life of the enemy was the blockade. The British controlled the North Sea and prevented Germany from receiving supplies from the other side of the Atlantic. The Germans

suddenly recognized that their strongest weapon in sea warfare was the submarine and they declared the entire British Isles to be blockaded territory and claimed the right to search and sink all ships approaching British ports.

In the First World War the activities and the morale of the civilian population acquired crucial importance. There now existed not only a military front but also a home front. And to maintain the spirit of the home front became essential. In all countries censorship was used, both to prevent the spreading of news which might be helpful to the enemy and to control and direct all news media toward the strengthening of civilian morale. It was as a consequence of the First World War that "propaganda" came to be a pejorative term: all governments installed propaganda offices and all of them falsified news. One of the chief duties of the war propagandists was to discredit the enemy, to paint him in the darkest colors, so that the populace would become convinced that defeat would mean the destruction of all that was worth living for. The practice of viewing the war as a struggle against evil increased steadily. Anti-German propaganda was particularly effective because the conduct of the Germans provided a factual basis for reports of their atrocities. The brutal behavior of the German armies in Belgium was undeniable. Because they had expected to pass through unmolested, the Belgian resistance infuriated them. The suddenness of the German invasion made it impossible for the Belgians to mobilize and many fought in civilian clothes, identified as soldiers only by armbands. This practice was accepted in international law, but the Germans considered all those fighting out of uniform as *franc-tireurs*, to be shot when captured. The impression that the entire civilian population of Belgium was resisting made the Germans jittery; they took hostages and executed them when they found opposition. In the last week of August the London *Times* called the Germans "Huns," in reference to events in Louvain. There, in the belief that sniping had occurred and that Louvain was full of *franc-tireurs*, the Germans shot a large number of citizens and set the town on fire. The famous old library of the university was entirely destroyed. The "vandalism of Louvain" was soon aggravated by the "crime of Rheims." In September, 1914, the Germans, convinced that the tower of the cathedral of Rheims served as a French observation post, fired on the cathedral, severely damaging the roof and the nave. Even if the tower was being used, the destruction wrought on a great monument of European art was indefensible. The Germans provided further food for propaganda against them by their ruthless occupation policy in Belgium. They executed Edith Cavell, a nurse who had helped British and French soldiers to escape over the borders into the neutral Netherlands, ignoring the fact—recognized by some of their own occupation officers—that as head of a hospital she had selflessly worked to mitigate the sufferings of soldiers of all nations, and deserved mercy rather

THE VETERAN'S FAREWELL.

"Good Bye, my lad.
I only wish I were young enough
to go with you!"

ENLIST NOW!

War enthusiasm in Great Britain. *A famous enlistment poster.*

than justice. Another incident, called by President Wilson "one of the most distressing and I think one of the most unjustifiable incidents of the present war," was the deportation of more than 100,000 Belgian workers into Germany.

The War Aims

The ideological and moralistic approach which determined the attitude toward the war in all countries made impossible a negotiated peace aimed at reestablishing a balance of power and restoring international collaboration. Each side was convinced that the war could end only with the complete defeat of the enemy, so that an entirely new world could be created. Each therefore attempted to present its war aims in generalized idealistic terms showing that victory would serve the interest of all mankind. Formulation of such war aims was relatively easy for Great Britain, France, and their allies in the last two years of the conflict. The war was declared to be a struggle for a new world order based on the principles of democracy and national self-determination, its purpose succinctly summarized in the famous slogan "to make the world safe for democracy." As long as Russia with its authoritarian government, was a member of the coalition against Germany, the assertion about fighting for democracy had a hollow sound. But after the overthrow of the tsar in March, 1917, the notion of a struggle between democracy and authoritarianism gained meaning, particularly since the overthrow coincided with the entrance into the war against Germany of the greatest democracy in the world, the United States. The fact that men and women of all classes contributed to the military effort gave force to the demand that they should have the right to decide the political fate of their country. Where before the First World War the demand for suffrage for women had been regarded as utopian and even ridiculous, it now became more urgent. In Great Britain, Germany, and the United States, female suffrage was achieved soon after the war. In Italy and France its adversaries were able to delay giving women the vote until after the Second World War. But even there the final victory of female suffrage was never seriously in doubt.

It was difficult for Germany and its allies to place the war on a broad ideological level. The German Social Democratic party had been the largest and best organized of all socialist parties. Socialist approval of the money bills required for the financing of the war was the most striking and also the most surprising example of the abandonment of revolutionary international-ism by Social Democrats in favor of defense of the homeland. The German government gained the support of socialist and progressive forces without taking them into the government. Thus, during most of the war Germany continued to be ruled by the members of the conservative bureaucracy Their innate resistance to liberal and democratic reforms was reinforced by the military, whose power now increased immensely. William II, who even in peacetime had failed to exercise steady leadership, did not dare to challenge the men of the hour. Thus the German military leaders Paul von Hindenburg (1847–1934) and Erich Ludendorff (1865–1937), who were enormously popular because of victories against the Russians, began to exert—if not in form, at least in fact—a military dictatorship. As allies of the Conservatives they resisted political reforms, and the tensions which had existed in peacetime came again out into the open during the last few years of the war, expressing themselves in a bitter struggle about the war aims between those who wanted to fight for total victory so that Germany could make extended annexations and those who believed that peace ought to be concluded on the basis of the *status quo* and that every effort should be made to reach a peace of understanding. Thus in Germany the united front which had been established in August, 1914, began to show fissures, which became deeper month by month.

THE TIDES OF BATTLE

The Expanding Theater of War

The conflict that took place between 1914 and 1918 is rightly called a world war, for it assumed global dimensions. At the start, however, it was confined to the great European powers: Great Britain, France, Russia,

The German Military High Command. *Hindenburg, William II, Ludendorff.*

Germany, and Austria-Hungary. Only two of the smaller European states participated from the outset in this struggle of the great powers: Serbia, whose conflict with Austria had led to the explosion; and Belgium, which had been forced to resist by the German violation of its internationally guaranteed neutrality. The first non-European power, Japan, entered the war in August. But its military contribution was limited to the conquest and occupation of the German colonial possessions in the Far East. A real enlargement of the theater of war took place with the entry of Turkey on the German side in November, 1914. Turkey occupied a key position. By allying itself with the western powers and Russia, it could have closed the ring around the Central Powers—as Austria and Germany were called—and ensured coordinated action against them from the west, east, and south. On the other hand, as an ally of Germany and Austria, Turkey could prevent the shipping of supplies to Russia through the Mediterranean and the Black Sea. Hence, a fierce diplomatic struggle for the favors of Turkey took place in Constantinople, but the hold which Germany had developed over Turkey through the building of the Baghdad Railway, reinforced by the appearance of two German naval ships in the Dardanelles, proved to be the stronger. The entry of Turkey extended the war into Mesopotamia and Persia, where British and Russian forces on the one hand and Turkish troops under German command on the other fought with alternating success. In order to relieve the pressure on Turkey, Germany and Austria became anxious to establish direct communication with the Ottoman Empire. Promising the cession of large parts of Macedonia, now in Serbian hands, they persuaded Bulgaria to enter the war in October, 1915. In counteraction, the Allies—France, Great Britain, and Russia—induced Rumania in August, 1916, and then Greece in June, 1917, to declare war on the Central Powers, although by that time Serbia had succumbed to the joint attacks from the west and the north, so that the Central Powers dominated a broad connected stretch of territory from the North Sea to Mesopotamia and the Suez Canal. However, in 1915 the Allies had gained an important partner in Italy. Originally the Italians had declared themselves to be neutral because in their view the Austrians had started the war and had not acted in self-defense, requiring Italian assistance under the Triple Alliance. The Italians were courted by both sides, but the Central Powers could not make any promises that outweighed Italy's interest in using this war for the liberation of people of Italian nationality living under Austrian rule. The Allies in a secret agreement concluded in London in April, 1915, promised Italy, in addition to the Austrian provinces inhabited by Italians, a wide expanse on the eastern side of the Adriatic Sea, including northern Albania; the Dodecanese in the Aegean Sea; and—if Turkey was partitioned—a part of Asia Minor. Later, even Portugal and San Marino entered the war; by 1917, with exception of the Scandinavian countries, the Netherlands, Switzerland, and Spain, all the European nations were engaged on one side or the other. With the entry of the United States in April, 1917, the war finally took on a global character. Then a number of Latin-American states, among them Brazil, declared war on Germany, and others, such as Bolivia, Peru, and Ecuador, severed relations with Germany. In Asia, China and Siam and in Africa, Liberia joined the coalition against the Central Powers. In many of these cases the reason for participation was purely economic. The rupture with Germany served to tighten loopholes in the blockade, to prevent the transference of German capital, and to permit the confiscation of German assets. In any event, the war had become global.

The small size of the area occupied by the Central Powers in comparison with the vast extent of the territory represented by their enemies might lead one to believe that the defeat of the Central Powers was almost inevitable. But the actual fact is that many times Germany seemed near victory and the German collapse in 1918 was sudden and unexpected.

Stalemate in the West

When the war broke out, the German general staff planned to defeat France within six weeks and then to turn against Russia. A quick victory in the west was to be attained by concentrating almost all the German forces against France, most of them on the right wing, which was to advance in a great wheeling movement through Belgium and northern France and then turn south and finally east, trapping the French forces in a gigantic ring. The strategy used by Hannibal in his defeat of the Romans at Cannae was to be repeated on an immensely enlarged scale. This was the famous Schlieffen Plan, named after the German chief of staff who had conceived it about 1905. The plan failed; the German advances were halted in the Battle of the Marne, which takes its place as one of the decisive battles of history.

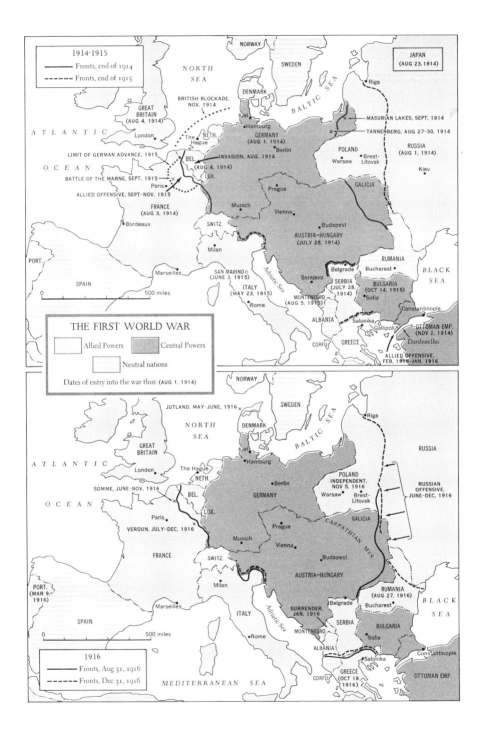

THE FIRST WORLD WAR

1914-1915

Fronts, end of 1914
Fronts, end of 1915

Allied Powers
Central Powers
Neutral nations

Dates of entry into the war thus: (AUG 1, 1914)

NORWAY
SWEDEN
NORTH SEA
DENMARK
BALTIC SEA
JAPAN (AUG 23, 1914)
BRITISH BLOCKADE, NOV. 1914
GREAT BRITAIN (AUG 4, 1914)
Kiel
Hamburg
Riga
MASURIAN LAKES, SEPT. 1914
TANNENBERG, AUG 27-30, 1914
ATLANTIC OCEAN
London
The Hague
NETH.
GERMANY (AUG 1, 1914)
Berlin
POLAND
Warsaw
Brest-Litovsk
RUSSIA (AUG 1, 1914)
Kiev
LIMIT OF GERMAN ADVANCE, 1915
INVASION, AUG. 1914
BEL. (AUG 4, 1914)
LUX.
BATTLE OF THE MARNE, SEPT. 1915
Paris
ALLIED OFFENSIVE, SEPT-NOV, 1915
Prague
GALICIA
FRANCE (AUG 3, 1914)
Munich
SWITZ.
Vienna
Budapest
Bordeaux
Milan
AUSTRIA-HUNGARY (JULY 28, 1914)
RUMANIA
PORT.
SAN MARINO (JUNE 3, 1915)
Adriatic Sea
Belgrade
Bucharest
BLACK SEA
SPAIN
Marseilles
ITALY (MAY 23, 1915)
Rome
Sarajevo
SERBIA (JULY 28, 1914)
MONTENEGRO (AUG 5, 1915)
BULGARIA (OCT 14, 1915)
Sofia
Constantinople
0   500 miles
ALBANIA
Salonika
Gallipoli
OTTOMAN EMP. (NOV 2, 1914)
CORFU
GREECE
Dardanelles
ALLIED OFFENSIVE, FEB. 1915-JAN. 1916

JUTLAND, MAY-JUNE, 1916
NORWAY
SWEDEN
NORTH SEA
DENMARK
BALTIC SEA
GREAT BRITAIN
Kiel
Hamburg
Riga
RUSSIA
ATLANTIC OCEAN
London
The Hague
NETH.
GERMANY
Berlin
POLAND INDEPENDENT, NOV 5, 1916
Warsaw
Brest-Litovsk
RUSSIAN OFFENSIVE, JUNE-DEC, 1916
SOMME, JUNE-NOV, 1916
BEL.
LUX.
Paris
VERDUN, JULY-DEC, 1916
Prague
GALICIA
CARPATHIAN MTS.
Munich
FRANCE
SWITZ.
Vienna
Budapest
PORT. (MAR 9, 1916)
Milan
AUSTRIA-HUNGARY
RUMANIA (AUG 27, 1916)
SPAIN
Marseilles
ITALY
Adriatic Sea
SURRENDER, JAN. 1916
Belgrade
Bucharest
BLACK SEA
0   500 miles
Rome
MONTENEGRO
SERBIA
BULGARIA
Sofia
Constantinople
1916
Fronts, Aug 31, 1916
Fronts, Dec 31, 1916
ALBANIA
Salonika
CORFU
GREECE (OCT 18, 1916)
OTTOMAN EMP.
MEDITERRANEAN SEA

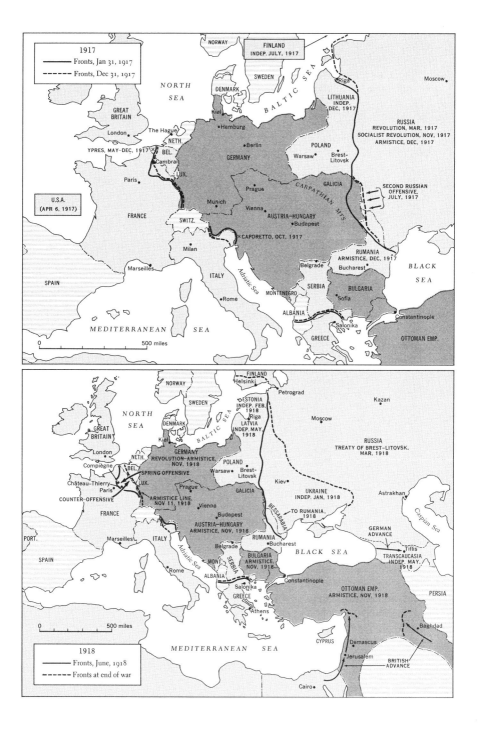

1917

— Fronts, Jan 31, 1917

--- Fronts, Dec 31, 1917

NORWAY

FINLAND
INDEP. JULY, 1917

SWEDEN

*NORTH
SEA*

DENMARK

Riga

Moscow •

BALTIC SEA

LITHUANIA
INDEP.
DEC, 1917

GREAT
BRITAIN

• Kiel

• Hamburg

RUSSIA
REVOLUTION, MAR, 1917
SOCIALIST REVOLUTION, NOV, 1917
ARMISTICE, DEC, 1917

London •

The Hague •

• Berlin

NETH.

POLAND

BEL.

GERMANY

Warsaw •

Brest-
Litovsk

YPRES, MAY-DEC, 1917

Cambrai

Paris •

LUX.

• Prague

CARPATHIAN MTS

GALICIA

SECOND RUSSIAN
OFFENSIVE,
JULY, 1917

U.S.A.
(APR 6, 1917)

• Munich

• Vienna

AUSTRIA-HUNGARY

FRANCE

SWITZ.

• Budapest

× CAPORETTO, OCT. 1917

• Milan

RUMANIA
ARMISTICE, DEC, 1917

*BLACK
SEA*

Marseilles •

ITALY

Adriatic Sea

Belgrade •

Bucharest •

SPAIN

• Rome

MONTENEGRO

SERBIA

BULGARIA

ALBANIA

Sofia •

Constantinople •

0   500 miles

MEDITERRANEAN SEA

GREECE

Salonika •

OTTOMAN EMP.

NORWAY

FINLAND
Helsinki •

Petrograd •

Kazan •

SWEDEN

*NORTH
SEA*

DENMARK

ESTONIA
INDEP. FEB.
1918

Riga •

Moscow •

GREAT
BRITAIN

BALTIC SEA

LATVIA
INDEP. MAY,
1918

London •

• Kiel

GERMANY
REVOLUTION-ARMISTICE,
NOV, 1918

RUSSIA
TREATY OF BREST-LITOVSK,
MAR, 1918

Compiègne •

NETH.

POLAND

BEL.

SPRING OFFENSIVE

Warsaw •

Brest-
Litovsk

Château-Thierry •

LUX.

• Prague

Kiev •

UKRAINE
INDEP. JAN, 1918

Astrakhan •

Paris •

GALICIA

Caspian Sea

COUNTER-OFFENSIVE

ARMISTICE LINE,
NOV 11, 1918

• Vienna

FRANCE

• Budapest

BESSARABIA

TO RUMANIA,
1918

AUSTRIA-HUNGARY
ARMISTICE, NOV, 1918

GERMAN
ADVANCE

PORT.

Marseilles •

ITALY

Belgrade •

RUMANIA

Bucharest •

Tiflis •

SPAIN

• Rome

MONT.

SERBIA

BULGARIA
ARMISTICE,
NOV, 1918

BLACK SEA

TRANSCAUCASIA
INDEP. MAY,
1918

Adriatic Sea

ALBANIA

Constantinople •

PERSIA

Salonika •

GREECE

OTTOMAN EMP.
ARMISTICE, NOV, 1918

0   500 miles

Athens •

Baghdad •

MEDITERRANEAN SEA

CYPRUS

Damascus •

BRITISH
ADVANCE

1918

— Fronts, June, 1918

--- Fronts at end of war

Jerusalem •

Cairo •

There were many reasons for the failure. First, the Belgian resistance delayed the German advance. Also, the Germans had not counted on the appearance of a British expeditionary corps which, although thrown back in the battles of Mons and Le Cateau, seriously retarded their movement forward. Alexander von Kluck, the commander of the German First Army, operating on the extreme right, believed that the presence of the British forces made it impossible to include Paris in the wide encircling movement which had been envisaged. He ordered his troops to turn sharply to the south, leaving Paris at their right. And this gave the French their opportunity. Although forced to retreat throughout August, the French army had not disintegrated. The commander of the French forces, Joseph Joffre, was an adherent of the doctrine of continuous attack and had been less concerned with arranging a defensive position than with seizing an opportunity to attack. Kluck's move to the south made it possible for Joffre to attack the German flank and rear. A famous episode of the ensuing battle was that under orders from Gallieni, the commandant of Paris, the city's taxi drivers transported men directly from Paris to the front. On September 9, Kluck's army was ordered to retreat from the Marne to the Aisne. The German campaign plan had failed.

The German military command contributed to the defeat. It had watered down the original Schlieffen Plan; the right wing was weaker than it ought to have been. Moreover, the German army on the left had been engaged in a battle in Lorraine and could therefore spare no troops to reinforce the right wing at the decisive moment. Helmuth von Moltke, the German chief of staff, following the precepts of his uncle, the great strategist of the nineteenth century, gave his field commanders freedom of decision. But he followed this principle too literally and too slavishly. There was little leadership from above, nor was there much communication among the various German commanders. Thus, between the First German Army, operating on the extreme right, and the Second German Army, operating further left, a gap opened at the critical time when the French counterattack began. And Moltke, alarmed by the dangers which might result from French advances into this gap, ordered retreat.

Whatever responsibility for the outcome of the Battle of the Marne one assigns to the energy and courage of the French and British generals, or to the mistakes committed by the German military leaders, the entire Schlieffen Plan was probably not feasible. In 1914 armies were not yet motorized and the distances involved in encircling the armed forces of an entire nation were too large to be covered by foot soldiers, at least with the speed and precision required for success.

The Battle of the Marne was followed by a race for the channel ports. Each side tried to regain freedom of movement by outflanking the other; but despite a bloody struggle along the seacoast in Flanders, neither was dislodged. The front now became stabilized: it began at the North Sea, in Flanders; then bulged out into France, with Germany retaining control of important French industrial areas; and then swung back to the Franco-German frontier along Alsace-Lorraine, ending at the Swiss border. The armies dug in. For the next four years, until the spring of 1918, the lines remained almost unchanged, although sporadic and bloody attempts were made to end the stalemate and break through the enemy's lines. In February, 1916, the Germans launched an attack on Verdun. This was intended to be a battle of attrition. The Germans wanted to draw the flower of the French army into this battle and destroy the morale of the French troops. But in June, when the battle was broken off, the German losses were hardly less great than the French and the German territorial gains were insignificant. In July, 1916, the French and the British attacked along the Somme, their main purpose being to draw German troops away from the eastern front, where the Russians were in dire straits; again, only small territorial gains had been made by November, when the battle at the Somme got stuck in the mud. The French and British attempted a breakthrough in the spring of 1917 by simultaneous attacks at two different points, Arras and along the Aisne; the general responsible for this offensive was the French commander in chief Nivelle. His main success was the conquering of the Chemin des Dames, a height in the center of the front line, but the losses were so terrible that mutiny broke out in the French army and General Henri Philippe Pétain (1856–1951), who was called in to replace Nivelle, decided on a purely defensive conduct of the war in the west. However the British commander, Douglas Haig, believed that Nivelle's offensive had failed because of tactical mistakes and that he, Haig could do better. Despite great doubts in the British cabinet, Haig ordered an offensive in Flanders, around Ypres, which began on July 31 and lasted until November. Again the territorial gains were small and the casualties staggering. The rain and mud of autumn slowed down every step so that the advancing troops offered easy targets. Passchendaele, as this battle is usually called, together "with the Somme and Verdun, will always · ɪnk as the most gigantic, tenacious, grim, futile and bloody fight ever waged in the history of war"[1]—an entirely useless slaughter. If any further proof was needed, Passchendaele showed that new weapons and new methods had to be introduced if the superiority of the defense over the offense was to be overcome.

German Success in the East

The failure at Verdun sufficiently proved to the Germans the futility of an offensive in the west. Those German military leaders who had believed

---

[1] David Lloyd George, *War Memoirs*, Vol. IV (London, 1934), p. 2110.

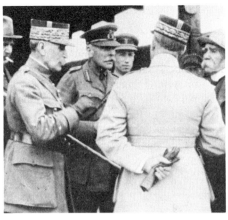

The political and military leaders of Great Britain and France. *Haig, Joffre, Lloyd George are shown on the left. Foch, Haig, Clemenceau, and Weigand on the right.*

since the failure in the Battle of the Marne that victory could be obtained only through defeat of Russia now gained the upper hand. The most influential and effective representatives of this view were Hindenburg and Ludendorff. They had acquired immense popularity in Germany because in August and September of 1914, in the battles of Tannenberg and the Masurian Lakes, they had defeated and annihilated two Russian armies advancing into East Prussia. Hindenburg's and Ludendorff's responsibility for these victories is somewhat diminished by the fact that they arrived— Hindenburg from retirement, Ludendorff from the west—when the German commanders on the spot had already made the arrangements for the battles. Nevertheless, Hindenburg and Ludendorff, as saviors of Germany from the Russian barbarians, became popular heroes. In September, 1914, Hindenburg was made commander in chief of the German armies in the east and in 1916 he became chief of staff, with Ludendorff as his main assistant. The German conduct of the war in the east was brilliant. In 1915 a great offensive was started in Galicia, which the Russians had occupied, and soon the operations extended over the entire eastern frontier; by the time military activity halted in the fall the lines reached from the eastern part of Galicia straight to the north, with the Central Powers having conquered Poland, Lithuania, and Kurland.

These German victories were facilitated by the Russians' lack of munitions and equipment. At the beginning of 1915 the British had made an ingenious attempt to open a direct route to Russia through the Dardanelles. This operation—the Gallipoli campaign—failed mainly through lack of cooperation between the naval and the land forces. Thus, materials could be sent to the Russians only through Siberia; the Russians were forced to rely on their own resources for the 1916 summer campaign, which became decisive for the war in the east. The Russians had planned an offensive which would be coordinated with the entry of Rumania into the war. But Rumania was quickly defeated and occupied by the Germans, and although the Russians drove the Austrians back more than eighty miles to the Carpathians and into Galicia, they suffered such serious losses that, with the coming of the winter, they were at the end of their strength. In March, 1917, revolution broke out, the tsar abdicated, and a republic was proclaimed. Since the new liberal leaders of Russia felt close to the parliamentary democracies of Great Britain and France and were anxious to continue the war, the change in government was of no advantage to Germany. The Germans were interested in weakening or overthrowing the new liberal government and the German high command agreed to permit a group of radical revolutionaries, among them Lenin and other principal Bolsheviks, to travel in a sealed railroad coach from Switzerland, where they were living in exile, through Germany to Russia. On April 16, 1917, the Bolshevik leaders arrived in Petrograd, the former St. Petersburg, whose name had been russified during the war. Their chance came in the summer of 1917 with the collapse, after some initial success, of an offensive ordered by the liberal Russian government. Making full use of the war-weariness of the masses, the Bolsheviks succeeded in seizing power. Shortly afterward an armistice was concluded, and militarily helpless and under the pressure of further German advances, the Bolshevik government was forced to sign a separate peace treaty with the Central Powers at Brest-Litovsk in March, 1918.

Thus, in the early spring of 1918 the Central Powers had freed themselves from the danger of a two-front war and seemed in a brilliant position. Half a year later the German high command was to declare to its government that

The signing of the armistice that ended the war in the east. *On the left, the German, Austrian, and Bulgarian representatives; on the right, Bolshevik representatives.*

the war must be considered lost. And in November, 1918, a Germany transformed by revolution into a republic agreed to an armistice which could only lead to a peace dictated by the western powers. What had happened to bring about this reversal of fortune?

Decision in the West

All of Germany's successes in the east could not outweigh the fact that its strongest adversaries were in the west and that victory was impossible without defeating them. It seemed clear that action at sea would be required to subdue Great Britain, the most formidable of the western enemies. Early in the war, a naval blockade to deprive Germany of raw materials had been instituted by Britain and France. In international law a distinction is made between contraband—munitions and raw materials needed for the manufacture of military equipment—and noncontraband, notably food and clothing. Only contraband is subject to confiscation by a blockading power. But the British refused to recognize this distinction. No ships of any neutral power were permitted to go to a German port, and imports into the Scandinavian countries and the Netherlands were limited to quantities which assured that the goods would be used in the importing countries and not be reshipped to Germany.

The British violation of recognized international law created serious trouble between the United States and Great Britain. But the United States finally sided with Great Britain against Germany because the Germans too violated international law—flagrantly and even more brutally than the British. The Germans felt that they could counterbalance the British blockade by a more effective form of economic warfare, a submarine blockade. Submarines could not remove goods or people from merchant ships; they could only sink the ships. The Germans declared the waters surrounding the British Isles to be a war zone in which all enemy vessels would be torpedoed and even those of neutral nations, if suspected of carrying goods, might be sunk. In February, 1915, a German submarine torpedoed the *Lusitania*, a British passenger liner; almost 1,200 people drowned, among them 118 American citizens. While it was true that the *Lusitania* carried ammunition, the death of more than a thousand civilians, many from neutral countries, seemed incredibly brutal. Indignation in the United States mounted. After a severe warning by President Wilson, the Germans relented and for two years they modified their conduct of submarine warfare. But pressure against Chancellor Bethmann-Hollweg and those of his advisers who advocated caution in using the submarine steadily mounted. It was difficult for the public to bear the hardships of the British blockade when Germany was believed to be in possession of a weapon with which it could retaliate. Moreover, the German navy had built many new submarines and the naval high command, supported by experts anxious to please the admirals, maintained that Great Britain could be starved out and forced to surrender in a short time. Hindenburg and Ludendorff gave full support to the demands of the navy. On January 31, 1917, the Germans proclaimed the resumption of unrestricted submarine warfare. President Wilson severed diplomatic relations with Germany, and provoked by the sinking of American ships, the United States declared war on Germany on April 6, 1917.

The effect of America's entry into the war was immense. British shipping losses, especially since the declaration of unrestricted submarine warfare, had risen dangerously. In April, 1917, alone, 875,000 tons of shipping were sunk. By organizing a convoy system, the British had tried to master this threat. But the entry of the United States into the war made the German submarine warfare an evident failure, because thereafter the number of ships convoyed and the number of ships protecting the convoys was increased steadily. Convoys of ships transporting food, war materials, and troops arrived safely in Britain, and the rate of shipping construction soon exceeded the rate of loss. Moreover, the entry of the United States into the war blunted the uplift in morale which the breakdown of Russia would otherwise have produced in Germany. Indeed, Wilson's insistence on a just and democratic peace increased internal tension in Germany. The demand grew for a guarantee that the war would not be fought to achieve the aims and ambitions of the ruling group but would be terminated as soon as the existence of the German people was no longer threatened. Both at home and abroad, distrust of the policy of the German leaders was reinforced by events connected with the negotiations in Brest-Litovsk about peace with the Bolsheviks. The Bolshevik delegation, under the leadership of Leon Trotsky (1877–1940), embarked upon a heated discussion of war aims with the foreign ministers of Germany and Austria, and widespread reports of this debate disseminated the Bolshevik formula of "peace without annexations or indemnities." The treaty which was finally forced upon Russia early

War in the air. *Two planes collide during a dogfight.*

in 1918 was dictated by the German military high command, and it was harsh. Its main effect was to push Russia out of Europe. Russia was forced to abandon Finland, the Baltic provinces, Poland, the Ukraine, and Transcaucasia. The Central Powers established in these countries regimes controlled by small wealthy groups: German landowners in the Baltic states, a small pro-German military clique in the Ukraine. German princes were placed on the thrones of such newly established states as Lithuania, Kurland, and Finland. The Treaty of Brest-Litovsk imposed a peace of annexation and of power politics.

Despite the apparent military advantage of the Central Powers at the beginning of 1918, their situation had grave weaknesses. The brutal German policy in the east kept the conquered areas restless and in revolt. Large military forces had to remain in the east, and the transportation of food, especially of wheat from the Ukraine, met many obstacles. Increasingly, the governments of the Central Powers were being criticized as overweening in their ambitions and unwilling or unable to terminate the war. The Allies had become strong enough to mount offensives at various fronts. In the fall of 1917 the British had thrown the Turks back from the Egyptian frontier and advanced into Palestine, taking Jerusalem on December 8, 1917. Greece's entry into the war in June, 1917, had made possible an offensive against Bulgaria. On the other hand in October, 1917, Austrian and German troops had broken the Italian front in the Battle of Caporetto, brilliantly described by Ernest Hemingway in A Farewell to Arms (1929). To stem the panic among Italian troops, Italian military police were ordered to shoot every tenth man of any formation that was fleeing. Significantly, even the German victory at Caporetto did not eliminate Italy from the war. The British and French were able to send in enough reinforcements to reconstruct an Italian front along the Piave.

Thus, at the beginning of 1918, despite the Treaty of Brest-Litovsk, Germany was not in an unassailable position, able to wait for the Allies to force the issue. The arrival of American troops and increasing disaffection within Germany necessitated action leading to a quick end to the war. The German military leaders responded with an offensive in the west which they believed, with the help of reinforcements from the east, would bring victory. But in its outcome this offensive, which started on March 21, 1918, was no different from previous ones in the west. Initially, territorial gains were large. But when the German soldiers advanced beyond the zone where they enjoyed protection from their artillery, they again found that in trench warfare defense was superior to attack, and the German offensive got stuck. German attacks in other areas of the front lacked even the force of the March offensive. The Germans were halted—by the French at Compiègne and by the Americans and the French at Château-Thierry. Starting in July, 1918, the Allies, now led by Ferdinand Foch, commander in chief of all the armies in France, began to attack. And their advances were power-

War on land. *Dugouts on the Western Front.*

fully supported by use of the tank—a new weapon which brought an element of movement into the war of position. At the same time, the Allied armies in Salonika and the Italians at the Piave began to advance and both the Bulgarian and the Austrian fronts collapsed; Bulgaria and Austria asked for peace.

At this point Ludendorff urged the German government to seek an armistice. German political leaders now lost all confidence in the German high command, and the German people and the troops were no longer willing to accept the leadership of the military or of the rulers who had supported them. Revolution spread from town to town. By November 9 all the German princes, William II included, had abdicated, and on November 11 the armistice was signed. The First World War was at an end.

A GENERATION LOST

In western Europe the losses and casualties of the First World War were considerably larger than those suffered by the same states in the Second World War. Altogether, about 8.5 million men were dead. More than twice that number were wounded, many of them maimed for life. The total number of casualties, including killed, wounded, and missing, is figured as 37.5 million. The greatest number of war dead and wounded— about 6 million—was suffered by Germany. France's losses were 5.5 million, but with a population less than two thirds that of Germany, France suffered proportionately more in the First World War than any other belligerent. The losses in single battles were horrendous. In the Battle of Verdun the Germans and the French each lost more than 300,000 men. Passchendaele cost the British 245,000 men. An entire generation rotted on the battlefields. Modern warfare does not lead to a survival of the strongest or the

War crimes. *The cathedral of Rheims after artillery bombardment.*

best. Many who might have been leaders in the coming decade never returned from the war.

In considering the developments following the holocaust, it is important to remember that the usual transition from one generation to the next did not take place in the interwar period. It is true that at the end of the 1920's a few men of the war generation did advance to political leadership: Anthony Eden in Great Britain, Edouard Daladier in France, Heinrich Brüning in Germany. But the distinction which they enjoyed as members of the war generation emphasizes how few of those who could become national leaders survived. Benito Mussolini and Adolf Hitler made a great play over having been frontline soldiers fighting in the trenches. They pretended to be the representatives of the generation which the old men tried to keep down and to suffocate. Exaggerated as such claims were, the leading statesmen of Europe, far into the 1930's, almost up to the Second World War, were for the most part men who had come into positions before the First World War. Moreover, because the memory of the events and experiences of this war persisted long after 1918, people continued to look upon the wartime military leaders as father figures to whom they could entrust their fate. Instead of fading away, the generals, the Hindenburgs and the Pétains—whether victorious or defeated—remained important personages on the political scene. There was a strange incongruity between the new issues which the First World War had created and the aged political leaders whose task it was to grapple with these problems.

CHAPTER 4

The World at the End of the First World War

THE CONFLICT which had begun in August, 1914, as a struggle between the great European powers had become a world war by the time it drew to a close. That the future of Europe was now linked with the future of the rest of the world was apparent at the Paris Peace Conference which met in January, 1919. Statesmen assembled from all parts of the world, and they redrew boundaries not only in Europe but also in Africa and Asia. The role which political leaders of other continents now played in the making of war and peace was a striking sign that the time when the European statesmen could arrange among themselves the affairs of the entire globe had passed. Moreover, the decrease of Europe's weight in international affairs was indicated not only by the weakening of European rule over other parts of the world, but by the fact that developments elsewhere began increasingly to impinge on the political situation in Europe; the impact of global events on the European political scene grew steadily during the twenty years between the two world wars. These events would contribute to the final breakdown of the European postwar settlement. Therefore, before we enter upon a detailed discussion of the European peace settlement we shall examine briefly the new forces which emerged in other continents and which undermined the rule of European powers over.

THE LEAGUE OF NATIONS

The most visible sign of the changed relationship between the European and the non-European parts of the world was the establishment of the League of Nations. In contrast to the nineteenth-century concert of a few great European powers, the League was expected to embrace all the states of the world, and large and small were to have the same voice. The idea of the League owed its origin to a widespread rejection of prewar diplomacy, which with its concern for the balance of power, its eagerness for secret treaties and systems of alliances, and its insistence on strong armaments was considered to have been responsible for the outbreak of the First World War. During the war the need for a "new diplomacy" was particularly

The Big Four. *The prime ministers of Italy, Great Britain, France—Orlando, Lloyd George, Clemenceau—and President Wilson.*

emphasized by writers and politicians of the Anglo-Saxon countries, and their ideas found an eloquent advocate in President Woodrow Wilson (1856–1924), who incorporated them in his peace program.

President Wilson provided the Allied cause with a persuasive justification. They were fighting for the creation of a new world. Boundaries should be drawn according to the principle of national self-determination, so that conflicts over expansion would not arise. Freedom of the seas and removal of economic restrictions should raise the level of economic well-being in all nations, and bind them together in cooperation. The single states should establish democratic forms of government so that the peaceful intentions of the people would prevail over the designs of small authoritarian militaristic groups. Abolition of secret treaties and "open diplomacy" would further assure the coming of a peaceful era in international relations, and a world-embracing organization of nations would supervise the maintenance of this new order. Wilson summarized these democratic war aims in his so-called "Fourteen Points" that made a deep impression all over the world.

At the Paris Peace Conference, Wilson regarded the organization of the League of Nations as his most important task; in return for agreement to this project he was willing to make many concessions, for he was convinced that if the League were established it would be able in the course of time to rectify any errors in the peace treaties.

The life of the League was short. Its first meeting took place in 1920 and its last in 1939, although the official dissolution did not occur until April 18, 1946. Since the League did not succeed in preventing war, it can hardly be called a success; nevertheless, as the first attempt to create a world-embracing organization of states for the preservation of peace it represented a landmark. Its original members came from every part of the globe. Moreover, in the League Assembly, which met regularly every year, each member—whether great or small—had the same rights. The executive business was entrusted to a Council whose composition did preserve something of the old idea of the rule of the world by great powers: Great

Britain, France, Italy, and Japan were its permanent members. But the Council also included a number of elected temporary members (originally four, later this number was steadily enlarged) and among them there regularly were representatives from Latin America, from Asia, and from the British dominions. Recognition of the equality of all nations and of their right to self-rule was also reflected in the fact that German and Ottoman territories in Asia and Africa which the victors had taken over were retained by them only as mandates, to be administered under supervision of the League with the aim of preparing their inhabitants for full independence.

Nevertheless, the League failed to prevent aggression and to preserve peace. And the reasons can be traced back to its beginnings. Although it claimed to be a world-encompassing organization, it was not. President Wilson was unable to overcome American fears that membership in the League might lead to involvement in "foreign quarrels," and the United States remained outside the League. Moreover, both Russia, because of its antidemocratic regime, and Germany, because of its role in starting the war and because of its war crimes, were excluded. The Bolshevik leaders of Russia therefore considered the League primarily as the center of a capitalist conspiracy for the encirclement of Russia and the overthrow of Communism; and the Germans viewed the League as an instrument for enforcing the peace treaty and keeping Germany down. Even when Germany (in September, 1926) and Russia (in September, 1934) finally entered the League, they did so primarily to strengthen their political position; neither the rulers nor their people ever became convinced believers in a new peaceful system of international relations which the League was to usher in. But the failure of the League has to be explained by more than the non-inclusion of important powers. Even those states which had participated in the founding of this organization and belonged to it from the beginning were hesitant to agree to arrangements which would limit their sovereignty. Thus, from the outset the League's chances of success in preserving peace were limited, for it had no "teeth." Membership involved commitments to avoid war, to respect the territorial integrity of other powers, and to submit disputes to investigation, arbitration, and settlement by the Permanent Court of International Justice in The Hague or by the Council of the League. If a government refused to honor these commitments and became an aggressor, the members of the League were to apply economic sanctions: to sever all economic intercourse with the aggressor state. Clear prescriptions for military action against the offender did not exist. Moreover, in questions of conflicts between states, decisions by the Council of the League required unanimity and were therefore almost impossible to obtain.

The most effective work of the League was done in promoting international cooperation in the technical and economic spheres. Its greatest successes were achieved by its health organization, which helped to control epidemics, to standardize drugs and vaccines, to promote worldwide studies

on nutrition, and to improve health services in Asia. The Economic Section of the League provided valuable analyses and statistics. The League Organization on Communications and Transit furthered collaboration concerning such matters as electric power and inland navigation. The International Labor Organization, working under the League, had some success in improving working conditions.

THE WANING OF EUROPEAN ECONOMIC SUPREMACY

The establishment of the League of Nations reflected the rise of the non-European countries, and this development was rooted in hard facts. Principal among them was the changed economic situation. The costs of the war had been fantastically high, and resulted in a wasteful drain on the economic resources of the states involved. For instance, in 1917 the German war expenditure amounted to two thirds of the total German national

income of prewar years. Only a small part of these vast sums could be obtained through taxation. All the governments resorted to loans; for the Allies a particularly important source of funds was the United States. By means of loans the European countries paid for the war materials which they bought from the United States; cash payments would have quickly exhausted their gold reserves.

Thus, in addition to the waste of capital and resources, there occurred a decline of the European economic position in comparison to that of the United States. The European powers were transformed from creditor nations into debtor nations. By the end of the war Great Britain's indebtedness to the United States government amounted to $3,696,000,000; that of France to $1,970,000,000; and that of Italy to $1,031,000,000. Altogether, the Allied powers of Europe owed the United States more than $7,000,000,000. In addition many loans were made in the period just after the end of the war; when the debt of the Allied nations to the United States was funded in 1922, the total indebtedness amounted to $11,656,932,900. The center of the world money market began to move from London to New York.

As a further consequence of the First World War, European investments in non-European countries diminished, and the opportunities of the European states for influencing economic development in other continents were lessened. Most German assets outside of Europe were confiscated by the governments of the countries in which they were located. Before the United States entered the war, loans were not easily obtainable, and Great Britain therefore paid for goods with gold and procured the necessary foreign exchange by mobilizing foreign securities held by British citizens. British and European holdings in non-European countries were thus considerably reduced. Moreover, because the European countries geared their industrial production to the war effort, their export trade ceased almost entirely, with the result that economic life in the non-European parts of the world was reoriented. For instance, before the First World War, the British and to a somewhat lesser degree the Germans dominated international trade with the states of Latin America. At that time agriculture was the economic mainstay of these countries, and manufactured goods were obtained from abroad. In the postwar period Latin-American trade with the United States, and investments by American firms in Latin America, increased steadily. The American economic influence accelerated industrial progress: the chief American investments were in mining, and American capital played a leading part in the development of oil fields in Venezuela, Peru, Colombia, and Ecuador. Now these countries were set toward industrialization, and in the 1920's they achieved a remarkable prosperity. Economic development in India was similar. During the war the government actively promoted industrial growth so that India could supply equipment for the troops fighting in Mesopotamia and the Near East. The Tata Iron and Steel Company in Bihar became the largest steel works in the world, producing almost a million tons annually. Production figures around the world revealed the diminished economic role of the European continent. In 1925 the world output of manufactured goods was 20 per cent higher than in 1913, and this rise can be attributed exclusively to the expansion of production in the non-European world.

NATIONALIST MOVEMENTS IN THE COLONIES

More important, however, than the weakening of the European economic position was the change which took place as a result of the First World War in the relationship between white men and natives, between the European rulers and the colonial peoples. Men of different races had fought side by side; the distance which the white men had kept from other races diminished. Where native movements for autonomy or independence had existed they gained a stronger impetus, and where nationalism had been sleeping it was now awakened. The areas in which antagonism between the European ruler and settler and the native population began to play an increasingly important role were Africa and southern Asia.

Africa

In Africa one must distinguish between the Northern Arc, which the Arabs had conquered many centuries ago, and central and southern Africa. In central and southern Africa the British and French governments tried to establish in their colonies advisory councils which would gradually give the native population some part in the government. These measures had to be taken because British and French control over the former German colonies in Africa (Tanganyika, Togo, the Cameroons) was exercised in the form of a mandate, carried out under supervision of the League of Nations, with the purpose of educating the natives for self-government. Naturally, the concessions made to the natives in the former German colonies had to be extended to other areas as well. But in these parts self-government or even independence was a very distant goal.

In North Africa and the Near East the movement against European imperialism had much deeper roots. Since the Egyptian Jamal-ud-Din al-Afghani (1838–1897) had raised national and liberal claims for the Moslems in the nineteenth century, nationalist movements had taken hold in North Africa and the Near East. Even before the First World War the Arabs had begun to react against Ottoman rule. When the Turks entered the First World War this Arab nationalism received support from the British and the French, and with the encouragement of agents like T. E. Lawrence (1888–1935), the famous Lawrence of Arabia, hopes were high for the establishment of a larger Arab kingdom reaching from Arabia to Damascus and Baghdad. But these hopes were crushed in 1920—the year which the Arabs called *âm an-nakba* ("the year of the catastrophe"). The French drove the Arabs out of Damascus and took control in Lebanon and Syria, which were assigned to them as mandates. Anti-Jewish riots were crushed in Palestine which the British government in the so-called Balfour Declaration (1917) had promised as a national home for the Jewish people and which the British administered as a mandate. The British tried to reconcile the Arabs by creating a number of Arab states—Transjordania, Iraq, and Hejaz—but Arab hostility to European imperialism remained alive, and the British and French could maintain their control in this area only by playing upon religious and racial antagonisms, like those of the Christian Arabs toward the Mohammedans and the Druzes toward the Moslems, or by using force. Nationalism also reached the westernmost of the Arab settlements. Starting in the 1920's the "young Tunisians," as the Tunisian nationalists called themselves, exerted increasing pressure, and in the 1930's a nationalist movement became active in Morocco as well. Nevertheless, only slowly and gradually, during the 1920's and 1930's, did these anti-imperialist movements become a serious threat to the control of this part of Africa by Great Britain and France; there was only one area—Egypt—where Arab nationalism became politically significant immediately after the war.

Anti-British feeling in Egypt had intensified during the war when the British entirely took over Egyptian rule and interfered in Egyptian life, requisitioning cattle and foodstuffs and forcing Egyptians to work on railroads and other installations needed for the campaign in the Near East. The resentment created by these harsh measures promoted the emergence of the Wafd, a well-organized movement whose goal was complete Egyptian independence. Disorders were frequent from March, 1919, when Britain refused the demands of the Wafd, until 1922, and under the impact of these revolts the British were forced in 1921 to release the organizer and leader of the Wafd, Saad Zaghlul Pasha (*c.* 1860–1927), whom they had exiled to Malta. After his triumphal return a certain stabilization was finally achieved. The British recognized Egyptian sovereignty but retained the right to intervene in Egyptian affairs. They kept the Sudan under their control and assumed responsibility for the defense of Egypt and the protection of foreigners living there. Even after this compromise the situation remained precarious. Zaghlul continued to press for the abolition of all the special rights which the British had preserved, and the Wafd was regularly victorious in elections. The British, however, had the support of the Egyptian king, who disliked the democratic tendencies of the Wafd. Although the British were forced to make further concessions, their retreat was slow. Nevertheless, throughout the interwar years Egypt remained a serious political concern for Britain, and the maintenance of a position there absorbed part of Britain's military strength.

India

While Arab nationalism was gaining ground only slowly, a most serious challenge to the rule of the white man arose in India at just about the time the First World War came to an end. The events in India provided the most striking example of the mounting strength gained by the movements of non-European peoples for liberation from the rule of the white man. More than half a million Indians fought in the First World War, and both princes and commoners distinguished themselves by their bravery. Even before the war ended, the British government realized that this active participation in battle gave justification to the Indians' claims for participation in the government of their country. In August, 1917, Edwin Montagu, the secretary of state for India, announced in the House of Commons that the British government planned "not only the increasing association of Indians in every branch of the administration but also the granting of self-governing institutions with a view to the progressive realization of responsible government in India as an integral part of the British Empire."

The British believed that in effecting changes in the status of India they would be dealing chiefly with the British-educated upper classes and with

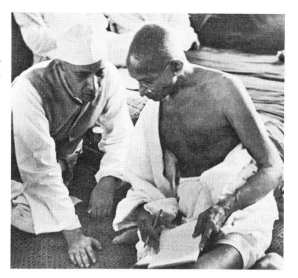

Nehru and Gandhi. *The leaders of the Indian independence movement.*

the rulers of the princely states. They felt sure that they could proceed slowly and cautiously. But the movement toward Indian independence assumed a quick tempo and became a dramatic conflict because of the inspiring personality of its leader, Mohandas Gandhi (1869–1948).

For twenty years Gandhi had lived in South Africa, where he had been the acknowledged leader of the large number of Indian workers who had gone there as indentured laborers. Gandhi had brought about remarkable improvements in their legal and economic position. The methods he had employed in achieving these gains had involved strikes, demonstrations, and hunger marches; but he had kept his followers from committing any violence, and when the police took action he and his followers had gone to prison willingly, without offering resistance. Gandhi's struggle for the Indians in South Africa had made him a well-known and highly respected figure, and when he returned to India in 1916, leadership in the nationalist movement devolved upon him almost automatically.

Gandhi infused two crucial new ideas into the movement for independence. First, its basis had to be broadened. It was not to be limited to the educated upper classes, but was to include members of all social classes, particularly the poor agricultural and industrial workers. Second, the method to be employed in obtaining independence was to be the one which he had successfully used in South Africa—nonviolence.

The broadening of the social basis required a revolutionary step: the breaking down of the barriers between caste members and "untouchables." When Gandhi began to live among "untouchables" and adopted an "untouchable" girl as his daughter, his people were deeply shocked. But gradually his moral courage aroused admiration and reinforced his political leadership. His insistence on nonviolence gave the movement a strong moral basis. Gandhi himself stated that his campaign constituted "an attempt to revolutionize politics and restore moral force to its organic station. We hope by our action to show that physical force is nothing compared to moral force and that moral force never fails." The instrument through which Gandhi hoped to obtain a withdrawal of the British without using violence was noncooperation. Again, this idea was powerful because it contained a strong moral element. As Gandhi said: "Non-cooperation with evil is as much a duty as is cooperation with good."

Noncooperation also implied practical measures which greatly weakened the British hold over India. Lawyers, among them future leaders such as Nehru (1889–1964) and Patel (1875–1950), left the courts; students left the universities; and like the *Narodniki* in Russia in the nineteenth century, professional men and intellectuals went into the villages, to educate the people and to preach noncooperation. For the success of noncooperation the rejection of all imported goods was essential, and the symbol of autarky became the wearing of homespun cloth. Gandhi admonished every Indian to spin daily. He attributed particular value to this work because while spinning one had time for religious contemplation.

Organization of the movement for Indian independence was in the hands of the All-India Home Rule League, of which Gandhi became president in 1920. Under him a democratic mass organization was created, with village units, city districts, and provincial sections, all culminating in the All-Indian Congress Committee. The fight for Indian independence became a struggle between Congress and the British. Congress adopted the policy of noncooperation, declaring that "it is the duty of every Indian soldier and civilian to sever his connections with the government and find some other means of livelihood." Noncooperation, however, developed into civil disobedience, and the latter was frequently accompanied by riots and violence. Gandhi's response to the outbreaks of violence was a fast, which he ended only when the disturbances had stopped. Indicative of the religious veneration in which the Indians held Gandhi is the fact that he could almost always control them by means of a fast; the people accepted Gandhi's demands because a prolonged fast might endanger his life.

The British were rather insecure in their handling of Gandhi. In 1922 they arrested him as the author of a number of seditious articles, and condemned him to six years in prison, but they released him after two years in order to quiet the resentment which his imprisonment had caused.

A crisis occurred in 1930. Because the British government had refused to give a definite promise of independence, a new campaign of civil disobedience was started, and Gandhi, after some years of withdrawal from politics, agreed to lead it. He decided to dramatize this campaign by an action breaking the government's salt monopoly, and accordingly he organized and led a march to the sea, covering two hundred miles in twenty-four days. At the shore he picked up and ate some salt which the waves had left, as a demonstration that he did not feel bound by the regulations concerning it. Again, Gandhi was arrested. But the British government realized that some agreement had to be reached, and released him. In appreciation of this gesture Gandhi expressed the wish to see the viceroy, Lord Irwin, later earl of Halifax (1881–1959). In the course of this famous visit, the viceroy offered Gandhi a cup of tea and Gandhi, taking a paper bag out of his shawl, answered: "Thank you. I will put some salt into my tea to remind us of the famous Boston Tea Party." Gandhi's meeting with Lord Irwin resulted in the cessation of civil disobedience, the release of all political prisoners, the abandonment of the British salt monopoly, and the agreement of the Congress party to participate in a round-table conference in London. Gandhi himself went to London as a Congress representative. In London the immense difficulties which the internal situation of India put in the way of independence became strikingly apparent. The conference produced a dramatic split between Hindus and Moslems; the Moslems, a minority in India, demanded separate electorates, an arrangement which would prevent them from being outvoted; the Hindus insisted on a single electorate. The British government's decision for separate electorates inflamed the struggle anew, and it moved in a quickened tempo through the 1930's: campaigns of civil disobedience, arrests, fasts by Gandhi, British concessions, followed one upon the other. The solution—independence accompanied by the division of India into two states, one largely Hindu, the other largely Moslem, within the British Commonwealth of Nations—was achieved only after the Second World War.

THE CHANGE IN THE FAR EAST

As a consequence of the First World War, two non-European powers—the United States and Japan—became equal in strength and importance to the European great powers; without their participation the affairs of the globe could no longer be decided. Indeed, developments in the Far East showed the extent to which in this particular area the United States and Japan now not only equaled the European great powers but even overshadowed them.

The involvement of the European nations and the United States in the European theater of war had given Japan opportunities of which it knew how to make full use. Japan was particularly anxious to strengthen its hold over China. China was forced to recognize Japan as the heir of Germany's rights in China and to give Japan extended economic privileges in Manchuria. Moreover, having taken over Germany's island possessions in the Pacific, Japan intended to keep them.

But Japanese policy ran counter to the interests of the United States. The occupied islands, particularly Yap, were so situated that control of them implied control of communications in the Pacific, and the Japanese hold over China nullified the American open-door policy. A naval armament race seemed unavoidable. But in the difficult economic circumstances after the First World War this aggravation of financial burdens seemed so senseless that the great naval powers were willing to make a serious attempt to settle their differences by negotiations. Accordingly, on December 12, 1921, they met in Washington, D.C. to discuss naval armament and the situation in the Pacific. In the opening speech, the American secretary of state, Charles Evans Hughes, made a number of concrete proposals for the limitation of naval armaments. On February 4, 1922, the conference ended with a settlement which in essence embodied these proposals in a series of complicated arrangements. One was the establishment of a definite ratio controlling the tonnage of the battleships of the great naval powers. Great Britain abandoned its claim to having the strongest navy in the world, and agreed to an American navy equal to its own. Britain and the United States were each allowed 525,000 tons of capital ships, Japan 350,000 tons, and France and Italy 175,000 tons each. Moreover, during the next ten years no new capital ships, i.e., ships of 10,000 or more tons, were to be built. This naval agreement was supplemented by the Nine Power Treaty, signed by the United States, Great Britain, France, Italy, Japan, Belgium, the Netherlands, Portugal, and China, guaranteeing the integrity and sovereignty of China and promising maintenance of the open door. In consequence of this treaty, Japan returned the former German colony of Kiaochow to China. Finally, in another treaty—the Four Power Treaty—the United States, Great Britain, France, and Japan acknowledged one another's insular possessions in the Pacific and agreed to mutual consultation if their possessions were threatened. The Four Power Treaty is usually regarded as the most important diplomatic achievement of the Washington conference. At the time of the conference the old alliance between Japan and Great Britain was due for renewal. The United States looked with distrust upon this special bond between Great Britain and Japan, and the British were reluctant to retain a commitment which might place them in opposition to the United States. The Four Power Treaty was to replace the British-Japanese alliance and initiate an era of cooperation among all the powers interested in the Far East, preventing Japan from taking isolated action.

Taken together, these agreements reveal a remarkable shift of power in the Pacific. In that area Great Britain clearly had become secondary to the United States. It had bowed to American wishes in abandoning its old alliance with Japan, and because it could keep only a part of its navy in the Far East, the arrangements about naval strength made any unilateral involvement of Britain in a Far Eastern war an impossibility. Britain's efforts now had to be directed toward gaining cooperation, and if necessary common action, among all the powers interested in the Far East. But it is very doubtful whether the policy worked out at the Washington conference was suited to this goal and whether the consequences of the replacement of a British-Japanese alliance by the Four Power Treaty were beneficial.

The Japanese withdrew from China and for a number of years adhered scrupulously to the Washington agreements. But feeling became strong in Japan that the nation had gained little from its participation in the First World War, and the moderate Japanese statesmen anxious to cooperate with Great Britain, the European powers, and the United States, lost influence, while a militaristic group bent on imperialist expansion and opposed to the parliamentary regime gained in appeal.

These developments were furthered by events in China itself. The Revolution of 1911, brought about by the Chinese resentment against foreigners and indignation about the impotence of the imperial regime, was followed by a confused period of civil war, with the various provincial governors, the so-called warlords, fighting one another. The First World War gave events a new turn. For China the crucial development was the seizure of power in Russia by the Bolsheviks, which meant that instead of being faced by a united front of powerful foreign states, China now had a defender among them. While the other nations were slow to give up the concession made to them by the Chinese imperial government, the Bolsheviks gained popularity by abandoning these privileges without hesitation. Moreover, the intellectual leader of the Chinese revolution, Sun Yat-sen (1866–1925), regarded many of the revolutionary changes which had been made in Russia, particularly in the distribution of land, as a pattern for China. Thus, Communists were admitted to the Kuomintang, the party which had led the overthrow of the imperial regime; the assistance of Russian advisers was accepted in the reorganization of the party and the reform of the army. With Russian help the process of political disintegration was halted and a central government was established in Nanking. But conflict broke out between the Communists and the more conservative members of the Kuomintang under Chiang Kai-shek (born 1886), and the Communists were driven out of the party and the government, although—under the leadership of Mao Tse-tung (born 1893) and Chu Teh (born 1886)—they remained in control in various areas. By 1928 the Nanking government was powerful enough to begin a series of political and economic reforms. The western powers, anxious to maintain trade with China, and to avoid this time the mistake of throwing the Chinese into the arms of the Bolsheviks, gave up their special privileges and evacuated the harbors which they had occupied in their imperialist days. But in contrast to the western powers, the Japanese did not consider a consolidation of the Chinese government as being in their interest. They *Japanese* feared that a politically strengthened China pursuing a nationalistic economic policy might exclude Japanese industrial goods from the Chinese market and make the Japanese economic situation critical. Thus, tension between China and Japan increased until, after a number of clashes along the Korean-Chinese border, there occurred in September, 1931, the so-called Mukden Incident—a railway explosion for which the Japanese made the Chinese responsible; this led to the Japanese invasion of Manchuria and to the beginning of a war which ended only with the Second World War. The European powers were unable to prevent the outbreak of the conflict or—even with the help of the League of Nations—to compose it. The helplessness which the European powers showed in this Far Eastern crisis is the most striking indication of the reduction in European influence and power.

RUSSIA UNDER THE BOLSHEVIKS

The interwar years were characterized not only by the rising antagonism of the colonial peoples toward European rule and by the emancipation of non-European powers from the European hegemony but by changes in Europe itself which had the effect of making it smaller. Probably most decisive in the weakening of European rule, and in the entire international situation in the postwar world, was the fact that Russia could no longer be counted as a member of the concert of Europe, that, on the contrary, it gave assistance to those who, like China, revolted against the European hegemony.

Since the Bolshevik take-over in 1917, Russia had been separated ideologically from the rest of Europe. But the peace settlements removed it to the periphery of the European scene geographically as well.

First, in the Treaty of Brest-Litovsk the Germans separated so much territory from Russia in the north—the Baltic provinces and Finland—and in the south—the Ukraine—that it became almost an inland state, isolated from the rest of Europe. After the German defeat, the arrangements of the Treaty of Brest-Litovsk were changed, but the Paris Peace Conference, to which Russia was not invited, confirmed the formation of a number of independent states in those areas of Europe which before 1914 had formed part of the Russian empire. In the bitter fighting of the so-called Great Civil War from 1918 to 1920 the Russians succeeded in reestablishing their authority over the Ukraine, the Caucasus, Siberia, and eastern Russia. And finally, in a war against Poland they regained some territory which had been assigned to Poland. Nevertheless, the Baltic states, Finland, Poland—all formerly parts of the Russian empire—remained independent, and Russia was thrown back to the edge of the European continent.

The victorious western powers sought to keep Russia as weak as possible because of the antidemocratic, anticapitalist character of the Bolshevik regime. With Lenin and his group, the most revolutionary and radical wing of the Russian prewar Social Democratic party came to power in Russia. During the war, which he had spent in exile in Switzerland, Lenin had not

0   500 miles

NORWAY

SWEDEN

FINLAND

Murmansk

White Sea

Archangel

WHITE RUSSIAN ADVANCE 1919

Gulf of Finland   Petrograd

ESTONIA

LATVIA

B A L T I C   S E A

LITHUANIA

U N I O N   O F   S O V I E T

S O C I A L I S T   R E P U B L I C S

(1922)

Moscow

GERMANY

(TO POLAND, 1921)

Minsk

POLAND

Brest-Litovsk

Volga R.

1919 WHITE RUSSIAN ADVANCES

1918

Kiev

AUSTRIA-HUNGARY

BESSARABIA

Kharkov

UKRAINE (TO SOVIETS, 1920)

Tzaritsyn (Stalingrad)

Dnieper R.

(TO RUMANIA, 1918)

Sea of Azov

1919 WHITE RUSSIAN ADVANCES

1918

CRIMEA

Sevastopol

(TO SOVIETS, 1920)

C A S P I A N   S E A

RUMANIA

SERBIA

BULGARIA

B L A C K   S E A

GREECE

Constantinople

TURKEY (OTTOMAN EMPIRE)

(TO TURKEY, 1918)

PERSIA

MOVEMENTS OF COUNTERREVOLUTIONARY FORCES

GER.

1919

Moscow

1918

RUSSIA

Ural Mts.

1919

S I B E R I A

1918

1919

Omsk

1919

1918

1918

1918

Irkutsk

OUTER MONGOLIA

Vladivostok

JAPAN

PERSIA

CHINA

RUSSIA IN REVOLUTION 1917-1922

—··—··— 1914 boundaries

‑ ‑ ‑ ‑ ‑ ‑ 1921 boundaries

———— Brest Litovsk Treaty Line, 1918

 Territory lost by Russia in 1918

▲ ▲ ▲ ▲ 1918 ⎫ Limits of counterrevolu-
△ △ △ △ 1919 ⎬ tionary movements

only scorned those socialists who backed the war effort of their countries, but had also opposed the policy of those small socialist splinter groups which refused to support the war and urged a quick restoration of peace. To Lenin the only correct Marxist approach was to use the war to bring about revolution. At the time of the tsar's abdication, Lenin was fretting impatiently in his Swiss isolation. Then by taking advantage of the offer of the German military to transport him and his close associates through Germany, he reached Russia by way of Sweden. On April 16 Lenin, with a small group of followers—Grigori Zinoviev, Karl Radek, Anatoli Lunacharski—arrived in Petrograd, at the Finland Railroad Station. Greeted by a leader of the Mensheviks who in his speech demanded "a closing of the ranks of democracy" in defense of revolution, Lenin turned away from the official welcoming party and said to the crowds: "Any day, if not today or tomorrow, the crash of the whole of European imperialism may come. The Russian Revolution made by you has begun it and opened a new epoch. Hail the world-wide socialist revolution." Thus Lenin indicated that he regarded what had happened in Russia so far as a bourgeois revolution, which ought to be followed immediately by another revolution, giving power to the workers and peasants. Within six months the Bolsheviks would have achieved this aim.

Throughout the summer they gained steadily in appeal among the war-tired masses because they emphasized that Russia should conclude peace, while the government insisted on continuing the war. In addition, the Bolsheviks supported immediate seizure of land by the peasants, while the other political groups tended to postpone the issue of agrarian reform. Moreover, the government had failed to establish effective authority. In September, Kornilov, a popular war hero who had been appointed commander in chief, attempted a military coup to overthrow the government controlled by Mensheviks and Social Revolutionaries under Prime Minister Alexander Kerenski. The help of the Bolsheviks was needed to defeat this counterrevolutionary attempt. And as defenders of the revolution, the Bolsheviks now gained a majority in the workers' councils of Petrograd and Moscow. Rightly, Lenin thought that the time was ripe for a Bolshevik seizure of power. Trotsky played a leading part in the preparation of this coup. All the government buildings were quickly occupied, and the members of the previous government were arrested. In Petrograd and Moscow the central administrative apparatus of Russia, insofar as it existed and functioned, fell into the hands of the Bolsheviks; at the head of the government they placed a Council of People's Commissars, with Lenin as chairman.

For the next seven years, until his death in 1924, Lenin dominated Russian politics and exerted a crucial influence over developments in the rest of the world as well. The reasons for Lenin's success in achieving and

The Russian Revolution. *Street fighting in Petrograd.*

exercising power are complex. Before he came to office his study of Marxist theory had provided him with what he considered an infallible guide to the course to be followed, and his work as a party organizer had taught him to use men as instruments for definite purposes. Hence, after his return to Russia he was able to pursue the conquest of power, the secure establishment of his regime, and the social and political transformation of Russian life with ruthless single-mindedness and with a complete disregard for human life and legal restrictions. Furthermore, Lenin could count on a large number of followers who had studied his writings and accepted his leadership because they recognized his intellectual superiority. He demanded complete obedience only after a line of policy had been established; before any decision was made, he was willing to hear the views of his close followers and to discuss with them the various possibilities. Unlike Stalin, Lenin did not harbor resentment against those who gave advice contrary to the line finally adopted. However, after the decision had been made, opposition was no longer tolerated.

His hold over the masses of the workers is more difficult to understand than his eminent position among Bolshevik leaders. He was no great orator and his speeches, when read, seem monotonous. However, he never spoke down to the masses; he revealed to them with brutal frankness his views about the demands of the hour, explaining rather nakedly, but with strict logic, how he had arrived at his proposals; the masses had reason to believe

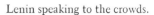
Lenin speaking to the crowds.

that he took them into his confidence and that they could rely on him. They had no doubt of his selflessness; even as ruler of Russia he continued to live modestly, claiming no exceptions or privileges. Thus, the most powerful man of Russia wrote humbly to the director of the library and asked for permission to keep a book overnight, against the rules of the library, because he had no other time for reading. Lenin inherited something of the father image which the tsars had possessed. But a principal reason for his rise to power was that he recognized, first in contrast to the revolutionary governments preceding the Bolsheviks, and later in contrast to some of his own adherents, that what the masses wanted above anything else was peace.

This resolution to end the war brought the Bolshevik regime immediately into conflict with Russia's former allies. They were anxious to prevent the supplies and ammunition which they had been sending to Russia from falling into the hands of the Germans. Thus, British and French troops were sent to such harbors as Arkhangelsk and Vladivostok. Inevitably, in the areas occupied by the Allies and therefore outside Bolshevik control, the enemies of the Bolsheviks began to organize. From the north and from the east, later also from the Baltic states and from the Ukraine, tsarist generals advanced, halfheartedly supported by the western powers. For two years, from 1918 to 1920, civil war raged. The Bolsheviks had the advantage of controlling the interior lines, which permitted them to move their troops rapidly from one threatened frontier to another. On the Bolshevik side the military hero of this civil war was Trotsky, the commissar of war. He succeeded in organizing an efficient and disciplined Red Army. He personally appeared at the most threatened points of the front, living in a railroad car which moved from one endangered sector to the other. Moreover, the leaders of the White Russians, as the opponents of the Bolsheviks were called, were disunited. Some, like Admiral Kolchak who advanced through Siberia into eastern Russia, wanted to restore the tsarist regime. Others realized the necessity for a more liberal and democratic program. Against the White Russians with their contradictory aims, the Bolsheviks were able to keep the support of large parts of the population. The peasants feared that if reaction were victorious they would have to return the land which they had seized to its former owners. The assistance which the White Russians received from Great Britain and France, though minor and insufficient, made the Bolsheviks appear to be defenders of Russian national interest against foreign intervention. Officials of previous governments placed themselves at the service of the Bolsheviks and, strictly supervised by political commissars, were used by them as "technical experts." Bolshevik attempts—with the help of native Communist parties—to reconquer Finland, the Baltic states, and Poland failed. But in the rest of the former tsarist territories, the Bolsheviks gained control.

When the civil war ended, no reintegration of Russia into the European state system occurred. The internal policy which the Bolsheviks had pursued since coming to power had opened a wide, almost unbridgeable gap between Russia and the western world.

The Bolsheviks had started their rule with a number of startling and, to the rest of the world, shocking measures and decrees. They retained civil servants who accepted the new government, but they also gave positions in the bureaucracy to reliable party members without demanding examinations or special knowledge. Likewise, courts were staffed by judges who lacked legal training. Thus the obstacles which a conservative bureaucracy usually places in the path of a revolutionary regime were immediately removed—to the horror of the rest of Europe, which regarded civil servants as members of an exclusive higher order. But the measures which of course caused the greatest abhorrence outside of Russia lay in the economic field. The Bolsheviks confiscated all private bank accounts and nationalized all banks. They repudiated the entire national debt. Factories were handed over to the workers; all land was declared national property; private trade was abolished, and retail shops were closed. To be sure, the economic policy announced in these early decrees was soon modified. Larger estates were divided up, but the peasants remained in possession of their land, although they were forced

A Russian poster. *The Bolshevik knight slaying the capitalist dragon.*

to give certain quotas of their production to the government for distribution among other sectors of the population. The chaos which resulted when the workers directed the factories was soon replaced by planning. In 1921, after the civil war had ended, there was even an openly acknowledged change from the early Communism to a New Economic Policy (NEP), which permitted a remarkable amount of freedom of trade within the country. However, heavy industry, transportation, and the credit system remained nationalized, and foreign trade remained a government monopoly. Russia had abandoned the principles of capitalist economy, and the government's grip over economic life was firm enough to permit an enforcement of stricter controls at any time. Moreover, the original measures confiscating bank accounts, socializing factories, and nationalizing land had completely impoverished the middle classes and the nobility. The appropriation of industrial enterprises and the repudiation of state loans also hit foreigners—individuals, banks, governments—who had investments in Russia. And in all further negotiations with the Bolshevik leaders the claims of these foreign investors for compensation and for the repayment of debts contracted by tsarist Russia formed an insurmountable obstacle. In particular the French, because of the large loans which they had given to the tsarist government, for a long time remained adamant in refusing contact with the Bolshevik regime until they had received compensation for their losses.

But these conflicts over financial matters were only one aspect of the differences between Bolshevik Russia and the rest of the world. The Bolsheviks rejected all the liberal and democratic values for which the western powers had claimed to be fighting. Like the tsars, the Bolsheviks refused to permit freedom of the press and freedom of expression. The Russian leaders pursued a sharply antireligious policy, and church property was confiscated. Furthermore, attempts to establish a democratic basis for the regime were soon abandoned. After their seizure of power the Bolshevik leaders had been proclaimed the legitimate Russian government by a Congress of Soldiers' and Workers' Councils (Soviets). But the previous government had ordered elections to a constituent assembly which would create a final constitution, and before seizing power the Bolsheviks had accused the government of delaying these elections; they therefore felt constrained to let them take place. But the voting, on November 25, 1917, left the Bolsheviks still a minority. When the constituent assembly opened on January 18, 1918, they declared that, because the voter lists had been made out before the Bolshevik revolution, the constituent assembly "represented the old order." With the help of troops the assembly was dissolved. The soviets remained the popular basis of the regime. Within the soviets the Bolsheviks, who represented the industrial proletariat, shared power with the left-wing Social Revolutionaries, who represented the peasants.

The dissolution of the constituent assembly sharpened internal tensions. The Bolsheviks saw themselves as surrounded by enemies within the nation. In December, 1917, they had established the All-Russian Extraordinary Commission (Cheka) for the purpose of "combating counterrevolution and sabotage." With the organization of the Cheka, terror became a consciously used, openly recognized instrument of government. In the summer of 1918 the Bolshevik leaders broke with their only partner in government, the Social Revolutionaries. As representatives of the peasant population the Social Revolutionaries had opposed the acceptance of the Treaty of Brest-Litovsk, which deprived Russia of the Ukraine, one of its most important agricultural areas. In an effort to nullify this treaty and to effect a break with Germany, Social Revolutionaries on July 6, 1918, assassinated Count Wilhelm von Mirbach, the German ambassador in Moscow. There remain puzzling questions about this event. It is difficult to understand how the murderers could get easy access to Count Mirbach, and it has been suggested that the Bolsheviks themselves, who had received information about the plans of the Social Revolutionaries, made this possible. Lenin and the Bolsheviks were eager to effect a break with the Social Revolutionaries; the murder of the German ambassador would give justification for such a break. At the same time, the Bolsheviks would have gotten rid of an ambassador whom they knew had reported home that their regime was weak and near collapse. Even if not true, such rumors were indicative of the

The Communist International. *Lenin presiding at its first meeting in 1919.*

confused and desperate situation in Moscow at this time. The Bolsheviks succeeded, however, in defeating the attempt of the Social Revolutionaries to overthrow the government, to which the assassination of Mirbach had given the signal. But the struggle went on. Like the revolutionaries of tsarist times, the Social Revolutionaries tried to shake the regime through a series of assassinations. On August 30, 1918, Lenin himself was severely wounded. The Bolshevik answer was increased terror, directed by the Cheka. Exact figures about the number of victims of this Red Terror are lacking. From Bolshevik sources we know that at the beginning of September in Petrograd 512 "counterrevolutionaries and White guards" were shot in one day. Many were killed not for the commission of a specific crime, but because as members of the propertied classes they were regarded as enemies of the state. The indignation of the non-Russian world was great; representatives of foreign powers in Petrograd and Moscow protested, accusing the Bolsheviks of "barbarous oppression" and "unwarranted slaughter" which aroused "the indignation of the civilized world."

In the fall of 1918, when the weapon of terror was unleashed with utter ruthlessness, the Bolshevik position was precarious. The conflict with the Social Revolutionaries coincided with the beginning of the civil war—the attacks of the tsarist generals, supported by the western powers, from the north and east. But although circumstances were almost desperate, the Bolshevik leaders believed that if they could hold on somewhat longer the entire situation might be reversed. For the European war was drawing to a close. The German government was tottering, dissatisfaction was widespread in other countries, and there was some reason to assume that the end of the war would be accompanied by revolution in several European states. At this time the Russian leaders could not imagine that Russia could become a socialist country while the rest of the world remained capitalist. As Lenin had proclaimed at the Finland Station, they supposed the Bolshevik revolution in Russia to be the first step of a revolutionary process which would extend over the whole globe. They believed that their own position depended quite as much on the spread of the revolution into other countries as on their staying in power in Russia. Thus, while involved in a deadly struggle within Russia, they established a Communist International, intended to stimulate revolution elsewhere. The First Congress of the Communist International, or Comintern, took place in Moscow in March, 1919; it was a rather tame affair, for the only delegates from abroad were a few leaders of extremist groups that had split off from the socialist parties. More important was the Second Congress of the Communist International, which met in Moscow in August, 1920. Including representatives of the extreme left from a large number of countries, this congress gave a more definite form to the organization of the Communist International.

The establishment of the Communist International had far-reaching consequences. One of these was a definite split within the various Marxist-inspired workers' movements. Even before the First World War most of the socialist parties in Europe had included a left and a right—a revolutionary and a revisionist wing—but the unity of the socialist movement had been maintained. From 1919 on, there were two different Marxist parties: Socialists and Communists. Moreover, the structure of the Communist International was essentially different from that of the Second Socialist International. In the latter, the socialist parties of the various nations remained sovereign; the organization which included them all—the Second International—gave advice only. In the Communist International, supreme authority was held by the World Congress of the Communist Parties which met every year, or more precisely, by an executive committee which this congress elected. The decisions of this congress or its executive committee were binding upon all Communist parties; they had to follow the "line" laid down by the Communist International. The influence of the Russian Bolsheviks was predominant because the headquarters of the executive committee were in Moscow and its permanent secretary, Zinoviev, was a Bolshevik leader. One of the basic principles of the Communist International was that all Communist parties must regard the maintenance, defense, and strengthening of the Bolshevik regime in Russia as their paramount aim. The goal of the Communist International was world revolution, and the Communist parties in the various countries were to build up support for the revolutionary movement by forming special youth organizations, Communist trade unions, and the like, all subject to the same discipline as the Communist parties themselves. Whether these organizations would work openly and freely or secretly and illegally, or whether open and clandestine organizations would work side by side, was to be determined by the situation in each country.

At the time of its formation the Communist International had as its chief goal the overthrow of the governments in the great capitalist states of western Europe. From the beginning, however, the Communist leaders were aware that the European nations drew much of their strength from the control which they exerted over the non-European parts of the world. Therefore, the undermining of European rule over colonial areas was from the outset an openly declared aim of the Communist International. Its first manifesto, issued on April 6, 1919, already included the statement that "the colonial question in its fullest extent has been placed on the agenda.... Colonial slaves of Africa and Asia! The hour of proletariat dictatorship in Europe will also be the hour of your own liberation." This point was emphasized and elaborated in 1920, when special "theses on the national and colonial question" were presented. It was proclaimed that "our policy must be to bring into being a close alliance of all national and colonial liberation movements with Soviet Russia.... The task of the Communist International is to liberate the working people of the entire world. In its ranks the white, the yellow and the black-skinned peoples—the working people of the entire world—are fraternally united."

In the West, the existence of the Communist International was interpreted as the sign of a Communist effort to continue the war against the West even after peace had been restored along the borders. The western states were hesitant to recognize the Bolsheviks as constituting the legitimate government of Russia. On the other hand, the Russians considered the reluctance of the western nations to enter into normal diplomatic relations with Russia to be a sign of their resolution to resume military intervention at the first favorable opportunity. Russia and the rest of Europe remained in opposite camps, and Russia was the ally of all those movements which were directed against European control of the globe.

THE PARIS PEACE CONFERENCE

The new forces which the First World War had released in all parts of the world contributed to the weakening and ultimately the destruction of the peace settlement which was made after the war. At a distance of fifty years the work and the procedures of the Paris Peace Conference appear rather futile and anachronistic. Many aspects of the peace settlement originated in attitudes which now seem inappropriate or obsolete. But the conference did represent a serious effort to come to grips with the needs of modern industrial society. The Europe which existed before the First World War could not be restored; and the question that hangs over the entire interwar period is whether the transition into a new world could have been achieved without the catastrophe of a Second World War.

The problem of whether a traditional or a progressive outlook would determine the nature of the peace settlement was reflected in the great differences among the leaders who assembled in Paris at the end of 1918.

Arthur Balfour, the British foreign secretary, had attended the Berlin Conference of 1878, and regarded the proceedings in Paris with the detachment of an old man; as a diplomat of the old school he was chiefly concerned with the reestablishment of a balance of power. But Balfour's attitude was an exception. The prevailing mood at the Paris Peace Conference was that of nineteenth-century nationalism. This emotion burned, for example, in the French prime minister, Clemenceau, for whom the French defeat in 1870–1871 was still a personal, unforgotten experience, so that his main concern now was to make a resumption of the Franco-German duel impossible. The principal representatives of nationalism, however, were the leaders and delegates of those nations which as a result of the war had emerged from the rule of—or dependence upon—other powers, and now strove to establish independent national states. Nikola Pasic (c. 1845–1926), the Serbian Bismarck, and Eleutherios Venizelos (1864–1936), the popular and influential Greek statesman, worked for the fulfillment of Greek and Serbian national aims; they wanted to create a greater Serbia and a greater Greece. The Czech and Polish representatives, Eduard Beneš (1884–1948) and Ignace Paderewski (1860–1941), based the demands for their new states on the new principle that each nationality had the right to self-determination. But they could be obdurate and ruthless when the interests of their nations clashed with those of others.

At the same time, advocates of the "new diplomacy"—those who aimed at overcoming old conflicts and tensions by building a supranational organization and strengthening international law—were also strongly represented. They came chiefly from non-European countries, as did General Jan Christiaan Smuts (1870–1950), the influential South African statesman. The leader of these idealists was, of course, Woodrow Wilson. For the first time an American president went to Europe while in office. Wilson was enthusiastically and tumultuously received in Paris, in London, and in Rome. He was welcomed as the savior who would bring about a new and better age. And though many of the leaders of the European states may have been skeptical, Wilson had numerous adherents among the younger members of their delegations. However, the variety of views and approaches represented at the Paris Peace Conference meant that the settlement which would result could not be a full realization of Wilsonian ideals, but a compromise in which the principles of a new diplomacy would be watered down by considerations of power politics and nationalist passions.

Decisive in weakening the influence of Wilsonian idealism and reinforcing the weight of political realism was the absence of Russia. A new global system could hardly be established without the inclusion of a country which covered so immense an area of the globe. The existence of Communist Russia also had a very important indirect effect on the shape which the peace settlement took. Fear of Bolshevism and of the spread of Communism into central and western Europe weakened the forces supporting Wilson's ideas of a magnanimous peace and an international peace organization. In all countries the workers now were split into two groups: the Communists, who actively sought world revolution; and the socialists, generally much more numerous, who violently opposed the extremists on their left and were willing to operate within a democratic framework. Moreover, the appeal of the left-wing bourgeois parties in England, France, and Italy diminished because they seemed to lack the hardheadedness needed to suppress subversive movements. In reaction to the fear aroused by the ruthless political proceedings and the confiscatory economic measures of the Bolsheviks, a trend toward conservatism developed in Great Britain, France, and the United States, and the statesmen in Paris were aware that the stability of their governments depended on their paying heed to nationalistic and counterrevolutionary tendencies at home. Thus, domestic policy exerted a powerful impact on the making of the peace.

Adherents of a Wilsonian peace were aware of the difficulties created by the absence of Russia, and several attempts were made—for instance, through a mission of the American diplomat William Bullitt—to get in contact with the leaders of Russia. But these efforts were not followed up energetically, for every attempt to come to an understanding with Russia immediately aroused the opposition of the influential groups in France and Great Britain which advocated intervention to overthrow the Bolshevik regime. Furthermore, just at the time of critical negotiations at the Paris Peace Conference, the fear of world revolution did appear to have some reality behind it. Communist revolts broke out in various parts of eastern and central Europe. From March to August, 1919, the Communists, under Béla Kun, ruled in Hungary. Throughout April, 1919, a Soviet republic existed in Bavaria. It was believed in Paris that only a decided anti-Bolshevik stand could save large parts of Europe from falling to the Communists. Hence the Paris Peace Conference adopted the policy of constructing a stout dam against the Bolsheviks in eastern Europe, a *cordon sanitaire* which would separate Bolshevik Russia from the democratic states. Finland had acquired independence by its own efforts. But the various Baltic nations—Estonia, Latvia, Lithuania—needed and received support in their resistance to Russian attempts at reconquest. Because it was believed that Poland and Rumania could become firm bulwarks against Communism, these states were deliberately strengthened by the makers of the peace settlement, even in violation of the principle of national self-determination. Rumania received what had been Russian Bessarabia; Poland tried to push its eastern frontiers as far as possible into Russia and claimed the entire Ukraine. Although the Russo-Polish War of 1920 stemmed the Polish advance, western diplomatic help and economic aid gave the Poles a border extending far into Russian territory.

These arrangements and considerations also influenced the main business of the Paris Peace Conference: to conclude treaties with the Central Powers—Turkey, Bulgaria, Austria-Hungary, and Germany. These settlements bear elegant-sounding and historic names because they were signed in various palaces in the suburbs of Paris. The short-lived Treaty of Sèvres (1920) terminated the war with Turkey. The Treaty of Neuilly (1919) established peace with Bulgaria. The situation resulting from the disintegration of the Habsburg empire was resolved by the Treaty of St.-Germain (1919) with Austria and the Treaty of Trianon (1920) with Hungary. The most important of the peace settlements was the Treaty of Versailles (1919), ending the war with Germany.

The Treaty of Sèvres and Developments in Turkey

The Treaty of Sèvres was the last treaty arranged at the Paris Peace Conference, being signed only on April 20, 1920. It is treated here first, however, for the reason that, strictly speaking, it dealt not with Europe, but with a non-European part of the world. Hence this treaty—or, to be exact, the failure of this treaty—was closely connected with the rise of antiimperialism and anticolonialism in the Near East and with Russia's efforts to emancipate the nonwhite races from the tutelage of the great capitalist powers of the West. In the settlement of the peace with Turkey the last chapter of one story, that of the First World War, is immediately joined with the first chapter of a new story, that of the anti-European revolt.

When the victors, absorbed in the disposition of the European situation, finally came around to deciding the fate of the Ottoman Empire, they dealt with it as if it were a colony, although actually they were facing a nation which was conscious of its great past and in addition was now inspired by the new anti-European nationalism. During the war the western powers had made a number of agreements concerning the partitioning of the Ottoman Empire. There had been a general understanding that the Arab portions would be separated from Turkey, but the arrangements made by the Allies during the war also envisaged a partition of the Turkish heartland of Asia Minor. Even after the collapse of tsarism had made the details of this agreement obsolete, the notion of a partition was maintained. In April, 1919, the Italians appeared in Adalia, in southern Asia Minor, and a month later the Greeks landed in Smyrna. The Greek occupation bore, to quote from an official report of an investigating committee, "more resemblance to a conquest and a crusade than to any civilizing mission." An Allied force controlled Constantinople and its surrounding areas.

In the Treaty of Sèvres, Smyrna and Thrace were given to Greece, large areas in Asia Minor were assigned to Italy and France as their spheres of interest, and Constantinople was internationalized. The sultan, residing in occupied Constantinople, signed the treaty under protest. But the foreign advances into Asia Minor encountered a vehement Turkish reaction, and Turkish nationalism found a leader in a hero of the First World War, Mustafa Kemal Pasha (1881–1938), who began to organize resistance in the interior of the country. Kemal Pasha set up a countergovernment in Angora (now Ankara) and refused to recognize the treaty. To enforce the treaty, the Allies permitted the Greeks to advance from Smyrna into the interior. The Turco-Greek war, lasting from 1920 to 1922, ended with the complete defeat of Greece. The Turkish success was chiefly due to the brilliant military and political leadership of Kemal. But Turkey was also aided by supplies from Bolshevik Russia, which was glad to help this revolt against the dominance of the western powers. Most important, instead of rallying to the support of Greece, the Allies were competing against one another. Italy resented the increase of Greek power in Asia Minor, and France wanted to limit the British influence in the Near East. Hence, Italy and France were willing to withdraw from Asia Minor when they received the promise of economic concessions by the Turks. Only the British, particularly the prime minister, Lloyd George, remained passionate supporters of the Greeks. But although Lloyd George was inclined toward active intervention to assist the Greeks and to hold Constantinople, the British people were too tired of war to accept this policy. Left alone, the Greeks were defeated, and in the summer of 1923 the Treaty of Lausanne, replacing the Treaty of Sèvres, was concluded. The Turks lost most of the Aegean Islands, some to Italy, others to Greece. The Straits remained demilitarized and open to ships of all nations, but the Turks regained the strip of European territory, including Adrianople, which they had possessed before the First World War. They were again complete rulers all of Asia Minor, including Constantinople.

Kemal became the creator of a modern state. The close association between the Turkish government and Islam was ended; indeed, the wearing of the fez was forbidden, and women were encouraged to abandon the veil. The Latin alphabet was introduced, school attendance became compulsory, and a policy of industrialization and of agricultural modernization was initiated. The Turkish republic became officially a parliamentary state based on popular elections, although for many years no opposition party existed and Kemal and his group of victorious officers ruled. Turkey proved that, despite European claims to the contrary, the nations of the Near East were able to develop quickly to the levels of political, economic, and social life which existed in the western world.

The Treaties of Neuilly, Trianon, and St.-Germain and the Interwar Developments in Southeastern and Eastern Europe

The immediate purpose of the treaties of Neuilly, Trianon, and St.-Germain was to conclude peace with Bulgaria, Hungary, and Austria. But these treaties involved the settlement of the entire area of eastern Europe, from the Aegean Sea in the south to the Baltic Sea in the north. The political, territorial, and economic questions with which the treaties had to deal were extremely complex. For one thing, the area was inhabited by a large number of different nationalities, with relations between some of them poisoned by the fact that before the First World War certain groups, such as the Magyars and the Germans, had dominated the others. Moreover, the reorganization of this area cut deeply into the existing economic structure. Austria-Hungary, which the treaties of Trianon and St.-Germain destroyed, had formed a natural economic unit that was now torn into parts. The various sovereign states among which the territory of the former Danube monarchy was divided needed financial resources, and the settlements therefore involved a distribution among them of the economic assets of the former Austria-Hungary.

The postwar settlements were to be made in accordance with the principles which Wilson had outlined in his Fourteen Points—national self-determination and democracy—and the victors regarded the treaties of Neuilly, Trianon, and St.-Germain as applying these principles. But in the course of time they did not pass the test: in fifteen years, with the exception of Czechoslovakia, not one of the states created or reorganized at the Paris Peace Conference remained a democracy. What were the reasons for this situation? What were the weaknesses in the peace settlement which allowed developments so different from those envisaged at the end of the war?

It is easy to understand that democracy was a weak plant in those countries which, having been defeated, had to cede territories and pay damages. Actually the territorial renunciations which the Treaty of Neuilly forced upon Bulgaria were not considerable. In addition to a few small border revisions in favor of Serbia, Bulgaria had to surrender to Greece an area along the Aegean Sea which she had conquered in the Balkan Wars and which had provided Bulgaria with an access to the Mediterranean. Bulgaria also had to pay reparations and to accept the limitation of her army to twenty thousand men. Although not crippling, these conditions were sufficiently hard to keep alive in the proud and ambitious Bulgarian nation a feeling of resentment against neighboring Rumania and Yugoslavia (the enlarged kingdom of Serbia). The officers of the diminished Bulgarian army were particularly eager for revenge. They kept a protecting hand over Macedonian nationalists who, dissatisfied because Macedonia had not been established as an independent state but had been divided between Yugoslavia and Greece, had fled to Bulgaria and operated from Bulgarian soil against Yugoslavia. Bulgarian officers allied to Macedonian nationalists

TERRITORIAL CHANGES AS
A RESULT OF WORLD WAR I

——— Line of Treaty of Brest–Litovsk

TERRITORIES LOST:

By Russia

By Austria–Hungary

By Germany

By Bulgaria

Plebiscite areas

— · — · — 1914 boundaries

TERRITORIAL SETTLEMENTS
AFTER WORLD WAR I

—— 1926 boundaries

New independent nations

Zone of Allied occupation

Demilitarized zone

NORWAY

Oslo

Stockholm

SWEDEN

FINLAND

Helsinki

Petrograd

Murmansk

White
Sea

NORTH
SEA

DENMARK

ESTONIA

LATVIA

LITHUANIA

Moscow

U.S.S.R.

UNITED
KINGDOM

London

The
Hague

NETH.

BELGIUM

Hamburg

Danzig
(Free state)

EAST
PRUSSIA

BALTIC SEA

Berlin

GERMANY

Warsaw

Brest-
Litovsk

Kiev

Paris

LUX.

SAAR

ALSACE

LORRAINE

Prague

CZECHOSLOVAKIA

POLAND

Cracow

Lemberg

UKRAINE

FRANCE

Munich

SWITZ.

Geneva

Milan

Vienna

AUSTRIA

HUNGARY

Budapest

RUMANIA

Venice

Trieste

Fiume

YUGOSLAVIA

Belgrade

Bucharest

BLACK   SEA

Marseilles

ITALY

ADRIATIC SEA

Sofia

BULGARIA

Barcelona

CORSICA

Rome

Naples

ALBANIA

Constantinople

SARDINIA

GREECE

Aegean
Sea

TURKEY

CORFU

Athens

Algiers

SICILY

CRETE

Tunis

MALTA (Br.)

MEDITERRANEAN   SEA

ALGERIA

TUNISIA

0   500 miles

vehemently opposed any policy which implied recognition of the peace settlement, and hence clashed with those who wanted to concentrate on domestic reforms.

Discredited by defeat, Bulgaria's leaders were replaced when the war ended. King Ferdinand abdicated in favor of his son Boris (ruled 1918–1943) and a new party, the Agrarian party, came into power. The Agrarian leader, Alexander Stamboliski, advocated cooperation among the peasants of southeastern Europe and aimed at a Balkan federation in which Serbians and Bulgarians would be reconciled. In Bulgaria, he introduced land reforms, dividing the extended agrarian estates. Although the number of large landowners hurt by these measures was small, Stamboliski's agrarian program was widely considered as a step toward Communism, especially since many members of his party expressed sympathy for the Bolshevik social and economic policy. Hence, the Bulgarian bourgeoisie, the military, and the king all became upset by Stamboliski's reforms. But since he had a firm grip over the peasants, who formed 80 per cent of the Bulgarian population, he could not be removed by democratic means. His enemies therefore resorted to violence. In the early summer of 1923 his government was overthrown by a military coup. Stamboliski was captured by Macedonian terrorists, cruelly mutilated, tortured, and finally killed. This military coup ended democracy in Bulgaria. Behind the façade of a series of impotent bourgeois governments, Macedonian nationalists and Bulgarian officers, sometimes in alliance, sometimes quarreling, maintained control and terrorized the country. Finally, in 1935, King Boris, who had played an important role behind the scenes all along, came into the foreground and established a dictatorship, supported by the army and the police.

In the peace settlements, Hungary suffered more extensive territorial losses than Bulgaria and Austria. The Treaty of Trianon provided that in addition to paying reparations and limiting its army to 35,000 men, Hungary would have to cede to Czechoslovakia, Yugoslavia, and Rumania, three quarters of its former territory, with two thirds of its population. These harsh conditions could hardly arouse in the defeated nation great enthusiasm for the principles, such as democracy, advocated by the victors. Moreover, through a change of regime in the last stages of the war the Hungarians had expected to gain the favor of the western democracies. Two weeks before the end of the war they had pronounced the union with Austria dissolved and had declared themselves independent. Power had been taken over by Count Mihely Károlyi, who as an enemy of Tisza and a sympathizer with democratic western ideas had been a lonely figure among the Hungarian aristocrats. Károlyi had immediately taken steps to initiate a radical land reform; he ceded himself his own vast land holdings —more than fifty thousand acres—to his peasants for distribution among them and his government began to arrange for the dissolution of large estates. Károlyi also supported the convocation of a constitutional assembly, to be elected by universal and secret suffrage of men and women. But the elections for this assembly never took place. Károlyi, who had opposed Austria-Hungary's participation in the war, was a sincere believer in Wilsonian principles, and his popularity declined when the victors treated Hungary not as a newly arisen nation, but as a defeated enemy, and supported the claims of Yugoslavia, Rumania, and Czechoslovakia to Hungarian territory. Under these circumstances Károlyi felt that he could no longer be useful, and in March, 1919, he resigned in favor of the radicals of the left. From March to August, 1919, Hungary was a Communist republic, with Béla Kun as the leading political figure. Although representing a small extremist minority, the government of Béla Kun originally enjoyed broad support. The Hungarians hoped and expected that with the help of Bolshevik Russia they might be able to repulse Rumanian and Czechoslovakian encroachments on what they regarded as Hungarian territory. Officers and soldiers of the old Habsburg army served under Kun, whose government was careful not to antagonize the non-Communist groups of society. The great landed estates were collectivized, but the management of these collectives was frequently entrusted to the former landowners or their administrators; thus, at first the old ruling group and the bourgeoisie were willing to tolerate the Communist government. However, after a few initial military successes, the Kun government was forced by Allied pressure to evacuate Slovakia, and Rumanian troops, backed by the French, advanced toward Budapest. Realizing that even the Communists were unable to save the territorial integrity of Hungary, the old ruling group and the bourgeoisie withdrew their support from Béla Kun and rallied around a former officer of the Austro-Hungarian navy, Admiral Nicholas Horthy (1868–1957). The Communists tried to retain power through terrorist measures, but under the pressure of external and internal foes their regime collapsed; Kun fled to Russia, where he was later executed in one of Stalin's purges. Horthy and his reactionary supporters took over; by the autumn of 1919, the old ruling group was in power again in Hungary, and Communists, those suspected of radical views, spokesmen for workers and peasants, and particularly Jews, were rounded up, tortured, and killed. After some months the terror ended and political life returned to its prewar pseudoconstitutionalism. Horthy reigned as regent. Legally the monarchy was restored, but Hungary's neighbors vetoed the return of the last Habsburg ruler as king, so the throne remained empty. Parliament was reestablished, but the right to vote remained limited and the elections were managed by the group in power. The landowners, large and small, were all-powerful in Hungary until the Second World War. Horthy and his group had bought the assistance of the Allies against the Communists by accepting the Treaty of Trianon, which was signed on June 4, 1920. Yet indignation about the treaty was immense. Hungarians resented the reduction of their nation to a minor power. Moreover, the loss of many of Hungary's former markets created great difficulties for industry and agriculture. The constant aim of Hungarian foreign policy was to change the peace settlement and to regain the areas which once had been under the crown of St. Stephen. During the interwar period, Hungary remained a constant factor of unrest and was the natural ally of any power seeking to revise the peace settlement.

In contrast to Bulgaria and Hungary—nations with strong national traditions—the Austria which emerged from the First World War had little relationship to the Austria of the Habsburgs. Since its territory was limited to the German-speaking part of the Habsburg empire, it became a small country, with about 6.5 million inhabitants. One German-speaking area, South Tyrol, was given to Italy. And the unwillingness of the South Tyroleans to adjust themselves to Italian rule created continual friction between Austria and Italy. In other respects, the Austrians had little cause to resent the manner in which their frontiers were drawn. The complaint which they could make against the Treaty of St.-Germain was that their nation was not permitted to join Germany, that it was deprived of the right of self-determination. This prohibition against *Anschluss* created a festering wound, for though the enthusiasm of the Austrians to become part of the German Reich may have been limited, they recognized that as a separate state Austria was economically hardly viable. Vienna, formerly the capital of an empire, was one of the world's larger cities, much too large now for the small state of which it was the capital. After the war the inhabitants of Vienna formed a third of the entire population of Austria. This disproportion between the rural and the urban populations created constant economic difficulties and political tensions. In Vienna the socialists prevailed and established an effective municipal administration. The rest of the country was conservative and Catholic and this outlook dominated the government of the republic. Thus, the political situation was inherently unstable, and when in the 1930's economic difficulties and pressure from the north endangered Austrian independence, the rulers dared no longer trust the fate of Austria to the outcome of popular elections but turned to dictatorial forms of government.

The disposition of the non-German parts of Austria and the territories relinquished by Hungary resulted in the creation of a new system of states in eastern and southeastern Europe. Galicia was given to Poland; Transylvania and part of the Banat to Rumania; another part of the Banat, Bosnia, Herzogovina, and Dalmatia to Yugoslavia, which also absorbed Montenegro. Finally, out of Bohemia, Moravia, and Slovakia a new state was formed, the republic of Czechoslovakia. Poland, Rumania, Yugoslavia, and Czechoslovakia were known as the Successor States because, through the possession of territories which had formed part of the Austro-Hungarian empire, they inherited claims and obligations which were only slowly settled in international negotiations. The justification for the distribution of these territories in the Balkans and eastern Europe was the principle of self-determination. Whether newly formed, like Poland and Czechoslovakia, or already in existence, like Rumania and Serbia, each of these states was supposed to be the independent homeland of a previously suppressed nation. Actually, however, the application of the principle of self-determination in this area was complicated; it raised as many problems as it was assumed to solve.

A case in point is Yugoslavia, the enlarged kingdom of Serbia. The new name was intended to indicate that all the people living in this state were South Slavs—Yugoslavs—members of the various branches of the South Slav family. But though they were all South Slavs, the Serbs, Croatians, and Slovenes of Yugoslavia regarded themselves as distinct national groups, and this attitude created problems which impeded the working of democracy there. The Serbs and their leader, Pasic, considered themselves the creators of this new national state and were not ready to share power with the others. They clamored for a Greater Serbia, not for a federal state of several nationalities. Because a federal principle was rejected by the government, the Croatians refused to take seats in the constituent assembly elected in November, 1919, and in their absence a constitution was adopted which established a centralized state dominated by the Serbs. The consequent resentment of the Croatians and Slovenes was reinforced by religious contrasts and social friction. While the Serbs were Greek Orthodox, the Croatians and Slovenes were largely Roman Catholic. Moreover, the great majority of the Croatians were peasants, while the controlling element among the Serbs was a bourgeoisie favoring industrialization. When in 1928 the political leader of the Croatians, Stefan Radic, was assassinated, disintegration threatened and the king, relying on the support of the army, ended parliamentary rule and established a military dictatorship. The ensuing quiet in the political scene was deceiving, for although the Croatians were forcibly suppressed, they remained dissatisfied. Throughout the 1930's, the choice seemed to be between political disintegration and the continuation of a brutal dictatorship.

Democracy did not long survive either in Poland or in Rumania. There was no nationality problem in these countries, for the minority peoples (some Magyars and Germans in Transylvania) were powerless. A virulent anti-Semitism existed in both states; governments even tried to gain popularity by permitting and stimulating anti-Semitic disturbances. But the Jews carried little political weight and could defend themselves only by economic means. In Poland, as in many countries, a primary source of unrest and dissatisfaction was the agrarian problem. New regulations limited the maximum area which a single owner could hold to a hundred hectares (or well over two hundred acres), with a total of four hundred hectares permitted in the eastern border region. But the application of these laws encountered the obdurate resistance of the Polish nobility, who owned immense landed estates, and the laws remained chiefly on the books. The landowners found allies in the members of the bourgeoisie, who feared Communist influences among peasants and workers and were reluctant to allow them greater power. The deadlock resulting from this division of Polish political life into two hostile camps provided the opportunity for a *coup d'état* in 1926. Its leader was Józef Pilsudski (1867–1935), who was recognized as a patriot and military hero by all groups of society. He had struggled for Polish independence under tsarism; he had organized a Polish legion during the First World War; and with its help he had established an independent Polish government in the last phase of the war. In 1920, as leader of the Polish army, he had stopped the Russian advance before Warsaw and saved the country from Bolshevism. In his early years Pilsudski had been a socialist, and when he undertook the military coup of 1926 he was supported by the workers of Warsaw, who expected that he would reactivate the stalled movement toward democracy and social reform. But Pilsudski disappointed them. Once in power he allied himself with the bourgeoisie and the landowners, and the rule of these relatively small groups inevitably led to restrictions on liberty. In 1935 a constitution was forced upon the people which gave the president and the government unlimited powers. In the same year Pilsudski died, and power now remained in the hands of his confidants, chiefly men who had been officers in his Polish legion during the First World War. This group of colonels, less selfless than Pilsudski, and not beyond corruption, ruled in Poland in the years before the outbreak of the Second World War.

In Rumania, as in Poland, there was antagonism between the peasant party—anxious for agrarian reform and protective tariffs—and the wealthy urban bourgeoisie, who sought to maintain lower tariffs so that other nations would reciprocate and Rumania's industrial products, particularly oil, could be sold easily on foreign markets. The bourgeoisie could produce a parliamentary majority only by rigging elections, and retained power chiefly by using force. On the other hand the agrarian party, when it acquired control, showed itself remarkably inept in conducting political affairs. In this situation, in 1930 King Carol II returned from exile, into which he had been forced because of a morganatic marriage, so that his small son Michael had ruled under a regency. King Carol's hostility to the political leaders who had opposed him led him systematically to diminish their prestige by playing one against the other. The resulting stagnation of political life made the abolition of parliament and the establishment of a dictatorship appear to be the simple solution for getting things done.

But by the time the royal dictatorship was established in Rumania, Fascism and Nazism had already appeared on the scene; imitating the Italian and German leaders, Carol tried to establish a one-party system. He believed that he was riding the wave of the future, and certainly the Rumanian dictatorial regime was not far behind Fascism and Nazism in brutality and terror.

Only in Czechoslovakia did democracy continue to function throughout the entire interwar period. Like Yugoslavia, Czechoslovakia included people of several different nationalities: Czechs, Slovaks, Ruthenians, Germans. If in Czechoslovakia nationality conflicts were less sharp than in Yugoslavia, one reason may be found in the developments which preceded the foundation of the state. During the war, leaders of the Czechs and the Slovaks, among them Tomás Masaryk (1850–1937), an internationally known scholar of proved political courage and integrity, formed a committee which propagandized the cause of Czech independence and organized a military force fighting on the side of the Allies. Even before the war had ended the Allies recognized this committee as a provisional government. From the outset Czechs and Slovaks had worked together on this committee, and they were aware of the need for building a state based on cooperation among different nationalities. Thus, when parties were formed and parliamentary elections took place, the largest and most important political parties—the Social Democrats and the Agrarian party—included members of all nationalities, from all parts of the republic. One of the first measures of the new state, the dismemberment of the large landed estates, created among the peasants throughout the country a vested interest in the maintenance of the new republic. Furthermore, since Czechoslovakia had coal and iron mines and modern brewing and textile industries, its economy was better balanced between industry and agriculture than that of any other country in this area. Finally, as president of the republic, Masaryk, himself a Slovak, worked steadily for fairness toward all sections of the population. As a professor at the University of Prague before the war, Masaryk had educated the intellectual elite of the entire area, and he enjoyed immense respect and authority. Nonetheless, Czechoslovakia was by no means free of internal tensions. The Ruthenian and Slovak parts of the country were chiefly agrarian, and their inhabitants believed that the government neglected the agrarian sector of the economy in favor of the industrial parts in Bohemia. Moreover, most of the Ruthenians and Slovaks were Roman Catholic; their antagonism to the administration was sharpened by friction which developed between the anticlerical government and the Roman Catholic Church. Finally, many of the Germans living in Czechoslovakia, particularly in the Sudeten area, had before 1918 regarded themselves as the ruling element of the population; they accepted their sudden demotion with bad grace. But these centrifugal forces became dangerous and destructive to Czech democracy only when in the second part of the 1930's they were supported and stimulated by an outside power—Nazi Germany.

Thus, in the Balkans and in the former Habsburg empire two groups of powers developed as a result of the war: on the one hand were the defeated—Bulgaria and Hungary—both dissatisfied with the peace settlement; on the other were the victors—Rumania, Czechoslovakia, and Yugoslavia—who wished to maintain the *status quo* and formed a little entente to defend the situation created by the peace settlement. The antagonism between these two groups in foreign affairs increased the internal political instability of the various states because it prevented economic cooperation. An attempt to obtain through a Danube federation the economic cohesion formerly provided by the empire was in vain. The defeated saw in such an organization an effort to stabilize the *status quo*. The victors feared that it might be a first step toward the restoration of the Habsburg monarchy. In the end each country directed its economic policy toward autarky, in the hope that it could become independent of its neighbors. The artificial stimulation of industry resulted in stiff competition and low prices— a precarious and vulnerable economic situation.

The situation in the Balkans and eastern Europe held two particular dangers for the stability of Europe as a whole. Democracy there had succumbed because of contrasts between nationalities, conflicts between a radical peasantry and a bourgeoisie anxious to foster industrialization, resistance of a landowning class to agrarian reform, fear of revolution and of Communism. The dictatorial or pseudodictatorial regimes which followed the democratic governments clamped the lid on these problems; they did not solve them. Thus, they were themselves unstable, and having come to power by force, they were threatened by force. They would rather take risks than endanger their position by retreat.

If the great powers of Europe had been united, they might have been able to work out a common policy for this area which would have improved the economic situation and relieved tension. But the great European powers were divided, and each side sought for support among the eastern European states, with the result that the antagonisms in eastern Europe deepened. On the other hand, the prestige of the great powers became tied up with the fortunes of their Balkan allies, and the conflicts over the Balkan area placed a severe handicap on all attempts to overcome tensions among the great powers.

The Treaty of Versailles and Its Aftermath

In its various provisions, the settlement concluded at the Paris Peace Conference affected the entire world. But most attention has doubtless been directed to the part of the settlement which arranged the peace with the western powers' principal enemy—Germany. This treaty was signed at

Versailles on June 28, 1919, in the Hall of Mirrors, where in 1871 the German empire had been proclaimed. Its territorial provisions included the return of Alsace-Lorraine to France and the cession of areas with Polish populations—notably Poznán and the larger part of West Prussia—to Poland, so that a stretch of territory under Polish sovereignty, the so-called Polish Corridor, would separate East Prussia from the rest of Germany. Danzig, a German seaport at the northern end of the Polish Corridor, was established as a free city under supervision of the League of Nations, which was intended to guarantee Poland unimpeded access to the Baltic Sea. Memel, at the northern tip of East Prussia was also placed under the League of Nations; later it was seized by Lithuania. Plesbiscites were ordered in Schleswig and Upper Silesia and the southern part of East Prussia, and as a result of these, Germany had to give up some additional territory, although only the loss of the rich coal mines of Upper Silesia was of significance. Finally, Germany had to relinquish its colonies. Altogether, 13.1 per cent of Germany's prewar territory and 10 per cent of its population in 1910 were lost.

These territorial arrangements were complemented by clauses dealing with military and economic matters. The German army was limited to 100,000 officers and men. It was not to utilize aircraft, tanks, or aggressive weapons, and their production was prohibited. Artillery, aircraft, and tanks still in German possession were to be handed over to the victors. Also, the German navy was to be surrendered to the British; however, the Germans succeeded in scuttling most of their ships. In the future the German navy was to be restricted to twelve ships, none more than ten thousand tons; submarines were forbidden. The general staff and the officers' schools were to be abolished. Finally, as a guarantee for the fulfillment of the military clauses, the Rhineland would be occupied by Allied forces for up to fifteen years and would remain permanently demilitarized.

The Allies had great difficulty in reaching agreement about the economic aspects of the settlement. In the end, Article 231 of the Treaty of Versailles stated that the Germans must accept "responsibility of Germany and her allies for causing all the loss and damage to which the Allied and Associated Governments and their nationals have been subjected as a consequence of the war imposed upon them by the aggression of Germany and her allies." The far-reaching nature of this formulation was obvious. It might be interpreted as requiring Germany to finance pensions for officers, demobilization payments, and compensations for the wounded and maimed. The exact determination of how much, on the basis of this article, Germany would have to pay was difficult to reach, and no figure was specified in the treaty because the amount the experts believed Germany could pay was very different from the sum the people in the victorious countries had been led to expect. The treaty did state that in the next few years Germany was to pay five billion dollars, pending a definite settlement in 1921. However, the treaty included various provisions which weakened the German economy and hence reduced the nation's subsequent capacity to make payments. Germany had to hand over to the Allies most of its merchant marine, a quarter of its fishing fleet, and a good part of its railroad stock. For five years Germany had to build annually 200,000 tons of shipping for the victors. It had to make yearly deliveries of coal to France, Italy, and Belgium, and to pay the costs of the occupation of the Rhineland by the Allied armies. In addition, France received economic control over the Saar area, rich in coal and iron; for fifteen years this area was to be administered by the League of Nations; then a plebiscite was to decide its fate.

The strong moral condemnation of Germany and the German people that was contained in Article 231, with its statement that the war had been caused by German aggression, was also implied in other arrangements. Germany was not permitted to join the League of Nations; the Germans were to hand over their former political and military leaders to the Allies so that they could be judged by an international court for their crimes against international morality; the political union of Austria and Germany was prohibited, that is, the German-speaking people were not permitted to exert the principle of national self-determination. The impression that the Germans were treated as outcasts was reinforced by the manner in which the treaty was presented to them. The German delegation which had come to Versailles on April 29 was kept in isolation behind barbed wire. On May 7 the treaty was presented to the Germans without previous negotiations, and after they had received it, only an exchange of written notes took place. On June 16 the Allies presented an ultimatum in which they declared that they would resume hostilities if the Germans had not agreed to sign the treaty within a week. They did so on June 23, and five days later the ceremony in the Hall of Mirrors took place.

The harshness of the Treaty of Versailles has been sharply criticized and is frequently mentioned as a reason for the rise of Nazism in Germany. It is probably more correct to say that the fault of the Treaty of Versailles was that it was a compromise, neither fully generous nor totally destructive. The French wanted to destroy German unity, or at least to separate the Rhineland from Germany, and to keep Germany disarmed and economically weak in the foreseeable future. Great Britain and the United States were opposed to these French aims, partly because they considered them to be immoral, partly because they regarded them as impossible to realize. All the victorious powers were agreed that if the conditions were unbearably harsh Germany might throw itself into the arms of the Bolsheviks and Communism might penetrate into the center of Europe. Thus the French aims were resisted by Great Britain and the United States. But in order to persuade the French to abandon their plans, the British and the Americans had to make concessions. The result was a treaty which appeared to be an attempt to cripple Germany permanently rather than to make possible its further existence in the society of states.

In view of the hatreds aroused in the war, perhaps nothing better than the Treaty of Versailles could have been arranged. By and large, it did establish frontiers according to the principle of national self-determination. And the necessity of revising and mitigating the military and economic clauses of the treaty was soon accepted. But the impression received by the Germans in the summer of 1919, when the treaty was presented to them, was that of unrelenting harshness. This impression was particularly strong because they believed that they had been assured generous treatment. The Germans thought that they had laid down their arms under the condition that the peace treaty would be concluded on the basis of Wilson's Fourteen Points. Actually, at the signing of the armistice, the Germans were hardly in a position to make conditions. Their armies were in full retreat, their people were in revolt, and further resistance was hopeless.

BEGINNINGS OF THE WEIMAR REPUBLIC

When in October, 1918, the German front in the west began to weaken, a new German government was formed, headed by Prince Max of Baden, a man of humane outlook and liberal principles whose activities on behalf of prisoners of war had earned him a high reputation even in the non-German world. His task as chancellor was to direct the political transition of Germany; the military failure had compromised the existing ruling group in the eyes of the German people. The constitutional changes made during October transformed Germany into a parliamentary democracy. Its government was made dependent on a vote of confidence in the Reichstag. The introduction of universal suffrage in Prussia meant that the dominating influence of the *Junkers* on the policy of the Reich was broken. Moreover, the leaders of the political parties of the center and left of center—the parties that had always urged a democratization of German political life—entered the government. Given time, perhaps the government could have persuaded the world that a new democratic Germany had arisen. But these changes and reforms took place under the shadow of imminent military catastrophe. When Prince Max of Baden formed his government, Ludendorff, despairing of the military situation, demanded the opening of negotiations which would lead to an immediate ending of hostilities. The government therefore informed President Wilson of its readiness for peace negotiations based on the Fourteen Points. An exchange of notes followed, lasting through October. Because the European allies distrusted the sincerity of this sudden conversion to democracy at the moment of defeat, Wilson demanded clear proof of the change in Germany. But meanwhile the government's appeal to Wilson was having an immense impact on the German people. They became suddenly aware of what had been concealed by optimistic military communiqués—the fact that the war was lost. The belief became widespread that the old leaders ought to give up power so that Wilson and his allies would have undeniable proof of the change in Germany. When William II hesitated to abdicate, mutinies—first in the navy—broke out. Unrest spread in the cities. Demonstrations and strikes indicated that the government could no longer rely on police or military force. On November 9, 1918, a republic for Germany was proclaimed in Berlin. Two days later the armistice was signed.

The revolution within Germany threw power into the laps of the socialists. But if they wanted to use the fall of the monarchy for a transformation of their country into a socialist state, the chaotic situation in Germany frustrated them. The socialists themselves were divided, and the next month saw a struggle between moderates and radicals. The moderate majority of the Social Democratic leaders, known as Majority Socialists to distinguish them from the dissident Independent Socialists, believed that radical social changes would result in the dissolution of the Reich, especially since separatist movements had begun to arise in Bavaria and the Rhineland. The Majority Socialists pushed the radicals out of the government, and the latter resumed revolutionary action. The driving force toward this revolutionary action was an extreme leftist organization, the Spartacus group, from which later the German Communist party developed. In the winter of 1918–1919 its leaders were Karl Liebknecht and Rosa Luxemburg, both of whom had been influential in the socialist movement before the First World War. There was fierce street fighting in Berlin, particularly vehement in the last weeks of 1918 and the first weeks of 1919. Uprisings spread in the Ruhr area and in Hamburg and in April a Soviet Republic was established in Bavaria. All these revolutionary movements were defeated.

In order to fight off the radical left, the Majority Socialists felt constrained to accept help from the elements to their right. They were particularly anxious to gain control over an organized military force. Immediately after the proclamation of the republic in November, 1918, Friedrich Ebert (1871–1925), the leader of the socialists and head of the new federal government, approached Field Marshal von Hindenburg and General Groener, of the military high command—the latter having replaced Ludendorff—and the generals agreed to cooperate with the socialist leaders in order to maintain German unity.

The alliance between the Majority Socialists and the military high command had important consequences. Following Hindenburg's example the German civil servants recognized the legitimacy of the new government and placed their services at its disposal. The resulting administrative

Revolution in Germany. *Adherents of the Spartacus group occupying a government building in Berlin.*

continuity helped to overcome the difficulties of demobilization and to ease the transition to a peacetime economy. But the advantages to the new government of gaining the support of the military high command for military action against the extremists on the left were less than might have appeared at the time of the proclamation of the republic and had a fatal influence on future developments. When the troops returned to German soil from the occupied territories in the west and east, discipline dissolved; they left the ranks and went to their homes. This created a critical situation in the last months of 1918. The high command responded by starting to organize volunteer units (*Freikorps*) in which former officers had a leading role; these *Freikorps* played their part in the fight against the extremists. The weight of the conservative allies pushed the government strongly in the direction of ending the revolutionary situation in which Councils of Workers and Soldiers interfered in the process of government. The government was urged to arrange as soon as possible elections through which the bourgeoisie and the more conservative part of the population could make their voices heard. At the end of January, 1919, when most of the revolutionary movements of the radical left had been defeated, elections to a constituent assembly took place. The new assembly met in Weimar on February 6, 1919.

However, the shotgun wedding between the socialists and the high command had consequences which extended far beyond the winter of 1918–1919, and stultified the development of democracy in Germany. Because the socialists relied on the old civil servants, the republic was obligated to preserve the rights which these functionaries had possessed under the empire. Thus, during the entire existence of the republic its administrative apparatus was in the hands of conservative, usually monarchist, civil servants who could not be dismissed and who exerted a controlling influence on the admission of new members to their ranks. Furthermore, when the new 100,000-man army was created, the task of selecting its officer corps remained in the hands of the officers of the old general staff. This reliance on conservative forces prevented the destruction or even the weakening of the powerful position of the landowners and industrialists. Promises of agrarian reform, made in the initial burst of revolutionary enthusiasm, were not kept. The industrialists fended off all attempts at socialization, although the trade unions did gain the assurance that employers would accept the principle of collective bargaining and refrain from obstructing the functioning of the unions in the factories. It has been argued that the socialists were unable to undertake a thorough transformation of German society because if they had acted against the bourgeoisie the resulting conflict would have destroyed the unity of the Reich. But the unity of the Reich withstood severe crises in the following years. The fact is that most of the leaders of the Majority Socialists were bureaucrats rather than revolutionaries and did not know what to do with the power which had fallen to them.

That in November, 1918, the German people were ready for far-reaching changes was shown by the elections which took place when reaction had already begun to set in. In the constituent assembly, those who advocated democratization of German political life obtained a striking majority: 328 deputies out of a total of 423. Within this republican group the moderate socialists, with 165 members, were strongest, but lacking a majority, they had to collaborate with the two bourgeois republican parties, the Catholic Center party and the left-liberal Democratic party, which together were not quite as strong as the socialists. Thus the constitution resulting from the deliberations of this assembly established not a socialist system, but a parliamentary democracy. All power was concentrated in the hands of a parliament (the Reichstag), elected through secret ballot by all men and women of at least twenty-one years of age, on the basis of proportional representation. The federal government of the republic was given more power than had been enjoyed by its counterpart in the empire; a provision for which a member of the Center party, Matthias Erzberger, was mainly responsible gave the right to raise direct taxes to the federal government, which then assigned funds to the various states. As in the United States, the president—the head of the republic—was to be elected directly by the people. The government, with a chancellor as its head, was responsible to the Reichstag. Thus, both the Reichstag and the president could claim to represent the people and to enjoy democratic legitimation. When they clashed, the door was opened for the overthrow of parliamentary democracy: in emergency situations the president had the right to rule by decree without previous approval of the parliament, and no law ever defined

Acceptance of the Republican Constitution in Weimar in 1919. *President Ebert and other leaders of the Republic on the balcony of the building in which the Constituent Assembly met.*

what an emergency situation was.

Despite internal conflicts and economic misery, the changes in the forms of political life and the emergence of new political leaders raised hopes in Germany. But when the draft of the peace treaty was handed to the German delegation in Versailles, these hopes turned into disappointment and vehement indignation. In the face of violent opposition, the treaty was accepted in the Reichstag by a small majority consisting of the moderate socialists and the Center party. A resumption of hostilities, as the military leaders admitted, was impossible. And it was feared that an occupation of Germany by the Allied armies might result in the disintegration of the Reich. The acceptance of the peace treaty led to a strengthening of the monarchical right and the radical left, the right accusing the republican government of a lack of feeling for national honor, the left advocating cooperation with Bolshevik Russia as a means of "liberation." After the summer of 1919 those parties that were the protagonists of a democratic republic and the true authors of the new constitution—the Center party, the Democratic party, and the Majority Socialists—did not again constitute a majority in the Reich. It has been said about the rise of the Nazis that, as long as there were free elections in Germany, the Nazis never gained a majority among the voters. And this is true. But it must also be said that after 1919, during the fourteen years of the Weimar Republic, those parties that were convinced supporters of the republican regime never had a clear majority either.

The parliamentary system never really functioned in Germany. The governments changed frequently; several of them were minority governments or governments of experts, ruling with ever-shifting majorities. Those which were based on a parliamentary majority, such as the two governments of the Great Coalition, in 1923 and 1928, were possible only with right-wing support: these governments included—in addition to the three republican parties (Social Democrats, Democrats, Center party)—the monarchist German People's party. And the governments of Heinrich Brüning and Franz von Papen, preceding Hitler's rise to power, ruled by presidential emergency decrees without a secure parliamentary basis.

THE STRUGGLE OVER FULFILLMENT OF THE PEACE TREATY

Problems connected with the execution of the peace treaty dominated the policy of the Weimar Republic throughout its existence. In the first five years after the signing of the Treaty of Versailles the two principal issues concerned the reduction of the army to 100,000 men and the payment of reparations. These questions kept alive the conflicts which had developed over the acceptance of the peace treaty. Opponents of the treaty recommended an obstructionist policy, suggesting that changes in the world situation would make enforcement of the terms impossible. The republican parties believed that Germany should attempt to fulfill the clauses of the peace treaty and hereby create a confidence in German trustworthiness that would lead to the mitigation of the treaty's requirements.

The most vehement opponents of adherence to the military clauses were the career officers, who had in the defense minister, the socialist Noske, an all too trusting chief. The general staff continued to function in disguised form as a section of the defense ministry. The military assisted the formation of unofficial, secret military organizations, provided them with weapons, and participated in their training. Among the men used by the army for keeping alive the military spirit was a corporal named Adolf Hitler, whose oratorical gifts seemed suited for this task.

The wave of military obstructionism reached its high point in March, 1920, when the reduction of the army to its accepted size could no longer be delayed. In a putsch organized by a former imperial civil servant, Wolfgang Kapp, the generals attempted to overthrow the government. Although the government had to flee Berlin, a general strike forced the putschists to surrender. The army was reduced to its prescribed strength and the illegal military organizations gradually disbanded. But the disorder of the Kapp Putsch led to Communist revolts, particularly in the Ruhr area, that could be suppressed only with the help of the military. The republican government, therefore, felt unable to take advantage of its victory over the rightists for a purge of the army of monarchist elements. The new 100,000-man army, the Reichswehr, remained firmly in the hands of the old officers' group.

The Treaty of Versailles had left determination of the exact amount of reparations and the details of their payment to later negotiations. These questions were thrashed out in a number of meetings and conferences which showed a wide gap between Allied demands and the Germans' estimate of their ability to pay; this disagreement served to maintain a poisoned atmosphere between the opponents. Germany was finally forced to accept an ultimatum in which the amount of damages for which reparations were required was fixed at 132 billion marks (31.5 billion dollars), due in annual installments of 2 billion marks (close to 500 million dollars).

All the German political parties were convinced that their country could not pay this sum. But German politicians disagreed on how a reduction could be achieved. Once again the rightist parties advocated obstruction; the republican parties wanted to go as far as possible in fulfilling the demands of the victors. The most prominent protagonist of this fulfillment policy was Walter Rathenau (1867–1922). Rathenau was an uncommon figure: an aesthete who was close to many figures of modern art and literature, and a writer who in a number of widely read books had discussed the impact of modern technology on human existence, he was also a man of action who had proved his practical abilities as chairman of the great German electricity trust. And Rathenau was a good German patriot. At the beginning of the war he had suggested that the government inventory all raw materials—a most necessary measure—and had been entrusted with the task. In the difficult postwar situation Rathenau again put himself at the disposal of the government, serving as minister of reconstruction (May, 1921) and subsequently as foreign minister (February, 1922). His primary aim was to halt the inflationary trend of the German economy by substituting deliveries of goods for payments in gold; he hoped that economic cooperation, particularly between German and French industry, would gradually lead to a feasible reparations settlement. However, Rathenau was not master in his own foreign ministry, in which influential officials believed that western pressure on their nation would be weakened only if Germany exerted some counterpressure; they favored close connections with Soviet Russia. On April 16, 1922, when no improvement in the reparations arrangements seemed obtainable, Rathenau, the advocate of a western orientation in German foreign policy, was persuaded to conclude at Rapallo a treaty with Russia which provided for closer political and economic collaboration with the East. Nevertheless, because the German public regarded Rathenau as the embodiment of a policy of concessions to the victor, he became the chief target of the extremists of the right. On June 24, 1922, he was assassinated by members of a secret organization consisting chiefly of former officers who sought to eliminate as traitors the principal exponents of the fulfillment policy. Rathenau's assassination was only one in a long chain of political murders. Early in 1919, Karl Liebknecht and Rosa Luxemburg, who as leaders of the Spartacus group had been involved in the extremist revolt against the Majority socialists, had been killed without trial after falling into the hands of the military. Matthias Erzberger, the leader of the Center party who had signed the armistice, had been asassinated in 1921, and in 1922 an attempt had been made on the life of the socialist Philipp Scheidemann, who in November, 1918, had proclaimed the republic in Berlin from the balcony of the Reichstag building. The members of the judiciary were conservative and nationalistic and refrained from probing the nationalistic organizations to which the murderers belonged.

With Rathenau's elimination, the enemies of the fulfillment policy gained the upper hand. A government of experts under the business leader Heinrich Cuno, supported by the parties of the right, deliberately refused to make the deliveries to which Germany was obligated. The French reaction was quick and sharp. French troops moved into the Ruhr area, so that the mines of the district would now produce for France. But encouraged by the German government, the miners refused to work and embarked on a policy

The occupation of the Ruhr area in 1923. *French troops enter Essen.*

of passive resistance. To provide the money which the workers needed to live on, the German presses began to turn out currency with accelerated speed, and the mark plunged to unimaginable depths. At the beginning of 1923, the American dollar, which in 1914 had been the equivalent of 4.2 marks, brought 1,800 marks. By the fall of 1923 one American dollar was worth 4.2 trillion marks. Currency of this sort had no real value. When people received their wages they hastened to transform them into goods before their buying power diminished even further. Workers were hard hit because their wages, although steadily increased, did not keep up with the rising prices. Civil servants, with fixed salaries that only slowly adjusted to the upward trend, were in dire straits. Those dependent upon pensions, rents, or investment in government loans existed by selling whatever pieces of value they possessed. That the middle classes, usually a stabilizing social force, suffered most gravely and became embittered and increasingly radical was a fatal blow to the prestige of the republican regime. The inflation had a deeply demoralizing effect. While most people did not understand what was going on, those who did were able to make great amounts of money. Boys of seventeen and eighteen left school, turned to financial speculation, and quickly earned ten times as much as their fathers, who had been slowly working their way up through the bureaucratic hierarchy.

Conditions in Germany became chaotic. Separatist movements sprang up in the Rhineland. In Saxony, the radical left came into power. Bavaria was dominated by Bavarian monarchists and radical rightist organizations led by Ludendorff and Hitler. If a unified Reich and an ordered social life were to be maintained, the printing of money would have to be stopped, the passive resistance in the Ruhr would have to be abandoned, and Germany would have to resume reparations payments.

The necessity for admitting defeat was realized not only by those who had advocated the fulfillment policy but also by a leader of the rightist German People's party, Gustav Stresemann (1878–1929). Stresemann looked like a typical German petit bourgeois. Before 1914 he had been an enthusiastic admirer of William II and as a member of the Reichstag during the war years, he had been a rabid nationalist and annexationist and supported the high command in all its demands. But Stresemann had been deeply shaken by the way the military leaders had deceived themselves and the German people about their chances in the war. He became convinced that a reorganization of German political life on a democratic basis was unavoidable, and when the republican German Democratic party failed to accept him, he founded his own party, which aimed at the restoration of the monarchy but accepted the parliamentary system of government. In asserting the hopelessness of the contest over the Ruhr, Stresemann risked his popularity, but he was aware that by assuming leadership in this matter he was opening the door to a positive role for

Inflation in Germany. A *kohlrabi (a type of turnip) cost fifty million marks in 1923.*

himself in the political life of the Weimar Republic. In a number of speeches made all over Germany during the early summer of 1923, he prepared the public for the necessity of abandoning the Ruhr struggle. And in August, 1923, he became chancellor, with the program of stabilizing the German currency and resuming the fulfillment policy. As a first step he ended the passive resistance in the Ruhr. He was helped by the fact that the chaotic situation which had developed in central Europe was having a damaging economic effect throughout the continent. All the great powers now recognized that for the sake of their own economic stability some compromise about German reparations payments had to be worked out; they agreed to the reopening of the question by a committee of experts headed by an American, Charles G. Dawes

Defects and Strengths of the Weimar Republic

Between the proclamation of the republic in 1918 and the economic collapse of 1923, events in Germany crowded one upon the other. There was a long procession of personalities who came forward and then disappeared from the scene after a short time: Liebknecht, Noske, Rathenau, Erzberger, Cuno, Kapp. There were strikes and unrest, sometimes developing into civil war, in Berlin, in Bavaria, in the Rhineland, and in Saxony. There were moments when it seemed questionable whether the federal government could enforce its authority in all parts of the Reich, especially since the army and the judiciary kept their protecting hands over secret military organizations bitterly hostile to the republic. In critical situations like that of the Ruhr occupation, hostility to the western powers created an alliance—called National Bolshevism—between the extreme right and the extreme left. The economic upheaval brought new economic leaders into the foreground. The most powerful of these was Hugo Stinnes (1870–1924), a coal merchant, an owner of coal mines in the Ruhr, who built up a gigantic concern consisting of ironworks, banks, merchant ships, newspapers, and hotels, and who was one of the strongest adversaries of the fulfillment policy; however, Stinnes' phenomenal rise to economic power and political influence was quickly followed by the disintegration of his firm after the stabilization of the mark: the debts which he had contracted in building up his enterprises, easily repaid during the inflation, became a stifling burden after stabilization.

It was a turbulent period, but the very turbulence of these years concealed the fact that the changes which the overthrow of the monarchy had brought about were not very far-reaching. Germany had become a republic, with a parliamentary system. The functions of the Reich had been enlarged at the expense of the individual states, and the power of the Reichstag had been increased so that the government—the executive branch—was now dependent on the legislative branch. General suffrage and the parliamentary system had also been introduced in the individual German states, so that, for instance, Prussia had a government headed by a Social Democrat until 1932. The position of the trade unions had been legally fortified, and as a result of the influence of the Social Democrats, governmental intervention and arbitration in labor conflicts secured a fair hearing for the cause of the trade unions. These were much-needed reforms and improvements. But they did not represent a revolutionary change, the creation of a new truly democratic society; and they left the social structure of Germany almost untouched. The strength which the traditional organizations and institutions preserved would be a serious danger to the existence of the Weimar Republic in years to come.

However, German life did assume a new shape in one area—that of culture. Frustrated in more far-reaching plans by the consequences of defeat and economic difficulties, the liberal and socialist ministers were anxious to demonstrate that at least in the field of culture a new era had opened. They supported the modern tendencies in art and literature which had been fought by conservative ministers of education under the empire. At the same time, the turmoil and the insecurity of these years created an excitement which was a spur to artistic and intellectual experiments. Furthermore, inflation had somehow shaken the belief in traditional values. And as we have seen, some people profited considerably from speculations during the inflationary period. They put their money into things of lasting worth, such as works of art; they spent freely and quickly, anticipating the rapid depreciation of paper money. Thus, masking the grimness of the social reality there was a glittering façade, particularly in Berlin and other large cities. The amusement industry flourished. Art exhibitions, operas, theaters, and concerts were well attended. There was much experimentation in opera, drama, and art. At this time the first plays of the young Bertolt Brecht appeared on the German stage; the opera *Wozzeck*, by Alban Berg, had its first triumph; movies like *The Cabinet of Dr. Caligari* demonstrated the possibilities inherent in this new form of art; and the Bauhaus, first

Modern architecture in Germany. *The Bauhaus in Dessau.*

in Weimar and later in Dessau, inaugurated a new functional style in architecture and interior design. The absence of social stability fostered cynicism, as well as a sharpening of social criticism, both reflected in the drawings and paintings of George Grosz. Even after the economic crisis of the immediate postwar period had been overcome, a critical spirit remained alive and eagerness for experimentation continued. The intellectual atmosphere of Berlin after the First World War was electrifying; it attracted journalists, writers, and artists from all over the world. Such figures as Sinclair Lewis, Dorothy Thompson, Stephen Spender, Christopher Isherwood, and Ilya Ehrenburg were to look back nostalgically upon life in Berlin in the 1920's as one of their great experiences.

But because of their rejection of traditional forms of art, and because of their conscious cultivation of contacts with the most advanced intellectual movements in other countries, these cultural activities aroused opposition among many Germans. Conservatives regarded them as further proof that the Weimar regime represented a break with German tradition and was an alien element in German history. The distance widened between Berlin, the modern capital of the republic, and the rural areas, far removed from the rapid changes of modern life. This alienation of Berlin and other large urban centers from the rest of the country strengthened the appeal which in later years the Nazi propaganda against the Weimar "system" would have among wide circles of the population.

CHAPTER 5

Era of Stabilization and Its Breakdown

IN 1923 THE POLICY of the victorious powers changed direction. Until 1923 unrest and tension had been increasing, and pressure on Germany had been mounting steadily, but now steps were taken toward liquidating the consequences of the war and restoring cooperation among the European powers. This shift in attitude must be explained partly as an attempt to end the rifts which had developed among the wartime allies, and partly as a consequence of economic and social developments within the victorious states.

ITALY IN THE POSTWAR WORLD

The postwar relations between France and Great Britain were not smooth. Still, the distance between these two states was less wide than that which separated Italy from them both. In the postwar world Italy did not regard itself as a victorious power; it was anxious to see the peace treaties modified, and tended to support revisionist movements. This separation from the other Allies, already evident at the Paris Peace Conference, had its roots in the events accompanying Italy's entry into the war in 1915.

Unlike the other great powers, which were drawn into the hostilities in consequence of a chain of events over which they had lost control, Italy entered the war deliberately, with the aim of aggrandizement. In the secret Treaty of London of 1915, Great Britain, France, and Russia had promised Italy wide territorial gains. But the fulfillment of this treaty had encountered difficulties at the Paris Peace Conference, especially with regard to the extended Austrian territories which Italy was to receive: the Trentino and South Tyrol up to the Brenner Pass, Trieste, Istria, the islands along the Dalmatian coast, and a great part of Dalmatia. These acquisitions were intended to give Italy security against the Habsburg empire, which in 1915 nobody expected to disappear. But when the war ended, Austria-Hungary no longer existed and adherence to the arrangements of the Treaty of London was incompatible with the principle of self-determination for it would have placed more than a million Yugoslavs under Italian rule. Nevertheless, the Italians occupied Austrian territory up to the line assigned to them in the treaty of 1915, and when the Paris Peace Conference convened they insisted on their pound of flesh—the fulfillment of the treaty. Aware, however, of the obstacles which in these changed circumstances the execution of the early promises would encounter, the Italians intimated that they might be willing to accept less if they were given Fiume, which had not been assigned to them in the Treaty of London. But Fiume had a large Yugoslav population, and the Yugoslavs vehemently refused this Italian demand, since they did not want to see the two good ports on the eastern side of the Adriatic Sea—Trieste and Fiume—in Italian hands. The question of Fiume became one of the stumbling blocks at the Paris Peace Conference. President Wilson's appeal to the Italian people to accept the principle of self-determination was rejected. For three weeks the Italian delegates absented themselves from the negotiations. Even after their return, the Fiume question remained undecided.

The Paris Peace Conference allowed Italy to extend its frontiers to the Brenner Pass and to take over the Istrian Peninsula, including the city of Trieste. Italy thus acquired all the Habsburg territories which had been regarded as *Italia irredenta* in the prewar years, but the government, in order to get backing for its additional claims, had whipped up nationalist excitement to such a degree that the joy over the fulfillment of these national aspirations was overshadowed by disappointment over the failure to obtain Fiume and Dalmatia. All over Italy, people spoke of "the mutilated victory." Contempt for the feebleness of parliamentary politics had arisen in Italy before the First World War and these events reinforced this attitude. Nationalist organizations of an antiparliamentary character sprang up everywhere. The fiery poet Gabriele D'Annunzio became an influential political leader in Italy. In the fall of 1919, while the negotiations over Fiume were still going on, he organized a troop of volunteers, who seized power in Fiume. There they remained until December, 1920. By then, Italy's foreign minister, Count Carlo Sforza (1873–1952), had negotiated a treaty according to which Fiume became an independent city-state and in compensation Italy received a number of islands on the Dalmatian coast. Now Italian troops turned D'Annunzio and his volunteers out of Fiume. But D'Annunzio had exposed the weak and vacillating character of the Italian government, which first made great demands and then hesitated to enforce them. Among the nationalist leaders of this period, the most efficient was the former Socialist leader Benito Mussolini (1883–1945), who had left the Socialist party because it had resisted Italian entry into the war. He had served in the war as a volunteer and was now seeking a platform from which to reenter political life. On March 23, 1919, in a building on the Piazza San Sepolcro in Milan, he founded his own organization, the *Fasci di Combattimento*, whose members came to be known as Fascists.

Resentment over thwarted nationalist aims was fed by economic misery and discontent. In Italy more than 50 per cent of the country's tax revenues came from consumer taxes, which fell off when the war caused a decrease in the production of consumer goods. An attempt was made to finance the Italian war effort through internal and foreign loans, and when these proved insufficient the government resorted to the printing of paper money. The consequence was inflation; in 1920 the lira had less than a fifth of its prewar value. The financial problems were increased by a growing deficit in the balance of trade. During the war, agricultural production had decreased drastically, and after the war Italy had to import not only coal and oil but also great quantities of grain.

Most directly hit by the inflation were the members of the middle classes: people with fixed incomes, such as civil servants, landlords prevented by law from raising rents, and rentiers who had invested their money in government bonds. But economic distress was also felt by the rural classes and the workers. After the war more than 50 per cent of all Italians were engaged in agriculture. Nine tenths of those who owned land possessed less than three acres, not nearly enough even for subsistence. And a great part of the rural population was entirely landless, working for wages on the great estates. During the war the government had promised a redistribution of the land; rumors—many exaggerated—about what had been done in Russia stimulated the impatience of the Italian peasants and raised their expectations. The war also increased unrest among the industrial workers. Hitherto industrial activity had largely taken the form of very small enterprises, employing less than ten workers. But in response to the needs of war production, large-scale industrial establishments had become much more numerous. News from Russia, coupled with the inflationary price rise with which wages could not keep up, intensified the demand for social reform by the workers, and the long-standing influence of syndicalism and anarchism contributed to their radicalization. Dissatisfaction among the rural and industrial proletariat erupted in direct action. In dramatic fashion bands of peasants and agricultural workers, marching to the accompaniment of martial music and the pealing of church bells, occupied uncultivated land belonging to the great landowners. In cities and towns strikes increased. The strike wave reached its high point in the summer of 1920, when dismissals in the metallurgical industries led to an occupation of the factories by the workers in industrial regions. However, these demonstrations had no long-lasting effect. The police removed the peasants from the land which they had appropriated, and the workers, lacking raw materials, capital, and salesmen, were unable to keep the industries going and evacuated the factories. Nevertheless, the political activity of peasants and workers contributed significantly to the transformation of the Italian party system. Before the war the Italian political parties were rather loose in structure; the individual deputy owed his election to his reputation and his standing in his own district, not to his party label. After the war, the socialists, in close alliance with the trade unions, built an efficient, centrally directed organization. Furthermore, Pope Benedict XV gave permission for the foundation of a Catholic political party, and the Catholic People's party appeared on the scene. Eager for mass support, it looked beyond the Catholic bourgeoisie for adherents, seeking to attract the peasants of the south and the industrial workers, among whom Catholic trade unions began to compete with socialist trade unions. The guiding spirit of the Catholic People's party was a Sicilian priest, Don Luigi Sturzo, whose experience in the stagnant Italian south had made him aware of the need for social —particularly agrarian—reform. The influence of the two mass parties —the Socialists and the Catholic People's party—was strengthened by the adoption of the proportional voting system, which the government had introduced as a concession to the demands for reform: the number of deputies allowed each party was determined by the total number of votes received by the party throughout Italy. The bourgeois parties of the center and the left, Liberals and Democrats, were seriously threatened. This was the situation when the Fascists came to power in October, 1922.

Mussolini's claim that Fascism saved Italy from Bolshevism is palpably untrue. If there ever was danger of a successful Communist take-over in Italy after the First World War—and this is most doubtful—the revolutionary wave had certainly passed its crest by the spring of 1921. The new mass parties, now firmly entrenched, did not advocate revolution. However, they did agree on the need for far-reaching social and economic reform. Reform was deeply feared by the industrialists and landowners, still suffering from the shock of the occupation of factories and land by workers and peasants. In their anxiety they turned to the opponents of parliamentary democracy, hoping to gain support in their fight against reform. Mussolini's Fascists offered themselves as a most suitable instrument. Throughout Italy the party had formed paramilitary organizations, consisting chiefly of young unemployed war veterans. In the industrial centers of the north these Fascist organizations made themselves popular with the bourgeoisie by protecting strikebreakers and disrupting Socialist street demonstrations. The young Fascists were ruthless but effective. Moreover, Mussolini, their leader, inspired some confidence; he was a journalist of gifts and a remarkable orator. Although his boasts of intensive study of Marx and Nietzsche were considerably exaggerated, his acquaintance with Marxist thought and modern philosophy was sufficient to give his writings and speeches intellectual respectability. Through his advocacy of Italy's entry into the war, and through his war service, he had demonstrated his patriotism, but Mussolini was too much of a Marxist to believe that the world could stand still and be satisfied with the same old ideas. He was therefore not only a nationalist but also a revolutionary activist. And this combination constituted his strength in the eyes of the Italian upper classes. On the one hand Mussolini seemed to have a hold over the masses which they had lost; on the other, he seemed to share their own nationalist ideals and their rejection of international socialism. They expected that Mussolini might develop his organization into a counterforce to the new mass parties. Leaders of the old political groups, such as Giolitti, regarded Mussolini's rise with benevolence. They believed that he would be useful and that cooperation with him would be feasible.

The test came with the Fascist seizure of power—the March on Rome on October 27, 1922. The version of this event which the Fascists later spread was that the Fascist organizations had converged on Rome and the government, faced by this revolutionary force, capitulated. Actually, negotiations about Fascist participation in the government had been going on for some time. Leaders of various political parties—Giolitti as well as the more conservative Antonio Salandra (1853–1931)—were willing to form a coalition government which included the Fascists. To clinch these negotiations Mussolini organized the March on Rome; his paramilitary organizations approached the capital from four directions. The government felt sure that it could defeat this Fascist revolt with the help of the army, and the king was willing to sign the order declaring a state of siege. But on the night of October 27, he changed his mind because—as he revealed after the fall of Mussolini—he had received exaggerated reports of the Fascists' military strength. When Mussolini heard of the king's attitude he was no longer content with a subordinate partnership in a coalition government, and insisted that he be made prime minister. Only after this demand had been granted did he come to Rome; arriving on October 30 after traveling from Milan by sleeping car, he appeared before the king and was commissioned to form a government. The Fascist organizations now entered Rome and held a victory parade. Mussolini's government included, in addition to Fascist leaders, members of the parties of the right and even some members of the Catholic People's party. The March on Rome shows all the features characteristic of Mussolini's policy in the first decade of Fascist rule: on the one hand, the dramatic gesture directed toward the outside world; on the other, cautious preparation and careful calculation.

In the first years of his regime Mussolini's policy was rather ambiguous. The Fascist paramilitary organizations became a militia paid by the state and were effectively used to eliminate opposition. Mussolini placed Fascists in key positions in his administration, and they controlled the police. But since his government included not only Fascists but also Liberals, Conserva-

The March on Rome. *Mussolini in the middle; on the extreme left, Balbo, later Italian air minister.*

tives, and some members of the Catholic People's party, parliament continued to function, and Mussolini gave repeated assurances that he would remain within the framework of the constitution in his conduct of affairs. Thus in the first few years of his prime ministership, Mussolini's system of government was not very different from that of Giolitti in the prewar years. However, because the mass of workers and peasants had become more vocal and better organized, such a parliamentary dictatorship was now much more difficult to maintain, and accordingly the men in power had fewer hesitations about the use of ruthless and brutal methods. Moreover, Mussolini was determined to remain in power, and in 1923, under the threat of a second wave of revolution, he forced parliament to accept a change in the electoral law according to which the party with the largest number of votes would receive two thirds of the seats in the Chamber of Deputies. Hence, in the elections of 1924 the government received 374 of the 535 seats.

The abandonment of the parliamentary façade and the establishment of an undisguised dictatorship came in 1924 as a result of the conflict following the assassination of Giacomo Matteotti, a young, highly respected Socialist deputy; in his writings and speeches Matteotti had presented extended proof of Fascist terrorist acts. In particular, he had demonstrated how violence had been used to intimidate voters in the recent election. And Matteotti's revelations had been highly compromising to several members of the Fascist hierarchy. It soon emerged that Matteotti's abduction and murder had been instigated by prominent Fascists, close to Mussolini. Even if Mussolini was not directly involved, the murder was a manifestation of the atmosphere of brutality and violence which had developed with the toleration and encouragement of government leaders. The excitement over these disclosures was immense. The parliamentary opposition—about a hundred deputies, among them the various socialist groups, some members of the Catholic People's party, and left-wing liberals—demanded the dissolution of the Fascist militia and refused to have any contact with the Fascists, members of a party including murderers. They therefore withdrew from the Chamber of Deputies and set up their own counterparliament on the opposite side of the Tiber, on the Aventine. The demands of the opposition were strongly supported by the large Italian newspapers, which called for Mussolini's resignation. He seems to have thought of retirement, but the king, whom the opposition expected to take the initiative in dismissing Mussolini, did not act. Mussolini remained in power, and from this time on he steered energetically toward a one-party system and a totalitarian dictatorship.

The powers of parliament were increasingly curtailed and finally almost eliminated. It could no longer overthrow a government by a vote of lack of confidence. Its members could not propose a question for discussion, the head of the government determined the subjects to be debated in parliament. The position of the head of the government, or prime minister, was raised above that of other members of the cabinet. He was to appoint and dismiss the ministers and to direct their work. Neither individually nor collectively could the ministers remonstrate against his decisions. The prime minister also became almost independent of the crown, for if it should be necessary to appoint a new head of the government, the king was now obliged to choose him from a list of candidates put together by the Great Council of the Fascist party. Thus the Fascist party became an officially recognized institution and the decisive element in Italian political life. Soon it was the only legal political party; the other parties, having become entirely impotent, were forcibly dissolved. Since the list of candidates which the voters could accept or reject was put together by the Great Council of the Fascist party, only Fascists were elected to the Chamber of Deputies. The Fascist party was carefully organized at local and provincial levels as well as nationally; all party officials were appointed, not elected. The highest authority in the party was the Great Council, consisting of about thirty members selected by Mussolini as his most loyal followers.

Mussolini was at once the prime minister—chief executive of the government—and the leader (*duce*) of the party. Through the channels of the party organization, local party officers reported to him about the efficiency and loyalty of government officials. By "supervising"—or informing on—administrative functionaries at all levels, the Fascists held a heavy club over the heads of civil servants, who soon saw the futility, if not the danger, of questioning the actions of party members. Little or nothing was done when members of the Fascist militia committed acts of violence. Terror became an instrument of rule. Many prominent political leaders of the pre-Fascist era went into exile. Some who remained in Italy were physically attacked and gravely wounded; some were imprisoned without trial, or banished to small islands in the Mediterranean or to isolated villages in the Calabrian mountains. Among the prominent political exiles were the brothers Carlo and Nello Rosselli, who in France founded a journal advocating liberal and socialist ideas. But the long arm of Mussolini reached even into France, and in 1937 the brothers Rosselli were assassinated by men hired by the Fascists.

Police supervision, reinforced by terror, was supplemented as a means of control by censorship, introduced immediately after the assassination of Matteotti. The censorship laws created so many obstacles in the way of privately owned and independent newspapers that these publications began to disappear. The owners were forced to sell them; some were taken over by the government; local papers were bought cheaply by local party officials. And censorship extended to every aspect of literature and scholarship. Writers and scholars were forced either to desist from writing on contemporary issues or to promote Fascist ideas. And the Fascists were very conscious of the importance and value of propaganda. They offered great spectacles to the masses; they embodied their doctrine in slogans, which appeared on posters all over the country; they impressed intellectuals by demonstrating interest in modern literary and artistic movements, such as Futurism; and by having the railroads run on time they showed foreigners that order had been restored.

Mussolini was aware that his regime needed support beyond what could be provided by police, terror, and propaganda. Despite the repeated assertions in his speeches that Fascism represented neither capitalism nor Marxian socialism but a new social system, Mussolini kept close to the financial and industrial leaders who had helped him into power. His famous "corporate state," which was supposed to realize the new Fascist ideas in social and economic life, actually served the purposes of the wealthier classes. According to the charter which established this corporate state, the employers and employees of each branch of industry were to form a corporation; for each corporation, committees including representatives of the employers, the employees, and the government would decide questions of wages, working hours, and the like. The decisions of the committees were to be binding, and therefore strikes were forbidden. But since only Fascist trade unions were permitted to exist, the union leaders who represented the workers in the committees followed the line set by the government representatives, who usually sided with the industrialists. The economic recovery which took place all over Europe in the 1920's caused a reduction in unemployment and disguised the fact that the workers had become powerless. Moreover, impressed by Mussolini's claim to have saved his country from Bolshevism, both Italian and foreign bankers regarded Fascist Italy as trustworthy and stable and gave loans to the Fascist government which provided additional stimulus to Italian economic life.

The respectability of the regime and its popularity among the various groups of Italian society was also increased by the reconciliation, sealed in the Lateran Treaty of February 11, 1929, of the Italian state with the Roman Catholic Church. Mussolini had initiated negotiations with the Vatican almost immediately after coming to power. In the 1929 agreement the pope was recognized as the independent ruler of a small state—Vatican City—and the Church received a large financial sum as restitution for the expropriations at the time of Italy's unification. The relations between the Church and the state were regulated by a *concordate* which declared Roman Catholicism to be the official religion of the state, permitted the pope to appoint the Italian bishops after he had received the approval of the government for his candidates, guaranteed religious education in schools, and made a religious marriage ceremony mandatory. Two days after the conclusion of the Lateran Treaty, Pope Pius XI (pope from 1922 to 1939) declared that he regarded Mussolini as "a man sent by Providence."

Reconciliation with the Church may seem a strange step for one who in earlier years had flaunted his atheism and his contempt for the Church. But with the adoption of Fascism, Mussolini had accepted the view that the politician should not be bound by a system or principles. He emphasized the novelty of Fascist ideas, but when he came to power it was by no means clear what these new Fascist ideas actually were. In later years, when attempts were made to formulate the system of Fascism, this lack of a consistent framework of thought was justified by the assertion that thought independent from action did not exist.

It has always been easier to discover what Fascism rejected than what it stood for. In their statements about Fascist concepts of politics and government, Mussolini and his adherents emphasized that Fascism stood against the individualistic and rationalistic philosophy of the French Revolution. The law of politics, like the law of nature, was struggle; continued existence required continued growth and could be achieved only through action, not thought. Nations were living, viable units in politics, and man's function was to be an instrument in the hands of his nation's leader. Having turned from socialism and internationalism to nationalism, Mussolini preached the subordination of the individual to the nation with the excessive zeal of a convert. But he was also aware that the pursuit of a strictly nationalistic policy offered the best opportunity to conceal the contradictions of a regime which claimed to be revolutionary but actually defended and maintained the *status quo*. Thus personal inclination and political calculation combined to make the conduct of a forceful foreign policy, expressive of national egotism, the cornerstone of Mussolini's rule. He set the new tone of Italian foreign policy as early as 1923, when he used the assassination of a group of Italian officers on the Greek Albanian border as pretext for an ultimatum to Greece. He demanded an indemnity of fifty million lire, an inquiry with the assistance of the Italian military attaché, ceremonial apologies, and funeral honors. When the Greeks hesitated to comply he bombarded and occupied the island of Corfu, evacuating it only after the Greeks, on the advice of the Great Powers, had given in to the Italian demands. The tangible result of Mussolini's first adventure in foreign policy was small, and could have been obtained without force. But his aim had been to show the Italians that their state was no longer ruled by a weak, timid, internationally minded government, and he used every opportunity to demonstrate that Italy had embarked on a new active course in foreign policy. Through bilateral negotiations with Yugoslavia he obtained a further change in the status of Fiume. In 1924 the town became Italian, while the rest of the free state was given to Yugoslavia. Mussolini also took some concrete steps toward expansion through the establishment of an Italian protectorate over Albania, in 1927. He always emphasized his disbelief in eternal peace and stressed that Italy must possess not only a powerful army and navy but also "an airforce that dominates the skies." He was proud to have shown with his action in the Corfu incident that Italy had freed itself from the tutelage of Great Britain and France, and—as in his negotiations with Yugoslavia —he did not shy away from asking for the support of Germany.

Mussolini disliked collective action and stabilization and wanted a fluid situation in which, by making use of the changing relations among various states, Italy could advance its own national interests. He stressed that Italy was not a satisfied nation, but "a nation hungry for land because we are prolific and intend to remain so." But in the 1920's the bark of Fascism was more threatening than its bite. Mussolini was careful to avoid moves which might lead to serious complications, such as a conflict with one of the great powers. The fateful consequences of his emphasis on action and national prestige became apparent only in the 1930's, when the Nazis had come to power in Germany and pursued an aggressive course. Then Mussolini was hoisted with his own petard. He did not want to appear less virile and martial than the Fascist leader of Germany. By then the prosperity of the 1920's had passed and Italians had begun to notice how little the Fascist regime had changed the economic and social life of their nation. The only way out, it seemed to Mussolini, was to tie the fortunes of his country to the rising power of Nazi Germany.

THE POSTWAR YEARS IN FRANCE AND GREAT BRITAIN

After the conflict over Fiume, and still more, after the Fascist seizure of power, Great Britain and France could no longer count upon Italy to join in common action to enforce the peace treaties. Great Britain and France in these years and throughout the entire interwar period were aware that in European affairs they were dependent upon each other. Nevertheless, rifts did develop in the relations between them. France entered the peace conference convinced that it had to avoid at any price a situation in which it would confront Germany alone. It had to have security, and therefore tried to obtain from the United States and Great Britain a commitment for common defense in the case of attack. When it failed to get such assurances, France next sought to weaken Germany beyond recovery, even to the extent of splitting it up. But Great Britain opposed French proposals for the dismemberment of Germany. The most the French were able to obtain was a compromise which left the final solution of the reparations question open and allowed Germany to retain the Rhineland, under the occupation of Allied troops.

Germany remained the center of friction between Great Britain and France in the following years, when the arrangements of the Treaty of Versailles—especially those about reparations and disarmament—had to be given practical shape. But tension between the British and the French extended also to other areas. Each of them wanted to prevent the other from growing in strength. The Near Eastern crisis of 1922, in which the British backed the Greeks while the French favored the Turks widened the rift. A year later the British denounced the French occupation of the Ruhr. But in 1924 close cooperation and a general European understanding was reached. These developments can only be understood in the context of the political and social situation which existed in the two countries after the war.

France

The end of the First World War was a high point in French history. Alsace-Lorraine had been regained and the defeat in the Franco-Prussian War of 1870–1871 had been revenged. The First World War had been won by Allied forces under the command of a French general, Marshall Foch. The French army was looked upon as the first army of the world. Before the First World War the German army had formed the model for the military forces of many of the smaller states, but now French officers became instructors in the newly organized states, and the officers and soldiers in these new armies wore uniforms patterned after French uniforms.

It was in recognition of the role which France had played in the war that the peace conference met in Paris. With statesmen and politicians from all over the globe assembling there, Paris could claim, at least for the duration of the conference, to be capital of the world. Through their presence in Paris men from all over the world learned that, with Marcel Proust, Paul Claudel, André Gide, and Paul Valéry, a new generation of significant French writers had emerged and that French civilization was entering a new era of greatness.

But there was a reverse side to this picture of a France radiant in the joy of victory. The nation had lost 1,320,000 military men and 250,000 civilians in the war. Because the French birthrate was low these losses would be replaced only slowly and it was evident that in the number of males of military age France would remain inferior to Germany. Moreover, for four years the northern part of the country had been a theater of war and on their retreat in 1918 the Germans had devastated much of this area in which France's most important industries were situated. French finances, like those of other belligerents, had suffered from the war. Despite foreign loans, chiefly from the United States but also from Great Britain, France had been forced to print money; by the end of the war more than five times as much money was in circulation as in 1914, and prices were three and a half times as high as they had been before the war.

It is not astonishing that a country that had suffered as much as France would expect that its material losses would be paid for by the defeated opponent—Germany. The French were not overly concerned about the hardships which such demands would cause in German economic life. Inferior to Germany in manpower and in natural resources, France advocated the use of Germany's economic resources for rebuilding the economy of the victors, a measure that would weaken Germany's competitive capacities. And if the pressure on Germany also destroyed the unity of the Reich, this was not a development which the French would regret.

A military mentality was reflected in the elections which took place in November, 1919: known as *horizon bleu* elections, after the color of French uniforms, they resulted in a great victory of the conservative *bloc national*, which obtained two thirds of the seats in the Chamber: 437 out of 613. The *cartel des gauches*, led by Édouard Herriot (1872–1957), and the Socialists lost heavily. This swing to the right was not purely the result of nationalist enthusiasm caused by victory; in France almost more than in any other country the coming to power of the Bolsheviks in Russia had aroused deep fears and hostility. The Bolshevik repudiation of the French prewar loans to Russia had provided the French bourgeoisie with some practical experience of what a revolution could involve. Alarm was reinforced by a change in the French economic system. The war had started a trend toward concentration

in industry, with large corporations overshadowing the small family enterprises characteristic of the prewar economy. The acquisition of Lorraine,
with its rich iron-ore mines, strengthened the position of heavy industry
within the industrial structure. A new social force in French political life
emerged as membership in the Confédération Générale du Travail, the
most important trade-union organization, soared from 600,000 in 1914 to
2,000,000 in 1920. In recognition of the strength of the workers the
government under Clemenceau pushed through an eight-hour day and legal
status for collective agreements before the 1919 elections. But this courting
of labor appeared dangerous to the other strata of society because, in 1919,
the French Socialist party was still in close contact with the Bolsheviks.
Only in 1920, at the Socialist congress in Tours, did the party split: the
larger group declared its adherence to the Communist International; the
smaller, under Léon Blum, remained loyal to the Second Socialist International as it had been reconstructed after the war.

In the triumphant *bloc national* the most influential leader was Raymond
Poincaré. His term as president of the republic ended in February, 1920,
but he was elected to the Senate and continued political activities. As
president he had supported Foch, who advocated separation of the Rhineland from Germany, and he had been hostile to Clemenceau because of the
latter's willingness to make concessions to the British and the United States
and to content himself with a long-term occupation of the Rhineland.
Poincaré favored the most adamant enforcement of the Treaty of Versailles.
When the negotiations about reparations dragged on, he took over as prime
minister and foreign minister, in 1922, and embarked on a policy in which
France abandoned common action with its former allies, and followed an
independent course. This policy culminated in the invasion of the Ruhr in
January, 1923. Poincaré expected that this combination of military and
economic pressure would strengthen the centrifugal forces in the Reich and
might lead to the foundation of a separate republic in the Rhineland. In
such aims, his policy was unsuccessful. The Germans were forced to give up
their passive resistance in the Ruhr and to declare their intention in
principle to resume payments and deliveries under the Versailles treaty, but
the Reich remained unified, and capitulation was followed in December,
1923, by the establishment of an international committee of experts to
examine the German economic situation and the possibilities for reparations.

With his agreement to the formation of this committee Poincaré
abandoned his policy of single-handed French action. Probably he had
underestimated the "painful impression of intransigence"—to quote from a
note to the French government by the British foreign secretary, George
Curzon—which French policy had made all over the world. Poincaré and
his adherents also had misjudged the French economic position. Recon-

struction had given a stimulus to the French economy and France had withstood relatively well the postwar depression of 1921, which had severe effects in Great Britain and the United States. But the reconstruction of the devastated areas in France was financed by extensive government credits and it was expected that these outlays would be paid for by German reparations. When German cash payments did not take place or only in much smaller amounts than had been expected, and when the occupation of the Ruhr area resulted in a considerable rise in government expenses, the inflationary tendency which was part of the legacy of the war was reinforced. In 1914, 5.2 francs would buy a dollar, but 16.5 francs were required in 1923, 18.5 francs in 1925, and 26.5 francs in 1926. Although the loss in the value was moderate, the psychological impact on the French bourgeoisie who had suffered greatly through the default of the Russian loans was very strong. This was probably the decisive factor in forcing Poincaré back into a policy of cooperation; a great change in French public opinion certainly had taken place. In the elections of the year following the Ruhr occupation the *cartel des gauches* won: Poincaré resigned. The new prime minister was Herriot, and the foreign minister in the government of the left was Aristide Briand (1862–1932).

Briand remained foreign minister from 1925 to 1932. The early years of his political career, when he had been feared as a radical for his role in effecting the separation of church and state, were far behind him. He had subsequently served in many French cabinets, as minister of education, minister of justice, and prime minister. As prime minister during the German offensive against Verdun, Briand had experienced the horrors of this battle and his interests in the postwar years turned toward foreign affairs and the problems of peace. Briand was no less convinced than his predecessors that France needed guaranties against attack, but he hoped to achieve them through agreements and alliances embedded in a system of collective security which would automatically align the members of the League of Nations against any aggressor. Briand was a great orator and his speeches, always high points at meetings of the League of Nations in Geneva, created a great deal of international good will for France. Nevertheless, the acceptance of his foreign policy in France represented a resigned acknowledgment of the limitations of French power. Despite victory in war, and despite possession of the greatest European army, France was not able to go it alone in foreign policy during the postwar years.

Great Britain

Although Great Britain came to advocate a more lenient treatment of Germany than France, the British people did not have any sympathy for the Germans at the end of the war. Indeed, the hatred had grown so strong that it took years before personal contacts between the British and German

Aristide Briand. *The French foreign minister delivers a speech during the great days of the League of Nations.*

people were resumed. The elections which took place in December 1918, and in which for the first time women were entitled to vote, were known as khaki elections, for the campaign and the voting both reflected the spirit of the khaki-clad soldier. In the campaign, the government promised to prosecute William II and all those Germans responsible for war atrocities and to make Germany pay the entire costs of war. With Lloyd George, the prime minister, assuring the people that he would "exact the last penny we can get out of Germany up to the limit of her capacity," the government gained an overwhelming victory, winning 478 seats while the opposition secured only 87. The government was a coalition of Conservatives (still called Unionists) and of Liberal adherents of Lloyd George and reflected the nationalist mood of this period in that the Conservatives, with 335 seats, were much stronger than their Liberal coalition partners.

Nevertheless, in Great Britain the expectations for the postwar world were different from those in France. The French had achieved concrete gains, such as the recovery of Alsace-Lorraine, and nurtured concrete aims, notably liberation from the incubus of German superiority and aggression. The British had much vaguer notions. They expected a peaceful world and a better life for all the people in the British Isles. The idea of a new order in international affairs went hand in hand with demands for reform in domestic life. The crucial importance of making the postwar world an era of social reforms was reflected in the address of the king at the opening of the postwar Parliament: "The aspirations for a better social order which have been quickened in the hearts of My people by the experience of the war must be encouraged by prompt and comprehensive action. . . .since the outbreak of the war every party and every class have worked and fought together for a great ideal . . . we must continue to manifest the same spirit. We must stop at no sacrifice of interest or prestige to stamp out unmerited poverty, to diminish unemployment, to provide decent homes, to improve the nation's health, and to raise the standard of well-being throughout the country." And these notions were underlined by Lloyd George in a speech in the House of Commons in February, 1919, in which he stated that there was no member in the House who was not pledged to the cause of social reform. "If we fail, history will condemn not merely the perfidy but the egregious folly of such failure."

The war effort had involved all classes of British society, and those who had participated in the war now expected fulfillment of their needs in peacetime. The government had given women of thirty and over the right to vote, and extended the male suffrage by removing property qualifications. But its record in instituting social reforms was unsatisfactory, despite such steps as the extension of unemployment insurance to almost all workers earning less than five pounds a week. The most important issue in postwar Britain was housing. Building had stopped during the war years, and it was estimated that at least 300,000 new houses were needed within one year after the war. But two years later the housing policy of the government had produced only 14,594 new houses, and when in 1923 budgetary cutbacks ended government subsidies for home construction, the shortage of houses was even worse than it had been in 1918. Slums remained an indelible and spreading blot on English industrial centers.

The disappointment of the expectations which victory and the promises of the government had aroused raised questions also about the past. It transformed enthusiasm for the wartime statesmen into doubts and criticism and aroused skepticism about the policy pursued toward Germany.

The failure to achieve social reform was partly a failure of the government, but also due in part to circumstances beyond its control. For one thing, the government was made up of prima donnas. Besides Lloyd George, who had acquired immense authority because of his war leadership, there were such formidable figures as the former prime minister Arthur Balfour, Alfred Milner of South African fame, and George Curzon, a former viceroy of India. Also included were the stars of a younger generation, among them the arrogant and witty F. E. Smith (later earl of Birkenhead),

Winston Churchill, and Austen Chamberlain, Joseph Chamberlain's son and political heir. These and other leaders seemed more interested in maneuvering against one another for public favor than in carrying out a unified policy. Their ambitions and intrigues were fed by the press, particularly by the newspapers belonging to the press "Lords"—Northcliffe, Rothermere, Beaverbrook—who themselves were eager for a political role.

As a coalition of Conservatives and Liberals the government was beset by conflicting principals whenever it strove to establish a definite line of policy. The old conflict about free trade revived with the Liberals eager to maintain an open trade policy and the Conservatives favoring preferential tariffs for the members of the British empire. There was also a conflict over the maintenance of government control over economic life within Great Britain. Without the possibility of some such control, the Liberals' demands for an active policy of social reforms could not be carried out. The Conservatives, however, used their strength in the House of Commons to force Lloyd George to abolish the economic restrictions and regulations introduced during wartime.

Other problems confronted the government as well. The turmoil which the war had raised did not easily subside; instead, unrest was widespread through the British empire. The peace conference, the question of the intervention in Russia, the struggle in the Near East absorbed much of the attention of British statesmen. Closer to home, a settlement of the Irish question, which had disturbed British political life for almost a century, could no longer be postponed. During the war the government had hesitated to take energetic steps toward the introduction of home rule in Ireland, and the result had been a rebellion at Easter time in 1916. It was quickly defeated, but the ruthlessness of its suppression destroyed the influence of the moderates in Ireland. The dominating force in Irish policy now became the Sinn Fein; the name, which means "we ourselves," indicated that the goal of this group was complete independence. The Sinn Fein engaged in guerilla warfare; British officers were attacked, manor houses belonging to those opposed to independence were burned, banks were robbed. To replace Irishmen who had resigned, the police force was strengthened by recruits from England, derisively called the Black and Tans, after the colors of their uniform. Their brutality aroused indignation even in England.

The Conservatives believed that dealings with the Sinn Fein should start only after the Black and Tans had reestablished order. But the Liberals wanted to enter upon negotiations immediately, and their view prevailed. In December, 1921, a treaty was signed which divided Ireland into a northern part, Ulster, which remained within the United Kingdom, and a southern part, the Irish Free State, with dominion status. Some members of the Sinn Fein, led by Eamon de Valera (born 1882), were not content with this arrangement; they fought bitterly against the moderate Irish government, and finally attained power. In 1937, they succeeded in gaining complete independence for the Irish Free State.

The most serious blow to all plans of social reform was an economic depression that engulfed Britain in 1921. The pent-up demand for goods that had not been available during the war had resulted in a boom which soon led to overexpansion and overspeculation. In consequence, a great rise in prices immediately after the war was suddenly followed by a decline, which led to a shrinking of production and a diminution of buying power. In 1921 British exports to France fell by 65.2 per cent and to the United States by 42.6 per cent from the previous year's level. Altogether, British exports in 1921 were less than half of what they had been in 1920. The nadir of this depression was reached in June, 1921, with 23.1 per cent (2,185,000) of Britain's workers unemployed. The full extent of this misery was not reflected in this figure, however. Certain industries suffered more than others and in some localities unemployment climbed to 40 or 50 per cent of the labor force. After 1922 the situation improved, but not until the outbreak of the Second World War did the number of unemployed in Britain drop below a million. One of the permanent features in British economic life became the "dole," the benefits which the unemployed received under the Unemployment Insurance Act. They were strictly limited to two periods of sixteen weeks each and were paid only to those who proved to be in need. Unemployment and the dole seemed strange compensation for the hardships and sacrifices of a victorious war.

The 1920's in Great Britain became a time of disillusionment. The most flamboyant of the war leaders lost much of their appeal. Winston Churchill had to struggle hard to maintain his place in politics. Lloyd George aroused the greatest distrust. In 1922, in a famous speech in the Carleton Club, the very heart of the Conservative party, Stanley Baldwin, then president of the Board of Trade, said of Lloyd George that he was "a great dynamic force" but that a dynamic force could be a "a very terrible thing." After the Conservatives then voted against continuation of the coalition, Lloyd George never returned to a position in the government.

The view that no victory could compensate for the losses and damages of war became widespread. Pacifist organizations proliferated. Expenditure for the armed forces became unpopular. The government required the military services to base their budget estimates on the assumption that "the British Empire will not be engaged in any general war during the next ten years and that no expeditionary force will be required." Disarmament was regarded as the panacea.

The country which profited most from this change of view was Germany. It was believed that wartime propaganda had painted an exaggerated and false picture of Germany. Back in 1919 Keynes's *Economic Consequences of the Peace* had opened the attack upon the peace settlement, and now German demands for revision of the Treaty of Versailles began to find a hearing in Great Britain.

Because so many young men had been lost in the war, the older men remained in power much longer than their counterparts in the prewar days. It seemed impossible to make a dent in their closed ranks. Viewing the traditions and customs of political life with disgust young men turned away from politics. Rejection of accepted forms and values became characteristic of the most gifted writers and artists of the new generation. The great literary monument of the disillusionment and desperation of the postwar world in England was T. S. Eliot's *The Wasteland* (1922).

The abandonment, in pursuit of victory, of attitudes deeply rooted in liberal beliefs, and the disillusionment of the postwar era, aroused skepticism toward the traditions and the achievements of the past, and this changed political mood played a role in what, from the point of view of political history, might be regarded as the most striking event in the years after the war: the rise of the Labor party. In 1914 the replacement of the Liberal party by the Labor party would have been regarded as most improbable. The war had favored the chances of the Labor party. With the ousting of Asquith as prime minister in 1916, and his replacement by the dynamic Lloyd George, the Liberal party had been split into two hostile groups. Moreover, the war had strengthened the power of the Labor party. The shift of industries to war production, and the need for using all available manpower, required cooperation of the government with trade unions. Their power and therefore also their appeal had increased. By 1919 the membership of the trade unions had almost doubled, and amounted to more than eight million. In order to assure the support of the workers, two leading figures in the Labor party, Arthur Henderson and John Robert Clynes, had entered the war government and their activities disproved the thesis that Labor leaders were wild radicals who could not be entrusted with government responsibility. On the other hand, the kind of opposition to the war which had existed in the Liberal party in 1914 continued to dominate the thinking of some groups in the Labor party. Most prominent among the opponents of the war was Ramsay MacDonald (1866–1937).

An intellectual who looked like a peer of the realm, MacDonald was rather removed from the down-to-earth trade-union leaders who dominated the party organization. But MacDonald showed remarkable courage during the war, struggling against the tide of national hysteria and sponsoring meetings at which conscientious objectors expressed their pacifist views. MacDonald argued eloquently that the war would have meaning only if it was the beginning of a changed and better world. In 1917, he greeted the Russian Revolution as an inspiration for labor movements all over the globe and advocated the formation of workers' and soldiers' councils in Britain.

In the disillusionment of the postwar years Labor benefited from the fact that, in contrast to the Conservatives and Liberals, it represented the possibility of change and, at the same time, the war seemed to have proved that Labor was able to govern. This worked to Labor's advantage in the elections which were held in December, 1923. The coalition government under Lloyd George had been succeeded by a Conservative government, headed first by Bonar Law (1858–1923) and then by Stanley Baldwin (1867–1947). Baldwin decided on new elections in order to get a mandate for the realization of the old Conservative demand for protective tariffs, which he believed would alleviate unemployment. In the elections the Conservatives remained the strongest party, but they lost their majority. The Liberals and Labor combined had more votes than the Conservatives, and since Labor held more seats than the Liberals, Ramsay MacDonald was asked by King George V to form the government. Because this first Labor government lacked a majority and needed the support of the Liberals, its potential for action was strictly limited, and its accomplishments were meager. A housing act, providing state subsidies for the building of houses with controlled rents, was the main domestic achievement. In foreign affairs, the government established diplomatic relations with Soviet Russia and promptly signed a commercial treaty with the Russians. Storms of protest greeted these moves. On a minor issue—the somewhat questionable dropping of the prosecution of a Communist journalist—the Liberals voted against the government, and in the elections which followed, Labor was defeated. This loss was chiefly due to anti-Communist hysteria. The middle classes, who had been upset by MacDonald's negotiations with Soviet Russia, were turned decisively against Labor by the publication during the election campaign of a letter allegedly written by Zinoviev, the head of the Communist International, outlining a strategy for revolution in England. Although a clever falsification, the letter did compromise the Labor party. The Labor government lasted only ten months, but its tenure, though short, established Labor as the alternative to the Conservatives. Moreover, although Labor's domestic record had been unexciting, it could claim that in foreign affairs its rule had been an undisputed success—a success which had to be primarily attributed to Ramsay MacDonald. MacDonald had been foreign secretary as well as prime minister, and it was while he was foreign secretary that agreement on the reparations question was achieved.

When Labor came to power a committee of experts was examining the reparations question but it was still not settled whether the states involved, and particularly France, would consider the result of the committee's deliberations as binding on them. In a letter to Poincaré in February, 1924, MacDonald made a statement almost undiplomatic in its frankness: "It is widely felt in England that, contrary to the provisions of the Treaty of Versailles, France is endeavoring to create a situation which gains for it

The first British Labor government. *In the middle of the first row, Ramsay MacDonald; in the last row on the extreme left, Lord Passfield, the former Sidney Webb.*

what it failed to get during the allied peace negotiations. . . . The people in this country regard with anxiety what appears to them to be the determination of France to ruin Germany and to dominate the continent without consideration of our reasonable interests and future consequences to European settlement." MacDonald clearly implied that England expected France to accept the report of the experts, and was not willing to bargain about this. The French people could have little doubt about the dangerous consequences of British hostility for French economic life in times of rising inflationary pressure. Fortunately for MacDonald, Herriot and the *cartel des gauches* came into power in May, 1924, and the new government participated in a conference in London over which MacDonald presided. The report of the committee of experts formed the basis for an agreement on reparations which was signed on August 31 by all powers concerned.

The policy of MacDonald was not very different from that of the Conservative foreign secretaries who preceded and followed him. But Labor and Conservatives arrived at the same policy from somewhat different points of departure. MacDonald's approach was idealistic. He had been an opponent of the war and he wanted to liquidate the consequences of the war as quickly and as thoroughly as possible as a prerequisite for the building of a peaceful international order. The Conservatives were more realistic. They were concerned about the deterioration and the difficulties of the British economic situation, and they regarded an improvement of the economic conditions in central Europe as necessary for Britain's own recovery. These considerations were particularly powerful among the Conservatives, who had become a party of businessmen. Moreover, financial circles in the United States which had been exerting a great influence on British economic policy since the war, were demanding a settlement of the reparations question. In the first months of 1923 Stanley Baldwin, then chancellor of the exchequer, had negotiated an agreement with the American government on the repayment of the loans which Britain had received from the United States during the war. Officially the American government maintained that there was no connection between German reparations and the repayment of war loans given to the Allies. But it was evident that the European states would not repay their war debts until they received reparations from Germany. Thus, a settlement of the reparations question which would allow an economic recovery of Europe was in the American interest, and became a common goal of the two English-speaking countries. American financial circles were willing to assume a positive role. They participated in the committee of experts, which was chaired by an American, Charles Dawes, and they were ready to make the proposals of the report work by giving a loan. It was this active interest and assistance which gave Europe the possibility of a breathing space.

THE ERA OF EUROPEAN STABILIZATION, 1925–1929

An era of political stabilization was achieved in Europe through two closely connected events. One was the attainment of agreement on reparations in the Dawes Plan; the other was the conclusion of a political agreement among the principal European powers, embodied in the Locarno treaties, arranged in Locarno, Switzerland, in October, 1925, and signed in London on December 1, 1925.

After abandoning passive resistance in the Ruhr, Germany stabilized its currency by introducing a new basic unit, the *Rentenmark*, equivalent to a trillion of the old marks. This was an operation on paper, purely an elimination of a number of zeros. It assumed some reality because Hjalmar Schacht, president of the German Reichsbank since December, 1923, managed to obtain credits from British banks and a loan from Montagu Norman, the governor of the Bank of England. On the other hand he started a strictly deflationary policy by refusing to give any further credits to the German government or to German economic enterprises. The printing of money had ended. However, renewed pressure for reparations payments would have restored the inflationary trend if the stabilization of the German currency had not been complemented by the acceptance of the Dawes Plan.

The Dawes Plan fixed the German reparations payments for the next five years; the installments were then gradually to increase as Germany's economy recovered with the aid of a large foreign loan. An American commissioner was to make certain that Germany paid to the limits of its capacity. He was to control the remittance of reparations and to establish the transfer of payments in gold. It would be in his power to exert a far-reaching influence on German economic life, for he would supervise the policy of the Reichsbank and the financial administration of the railroads, as well as other state-run enterprises. The presence of this commissioner assured the Germans of a hearing if the payments envisaged in the Dawes Plan went beyond their capacity. Furthermore, the existence of the accompanying foreign loan meant that the financial interests of other nations were connected with German economic recovery and prosperity.

John Maynard Keynes (1883–1946) described the reparations settlement as follows: "Reparations and interallied debts are being mostly settled on paper and not in goods. The United States lends money to Germany, Germany transfers its equivalent to the allies, the allies pass it back to the United States government. Nothing real passes—no one is a pennyworse." In this brilliant satirical summary Keynes did not mention one issue which in the following years would become highly important. The loans had to be repaid with interest and the Germans had to earn this interest through exports. Because German wages had been low since the end of the war, and because the world economy was again expanding, after the economic nadir of 1921, the earnings of German exports were sufficient to pay the scheduled amount of reparations and the interest on the loans. The system functioned for a number of years, but it ran into trouble when the requisite combination of low German wages and world prosperity began to disappear.

With the establishment of international interest in the economic recovery of Germany it became important for the victors of the First World War to tie Germany also to the political settlement made at the Paris Peace Conference. To the Germans this meant a chance to regain a place among the great powers. These were the considerations which underlay the arrangements made at Locarno. The most important of them was a treaty concluded by Great Britain, Germany, France, Belgium, and Italy. Germany recognized that its western frontier, as defined in the Treaty of Versailles, was permanent. If there occurred an "unprovoked attack" by Germany against France or by France against Germany, the victim would be helped by Great Britain and Italy; especially noteworthy was the stipulation that not only a violation of the frontiers but also a "flagrant violation" of the demilitarization of the Rhineland was regarded as an act of aggression. This stipulation became important after the occupation of the Rhineland had ended in 1930, for six years later, when German troops marched into the Rhineland, the expressions "flagrant violation" and "unprovoked attack" became loopholes through which remilitarization of the

Rhineland was condoned. Although nobody could deny that the Germans had broken the Locarno treaties, it was argued that this violation was neither "flagrant" nor "unprovoked." But in 1925 the general opinion was that the frontiers between Germany, France, and Belgium—and the permanent demilitarization of the Rhineland—were now recognized as final.

This treaty, the core of the Locarno arrangements, was complemented by a number of other agreements. Treaties concluded by Germany with France, Belgium, Poland, and Czechoslovakia established that all disputes which could not be resolved by diplomatic negotiations would be submitted to arbitration. Moreover, agreements between France and Poland and France and Czechoslovakia determined that if Germany refused arbitration, these states would assist one another against Germany, by force of arms, if necessary. Finally, Germany was to be admitted to the League of Nations and receive a permanent seat on the Council of the League. Germany declared, however, if the League imposed military sanctions on some state, Germany's participation would be limited by its military and geographical situation, because military clauses of the Treaty of Versailles had left the country too weak to join in military actions. Practically, this meant that Germany would not have to participate in military action against Soviet Russia.

To what extent did the Locarno agreements change the existing political situation, and to whose advantage were they? The admission to the League of Nations and the acquisition of a permanent seat on the Council meant that Germany was again recognized as an equal of other nations and as a great European power. For the Germans, abandonment of the claims to Alsace-Lorraine on their western frontier and the acknowledgment of restrictions on the exercise of sovereignty in the Rhineland were painful. However, there was no comparable acceptance of the permanence of the eastern borders; Germany abjured the use of force for revising these frontiers, but was not prevented from urging such revision. Moreover, Germany was able to maintain its special relationship with Russia, which had been established in 1922 with the Treaty of Rapallo; in April, 1926, in the Treaty of Berlin the two states confirmed the Treaty of Rapallo. Germany had not opted between east and west. It certainly was in no worse a bargaining position than before, perhaps in a better one.

France also had not lost. Ever since the end of the First World War, France had been insisting that its security demanded a firm alliance with the United States and Great Britain against Germany. Now it had finally obtained assurances of aid from Great Britain. To be sure, the Locarno treaty was not a special Franco-British alliance, just a guarantee of the existing frontiers of both France and Germany. But since nobody expected France to want to change the frontiers, it actually amounted to a promise of British support in case of a German attack. France would have liked a

similar guarantee of the eastern frontiers of Germany. But the demilitarization of the Rhineland, coupled with France's military alliances with Poland
and Czechoslovakia, had left Germany militarily powerless, unable to
expand either to the east or to the west. Thus the Locarno treaties did not
weaken the French position. If anything, they reinforced French military
security.

For both France and Germany two ways were open. They could regard
the Locarno arrangements as a new departure, the beginning of a cooperation which slowly and gradually might remove distrust and create a
European community. Or they could fall back into antagonistic positions,
their relative strength neither weakened nor increased.

The Locarno agreements were bitterly criticized in Germany and France.
Briand and Stresemann, the foreign ministers who had concluded them,
were accused of having abandoned essential national interests. Each of these
men trusted the other and was convinced of the other's good will. But each
had to demonstrate to his people that the treaties had advantages for their
nation. To bring about a gradual recognition of these advantages, much
could be done by Great Britain. If Britain cautiously balanced France
against Germany and Germany against France by opposing every resurrec-
tion of German military power and every French attempt to use its military
strength for keeping Germany economically weak, it might help to bring
the old antagonists together. For a number of years Britain did indeed
follow this course.

When the Locarno treaties were signed in London the portrait of
Castlereagh was brought down from an attic in the British foreign office and
hung in the room in which the solemn ceremony took place. The gesture
was appropriate. Castlereagh had been banished to the attic because during
the period of Britain's splendid isolation his policy of cooperation with the
great European powers had seemed contradictory to the British tradition.
But his aim of maintaining peace and stability in Europe by a diplomacy
based upon conferences with the continent's leading statesmen appeared
very similar to the policy which Austen Chamberlain, the British foreign
secretary, was now pursuing. Indeed, the effect of the Locarno agreements
was not limited to the mitigation of tensions between Germany and France.
Their main effect was to reestablish a concert of the great European powers
thereby restoring some order within Europe and extending the influence of
the European powers through the entire world.

Mussolini was well aware of this development; Italy had kept back from
the discussions preceding the Locarno agreements, but Mussolini had
appeared in person when the success of the negotiations was assured. He
realized that their result would be the creation of a kind of ruling group
among the European powers and he wanted to demonstrate that Italy
belonged to this group. The concert of powers which the Locarno agree-

ments established was less extended and less comprehensive than the nineteenth-century Concert of Europe had been. Spain was no longer counted among the great powers, Austria-Hungary no longer existed, and Russia was excluded. Moreover, the global influence of the new European concert depended on cooperation with non-European states, such as the United States. Nevertheless, in the years following the Locarno agreements Europe again played the decisive role in world politics. Officially the League of Nations was supposed to be the center of international decision making; but the three statesmen who had concluded the Locarno agreements—Briand, Chamberlain, and Stresemann—usually held preparatory discussions in which they agreed on a common line, and this was then generally accepted by the other members of the League. Even the Russians realized that the time of revolutionary upheavals was over; they made agreements with their neighbors—Poland, Rumania, Estonia, and Latvia—in which they rejected war, and they participated in a general pact renouncing the use of war which had resulted from negotiations between France and the United States—the Kellogg-Briand Pact (1928). In this relaxed atmosphere preparations for a conference on general disarmament went happily ahead.

Nevertheless, the sky was not without clouds. The Kellogg-Briand Pact did not provide for sanctions, if, in violation of the pact, a power resorted to war. Nor did it exclude wars undertaken in self-defense. A conference held in Geneva in 1927 to arrange further naval disarmament failed. Great Britain recognized Soviet Russia in 1924, but the commercial treaties following this diplomatic recognition were soon abrogated because of strong resentment aroused by Communist agitation in Britain. Finally, Franco-German relations remained precarious. The Germans demanded modification of the Dawes Plan. They stepped up their campaign to free themselves from the restrictions of the Treaty of Versailles by publicly repudiating the war-guilt clause and by building pocket battleships. The French, alarmed by Germany's quick recovery, were reluctant to consent to revision of the Dawes Plan and tried to delay the evacuation of the Rhineland. Nevertheless, between 1925 and 1930 such tensions seemed to be the unpleasant aftereffects of the upheavals caused by the First World War rather than signs of the beginning of a new period of political tension.

THE WORLD ECONOMIC CRISIS

The relative stability achieved after 1925 was soon shattered by a world economic crisis. As the 1920's passed, people had gradually become confident that the wounds left by the First World War could be healed, that the prosperity of the years before 1914 would again be reached, and that the march toward progress which the war had interrupted could be resumed. The economic crisis destroyed these expectations and hopes; the prewar world now appeared irretrievably lost, and many were convinced that the new course of events was leading inexorably downhill and would end in a holocaust more dangerous and devastating for the continuity of European life than the First World War had been. Thus the decade of the 1930's was a period full of anxiety and insecurity. A full recovery from the world economic crisis had still not occurred when the Second World War broke out in 1939.

The really acute phase of the economic breakdown lasted from 1929 to 1933; before its underlying causes are discussed, it might be well to recapitulate the dramatic events of these years. The actual beginning of the crisis was the collapse of the New York Stock Exchange under a wave of speculation in the last week of October, 1929, although some danger signs pointing to a decline in production had appeared earlier. In Europe the high point of the crisis occurred in the summer of 1931. In May, 1931, the most important Austrian bank, the *Kreditanstalt*, which was controlled by the Rothschilds, declared itself unable to fulfill its obligations. This failure shook confidence in the solvency of banks in Germany; there was an accelerated recall of money from them, and the main German banks soon found themselves insolvent and were forced to close. They were able to reopen only with the help of a government guarantee. In this critical economic situation the payment of international debts was clearly impossible, and the American president Herbert Hoover (1874–1964) suggested a one-year moratorium on reparations and war debts; after tedious negotiations, this was agreed upon in August. But the moratorium came too late to remedy the British financial situation, which had been seriously impaired by the economic collapse in central Europe. On September 21, 1931, Britain abandoned the gold standard; this event seemed to mark the end of an epoch, for hitherto the pound had enjoyed the reputation of being as good as gold. In the next years the level of economic activity remained low, although from 1934 on, slowly and gradually recovery began, especially in the industrial countries. Agricultural prices remained depressed, and the Balkan states, which were dependent on the export of agricultural products, continued to suffer severely. Moreover, France, which at the outset had seemed unaffected by the crisis, began to experience economic difficulties in 1933, and the French recession played its part in retarding recovery in the rest of Europe.

To understand the nature of this economic catastrophe—its severity, length, and spread—one must realize that two factors were at work. First, there was the decline in production, which led to a decrease in trade and created unemployment; second, there was the financial crisis.

The decline in production set in from what was a rather low plateau, for after the First World War production had remained sluggish. By 1929 the prewar level had indeed been reached, but the rate of economic growth ought to have been much larger to meet the needs of an increased population. Moreover, the European share in world trade was smaller than it had been in 1914, as European nations faced competition from the rising economies of the non-European nations. To the diminished share of Europe in non-European markets the elimination of Russia from the world economic system must be added as a further restricting and damaging factor. There was an economic boom in the second part of the 1920's, but it was built on a narrow base and lacked strength to resist any serious blow.

Even before 1929 falling prices for agricultural goods indicated the onset of an unfavorable economic trend. This decline in prices immediately affected the peasant countries of southeastern Europe—especially Rumania, Bulgaria, and Yugoslavia, where—by tradition or as a result of agrarian reforms after the war—small farms with rather high production costs were the prevailing form of land ownership. For the farmers of these countries the falling agricultural prices made competition on the European market outside the Balkans impossible. Even within these Balkan states the price of wheat fell by almost half. Since the prices of industrial goods did not decline to the same degree, the people of these countries were caught in a disparity between industrial and agricultural prices—a "price scissor"—and they were unable to purchase manufactured goods from industrial countries. Hence a shrinking of industrial production throughout Europe took place, and it was aggravated by the widespread introduction of protective measures against foreign goods, by which each country tried to defend its own industries at the expense of all others.

This crisis in production took an extraordinary and dramatic form because its difficulties were compounded by a financial crisis. Its center was Wall Street, where in 1929 a speculative boom ended in a stock-market crash which ushered in a long depression. The American economic collapse had its immediate repercussions in Europe, particularly in Germany. American loans had been granted not only to the German government for the settlement of reparations but also to many private and semipublic enterprises within Germany—industrial companies, public utilities, and municipal governments. Foreign capital had been drawn into Germany by high interest rates, which the German economy had been able to sustain because labor costs were relatively low. With the stock-market crash the influx of American money ended and American banks demanded the repayment of loans as soon as they became due. In a time of shrinking production and declining prices the abrupt withdrawal of American loans was a severe blow to the German economy; the situation was particularly critical because German businessmen, relying on the continuous availability of American capital, had used money borrowed on short terms for long-term investments. Despite the warnings of men like Schacht, the president of the

The Depression. *Workers' living quarters in northern France.*

Reichsbank, against this unsound practice, neither German businessmen nor foreign bankers had been able to resist the allure of easy gains.

With the withdrawal of American money from the German economy the liquid reserves of German banks and businesses came under steadily increasing pressure. In addition, because loans from abroad had to be repaid in foreign currency, the withdrawal endangered the German currency by absorbing the gold reserves of the Reichsbank; by 1931 they amounted to only 10 per cent of what they had been before the onset of the crisis. These developments reached their culmination in the summer of 1931 when the German public, becoming aware of the catastrophic financial situation, started a run on the banks. Because Germany had been the center for the investment of foreign money, the difficulties of the German banks meant great losses for the banks of other countries, particularly Great Britain and the United States. The result was a general restriction of credit, with capital for investments difficult or even impossible to obtain. The consequent lack of new investments prolonged the depression and slowed down recovery.

At this time the view of Keynes that in periods of depression new money ought to be pumped into the economy was regarded as a dangerous heresy by almost all economists. A deflationary policy marked by a balanced budget, with expenses limited to the absolute minimum, was the economists' prescription for the handling of both public and private finances in times of crisis; it was not realized that unemployment reinforced the depression because people without money could not buy goods. The generally sluggish economic development of the 1920's had created pockets of unemployment all over Europe; with the depression the numbers of unemployed increased rapidly. In Great Britain almost three million were jobless in 1931; in Germany at the beginning of 1933 industrial production was half of what it had been in 1929, while there were three times as many—six million—unemployed.

The economic crisis was a turning point in the interwar years because it changed the political climate and the political constellation in Europe. Even when economic life became less turbulent, there was no return to the situation which had existed before 1929.

With the end of the First World War the deep chasm, which before 1914 separated the workers from the ruling classes and the proponents of international socialism from the adherents of national states, seemed closed. The workers had supported their governments during the war and in acknowledgment of this show of willingness to recognize the value of the national state, the political rights of the masses had been extended: the lowering of the voting age, suffrage for women, elimination of property qualifications, proportional representation—some, or all, of these measures had been adopted in every state of western and central Europe after the war. Almost all the demands for political democratization which radicals had raised before the war were fulfilled.

With the struggle for political democratization eliminated as a major concern, the problem of reconciling the economic interests of all classes of society came to the forefront. In this area too the war seemed to have opened new perspectives. The socialists had lost some of their enthusiasm for revolution—partly because they rejected violently the theories and actions of the leftist radicals who had come to power in Russia, partly because the introduction of economic controls and regulations by the various governments during the war had demonstrated that the change from a free economy to a controlled and planned economy could be obtained within the existing system. Correspondingly, the members of the bourgeoisie had become aware during the war of the beneficial consequences of smooth collaboration with the workers, and they were frightened by the specter of the Russian Revolution, which seemed to show what might happen if the workers were driven to desperation. Hence the socialists and the bourgeoisie were willing to take some steps to meet each other. It was acknowledged that the workers were entitled to such concessions as the eight-hour day, increased unemployment benefits, recognition of the right to strike, and the establishment of the closed shop, which made trade unions the only legitimate representatives of the workers in the factories. In exchange, the socialists toned down their revolutionary propaganda, emphasized the possibility of achieving their aims by democratic means, accepted some arbitration machinery in labor disputes, and acknowledged the need for the maintenance of national armed forces until disarmament was achieved.

This period of compromise was short-lived. The economic crisis reopened the gap between the classes. With governments drafting budgets in which, to save money, unemployment benefits were cut, and with industrial enterprises dismissing workers ruthlessly, the hope of achieving socialist goals through a gradual transformation of the capitalist system appeared increasingly illusory. There was a renewed trend toward revolutionary radicalism. At the same time industrial entrepreneurs tended to become more antilabor, regarding the trade unions as obstacles to retrenchment by means of lower wages and a reduced labor force. Reactionary and authoritarian notions received new impetus, and their resurgence was accompanied by a revival of nationalism. In the grim climate of depression each government thought first of its own people and introduced measures of economic protection to fend off foreign competition. Concessions to other nations were condemned as signs of weakness.

Two areas of the European scene were particularly affected by intensified nationalist attitudes. In the Balkans hostilities among the various states sharpened and the exhortations of the greater powers for cooperation and toleration were no longer heeded, especially since they were no longer reinforced by loans. The French influence which had been predominant in this area lost ground and Italian and German influence increased. But tension also became more acute among the great powers of western Europe. Because the economic crisis had left Great Britain too weak to exert the role of intermediary and arbiter which it had assumed in the Locarno agreements, the resurgence of Franco-German hostility was almost unavoidable.

Thus all over Europe the economic crisis awakened and strengthened extremist tendencies on the left and on the right, and undermined the moderate center which clung to the ideals of democracy.

To understand the events of the 1930's, however, one must go beyond the effects of the economic crisis on the development of party politics. The entire political climate of the 1930's was different from that of the 1920's. One might say that only during the depression years did the full consequences of the shock represented by the First World War come to the surface. In large part this shock resulted from the collapse of assumptions once taken for granted. Before 1914 the steady progress of civilization had seemed assured, and the general principles of European morality were spread and accepted in widening areas of the world. The experience of the war, in which men ruthlessly attempted to create the most efficient machinery of death and destruction and to apply it against whole nations, disregarding conventions and morality when they stood in the way of national victory, could not easily be reconciled with the old principles, which with the return of peace were again proclaimed to be the acknowledged forms of civilized existence. Moreover, the young men who had been thrown straight from school into the conflict had learned that they had instincts and powers which the world of their parents seemed to have suppressed and which found no fulfillment or expression in the pattern of life to which their parents wished them to conform. It is no accident that after the war Lytton Strachey revealed the concealed hypocrisy of the Victorian age, that Freud's theories of repression and of the strength of the unconscious permeated art and literature, and that the views of Nietzsche, with his attack against conventional morality and his appeal to the new ethics of the Superman became a reigning philosophy. Nevertheless, in the period just after the coming of peace, the belief that the postwar years provided a chance for building a new and better democratic world prevailed over the mood whose essence was rejection of historical values and traditions. But when in the 1930's the disillusionment of the postwar world was combined with the miseries of the depression, it became much more difficult to deny the voices of those who preached that the forces which the experiences of the war had revealed—violence, ruthlessness, the drive for power—were the truly effective factors in society. In social and political life the use of war and warlike weapons seemed possible and permissible. With the strength of a delayed effect, the shock administered by the experiences of the First World War transformed the psychological approach to politics and social life.

This change in the European climate helps to explain a surprising and shocking development. Not much more than ten years after Great Britain and France had completed the arrangements which were meant to establish them safely as leaders of a democratic Europe, these two powers were in retreat; initiative had devolved to antidemocratic powers.

THE RISE OF NAZISM

The emergence of the Nazis in Germany signifies the great change which took place between the 1920's and the 1930's in Europe. This development received a decisive impetus from the economic crisis, but the economic crisis was certainly not the only—and perhaps not even the most important—cause for the rise of Nazism. To a large extent Nazism was an inner German phenomenon, reviving old political attitudes which had been dominant in imperial Germany: authoritarianism and nationalism.

Decline of Parliamentary Government in the Weimar Republic

As we have seen, the leaders of the Weimar Republic had felt constrained to retain the monarchical civil servants, antagonistic to parliamentarism and democracy, and to rely on an equally authoritarian officer corps which despised pacifism and internationalism. Thus a strongly antirepublican and antidemocratic influence emanated from men holding key positions in the republic. Furthermore, the popular support which the republic possessed at the outset was soon whittled down under the impact of the Treaty of Versailles.

Along with the Communists on the extreme left and some small parties on the extreme right there were five important political parties in Germany during the 1920's: three republican—the Social Democratic party, the Democratic party, and the Catholic Center party—and two monarchist—the German People's party and the German Nationalist party. The tenuousness of the hold of the republican regime became evident in 1925 when Friedrich Ebert, the leader of the Social Democrats, died and popular elections for a new president of the republic were held. The people elected Field Marshal von Hindenburg, who received 800,000 votes more than Wilhelm Marx, the moderate Catholic who was the candidate of the republican parties. The Communist candidate, Ernst Thälmann, won almost two million votes. The republican center was weaker than the combined forces of the right and the left.

Nevertheless, in the three or four years of increasing prosperity which followed the acceptance of the Dawes Plan and the conclusion of the Locarno agreements, the republican regime seemed to gain ground. The 1928 elections for the Reichstag strengthened the moderate left. It was a sign of the prevailing temper that after the election of 1928 the monarchist People's party entered a coalition with the three republican parties. However, the situation changed quickly. One year after the elections the economic depression began to make itself felt. In September, 1929, Germany had 1,320,000 unemployed; one year later, 3,000,000; in September 1931, 4,350,000; and in 1932 the peak was reached with over 6,000,000. In Germany the widespread poverty and wretched conditions caused by the depression had an especially devastating psychological effect because they came so soon after the hardships of the inflation. Republican governments seemed unable to create a secure economic foundation for society. Left-wing and right-wing radicalism increased, with a resultant sharpening of tension between the left and right wings of the ruling coalition. The socialists, fearful that their adherents would go over to the Communists, became increasingly unwilling to agree to economic measures which might increase unemployment; and the German People's party tried to strengthen its appeal by adopting a more nationalist line in foreign policy. Particularly unfortunate was the death in October, 1929, of Gustav Stresemann, who had exerted a moderating influence in the German People's party. Shortly before his death he had achieved an important success: the acceptance of the Young Plan developed by a commission headed by the American Owen D. Young, which reduced the amount of the annual German reparations payments, eliminated the international controls over German economy, and brought to an immediate end the military occupation of the Rhineland. But because this agreement had been preceded by bitter diplomatic struggles, its acceptance aroused nationalist passions and resentment and weakened rather than helped the advocates of a policy of international understanding.

With Stresemann gone, the gap between the right and the left in the government widened steadily, and in March, 1930, the coalition disintegrated. The parties were unable to agree upon measures to overcome the accelerating economic crisis. The particular issue which led to the resignation of the government was very similar to one which brought about the fall of the Labor government in Great Britain a year later: payments to the unemployed. The socialists wanted to maintain unemployment benefits but in order to minimize the budget deficit they proposed raising the contributions.

Although never concealing his monarchist convictions, Hindenburg carried out his duties in accordance with the constitution during his first years. But he was surrounded by monarchist officers and friends who believed that the collapse of the coalition government might afford an opportunity for a change to a more authoritarian system, paving the way for a new monarchy. In 1930 they picked a rather nationalist member of the Center party, Heinrich Brüning (1885–1970), as chancellor. Brüning's political views had been formed by the experiences of the war. Despite physical disabilities he had volunteered for the army and served as an officer at the front; he preserved an almost childish adoration for officers and for military values and virtues. A strict Catholic, he lived ascetically, and tended toward obstinacy and self-righteousness. He was an administrator rather than a politician, an authoritarian rather than a democrat. Although at first Brüning impressed people as a new and interesting figure on the political scene, his lugubrious character did not inspire confidence and hope. He had made his career in the Center party as an expert in financial affairs and was a strict adherent of orthodox views on economics. He believed that the crisis could be overcome only by deflation and strict economies, including cuts in unemployment insurance. Fully aware that such a policy would never be approved by the socialists, he expected to draw his support from the center and the right; he was willing to woo the right by effecting a constitutional change which would result in a more authoritarian form of government. When the Reichstag refused to approve his financial proposals, Brüning dissolved that body and put his financial proposals into effect by emergency decrees.

The elections which took place on September 14, 1930, showed the expected shift to the right, but not to the German People's party and the German Nationalist party, which might have coöperated with Brüning; instead, gains were made by the extremist National Socialists, or Nazis, who increased their seats from 15 to 107. From this time until January 30, 1933, when their leader, Adolf Hitler (1889–1945), became chancellor, German

From the early history of the Nazi movement. *Hitler and Ludendorff in 1924.*

politics was dominated by one issue: whether or not the National Socialists would come to power.

The outcome of the elections did not deter Brüning from his course; he rejected all suggestions that he resume cooperation with the socialists. The constitution in Paragraph 48 had provided that in emergency situations the president could rule by decree. It had hardly been envisaged that an emergency situation could last for several years, but Brüning, sure of presidential support, believed that if he could go on ruling by emergency decrees he would be able to demonstrate that the government would function much better with a less powerful parliament and a more independent executive. The ground would be prepared for a constitutional change in the direction of authoritarianism. He seems to have expected that such a fulfillment of demands of the right would take the wind out of the sails of the extremists and tame the National Socialists so that they would support his government. According to the constitution, emergency decrees became invalid if a majority of the Reichstag voted against them. However, Brüning anticipated correctly that although the socialists might not like this government they would regard it as a lesser evil than a government of the National Socialists. Thus, whenever the Reichstag voted on Brüning's emergency decrees the socialists abstained from voting, and the parties of the middle and the moderate right, which supported Brüning, defeated by a small margin the radicals of the right and left. A rather doubtful interpretation of the notion of emergency, combined with socialist tolerance, kept the Brüning government in power.

Brüning further ingratiated himself with the forces of the right by giving a nationalist turn to German foreign policy. In June, 1930, when the last French troops evacuated the Rhineland, official speeches celebrating this event expressed no appreciation of the French concessions, but instead raised demands for further revisions of the peace treaty. The British ambassador in Berlin wrote: "It is an unattractive feature of the German character to display little gratitude for favors received but when the receipt of favors is followed up by fresh demands there are grounds for feeling impatient." If the British government had followed the advice of its ambassador and had stood with France, the Germans might have become more cautious in making complaints and raising new demands. But Great Britain just tried to smooth things over without taking any definite stand and Germany went ahead with its policy of seeking revision.

The most disastrous German step in this campaign was the conclusion of a customs union with Austria in March, 1931. Such an agreement was hardly compatible with the 1919 prohibition against Anschluss, and it was in direct contradiction to stipulations which Austria had accepted in 1922 in order to receive financial support from France, Great Britain, and Italy. France brought the issue before the Permanent Court of International Justice in The Hague and the customs union was declared invalid. The prestige of the Brüning government waned in the face of nationalist resentment, of which the radical right made good use. Moreover, the political uncertainty created by the conflict over the customs union triggered in the summer of 1931 the dramatic explosion of the financial crisis which began in Vienna, then moved to Germany, and finally extended to London.

During that summer, Brüning and the president of the Reichsbank were forced to make desperate trips to London and Paris to plead for financial relief, and these appeals to former enemies further damaged the prestige of the government in the eyes of the nationalists. In the winter of 1931–1932, the nationalist opposition was still gaining in strength and unemployment reached frightening proportions.

Brüning was further handicapped by the fact that he could rule by emergency decrees only as long as he had the confidence of the president, to whom the power to issue the decrees actually belonged. In March, 1932, Hindenburg's first presidential term ended. In the subsequent election he received 53 per cent of the votes; Hitler received 36.8 per cent. Despite Hindenburg's imposing majority the result was a disappointment to him. The figures showed that right-wing radicalism had continued to grow; Brüning had failed to gain the cooperation of the rightist groups, and at the end of May, 1932, he was curtly dismissed by Hindenburg.

The details of what happened in Germany between Brüning's dismissal and Hitler's assumption of power in January, 1933, are intricate. There were intrigues centering around the president and the men who most influenced him: his son, Oskar, and his secretary, Otto Meissner. But the general pattern was constant. The continuing increase in popularity of nationalist extremism on the right made moderate conservatives less than ever inclined to resume cooperation with the socialists. Moreover, Hindenburg, getting old and dependent, decided against a return to parliamentarism. These authoritarian tendencies were strongly supported by the generals of the Reichswehr, particularly their representatives in the defense ministry, Kurt von Schleicher (1882–1934) and Kurt Freiherr von Hammerstein-Equord (1878–1943). They were sympathetic, if not to the National Socialist leaders, at least to the revival of nationalism and militarism which National Socialism preached. In their eyes the Nazis would be valuable material to be incorporated into the army when the hour arrived to break the chains of the disarmament clauses of Versailles. They were not willing to risk a serious political conflict in which the Reichswehr might have to fight the National Socialists with their paramilitary organizations. Indeed, they were not even sure that officers ordered to attack the Nazis would obey the command. Thus, all the men around the president wanted to cooperate with the National Socialists. The only stumbling block was the demand of their leader, Hitler, that he must be chancellor of any government supported by his party. Hindenburg's advisers wanted to use the National Socialists for their own purpose, but they did not want to get into a position in which the National Socialists might be able to call the tune. Brüning's successor, Papen, an ambitious and elegant former officer who through his great wealth had acquired newspapers and political influence, was disappointed in his lighthearted expectation that the National Socialists would cooperate with him. His successor, General Schleicher, was equally unsuccessful. By December, 1932, however, the situation began to change. Elections in November showed for the first time a slight decrease in the National Socialist vote; it became clear that the economic crisis had reached its peak. The conservatives and nationalists feared that if these trends continued, the occasion for the establishment of an authoritarian government and for a restoration of the monarchy might be missed. Likewise the National Socialist leaders began to feel that they might have waited too long. The masses might defect, having become convinced that National Socialism would never come to power. Under these circumstances, driven by ambition and stimulated by hatred of his successor Schleicher, Papen attempted once again to form a coalition with the National Socialists. He conceded to their leaders that Hitler should become chancellor, but only two other Nazis, Wilhelm Frick (1877–1946) and Hermann Göring (1893–1946), would become members of the cabinet, and Göring was to be minister without portfolio. The other members were to be either conservative politicians like Alfred Hugenberg (1865–1951), leader of the German

Nationalist party, or experts. Papen himself, as vice-chancellor, would be present at all Hitler's audiences with the president. In such a government, Papen and his friends believed, Hitler's chancellorship would be of no danger. Completely surrounded by sound conservatives, Hitler would have no freedom of action. With these arguments Papen, supported by Hindenburg's son and by his secretary, overcame the president's resistance. On January 30, 1933, Hitler was appointed chancellor.

Nazism in Germany

On the evening of January 30 the Nazis celebrated Hitler's appointment with a gigantic torch light parade in which they marched, along with organizations of military veterans, through the government quarter of Berlin. This demonstration was meant to emphasize that the formation of the Hitler government signified a new beginning and represented a revolution. The parallel with the rise of Fascism in Italy is striking. The formation of the government by Mussolini had been preceded by negotiations with other parties and by court intrigues; the outcome was a coalition. The traditional nature of the methods employed by Mussolini to gain office was concealed by the March on Rome, which made the seizure of power a conquest by force—a revolution. The torchlight parade on the evening of January 30 in Berlin was Hitler's "March on Rome." That the people around Hindenburg and the reactionary non-Nazi members of Hitler's government expected to control Hitler and to use the Nazis for their own purposes indicated that they had no understanding of Hitler's personality or of the reasons why so many people had been attracted to the National Socialist party. For though their final rise to power was due to the intrigues and subtle calculations of the military and the reactionaries, the Nazis had become a force in German politics because large masses of the German people approved of their radical demands for a new departure and saw in Hitler a messiah.

The rise of the Nazis reflected the disappearance of the bourgeois parties which had stood at the center in the German political scene. Among those who voted for the Nazis before 1933 were hardly any workers. There had been some shift of votes from the Socialists to the Communists, but the sum of votes given to these two parties remained constant even during the depression. The Catholic Center party too kept most of its adherents, but the German Democratic party and the German People's party disintegrated. Certainly the Nazis had many kinds of supporters. With the help of Hjalmar Schacht, who had turned against the government because in his opinion the Young Plan was still too burdensome and ought not to have been accepted, they received money from industrialists, who expected that the Nazis would put an end to concessions to the workers. Members of the nobility and of the Wilhelminian ruling group lent their prestige and their support to the

The Nazis in power. *Parade before Hindenburg on the evening of Hitler's appointment as chancellor.*

Nazis because they wanted to overthrow the despised republic. For the youth, particularly for students who believed they had little chance in the future and feared that they would become an academic proletariat, the Nazi demand for a new social order had great appeal. Farmers and small-town residents were antagonistic to the big cities and the trend toward industrialization, which they believed were dominating the policy of the republic. Most of the Nazi votes came from the middle classes, particularly the lower middle classes. They had been hit hard by the inflation. Despite some improvement in the later 1920's the economic situation remained precarious for the owners of small industries faced with overwhelming competition from large-scale industries organized into trusts and cartels. Shopkeepers found their businesses suffering from the increasing popularity of department stores. Moreover, the depression fell heavily on the white-collar workers in factories, offices, and stores, who did not even enjoy the minimum protection afforded by the trade unions. Most members of the lower middle classes became convinced of the incompetence and corruption of those whom the republican form of government had brought into power. This view of the republican government had been fed by the monarchist parties of the right, particularly the German Nationalist party. But the gains were harvested not by the Nationalists, but by the Nazis. The National Socialist party had a strong appeal because it claimed that it was entirely different from other political parties and that it took part in elections only in order to overthrow the entire existing political setup.

THE STRUCTURE OF THE NAZI PARTY

The character of Nazi propaganda and the form of the party organization emphasized the distinctiveness of National Socialism. At meetings, the paramilitary storm troopers first marched into the hall and flanked the podium; martial music was played until the main speaker appeared, greeting and being greeted by a raised right arm, the so-called Hitler salute. After an inflammatory speech he left immediately, again giving and receiving the Hitler salute. No questions were asked. Hecklers and people who tried to raise objections were thrown out of the meeting room by the storm troopers. The fact that such gatherings had the aspect of a religious revival meeting made them all the more appealing to Germans of the lower middle classes, who in their economic helplessness and isolation were drawn to a movement which seemed to make them part of a powerful world.

The structure of the party was hierarchical. At the top was the leader, Adolf Hitler. Below him was the *Gauleiter*, or subleader, having command of his own *Gau*, or region, and the *Gau* in turn divided into districts, each directed by a party official subordinate to the *Gauleiter*. The chain of command led strictly from above to below. Hitler gave the orders, and they were transmitted through the party hierarchy to the rank and file. From the beginning, Hitler considered this leadership principle to be crucial. Even in the 1920's, when the fortunes of the party were low, he refused to amalgamate with other small parties of nationalist extremism because such a move might threaten his position as the one and only leader. In the confusion of the German parliamentary system, with its numerous bourgeois parties and its many intrigues, the quality of decisiveness inherent in the leadership principle had attraction as promising a way out of chaos.

Resoluteness and decisiveness were communicated also by another feature peculiar to the National Socialist party: its paramilitary organizations, the *Sturmabteilung*, known as the S.A., or storm troopers, and the *Schutzstaffel*, or S.S. The S.S. gained importance only in later years, after Hitler's seizure of power; it began as a bodyguard for Hitler and his chief lieutenants. In earlier years the important and active military organization of the party was the S.A. Its original function was to protect Nazi speakers at open meetings. But this defensive role was soon superseded by an aggressive one, that of breaking up the meetings of Communists and other "enemies" of the nation. At first the S.A. men were given only uniforms and some food. Later, when the party became large and rich through membership dues and financial contributions, the storm troopers received regular wages. When unemployment was widespread, young men flocked to the S.A. The organization became strong enough to parade through the streets of the towns and to impede demonstrations of other groups and parties. Street fights, in which the S.A. excelled in roughness and violence, became frequent. The storm troopers committed a number of murders of political opponents, and their brutality—openly encouraged by Hitler—was one of the reasons why, until January, 1933, even nationalists who were sympathetic to Hitler's cause hesitated to entrust him with the government. On the other hand, the ruthlessness of the S.A. helped to strengthen the Nazis. In many smaller towns the S.A. became all-powerful, and citizens found it easier and less dangerous to go along with the National Socialists than to oppose them. Moreover, through the violence of the S.A. a kind of undeclared civil war developed in Germany and the local governments which did not seem able to keep peace lost in prestige to the National Socialists who guaranteed that they would maintain order if they came to power.

Hitler's Political Technique

Hitler's originality lay in his understanding of the art of directing the minds of the masses. He explained his views about the techniques of propaganda at some length in *Mein Kampf* ("My Battle"), written in 1924: "The driving force of the most important changes in this world had been found less in scientific knowledge animating the masses but rather in a fanaticism dominating them and in a hysteria which drives them forward." Thus the intellectual content of political propaganda must be as simple as possible: "All effective propaganda has to limit itself to a very few points and to use them like slogans. . . . It has to confine itself to little and to repeat this eternally." A political leader should not discuss an issue in all facets and complications. Everything ought to be painted in either black or white: a "suggestively biased attitude. . . . towards the questions to be dealt with." Because the masses are not acting upon intellectual considerations, are not "thinking," a political leader need not fear to speak a lie if this might be effective. But the lie must be a "big lie." Small lies the people might recognize, for they themselves tell them, but "it would never come into their heads to fabricate colossal untruths and they would not believe that others could have the impudence to distort the truth so infamously." Thus the effectiveness of a message depends not on its truth, but only on the fanaticism and the passion with which it is conveyed; to a properly presented appeal the masses will respond by accepting what they are told.

Hitler followed these rules carefully in his speeches. His oratory was his strength, and the important stepping-stones in his rise to power were the great mass meetings at which, among flags and uniformed men, under a sharp spotlight in an otherwise darkened hall, the leader spoke. Deliberately he built up an image of himself as the embodiment of the mission of the German nation. He represented himself as a man with no family and no women, living ascetically so that he could devote himself exclusively to the German nation. But he did not want to appear inhuman either. He loved dogs; he smiled at children and gave them chocolate. All this was artfully fabricated—a "big lie." Actually, his sister conducted his household. For fifteen years he lived with a mistress, Eva Braun. He spent hours looking at movies in his own theater. The photographs representing his private life which were published in German newspapers were carefully selected from the many taken by his official photographer.

Hitler's political ideas were crude and represented a mixture of Darwinism, Wagnerian romanticism, and Nietzschean philosophy, all simplified and vulgarized. "The whole work of nature is a mighty struggle between strength and weakness—an eternal victory of the strong over the weak," he said. Politics was to Hitler a struggle among races, but in his view the races were not equal; the "Aryan race"—and he never clearly defined this term—was superior to all others. Hitler believed in the importance of elites. Among the Aryans, the Germans were the elite. And among the Germans, the National Socialists were the elite, with the right and the duty to lead and to rule. Because struggle was the law of life, war was a necessity and the main task of a national leader was to make his state militarily strong so that it could win in battle and could expand.

In its political application this ideology resulted in certain concrete aims. Despite some shifts in his thought, Hitler always regarded France and Great Britain as Germany's enemies. However, he held them in contempt. As aging democracies they lacked the rule of an elite and were therefore weak and declining. The particular foe of the German nation, he believed, was Bolshevik Russia. For Russia was dangerous. It was not a democracy but a dictatorship. It showed no signs of age. Moreover, a military defeat of Russia would mean that its southwestern plains could provide the living space for which Germany had a great need. Finally, Hitler maintained that Communism was Jewish in origin, and to him the Jews were the most dangerous, the most fatal, enemies of the Aryans.

Anti-Semitism was central in Hitler's political thought. It was an effective propaganda device in Germany; the Jew could be blamed for those incomprehensible economic forces which destroyed the independence of small entrepreneurs and shop owners. But the usefulness of anti-Semitism as propaganda was secondary for Hitler; he was a convinced, passionate hater of the Jews. An admirer of Wagner's operas, Hitler was obsessed by the drama of Teutonic heroes, caught in a net by the dark dwarfs with their hoard of gold. There is no possibility of finding a rational explanation for such elements of Hitler's thought as anti-Semitism; it would be a mistake even to try to do so. As his whole career was to show, and as he himself frequently stated, in his crucial decisions he followed his intuition.

It is not difficult to determine where Hitler's ideas came from. He himself said in *Mein Kampf* that in his years in Vienna he "formed an image of the world and a view of life which became the granite foundation of my action.

Vienna was and remained for me the hardest but also the most thorough school of my life." Adolf Hitler was born in Braunau, Austria, on April 20, 1889. His father, who had been a customs official, died when his son was fourteen. His mother spoiled him; he grew up undisciplined and with a very spotty education. He was always distrustful of people with learning and imagined himself to be something better, an artist. The great tragedy of his early years was the death of his mother in 1908. Immediately thereafter, he went to Vienna, where, lacking financial resources, he drifted through various menial jobs without ever setting out on a definite career. He slept on park benches and in flophouses and wore shabby and torn clothes which people gave him out of pity. Hitler later said that the Vienna years had been very lonely. He had contact only with tramps and drunkards; he never learned to discuss or to exchange thoughts with others. His way of expressing himself was to monologize, and as the transcripts of meetings with his ministers and advisers during the Second World War would show, he retained this mode of speech to the end. But monologizing provided good training for a public speaker.

As an outsider without any special trade Hitler found himself unable to compete for jobs with organized labor, and he developed an intense hatred of Marxism. Moreover, at this time the Germans in the Habsburg monarchy were vehement nationalists, using racist theories to justify their right to rule over the other nationalities. All the German nationalist parties in Austria-Hungary were passionately anti-Slavonic and anti-Semitic. Hitler's opposition to Marxism, his belief in the value of race and in the superiority of the Germanic race, his anti-Semitism were all echoes, and mostly pure repetitions, of notions that flourished in Vienna around the turn of the century.

The one further element important in the formation of Hitler's mind was the war experience. In 1913, he moved from Vienna to Munich. As he later said, he preferred a real German city to Vienna with its "promiscuous swarm of foreign people." But in Munich his existence was quite as uncertain and miserable as it had been in Vienna. When the war broke out he volunteered for a Bavarian regiment. Hitler was a good soldier and for the first time he found some recognition and felt himself to be a member of a community. Indeed, he met in his regiment men who later became his most devoted friends and followers: Rudolph Hess, who became party secretary, and Max Amann, who was the press chief in Nazi Germany. The war experience made Hitler an admirer of all things military; he was impressed by the hierarchical structure of an army, with its chain of command. After years of rootlessness, he found a home in the army. The collapse of Germany was a personal catastrophe for him. He could not admit that the defeat had been caused by the admired military leaders; in his view it was the result of a stab in the back by those dark forces which he had seen in Vienna—Marxists and Jews. He returned to Munich, and as we have seen, was employed by the army as a propaganda speaker to keep the military spirit alive in the disheartened and defeated German nation. In the course of this activity Hitler came into contact with a small group calling itself the National Socialist German Workers' party, which pursued a somewhat confused mixture of nationalist and socialist ideals. Hitler became a member, and was soon the leader of this group. He had found his calling.

In Hitler's system of values those social ideas for which he had no feeling were no less significant than those which he emphasized. Hitler had no sense of the importance of morality or law. He was willing to stand up for murderers. He closed his eyes to the sexual aberrations of many of his companions, but he did not hesitate to make use of his knowledge of their weaknesses when he wanted to get rid of them. In politics, and probably also in his personal life, Hitler knew only friends and foes—and those who were his friends became his foes when they did not offer him blind allegiance. He used every weapon to eliminate his enemies. When in the summer of 1934 the S.A. had become an obstacle, he had the leaders—his enthusiastic followers—executed without recourse to the regular courts, explaining that he was "the supreme justiciar" of the German people. He had people placed in "protective custody" without giving them any opportunity to defend themselves in the courts. The result was the establishment of the dreaded concentration camps, where many were kept without legal recourse for unlimited periods. He established special courts, like those of the S.S., which made their own laws, and he issued retroactive laws. The lack of sense of morality, the inability to grasp the value of a system of law, were deeply rooted in Hitler's personality. In Vienna he lived as a lone wolf among outcasts fighting against each other for a minimum subsistence; his experience had been that "it is not by the principles of humanity that man lives, or is able to preserve himself above the animal world, but solely by means of the most brutal struggle." He never grasped that life in a community is possible only if recognized standards of morality and of law exist.

Almost inevitably Hitler's personality carried the seeds of his destruction. It has been debated why he could not be content with the success which he achieved. There were moments under his rule when Germany seemed to have obtained all that its people could have desired. But a halt would have meant the return to some legal order and the acceptance of some moral values permitting the existence of a stable communal life. In such a world neither the men who surrounded the leader, nor Hitler himself, would have fitted. Hence he drove restlessly on to new conquests until the chase ended in nothing. It is truly appropriate to call the Nazi revolution, as did Hermann Rauschning, at first Hitler's adherent and then his enemy, "the revolution of nihilism."

The Implementation of the Nazi Program

Hitler's aim was to obtain full power and then to launch Germany on a course of expansion, thereby fulfilling what he regarded as the natural law of politics. When he became chancellor in January, 1933, such an aim seemed far beyond his grasp. His government was a coalition in which the National Socialists were a minority. In foreign policy Germany's freedom of action was still restricted by the treaties of Versailles and Locarno. The size of the German army was limited and the Rhineland was demilitarized. One may reject Hitler's aims and detest his brutal methods, but still find remarkable the technical virtuosity with which he quickly freed himself from these internal and external restraints. A year and a half after he became chancellor, Hitler was the all-powerful dictator of Germany, and less than two years after that, in March, 1936, he made the treaties of Versailles and Locarno valueless pieces of paper.

At first, Hitler made use of the coalition with the German Nationalist party in order to stress the moderate and conservative character of his "national revolution." The black, white, and red of the German empire replaced the black, red, and gold of the national flag of the Weimar Republic; carefully staged celebrations emphasized the continuity between the old imperial Germany and the new National Socialist state. In March, 1933, the artfully contrived climax of the opening of the Reichstag in the Hohenzollern residence at Potsdam was Hitler's bow before President Hindenburg.

Hitler and the National Socialists had several reasons for the temporary adoption of a conservative line. First of all, Hitler had to win the confidence of old Hindenburg, who by refusing to sign emergency decrees could still bring about the fall of the government. Also, the new chancellor was anxious to avoid any obstruction by the bureaucracy and to make sure that the military leadership would not turn against him. Moreover, popular support of National Socialism would be strengthened if the members of the various conservative and nationalist parties and organizations, who had stayed away from the Nazis, could be lured into enrolling in the Nazi party. The conservative line also helped to secure the continuation of financial support for the Nazi party from the leaders of industrial trusts and banks, such as the Krupp metals empire and the I. G. Farben chemical works.

When the government was formed, Hitler insisted that the Reichstag be dissolved and new elections take place. The National Socialists entered the election campaign with immense advantages. They enjoyed the prestige of having their leader as head of the government. They could use the government machinery for propaganda, and on the basis of Paragraph 48 of the constitution they issued emergency decrees which limited the right of assembly of opposition parties and suppressed their newspapers and political publications. However, the decisive turn in the election campaign was

The burning of the Reichstag. *The main hall after the fire.*

brought about on the night of February 27, 1933, when the building in which the Reichstag met went up in flames. Though Marinus van der Lubbe, the young Dutchman who was caught in the building, never denied the deed, it was immediately assumed that he alone could not have caused the immense fire.

The Nazi leaders immediately accused the Communists, maintaining that the Reichstag fire was intended as the signal for a Communist revolt; but they never produced any proof, and it is certain that the Communists were not involved. We do know that the Nazis were only waiting for a Communist provocation which would give them the opportunity to suppress the Communist party and impose further restrictions on the other opposition parties. It has been suggested, therefore, that the National Socialists themselves used Lubbe as a cat's paw and were responsible for the Reichstag fire. In any event, the Nazi leaders welcomed the fire and utilized it most efficiently.

On February 28, the day after the burning of the Reichstag, the government issued a number of emergency decrees which were not rescinded until the end of Hitler's Third Reich in 1945. As a "defensive measure against Communist acts of violence," the government rescinded the guarantees of such basic rights as personal freedom, the free expression of opinion, the freedom of assembly and association, the privacy of postal and telephone communications, and the inviolability of property. In addition the number of crimes to which the death penalty could be applied was increased, and the spreading of rumors or false news was classified as treason. Finally, the Reich government was empowered to take over the government of the various federal states if necessary.

The elections, a week after the Reichstag fire, gave the National Socialists 43.9 per cent of the vote. It has been argued in favor of the political maturity of the German people that although the elections took place under severe pressure and restrictions, the National Socialists did not receive a clear majority. It is perhaps more significant that even after the dictatorial character of the Hitler regime had revealed itself, almost 44 per cent of the German people voted for the Nazis. Together with the German Nationalist party, with 8 per cent of the vote, the National Socialist party had the majority.

But application of the emergency decrees soon made this alliance unnecessary. The Communist deputies, representing 12.2 per cent of the vote, were arrested and not permitted to enter the Reichstag. Now even without the German Nationalist party the Nazis had a majority.

For Hitler this was only a first step. He wanted to eliminate entirely both parliament and elections. His government therefore proposed an Enabling Law, which would transfer the legislative power from the Reichstag to the government for four years; as a change in the constitution, such a law had to be approved by two thirds of the Reichstag. Hitler obtained the support of the Catholic Center party by threatening to use the emergency decrees against this party as he had used them against the Communists. The members of the Center party reasoned that by agreeing to the Enabling Law they might save their party and retain some influence. The Enabling Law was accepted on March 23; only the Social Democrats voted against it, while outside the hall the storm troopers shouted, "We want the bill or fire and murder."

With the emergency decrees of February 28 and the Enabling Law of March 23 all legislative and executive power was concentrated in the hands of the Hitler government, and all guarantees against transgressions by the executive had been removed. This was the "legal" framework for Hitler's dictatorship from 1933 to 1945.

However, the possession of the legal instruments for establishing a dictatorship did not overcome all obstacles to Hitler's unlimited control. Although his party now constituted a majority in the Reichstag, he was committed to retaining the coalition government. The prestige of the president, Hindenburg, was superior to his. Opposition parties and newspapers, though hampered, continued to exist. And the traditional spokesmen for educated public opinion—civil servants, professors, clergymen—could still make themselves heard. Hitler's technique for weakening and finally eliminating these remaining centers of independence was masterly. His approach was always the same. Instead of moving against all his opponents at once, he attacked one at a time, in each case proceeding gradually.

Characteristic was the way in which he ended the multiparty system. After the Communist party had been eliminated, Hitler's first target was the Social Democratic party. In this effort his coalition partners were willing helpers, and few objections were raised by the other bourgeois parties. The strength of the Social Democrats lay in their close relation to the trade unions, whose strikes could severely handicap the work of the government. Hence, Hitler's first move was to separate the trade unions from the Social Democrats; he did so by promising the unions undisturbed, continued existence if they abandoned political activities and concentrated exclusively on economic goals. Timid and bureaucratic, the union leaders fell into this trap and accepted the restrictions. Next, the Nazis declared that independent trade unions were unnecessary. The unions ought to become part of a great comprehensive organization which would include employers as well as workers. With a great celebration on May 1, which was declared to be a national holiday, a German labor front was founded. The next day the buildings of the unions were occupied, their funds were confiscated, and some of their leaders were arrested. With the elimination of the trade unions the Social Democrats lost all their remaining power to exert pressure. And when some important socialists, threatened by imprisonment, left Germany and attacked the regime from outside, the Nazis used their conduct as an excuse to declare Social Democratic activities treasonous; they prohibited the party and imprisoned many of its leaders.

Next, Hitler proceeded against the bourgeois parties outside his government. Most important among them was the Catholic Center party. Hitler again applied the tactics which he had used against the socialists: he destroyed his antagonist's source of power. A basic reason for the existence of the Center party was the need to maintain and protect the position of the Roman Catholic Church and its members. Hitler sent Papen to Rome to negotiate a concordat; for many years the Vatican had been eager for such an agreement, which would secure the legal status of the Catholic Church in Germany and would guarantee the bishops freedom of communication with the Vatican. But no previous federal government had been willing to conclude a concordat. The Vatican accepted Hitler's offer, probably as a result of the authoritarian inclinations of Pope Pius XI and the pro-German bias of his secretary of state Eugenio Pacelli, later Pope Pius XII. It was a fatal mistake. The concordat gave the first international approval to the Nazi regime and raised its prestige. It did not secure the position of Roman Catholicism in Germany, which Hitler went on to attack and undermine as soon as his immediate aim, the dissolution of the Center party, had been achieved. At the time, however, German Catholics, assured by the concordat that their religion would not suffer under the Nazi regime, abandoned membership in the Center party, and under pressure from the Vatican the party's leaders on July 8 agreed to its dissolution.

Hitler still had to dispose of his coalition partner—the German Nationalist party. When he became chancellor, he had promised not to change the composition of the government, which was to include, besides himself, only two National Socialists. However, he managed to increase the influence of his own party in the coalition by creating new departments headed by Nazis: Göring, who had distinguished himself in the war as pilot and was the most respectable of Hitler's close collaborators, became air minister; Joseph Goebbels (1897–1945), who had been head of the Nazi party in Berlin and was the most intellectual and also the most cynical of the Nazi leaders, became minister of propaganda. Moreover, members of the German Nationalist party who went over to the National Socialists were rewarded with advantageous positions in the administration and in the party. Those who refused, encountered endless difficulties. Therefore, strong pressure developed within the German Nationalist party to assure its members of continued influence in the government and administration by amalgamating with the Nazi party. Thus the party began to disintegrate and was finally dissolved. On July 14 a government enactment proclaimed that "the National Socialist German Workers' Party constitutes the only political party in Germany"; to attempt to maintain or organize any other political party became a crime. Germany was a one-party state. The elimination of the multiparty system was certainly Germany's most decisive step toward totalitarianism. But it was only one among many. Nazi commissars were placed at the head of the various federal states and appointed state governments dominated by Nazis. The press and the publishing houses were coordinated by the formation of a comprehensive Nazi-controlled association. Only members of this association were permitted to own, edit, or work on newspapers. A similar take-over occurred in the universities. New chairs were created for fields like racial science, and these were filled by National Socialists. The politically oriented newcomers were supported by the rectors of the universities, now not elected, but appointed by the Nazi minister of education. The expression of pronounced Nazi views became the prerequisite for obtaining tenure and promotion. No excuse is possible for the lack of resistance shown by the German intellectual community to the abolition of academic freedom. But because the Nazi infiltration of the universities happened gradually, many professors became aware of the systematic destruction of their independence only after it had been lost.

Similarly, the full aims of Hitler's anti-Semitic policy were only gradually apparent. It is certain that from the outset his mind was set on what during the Second World War became the "final solution"—the annihilation of the Jews. But at the beginning of the Nazi regime, Hitler created the impression that Jews would be permitted to continue their activities in economic life and in the professions; they were to be excluded from government service except for those who had done military service during the First World War. Soon, however, the screws were tightened. The exemption of war veterans from dismissal was rescinded. Doctors, lawyers, journalists, writers were organized in associations from which Jews were excluded; those who did not belong to these associations met increasing difficulties in the exercise of their professions. Admission to schools and universities was denied to Jewish youth. Gradually the same method was applied to business and economic life. Such activities required membership in organizations from which Jews were excluded.

The anti-Semitic policy reached a climax in the Nuremberg Laws of September 15, 1935, which deprived Jews and people with Jewish blood of German citizenship, prohibited marriage and sexual intercourse between people with Jewish blood and non-Jewish Germans, and denied Jews the right to employ non-Jewish female servants. Jews were forced to wear a yellow Star of David on their clothing whenever they went into the streets. They were pushed back into the ghetto. Protests against these measures were of no avail. As a matter of fact, few dared to endanger themselves by indicating disapproval.

All these changes were accompanied by a systematic policy of terror. When the Nazis came to power one of their first moves was to obtain control of the police. Since the ministers of the interior in the federal states were in command of the police the Nazis made sure that these posts were filled by reliable party members. Nazis also were appointed as police presidents in the larger urban centers. These officials arranged for the storm troopers to serve as an auxiliary police force. The emergency decrees passed after the Reichstag fire gave the police the right to arrest and keep in custody anyone suspected of disloyalty to the state. Nobody was secure; an incautious remark or the personal hostility of a storm trooper might result in imprisonment. People disappeared and were never heard of again. The police refused to interfere with Nazi demonstrations, as on April 1, 1933, when the Nazis marched unhindered through the streets of the center of Berlin, throwing stones into the windows of department stores and shops owned by Jews. Similar outbreaks by Nazi students in the universities forced professors regarded as unfriendly to the new regime to abandon their courses. In the atmosphere of terror, made more nightmarish by the official silence about these dark happenings, people gave up asking questions and closed their eyes and ears to what was going on around them. Moreover, the terror did not recede after the first few months; instead, it was embodied in an organization—the Secret State Police, or Gestapo—that developed into a large institution with headquarters in Berlin and offices all over Germany. The Gestapo devoted itself to the task of ferreting out the enemies of Nazism, who were arrested, interrogated, tortured, and placed in detention camps, without any legal recourse.

Under these circumstances the only serious threat to Hitler's leadership came from within—from the Nazi party itself. Many of those prominent in the party, like the fanatic but colorless Heinrich Himmler (1900–1945), the leader of the S.S., and the intelligent but generally despised Goebbels, the minister of propaganda, were aware that they had little personal following and were entirely dependent on Hitler. Göring, whose primitive enjoyment of luxury and power gave him a certain human appeal, was entirely satisfied with the power and riches he obtained as second in command and as Hitler's designated heir. But many of the early party members sincerely believed that the Nazi assumption of power would bring about a social revolution and that they would be the leaders of a new society very different from the old. A center of such aspirations was the S.A., and the main advocate of these ideas was the leader of the S.A., Ernst Röhm (1887–1934). His concrete aim was to have the S.A. become part of the army, with the S.A. leaders receiving officers' ranks. Such demands disquieted the generals of the Reichswehr, who did not want to see their control of the training and organization of the army disturbed by the "wild men" of the S.A. Hitler was anxious not to arouse the distrust of the military leaders because he anticipated needing army support for his plan to combine the position of president with that of chancellor after the death of Hindenburg, which in 1934 was imminent. The situation was further complicated by the activities of the conservatives, who were fully aware that without Hindenburg they would lack the power to halt a second revolution and were therefore trying to put a stop to Nazi radicalism before Hindenburg's death.

Out of this tangle of motives arose the blood bath of June 30, 1934. Hitler himself led the action against Röhm and other leaders of the S.A. whom he surprised in a small summer resort in Bavaria. Röhm and his associates were executed without trial; in his speech of justification Hitler emphasized his having discovered them in bed with young S.A. men. Actually he had known for a long time of the prevalence of homosexuality within the S.A. In Berlin, Göring proceeded not only against the leaders of the S.A. but also against other adversaries of the Nazis, like Schleicher, the former chancellor; he also arranged the execution of two of vice-chancellor Papen's secretaries, who had acted as spokesmen of the conservatives. Papen himself was placed under house arrest. Thus, Hitler shook off the radical wing of his party and earned the gratitude of the military leaders; he also demonstrated that he had not become a prisoner of the conservatives. The events of June 30 were both an expression of Hitler's utter disregard for law and morality and a sign of the omnipotence which he had reached. When Hindenburg died on August 2, Hitler combined the offices of president and chancellor without encountering objections.

In two sectors of social life—in economic affairs and in military affairs—the changes brought about by the Nazi dictatorship were less

The Nazi Party Congress in Nuremberg in 1934. *In the middle, Hitler, between Himmler, the leader of the S.S. (left) and Lutze, leader of the S.A.*

pronounced than in others. From the beginning the interests of the economic and military leaders harmonized with Hitler's aims. Economic life became strictly organized and controlled; industrial and commercial activities were coordinated by the trade associations to which all the entrepreneurs had to belong and from which, as we have seen, Jews—and also Freemasons—were excluded. The intermediary between the government and business was Hjalmar Schacht, who served Hitler as president of the Reichsbank and as minister of economics. Schacht abandoned the deflationary policy of previous governments; he pumped new money into the economy by initiating public works, such as the construction of the system of Autobahns, and by providing industry with armament contracts. The inflationary consequences of this policy were kept to a minimum by strict currency controls and import restrictions. Moreover, the secrecy with which German rearmament was surrounded kept the public in the dark about the extent of government expenditures and pump priming.

As the entire world has now learned, government support of economic activity—pump priming—can prove an effective means of overcoming economic depression. However, there are limits to the successful pursuit of an inflationary policy. Schacht himself believed that they had been reached by 1938, and he left the government because Hitler insisted on continuing this course. The damaging consequences did not come out into the open before the outbreak of the war in 1939. By then Germany was faced by the alternative of either a recession or a war and the Nazi leaders were entirely aware of this problem.

Once the danger of S.A. interference had been removed, the military leaders were quite content with Hitler's rule. In Hitler, Germany had a head of state who not only approved of rearmament but was anxious to accelerate the process. Thus, the military leaders no longer encountered government opposition to their desire for rearmament. However, their independence of the Nazi control was more apparent than real. The air force, created only after 1933, was under the command of Göring, and its officers were enthusiastic Nazis. Moreover, the quick promotions resulting from the expansion of the army made the younger officers favorably inclined toward the Nazi regime. In 1938, when the old army leaders began to fear that Hitler's foreign policy might be too risky, Hitler had no difficulty in replacing with more subservient generals those whom he regarded as obstructionists.

By 1936, Hitler could claim with justification that he had established a totalitarian state; with the exception of some pockets of resistance by small groups in the Roman Catholic and Protestant churches, all activities, organizations, and institutions had been adjusted (*gleichgeschaltet*) to the Nazi regime and were subject to the direction by the Nazi leader. But was there equal justification for the claim—which Hitler and the party chiefs made with still greater emphasis—that the Nazi conquest of power represented a revolution? "Revolution" may be understood as the overthrow of a ruling class and its replacement by another; in what respects, and to what extent, did the Nazi regime transform the basic structure of German social life?

The Nazi movement cannot be identified with a particular class or stratum of German society. Farmers and members of the lower middle class formed its backbone. But in the period of economic misery the unemployed swelled the Nazi ranks, and civil servants and white-collar workers joined them. Within these groups the younger generation in particular became Nazis; in 1930, the year of the party's first great electoral victory, more than two thirds of its members were under forty and more than one third under thirty years of age. Those who saw before them only a hard and bleak future were enticed by the Nazi promise of a complete change; the varied membership of the party was united only by common dissatection with the present.

Consequently, when the Nazis came to power they had no economic or social program aimed at changing the German social structure. They had promised their middle-class adherents protection against the absorption of small businesses by department and chain stores, and indeed they issued decrees which restricted the kinds of merchandise which these stores might sell and subjected them to a special tax. But the opposition of banks and other credit institutions which had invested in these enterprises led gradually to mitigation of the measures against chain and department stores. Beyond this somewhat ephemeral concession to the small middle-class businessman, the Nazis when they came to power had no concrete economic or social plans. Their "revolution" consisted in infusing a new "spirit" into the entire social body. Their apparently revolutionary actions were primarily propagandistic. They aimed at showing that a new nation had arisen in which all groups and classes harmoniously cooperated for the common good. The first of May became a national holiday intended to recognize the importance of the workers; this was only one of the many holidays created to emphasize the solidarity of the German nation. With the establishment of comradeship among the classes, "German Socialism," it was proclaimed, would become a reality. Organizations like the Hitler Youth and the Labor Service were meant to serve this purpose. The Hitler Youth consisted of boys and girls in their early years. The Labor Service was obligatory for students, voluntary for others; its disciplinary and educational effects were more highly appreciated by visiting foreigners than by those who had to undergo this training.

For Hitler the dividing lines in modern society were created not by differing education, differing professions, differing economic status, but by race. However, even within a superior race like the Germans there was an elite which alone had the right to rule; those few who came from the right stock and had excelled in their activities in the Hitler Youth were prepared for their tasks of leadership in special training schools, housed in buildings modeled after the castles of the knightly orders of the Middle Ages; the training—and these surroundings—were intended to awaken in the trainees the qualities of obedience, physical prowess, instinctivity, and will power.

The mixture of propaganda and racial romanticism in the social policy of the Nazis reflected the absence of concrete ideas about desirable changes in the German social structure. But this lack had its advantages for the Nazi regime. Since no revolution had occurred which changed the German class structure, and no ruling class had been toppled and replaced, each group of society seemed to have kept the position which it had held before the Nazis had obtained power. Except for the obvious victims of the change of regime—Jews, and politicians who had fought the Nazis—the individual did not experience an immediate diminution of status; the tenor of his life was not perceptibly changed, and this apparent stability was one reason for the lack of resistance to the Nazi regime in all levels of society.

The emphasis which Nazi propaganda placed on the establishment of a new national community was to a large extent directed toward mitigating the resentment arising from the realization of political powerlessness. The Nazi rulers took particular care to keep the industrial workers content. The

Hitler's artistic taste. *The Chancellery in Berlin built by Hitler's architect, Speer.*

labor front gave much attention to conditions in the factories, secured regular vacations for the workers, and through a special organization, called "Strength Through Joy," subsidized travel for the workers and their families during these vacations.

Nevertheless, it might be doubted whether propagandistic flattery and handouts would have been effective if employers and employees had not been consoled for their loss of political influence by economic prosperity. At the time the Nazis took over, recovery from the depression was beginning, and this trend the Nazis aided by their policy of military rearmament. In 1938 the federal budget was seven times as large as it had been before the Nazis came to power, and 74 per cent of this budget was used for military purposes. Enterprises carrying out government contracts were given credit or were assured of orders for a fixed number of years. For example, in December, 1933, the government contracted to buy motor fuel from the large German chemical concern of I.G. Farben for ten years at fixed prices. By such arrangements, industry gradually surrendered its independence and granted the government control over production and prices. But as a collaborator with the regime, industry—and particularly the large companies—began to flourish.

The spurt in economic life which resulted from rearmament also transformed the situation on the labor market. In 1936–1937 the number of employed was greater than the number of employed and unemployed together had been in 1933. Soon there was a labor shortage in Germany. Although on the average, wages were even lower than they had been in the 1920's, the unskilled worker in Nazi Germany in the 1930's had the advantage of being sure of finding a job, and the skilled worker was so much sought after that his wages were kept high. After the haunting experiences of the depression, economic security seemed to both employers and employees a benefit worth paying for.

The question was, however, how long the prosperity produced by rearmament could last. Necessarily, this economic policy was accompanied by currency restrictions and limitations on imports, and the Nazi rulers were all the more willing to utilize such measures because they cut off the German people from the outside world. Nevertheless, because rearmament is economically unproductive, the inflationary consequences of the extension of credit which this policy required could not remain concealed indefinitely. Hitler had little fear that an end of economic prosperity would disrupt the new spirit of national community which the Nazi revolution claimed to have created; he was not concerned with stabilizing the situation which existed. His economic measures were never intended to provide a lasting solution. They were aimed at a change through territorial expansion, for which the rearmament policy was the requisite.

CHAPTER 6

Toward the Inevitable Conflict

For HITLER the establishment of a totalitarian dictatorship was a means to a greater end: the expansion of Germany by war. In *Mein Kampf* he had written that along with the abrogation of the Treaty of Versailles and the restoration of the pre-1914 frontiers, Germany required additional "living space"; these goals were to be achieved, if necessary, by war. The rise to power of a man with such a program of expansion aroused fears in the non-German world. Yet Hitler succeeded in preventing common action, utilizing tactics very similar to those he had employed in domestic policy: proceeding slowly and gradually and dividing his enemies.

THE NEW POSTURE OF AGGRESSION

The Beginning of Nazi Foreign Policy

Hitler began his conduct of foreign policy with loud protestations of peaceful intentions: he was willing to disarm, if only Germany received equal treatment. Nevertheless, in October, 1933, he withdrew from the disarmament conference which had been meeting since 1932 because, as he stated, the plans for disarmament were still discriminatory against Germany. This first step toward a new foreign policy was simultaneous with Germany's withdrawal from the League of Nations. Hitler softened this blow by declaring that his nation would be willing to reenter if its claims to equality in armament were recognized. The British government, occupied with the pursuit of economic recovery, refused to participate in any strong counteraction and began to explore the possibility of coming to some agreement on armament limitations. The British felt encouraged in these attempts to bring Germany back to international cooperation when on January 26, 1934, in a sudden reversal of foreign policy, Hitler concluded a nonaggression pact with Poland. The German demands for a return of Danzig and the Polish Corridor had always been regarded as a serious danger to European peace. In coming to an agreement with Poland the new ruler of Germany, however brutal his domestic policy might be, seemed to show that he was aware that methods of violence were inappropriate in international relations. The first year of Hitler's conduct of foreign policy ended with a great plus for the Reich. Germany had indicated that it no longer felt bound by the military clauses of the Treaty of Versailles, and yet was still courted as a participant in international negotiations.

In 1934 the skies darkened for Germany. Himself an Austrian, Hitler felt emotional about the *Anschluss*. He reacted sharply to measures of the Austrian chancellor, Engelbert Dollfuss, who established a Catholic authoritarian regime with the purpose of keeping Austria independent. By prohibiting Germans from traveling to Austria Hitler ruined the Austrian tourist industry, and he gave active support to the Austrian Nazi party, which Dollfuss had outlawed. Austrian Nazis who fled to Germany were organized into a military legion stationed near the border. On July 25, 1934, the Austrian Nazis tried to seize power by force. They succeeded in assassinating Dollfuss, but the putsch failed. Another Catholic chancellor, Kurt von Schuschnigg (born 1897) took over and continued Dollfus' anti-Nazi policy. The German government tried to shake off responsibility for the putsch and dissolved the Austrian legion, but the disclaimers were not believed and the image of Hitler as a man of peace was severely damaged.

The revelation of Hitler's aggressiveness had two important consequences. France strengthened its bonds with the eastern neighbors of Germany and began to cooperate with Soviet Russia, which was thoroughly alarmed by Hitler's vehement anti-Communism and suspected that his pact with Poland might mean the preparation of a Polish-German war against Russia. Sponsored by the French, the Russians entered the League of Nations in September, 1934, and eight months later a Franco-Russian alliance was concluded in which each promised to come to the other's aid against unprovoked aggression.

Hitler's Austrian policy also brought about a change in Italy's attitude. Mussolini had regarded the rise of Hitler with satisfaction, and in the first months of 1933 had done his best to calm the fears which the Nazi seizure of power had raised in Europe and to dissuade France and Great Britain from taking action. Mussolini shared Hitler's dislike of disarmament and of the League of Nations. He saw definite advantages in a strengthened Germany, envisioning Italy as a balance wheel between Britain and France on one side and Germany on the other. But he recognized that the absorption of Austria by Germany would be counter to Italy's interests. Germany might then interfere in Italy's sphere of interest in the Danube Valley and the Balkans. Moreover, with a greater Germany on the other side of the Brenner Pass, the Germans under Italian rule in South Tyrol would become entirely intractable. Mussolini therefore helped Dollfuss to establish his anti-Nazi dictatorship, and when the news of Dollfuss' assassination came, he sent troops to the Brenner frontier, in order to show that

The Stresa Conference. *Laval, then French foreign minister; Mussolini; Mac-Donald; and the French prime minister, Flandin.*

he would not permit the *Anschluss*. From cautious support of Hitler, Mussolini had moved into the anti-Nazi camp. In January, 1935, negotiations in Rome with the French foreign minister, Pierre Laval (1883–1945), led to an agreement which even envisaged conversations between the French and Italian military staffs with the purpose of arranging for concerted action in case of war with Germany. The deterioration of the German position became evident when Hitler made his next move. In March, 1935, he declared the disarmament clauses of the Treaty of Versailles abolished, and announced a great augmentation of the German army and the introduction of general conscription. In a conference at Stresa, Great Britain, France, and Italy agreed to a sharp condemnation of this unilateral violation of an international treaty, declared their interest in the maintenance of Austrian independence, and threatened that further aggressive actions would evoke not only protests but counteraction. At this time Germany, except for the understanding with Poland, was isolated and seemed unable to move.

But the situation changed rapidly. Two months later, in June, Great Britain and Germany signed a naval agreement which defined the relative strength of their navies. Germany was permitted to have as many submarines as Britain, while the strength of the rest of the German fleet was to be restricted to one third that of the British fleet. Among the many mistakes of British foreign policy with respect to Nazi Germany the conclusion of the Anglo-German naval agreement is the most incomprehensible. The practical advantages for Britain were slight, for Germany was more interested in building a strong force of submarines than in creating a high-seas navy. The political disadvantages were immense, since by recognizing this departure from the military provisions of the Treaty of Versailles, Britain undermined the basis on which the Stresa front had been formed. Strangely enough, the British government seems not to have foreseen the implications of this naval agreement with Germany, and was apparently guided by purely technical considerations, notably the belief that the fixed strength of the German navy would facilitate negotiations with other powers about naval limitations.

The Italian Conquest of Ethiopia

Hitler, however, was encouraged to continue an aggressive foreign policy, and Mussolini began to realize that not much reliance could be placed on the western democracies. Military conversations between the French and Italian staffs were postponed. Moreover, although Mussolini had found cooperation with France and Great Britain useful for the preservation of Austrian independence, he expected to be paid for his support, and he decided to cash in as quickly as possible. The result was the Italo-Ethiopian War. The Italian conquest of Ethiopia, completed in May, 1936, in a sense constituted revenge for the old defeat at Adowa, a visible demonstration that Fascist Italy had become a great imperial power, stronger and more influential than democratic and parliamentary Italy had been. Also, Mussolini hoped to settle some of Italy's surplus population in Ethiopia. In his negotiations with Mussolini in January, 1935, Laval had indicated that France would have no objection to extension of the Italian influence over Ethiopia, and Mussolini expected a similar attitude from Great Britain. But strangely enough, while Hitler's actions had always found defenders in Britain, Mussolini's invasion of Ethiopia met vehement indignation. To the British people this seemed the occasion to set in motion the machinery of the League of Nations against aggression. When in December, 1935, it appeared that the British foreign secretary, Sir Samuel Hoare (1880–1959), was willing to make a bargain with Mussolini, popular excitement in Britain was so great that Hoare was dismissed and replaced by Anthony Eden (born 1897), a strong advocate of the League of Nations and of collective security. But this did not mean that, after the rejection of the bargain with Mussolini by the British public, the government had now decided to carry out a policy of collective security even if it should result in war. The British continued to pursue an ineffectual middle course; they were not too unhappy when the French tried to slow down their attempts to use sanctions against Italy, and they hesitated to insist on the application of the one effective sanction—the cutting off of Italy's oil supplies. The result was that in the League of Nations the British demanded only halfhearted measures, which embittered the Italians against Great Britain and France without preventing their advance in Ethiopia.

The March into the Rhineland

It was in this situation, on March 7, 1936, that Hitler ended the demilitarization of the Rhineland by ordering his troops to march into the region, and thus violated not only the Treaty of Versailles but also the Locarno pact. Hitler counted on the disarray into which the Ethiopian war had put the Stresa front to prevent action by the western powers. Nevertheless, he was aware that he was gambling. As he later stated, the twenty-four hours while he was waiting for the reaction of the French were the most exciting and nerve-racking of his life. If the French had answered by sending troops into the Rhineland, the German forces would have been withdrawn to the right bank of the Rhine. This was the condition which the German military leaders had forced upon Hitler before agreeing to this move. But there was no French military response. Hitler's gamble had come off, and the political balance in Europe was entirely altered. As long as the Rhineland had been demilitarized and the important industrial areas of the Ruhr had remained unprotected, France had held the military advantage and had been in no real danger of attack. Now, with German troops near the French border and the Ruhr area in the hinterland, a conflict with Germany would mean bitter and serious war. Germany was again the strongest military power on the European continent.

THE WESTERN DEMOCRACIES IN RETREAT

Why did the great western powers—Great Britain and France—permit this change in the balance of power? Why did they not crush the revival of German military might in the early years of Hitler's rule, when Germany was still weak? Why did they miss the opportunity for intervention which the Rhineland crisis offered, and why did they then embark on a policy of appeasement?

In both Great Britain and France, the weakness in foreign policy corresponded to internal weakness; hence understanding of their attitude to the rise of Nazism requires a consideration of their domestic situation in the 1930's.

Great Britain

In Great Britain the major domestic issue in this decade was recovery from the depression into which the nation had been thrown by the economic crisis of 1929. The seriousness of this crisis made people aware of an economic vulnerability with which Britain had actually been affected since the First World War. During the war, the diminution of foreign assets as a result of the overseas procurement of war materials had sapped the strength of an economy in which imports exceeded exports. Furthermore, after the war, the British government adopted two courses of action which, though they seemed safe and appropriate in the relatively prosperous period of the middle 1920's, turned out in the subsequent depression to have the effect of severely aggravating the economic crisis and retarding recovery: one was the industrial policy which centered in the handling of the general strike in 1926; the other was the return to the gold standard in 1925.

THE GENERAL STRIKE

The general strike of 1926 developed out of a crisis in the British coal industry, which had been lagging behind its German and American competitors even before the First World War and was now also hit severely by the increasing use of oil. During the war, coal mining had been controlled by the government; the return of the mines to private ownership led, unavoidably, to a crisis. The miners' trade union demanded guarantees that a general wage level would be maintained. The owners were not willing to give these guarantees because some of the mines were considerably less profitable than others and many were not profitable at all. Three fourths of all British coal was produced at a loss. With the help of government subsidies a showdown was postponed, and the French occupation of the Ruhr, which temporarily eliminated the competition of German coal, gave relief to the British coal industry. But in 1923, after the German passive resistance in the Ruhr had ended, a crisis could no longer be avoided. When wage contracts had to be renegotiated, the owners and the miners' trade union were at loggerheads about a reduction of wages, an extension of working hours, and so on. A commission established by the government under Sir Herbert Samuel, sided with the workers rather than the owners in its report and recommended a thorough reorganization of the coal-mining industry. But though in its general tenor the Samuel report was favorable to the workers, it did suggest that they accept wage reductions pending reorganization. On this issue negotiations broke down. The miners were backed by all the British trade unions and the consequence was a general strike lasting ten days, in May, 1926. Prime Minister Baldwin had probably been anxious to avoid this gigantic industrial conflict. But some members of his government, eager to put labor in its place, considered a showdown desirable.

The government was well prepared for a general strike. A state of emergency was declared; the country was divided into districts under civil commissioners supported by civil servants; and a force of volunteers trained for such an emergency was mobilized. The most urgently needed services were maintained and food supplies reached the cities. Thus the government gradually neutralized the major effects of the work stoppage, and some members of the cabinet, among them Neville Chamberlain and Winston Churchill, urged that the strike be declared illegal, its instigators imprisoned, and the funds of the trade unions confiscated. The union leaders

The general strike of 1926. *A street in London shows the impact of the lack of public transportation.*

feared that when the financial reserves of the unions were depleted, either the strike would peter out or the workers in their desperation would resort to force, perhaps causing civil war. Therefore, relying on a compromise formula which Sir Herbert Samuel had worked out and which envisaged wage reductions only after measures of reorganization in the coal industry had been effectively adopted, they called off the general strike. It was a defeat for the workers, all the more humiliating because the miners, infuriated by the suggestion of wage reductions in the compromise formula, continued to strike throughout the summer. But then their powers of resistance were exhausted. Increasingly discouraged, they returned to work. They had no national contract, only local and regional contracts; the overall result was that they had to work longer hours for lower wages.

In the prosperity of the second part of the 1920's English life took on something of the glamor of the prewar years, and the general strike soon seemed a thing of the past. But its consequences were far-reaching. The opportunity for a thorough overhauling of the coal industry had been missed; it continued to ail and the mining regions remained centers of low wages and unemployment. The bleakness, hardships, and dangers of life among British coal miners have found literary expression in George Orwell's realistic and moving *Road to Wigan Pier* (1937).

Moreover, the general strike increased distrust between the working class and the rest of the population. The failure of the government to force upon the employers concessions which would have prevented the stoppage raised suspicions about the intentions of the ruling group, and they were reinforced by the intransigent and vehement pronouncements of some of its members while the strike was in progress. After its collapse Baldwin took a conciliatory attitude, urging that industry reinstate the workers without reducing wages. But he lacked energy in the pursuit of this policy and was not able to restrain his antilabor colleagues. In 1927 the Conservative majority in Parliament struck a blow against the trade unions by passing a bill which limited the right to strike to trade disputes; sympathy strikes became illegal. Furthermore the unions were no longer allowed to collect money for political purposes. The intransigence of the government stiffened the resistance of the workers against all measures which might involve a temporary reduction in wages or a temporary increase in unemployment through the closing of unprofitable enterprises. To compete effectively on the world market British industry required modernization, but this was not feasible without the workers' cooperation, which was unobtainable after the general strike.

Equally fatal for Britain's economy was the return to the gold standard which Winston Churchill, Conservative chancellor of the exchequer, announced in his first budget speech, in April, 1925. At this time nobody questioned the principle that the basic unit in a currency must be defined as equivalent to a stated quantity of gold. The mistake of Churchill's measure was not so much that the pound was tied again to a fixed weight of gold, but that the ratio chosen, namely the prewar parity, was too high. Churchill was acting on the advice of the governor of the Bank of England, Montagu Norman, who hoped that by returning to the prewar standard London would regain the dominating position in the money market which it had lost to New York during the First World War. However, the result of this step was an increase in the price of British goods on the world market and hence a weakening of Britain's position in international trade. This effect was the more dangerous because of Great Britain's adverse balance of trade. Financiers would now view every further widening of the gap between exports and imports as seriously endangering British economic life. Furthermore, lulled into false security by the prosperity of the nineteenth century, British industrialists had been remiss in renewing and modernizing their equipment; now the decline in profits made investments for these purposes impossible. Keynes was one of the few who realized that the return to prewar parity represented a further "competitive handicap." In general, these difficulties were fully recognized only after it was too late, when the prosperity of the later 1920's had ended in depression.

From 1924 to 1929, a Conservative government was in power, headed by Stanley Baldwin. He had risen to a leading position in the Conservative party only after the war. He was very different from the great aristocrats, Salisbury and Balfour, who had been Conservative prime ministers earlier in

Stanley Baldwin. *"How Good He Is, How Just. And Fit for Highest Trust."* Motto of a Baldwin biography by Arthur Bryant published in 1937.

the century and who might have had a sharper understanding of the change in the distribution of political and economic power brought about by the war. Baldwin was a rich industrialist, and his assumption of the Conservative leadership indicates the importance which businessmen had gained in the party. However, Baldwin was not the conventional businessman—unsentimental, purposeful and efficient; he was lazy and had no clear program nor plans. He acted only when action was unavoidable, and then his conduct was determined by intuition rather than cold reason. In his expressions of longing for a quiet and peaceful life, remote from the turbulence of industrial society, he reflected perfectly the nostalgic mood of the middle classes, which were frightened by the size of the problems of the postwar world and constructed an idealized picture of the stability and prosperity of Victorian and Edwardian England. Thus, Baldwin was content to see some of the splendor of prewar England return in the later 1920's without questioning how firm and deep-rooted the prosperity of this period was. Moreover, Baldwin's easygoing attitude permitted his cabinet a free hand; energetic ministers were able to make their own policy. The tenure of Austen Chamberlain as foreign secretary was a success. His half brother Neville Chamberlain (1869–1940), minister of health, enlarged the system of social security by gaining passage of an old-age-pension bill. Churchill, chancellor of the exchequer, tried to stimulate industry by lowering income taxes and increasing death duties. But the manner in which, against Baldwin's expressed desire, Churchill and Chamberlain insisted on making use of the defeat of the general strike to obtain passage of legislation curtailing the power of labor showed the tension which existed below the surface during these few fat years.

When signs of an incipient depression appeared, the popularity of the Conservatives was immediately reduced, and as a result of elections held in June, 1929, another Labor government under Ramsay MacDonald came into power. Actually, the Conservatives still remained the strongest in the popular vote; but the boundaries of the electoral districts were drawn in such a way that Labor received 280 seats in the House of Commons and the Conservatives only 261; the 59 Liberal members turned the scales. Because, as in 1924, the Labor government relied on Liberal support, radical measures involving socialization were precluded, but Labor had no real program for solving the unemployment problem within the existing economic system. The government's freedom of action was further limited because MacDonald had given the chancellorship of the exchequer to Philip Snowden (1864–1937), an old member of the Labor party and a convinced adherent of free trade and economic orthodoxy. Meanwhile, with the spread of the depression unemployment increased until in December, 1930, it reached 2.5 million, about 1.5 million more than when Labor had come into power eighteen months previously. With income from taxation declining and payments to the unemployed rising, the budget became unbalanced. A committee which investigated the economic situation took a very gloomy view. Its report recommended economies in government and particularly a reduction in unemployment benefits. This pessimistic evaluation of the British economy coincided with the financial crisis in Germany, in which British banking interests were deeply involved. A panic followed, and the consequence was that those who owned pounds transformed them into other currencies: a flight from the pound set in; a currency crisis was added to the budget crisis. Because Labor had no majority in the House of Commons, negotiations with the leaders of the other parties became necessary; urged on by British and American bankers, these leaders made their further support contingent upon a reduction in unemployment benefits. This was a bitter pill, hard to swallow for members of a Labor government. When the members of the government could come to no agreement on whether to accept such a cut, resignation seemed inevitable; a coalition of Conservatives and Liberals was expected to take over. But instead of submitting his resignation, MacDonald astonished his party with the announcement that he had agreed to remain as prime minister, heading a national government which would include the leaders of all three parties. Most members of the Labor party refused to follow him; only two Labor politicians of reputation—Snowden and J. H. Thomas (1874–1949) —accepted positions in the new government. A national Labor party which

MacDonald founded remained insignificant. Nevertheless, MacDonald's "treason"—as his action was regarded by his former party associates—was a blow from which the Labor party began to recover only at the end of the 1930's.

MacDonald's behavior in this crisis is a puzzle. Many ascribe it to defects in his character, particularly to his vanity and social snobbery. When after the formation of the national government MacDonald was told that he would find himself popular in unfamiliar circles, he is reported to have exclaimed, "Yes, tomorrow every duchess in London will be wanting to kiss me." But it should not be forgotten that his socialist beliefs arose from a vague political idealism. He had never been a Marxist, and had never concerned himself with economic analysis. In economic questions he was accustomed to follow the views of experts, and he was probably honestly persuaded that he was placing country before party.

The new government began by introducing severe measures of economy: a reduction in the salaries of civil servants and a cut in unemployment benefits, which were now limited to twenty-six weeks a year and given only after a means test. Wage reductions in the armed services led to a mutiny in the British navy at Invergordon, Scotland, and although the mutiny ended quickly, it triggered a new financial panic. The government reacted with a step which a few months before would have been considered out of the question: taking the pound off the gold standard. As a result the share of British exports in world trade remained relatively stable. Elections held on October 27, 1931, to provide a popular mandate for the government resulted in its overwhelming triumph; Labor received 46 seats, while the parties in the national government now had 556, of which 472 were Conservative. Although the label of national government was retained and MacDonald ended his tenure only in 1935, actually the Conservative party ruled in Britain until the Second World War.

Stanley Baldwin remained leader of the Conservative party and as such was the most powerful figure in the national government, even while MacDonald was prime minister. After MacDonald's withdrawal, Baldwin took over the prime ministership. He resigned two years later, in 1937, at the height of his influence and fame. These had been immensely increased by his skillful handling of the crisis brought about by King Edward VIII's insistence on marrying a divorcee, a matter that ended with the abdication of the King. Baldwin's successor as prime minister was Neville Chamberlain, a son of Joseph Chamberlain. In his family Neville had been regarded as inferior in political talent to his older brother Austen; Neville therefore had been destined for a business career. When he finally entered political life, he became concerned primarily with affairs of economic policy. After he had been minister of health in the Conservative government of the 1920's, he served as chancellor of the exchequer in the national government; as such he was chiefly responsible for the manner in which the national government tried to lift Great Britain out of the depression.

The economic policy of the national government was strictly orthodox. The main aim was to keep the budget balanced and, as far as was compatible with this aim, to stimulate industry by keeping taxes low. Under the shield of a national government, the Conservatives were able to carry through a measure that symbolized the death of the liberal England of the nineteenth century: they introduced protective tariffs. For the party of Joseph Chamberlain, and especially for his son, this was a unique opportunity to establish closer economic ties between Great Britain and its empire by means of preferential tariffs. To do so seemed the more desirable because, in the course of the twentieth century, the cohesion of the British Empire had steadily weakened. The bond between Great Britain and the dominions (Australia, Canada, New Zealand, the Union of South Africa, and the Irish Free State) had become tenuous, sentimental rather than legal. A formula accepted by Great Britain and the dominions at a conference in 1926 stated that the dominions were "autonomous communities within the British Empire, equal in status, in no way subordinate one to another in any aspect of their domestic or external affairs, though united by a common allegiance to the Crown, and freely associated as members of the British Commonwealth of Nations." In 1931 the Statute of Westminster defined this new notion of a "British Commonwealth of Nations" in contractual constitutional terms. Because the dominions regarded themselves as fully independent in domestic and foreign policy, they gave a cool reception to the British government's suggestion to improve the economic situation by preferential tariffs among the members of the empire. The negotiations in Ottawa during the summer of 1932 were difficult, and the results fell far short of Joseph Chamberlain's dream of free trade within the empire; essentially, it was agreed that the dominions would retain their existing duties on industrial products from Great Britain but would raise duties on industrial products from other countries.

Thus the economic policy of the British government remained cautious. Neville Chamberlain himself called the course which he pursued a "pegging away." British economic activity reached its low-point in the late summer of 1932. Then, assisted by a general improvement in the world economic situation, a slow recovery took place. It was interrupted by relapses. The British industrial apparatus was never thoroughly overhauled; in the severely depressed areas people continued to live close to starvation and unemployment never went below a million.

The issues the British government had to handle in the 1930's— independence of the dominions, unrest in India, shocks like the abdication crisis, and, most importantly, the economic difficulties of Great Britain— were diverse and complex. Since a balanced budget was the cornerstone of

British economic policy, the government shied away from new, additional burdens that could easily unbalance the budget and might halt the march toward recovery. There was great reluctance, therefore, to embark on a policy of rearmament or to pursue a foreign policy that demanded a strengthening of Britain's military forces. To justify this reluctance, most members of the ruling Conservative party tended to minimize the dangers which threatened from the dictators, particularly from the rise of Hitler, and to take an overly optimistic view of the possibility of coming to peaceful terms with them. Churchill, almost alone among the Conservatives, raised a warning voice against Hitler's aggressive tendencies. But at this time his political influence was at its lowest. While Labor's opposition to the dictators was clear and definite, the pacifist tradition in the party made the Laborites unwilling to accept the necessity of military rearmament; their recommendation of relying on collective security was rather unrealistic.

There was an influential group in the British ruling class, however, which regarded the rise of Nazism with a favorable eye. To this group belonged Dawson, the influential editor of the London *Times* who since the early 1920's had been fighting a pretended pro-French orientation of British foreign policy; and empire-minded politicians like Lord Lothian, who wanted to free England from bonds to the continent; and Germanophile aristocrats like the Astors who saw Hitler as a restorer of the good German society of imperial days. The benevolent attitude of this group toward Hitler arose from a variety of sources. The members of the group accepted the revisionist thesis that Germany had been unfairly treated in the Treaty of Versailles and that Germany would be a satisfied and peaceful power if these injustices were removed. They had a certain admiration for the disciplined and orderly German ways which Hitler was supposed to have reintroduced; moreover, because Germany was the strongest nation in Europe, they believed that Germany was entitled to a hegemony in Europe and would then keep that restless continent orderly and quiet. They were inclined to believe the Nazi propaganda thesis which held that, before the Nazi seizure of power, Germany had been in danger of becoming Communist; and they were anxious to have on the European continent a powerful force that would form a dam against the spread of Communism. The importance of this group—the Cliveden set, as it has been called after the country place of the Astors—lies in the fact that it influenced, almost prescribed, the policy Neville Chamberlain followed after he became prime minister in 1937.

Neville Chamberlain turned his particular attention to foreign policy because he was impatient with the disturbances of economic life by political crises. He possessed a naïve arrogance that considered all other peoples inferior to the British, so that there was not much difference whether they were democracies or dictatorships. He saw no reason, therefore, why Britain should not come to an understanding with the dictators, and, lacking in imagination, he had no inkling of the dynamic expansionism inherent in Nazism. Neville Chamberlain approached the negotiations with Hitler as a businessman approaches a deal with other businessmen, trusting that among men of property and common sense a bargain to reciprocal advantage should always be possible. If Great Britain showed Hitler goodwill by a number of concessions, he assumed, Hitler would be willing to cooperate with Great Britain in maintaining peace. With such misconceptions, Neville Chamberlain embarked hopefully on a policy of appeasement. The original view of the Chamberlain family that Neville lacked political talents proved fully justified.

France

Although the French reaction to Nazi expansion was as weak as that of Great Britain the weakness of French foreign policy had very different origins. In the 1930's a net drop in population and a shift in the French economic structure contributed to a sense of national decline, unrest, and tension.

Although France had acquired Alsace-Lorraine as a result of the war, its losses had been so heavy that in 1921, when the first postwar census was taken, its population—39,210,000 people—was smaller than in 1914. This decrease, particularly the loss of young men, resulted in a decline in births, and just in the middle of the 1930's—in 1935—the number of births became smaller than the number of deaths. The following year the population began to increase again, but only because of the immigration of foreigners into France.

While the demographic statistics presented a somber picture, the tension which accompanied the shift in the French economic structure might be regarded as a kind of growing pains. At the beginning of the decade, in 1931, 45.1 per cent of the labor force was employed in industry, in contrast to 36.1 per cent twenty-five years before; clearly there had been a shift from agriculture to industry. Particularly noticeable was the growth of heavy industry, such as mining, iron and steel production, and the manufacture of machinery; for instance, in 1931 the iron and steel industry employed over 100,000 more men than in 1906. Accompanying this development, during the interwar years, was a trend toward industrial concentration. The increasing importance of the workers led to demands for an active social policy, while the French bourgeoisie, frightened by the Russian Revolution, the loss of Russian investments, and the inflation of the early 1920's, tended to regard labor's claims as the beginning of a dangerous revolutionary development.

During the 1930's these tensions were sharpened by a deterioration of the economic and financial situation. Throughout the preceding decade French economic development had been favorable. Reconstruction of the destroyed areas, completed by 1926, had resulted in a modernization of industrial installations. Poincaré, who in 1926 had returned as prime minister, though without influence on foreign policy, had quickly ended the inflation by drastic economies which balanced the budget. The nation entered the depression period in an economically strong position, and because France was more self-sufficient than other highly industrialized powers it remained, at least at first, relatively immune to the effects of the depression. The French government made use of this economic strength in the critical political and financial negotiations about the *Anschluss* and the Hoover moratorium during the hectic summer of 1931. In the following years, however, the general weakness of the international markets had repercussions on France. Exports declined rapidly. If those of 1912 are taken as a base and represented by 100, they had risen to 125 in 1929, but declined to 59 in 1936. The decrease in exports resulted in a steadily widening deficit in the balance of trade, reaching 64 per cent in 1936, and was accompanied by a lower rate of industrial production, which in 1935 was back at the prewar level. Because of the demographic situation unemployment was a less serious problem in France than in Germany or Great Britain; nevertheless, in 1935 the number of unemployed had reached half a million. A degree of waste in government spending, of slight consequence in the days of prosperity, now resulted in budget deficits. Fear of inflation led to a flight from the franc. The parties of the left regarded these problems chiefly as the result of the selfish attempts of the rich to save their own fortunes; economic difficulties would end if the flight from the franc could be stopped. Thus it was difficult, if not impossible, for the government to get parliament to accept measures of economy and tax increases. Because only stopgap actions were taken the situation continued to deteriorate, and the politicians were accused of incompetence and corruption. By the ·end of 1934 both Poincaré and Briand were dead, and the political leaders of this period—Édouard Herriot, Édouard Daladier, André Tardieu—lacked the prestige and the authority enjoyed by their predecessors—the heroes of the Dreyfus Affair and the French victory.

A striking indication of the tension which was developing in French society was the Stavisky affair of 1934. In comparison to the Dreyfus Affair, which had involved great questions of principle, this was a murky business, a small financial swindle revealing some corruption. But the Stavisky scandal has its place in history because it showed that the old conflict between right and left—existing since the French Revolution, surfacing in the Dreyfus Affair but seemingly overcome by the national revival brought on by the First World War—had broken out again, in renewed strength. The eagerness with which the scandal was blown up into a crisis of republican and democratic institutions was an expression of the desperate feeling of the French middle classes that they were losing out against the forces of big business and labor. The explosion caused by the Stavisky affair must also be regarded as a sign of the malaise arising from the impression that the successive French governments had wasted the brilliant position which France had gained with its victory in the First World War.

Serge Alexander Stavisky was a financial swindler of tremendous charm and ingenuity. He had managed to make many acquaintances among politicians, and because he had served as an informer, his relations with the police were good. If not for these contacts the fraudulence of his financial dealings would have been discovered earlier. When finally his enterprise collapsed, puzzling things happened. The police surrounded his house, but reached Stavisky only after he had shot himself. One of the judges investigating the scandal was found dead on the railroad tracks. Rumors spread that Stavisky had not committed suicide but had been shot by the police because he knew too much and that the investigating judge had been eliminated for the same reason. A high official, a brother-in-law of Camille Chautemps, one of the most influential leaders of the Radical Socialists, was suspected of responsibility for silencing the scandal. The rightists boiled over in indignation about the corruption among the parliamentary leaders of the left. When the prime minister, Daladier, dismissed the president of the Paris police, who with little justification was regarded as an embodiment of energy and integrity, war veterans and other organizations of the right arranged demonstrations, marched to the parliament building, and tried to storm it. The police fired, but Marshal Lyautey, one of France's most distinguished military leaders, announced that on the following day he himself would march at the head of the demonstrators. Unable or unwilling to face this outburst, Daladier resigned, and a new government of national unity was formed.

The head of the new government was Gaston Doumergue (1863–1937), who had been president of the republic from 1924 to 1931, and it included all the surviving former prime ministers as well as military heroes such as Marshal Pétain. It was a last—rather ephemeral—attempt to hold together the divergent forces of French society by an appeal to national solidarity, and to infuse new life into French foreign policy. Louis Barthou (1862–1934), the foreign minister under Doumergue, tried to make full use of the decline in Hitler's prestige in the summer of 1934 which had resulted from the purge of the S.A. and the murder by Nazis of the Austrian chancellor Engelbert Dollfuss. Barthou cold-shouldered British attempts to resume negotiations about armament limitations with Germany and visited the capitals of Czechoslovakia, Yugoslavia, and Rumania—which were allied in the so-called Little Entente—and of Russia in order to forge a firm alliance between these powers and France. An "eastern" Locarno, which would prevent German expansion toward the east, was to supplement the "western" Locarno, with its guarantee of the permanence of the Franco-German frontier. But on October 9, 1934, King Alexander of Yugoslavia, on a visit to strengthen his nation's ties with France, was assassinated in Marseilles by a Macedonian nationalist; another victim was Barthou himself, who was seated in the car next to the king. With Barthou's death French foreign policy returned quickly to a dependence on Great Britain.

The Doumergue government made an attempt to overcome the most evident weaknesses of French political life. It concentrated on plans to strengthen the executive at the expense of the legislative, chiefly by facilitating the dissolution of parliament and by depriving deputies of the right to augment suggested financial legislation. But Doumergue overplayed his hand; he tried to overcome resistance by appealing through radio addresses directly to the people. This authoritarian technique went against all republican tradition and the parliamentarians gained broad support as defenders of democracy against the penetration of "Fascist" ideas into French political life. The Doumergue government fell and the succeeding governments mainly marked time until the elections scheduled for the spring of 1936. In this period of weak transitional governments Hitler marched into the Rhineland. The French government in power was not strong enough to make a decision which would have demanded an abandonment of the dogma that France could not march alone, that she had to keep in line with England. So instead of ordering its troops into the Rhineland the French government acceded to the urging of England that the issue ought to be solved by negotiations.

The election campaign of 1936 was entirely a struggle between the right and the left. And the left fought the election as a Popular Front which reached from the middle-class Radical Socialists to the Communists. The Popular Front won an impressive victory. While the Communists agreed to support the government without actively participating in it, the Socialists, for the first time in French history, entered the government as a party, and their leader, Léon Blum (1872–1950), became prime minister. Blum was a strange figure to be leader of the Socialist party. He was neither a tough politician nor a Marxist. He was an intellectual, a man of wide culture, and a humanitarian. His sympathies with the underprivileged had brought him into the Socialist camp. His human qualities would shine brilliantly in his courageous stand against the Nazis during the German occupation of France. After the Second World War he would be prime minister again, and at the end of his life he was to be recognized as a major national figure. But when Blum became prime minister for the first time in June, 1936, his particular qualities were little suited to the situation. He was a pacifist, an internationalist, with little interest in the details of foreign policy. His main concern was social reform; he expected to improve the situation of the poorer classes by modernizing French life. A wave of strikes underlining the

Léon Blum, French prime minister, being interviewed during a meeting.

urgent need for social reform accompanied the formation of the Popular
Front government. These strikes were of a new type—the sit-down: the
workers refused to work but remained in the factories, making the use of
strikebreakers impossible. Removal of the strikers would have required
force, which the Popular Front government did not want to employ against
its own supporters. Hence the industrialists were forced to make a number
of concessions, granting the workers rights which their counterparts in most
other European industrial countries already possessed—compulsory collective bargaining, the forty-hour week, paid holidays—and also wage increases
of from 12 to 15 per cent. These arrangements were negotiated under
government auspices and were supplemented by legislative measures
intended to restrict the influence of high finance and big business on
French policy. The Bank of France was brought under government control;
its credit policy could no longer obstruct the financial measures of the
government. The armament industry was nationalized, and the government
inaugurated a series of public works to fight unemployment. Such reforms
were long overdue. Thus, if France was to develop a strong air force, the
nationalization of the armament industry was necessary, since it would
make possible concentration on a few types of mass-produced airplanes.
Even so, because time was needed to harvest the advantages of the change,
airplane production in France remained dangerously weak for some years.

Meanwhile, the direct consequences of the measures taken by the Blum
government were a sharpening of internal conflicts and then also a weakening of the coherence of the Popular Front. Industrialists and bankers,
deeply resentful of the concessions to which they had been forced, continued the flight from the franc and sharply attacked the government policy of
spending freely without attempting to balance the budget. The government
had promised to maintain the value of the franc, but was soon forced to
devaluate. This measure spurred fear of inflation among the middle classes,

and the Radical Socialists, their representatives in the government, became doubtful about continued cooperation with the parties on the left. First Blum had to declare a "breathing spell" in social reforms, in order to restore confidence among the bourgeois partners in his coalition; then he was replaced as prime minister by a Radical Socialist, although the Socialists still remained members of the government. Then the Socialists left the government, although they continued to support it in parliament. But in 1938 Daladier, the Radical Socialist prime minister, turned to the right, and the Communists and Socialists resumed their old roles as members of the opposition.

One reason for the formation of the Popular Front, and the main motive underlying the Communist participation in it, had been to establish a firm stand against the advance of Nazism and Fascism. Unavoidably, many of those who resisted the social program of the Popular Front also opposed its ideas on foreign policy; they complained that both the domestic reforms and the international action against Fascism served the aims of international Communism rather than the national interests of France. "Better Hitler than Blum" was a slogan which spread among the rightists. Only a few organizations, although rather noisy ones, favored a Fascist regime in France, but many adherents of the right believed that because of its terrible losses in the First World War their nation should avoid involvement in another conflict at almost any cost; they saw no reason why France should obstruct Germany's ambitions in the east. France had built along the German frontier a strong defense line, called the Maginot Line after the politician responsible for its construction. And the French military leaders expressed full confidence in the ability of their army to hold firm behind this line, which, it was believed, the Germans would not be so foolish as to attack. Officially no French government ever admitted that it was willing to write off the alliances with the eastern European states. But the governments of the right which succeeded the Popular Front were inclined to minimize French commitments rather than to reinforce them. French foreign policy remained strong in words but timid in deeds. Its only serious concern was to avoid separation from Great Britain.

FROM THE RHINELAND OCCUPATION
TO THE OUTBREAK OF WAR

The militarization of the Rhineland upset the assumptions on which European statesmen had based their foreign policy. Germany was no longer open to French attack, and the great industrial area of the Ruhr was no longer exposed to the fire of French guns. The weakening of the French position had immediate repercussions in eastern and southeastern Europe. Except for Czechoslovakia, which continued to rely on the support of Great

Britain and France, the states of this region began to drift into the German orbit; this development was assisted by the German economic policy under the clever direction of Hjalmar Schacht. The eastern European countries, suffering acutely from the slump in agricultural prices, welcomed the opportunity offered by Germany to conclude barter agreements by which they could exchange agricultural products for German manufactured goods. Moreover, the German success in the Rhineland and the Italian triumph in Ethiopia had increased the prestige and appeal of the totalitarian systems. Mussolini, who in the 1920's had declared that Fascism was not an export article, was now proudly proclaiming that the democracies were obsolete and decaying and that Fascism represented the wave of the future. The various dictatorial regimes in Poland, Yugoslavia, Hungary, Rumania, and Bulgaria, now began to imitate Fascist or National Socialist forms and methods, and claimed that their systems of government embodied a new political spirit, appropriate to the twentieth century.

Mussolini's praise of Fascism as a young international force which would triumph over the dying world of the democracies indicated that he had moved into the German camp. Close cooperation between Italy and Nazi Germany was established by October, 1936, after the trip to Germany of Count Galeazzo Ciano (1903–1944)—Mussolini's foreign minister and son-in-law. The so-called Rome-Berlin Axis was then confirmed by an exchange of visits, with Mussolini going to Berlin in September, 1937, and Hitler to Rome in May, 1938. The meetings of the two dictators were accompanied by immense military reviews, which were recorded on film so that the world could be impressed with the might of the Fascist powers. The western democracies were confronted by the alternatives of opposition by force and negotiations ending in concessions. Appeasement began.

The Spanish Civil War

The event in which the Axis powers first tested the democracies' will to resist was the Spanish Civil War. The contest in Spain was bitter, vehement, and long because it represented the clash of forces deeply rooted in Spanish social and intellectual life. Essentially a struggle of modern industrial and democratic forces against the continued existence of agrarian feudalism, it became enmeshed with the traditional movements for regional independence against Castilian centralism and with the age-old dispute about the position of the Church in Spanish social life.

In 1931 the inability of the Spanish army to put down a Moroccan uprising compromised the monarchy and the ruling group; revolt followed, and a republic was established in which full power was held by a democratically elected parliament. From the beginning the republican regime led a precarious existence. The new constitution separated church and state, but attempts to remove the Church from all activities which were not strictly religious aroused the resistance of the Catholic hierarchy and of many Catholics among the population. The workers, by tradition radical and anarchist, were dissatisfied by the failure of the republican government to put through anticapitalist measures. Riots, strikes, burnings of churches occurred in various parts of the country; violence led to a resurgence of rightist parties, and the counterrevolutionaries organized themselves into a movement on the Fascist pattern—the Falange. To fight reaction, all the parties from the center to the extreme left joined together in a Popular Front, which triumphed in the elections of February, 1936, more than two months before the victory of the French Popular Front.

The victors regarded their success as a mandate to purge the administration of reactionaries and to go ahead with a program of modernization and social reform. The Popular Front government took steps to divide up the great estates; it forced industrialists to take back workers who had been dismissed because of participation in strikes; and it closed Catholic schools. But the far-reaching nature of these measures spurred the rightist opposition to action. The military had been considering a *coup d'état* for a long time; now the Spanish antirepublicans received encouragement from Mussolini, who promised money and weapons. A putsch was planned for the middle of July, 1936. On July 12, 1936, the murder of the monarchist leader José Calvo Sotelo by a republican who was captain of the police played right into the hands of the conspirators. This crime seemed to show that the government was unable to guarantee order and security, and gave some justification for the rebellion, which erupted on July 17. Although the revolt was popular among upper- and middle-class groups and had the active support of organizations like the Falange, it began primarily as an officers' conspiracy. The officers ordered their troops to occupy government buildings and took over the administration of various towns, or entrusted it to rightist political leaders.

The course of the Spanish Civil War was long and confused. Originally the military coup was not a success. The generals seized power in extended areas of northern and northwestern Spain. But the entire southwest (except for a few small isolated areas), the center of Spain, and even the Basque coast in the north remained loyal to the republic. To strengthen their forces, the republican leaders, after some hesitation, distributed weapons to the workers. The resulting dependence on the masses led to a government shift toward the left, with the socialists, Communists, and anarchists becoming increasingly influential.

After the incomplete success of the military putsch both sides appealed for foreign aid: the republicans to France and Russia, the military to Italy and Germany. The Fascist powers were quick to respond. Mussolini sent bombing planes; Hitler authorized the immediate dispatch of some twenty transport planes. The acquisition of these airplanes was crucial; the Spanish

THE SPANISH CIVIL WAR
1936-1937

Territory occupied by Franco to July 1936

Gains by Franco to March 1937

Territory held by Loyalists

navy had remained loyal to the republican government, and air transport was the only means for bringing the well-disciplined Moroccan troops from Africa into Spain. Hitler said correctly, some years later: "Franco ought to erect a monument to the glory of the German transport aircraft. The Spanish Revolution of Franco has to thank this aircraft for its victory." By means of the Moroccan troops led by Francisco Franco (born 1892), one of the conspiring generals, the Spanish Fascists succeeded in extending their rule over the south of Spain and in establishing a bridge to the territory which they controlled in the north. By the end of September the republicans no longer had a common frontier with Portugal. But even though the Fascists advanced in four columns into the suburbs of Madrid and had a "fifth column" of adherents within the city, their attempt to take the capital failed as the Spanish republicans rose heroically to its defense in the winter 1936–1937. The Fascists halted outside Madrid, and from there extended their rule toward the west. Only three regions remained under republican control. One of these stretched from Madrid to southeastern Spain. It was connected by a small coastal strip with the second center of republican power, Catalonia. Finally, the Basque country in the north, along the Atlantic coast, remained republican. Isolated as they were, these centers of republican strength were no match for the Fascists, who conquered one after the other. The anti-Fascist regime in the Basque area fell in the summer of 1937. Then the war dragged on. Barcelona, the chief city of Catalonia, was taken in January, 1939; and thousands of freezing and starving Spanish republicans along with the remaining republican troops—altogether almost 400,000 people—crossed the frontiers to France, where on open land, fenced in by wires, lacking shelter and food, they dragged on their lives. Two months later, in March, 1939, Madrid surrendered. By then Spain was no longer a center of international politics.

The Spanish Civil War and European Diplomacy

The war was not just an internal Spanish affair. It was a struggle in which directly or indirectly the whole of Europe was involved. If the dispatch of German and Italian planes had been crucial in revitalizing the military revolt after its initial setback, the arrival of Russian tanks and aircraft in the fall of 1936 decisively helped the republican defense of Madrid against the renewed attack of the Fascists; moreover, Russian advisers gave coherence to the somewhat disorganized military effort of the republicans. Germany and Italy responded by boosting the Spanish Fascist regime with diplomatic recognition. But they also gave concrete assistance. The Germans sent more aircraft, and pilots as well—bomber squadrons of the so-called Condor Legion. The most famous—or infamous—exploit of the German fliers was the attack on Guernica during Franco's campaign against the Basque country (April, 1937). First they bombed the small rural town, then they machine-gunned the streets, killing and wounding about 2,500 of the 7,000 inhabitants. Later, the Germans would admit that this assault had been an experiment to test the effects of terror bombing. The Italian experiments were less devastating and less instructive; in trying out tank attacks they received a severe setback at Guadalajara, near Madrid (March, 1937). This loss of prestige impelled Mussolini to send additional Italian troops to Spain; at one point about forty thousand Italians were fighting there.

Undoubtedly the German and the Italian assistance to the Fascists was more effective than the Russian aid to the republicans, especially since the long route through the Mediterranean from the Black Sea was threatened by German and Italian submarines and warships. A balance could have been struck if the republicans had received airplanes, tanks, and supplies from the north, from France. But though Léon Blum, the French prime minister, was willing to send assistance, he was opposed by the British leaders and the nonsocialist members of his own government, who feared international complications, particularly the strengthening of Communism. Blum yielded to these pressures despite the indignation of the Communists and of many members of his own Socialist party.

Disagreement concerning the Spanish Civil War was an important factor in breaking up the French Popular Front. Hoping to localize the conflict, France and Great Britain suggested to the other powers a policy of nonintervention. The negotiations to implement this policy were long and drawn-out, and even after Russia, Germany, and Italy had been won over and a committee entrusted with the supervision of nonintervention had been established, Germany and Italy raised endless difficulties; they finally withdrew their troops only when they felt sure that doing so would not endanger the victory of Fascism in Spain.

For Hitler and Mussolini the Spanish Civil War was heartening proof of the weakness of their adversaries; they learned that although Russia, France, and Great Britain might be opposed to any disturbance of the *status quo*, they did not agree about how to control Fascist aggression. Evidently the main concern of the western powers was to avoid war.

But the Spanish Civil War did more than reveal the immense strength which the Fascist powers had gained. With the failure of the democracies, the opposition to Fascism lost its drive. When the Spanish Civil War began it had seemed evident that the democratic forces had right on their side and that democracy and Fascism met in Spain in a situation of equality—not prejudiced in favor of Fascism. It had appeared that if Fascism received a check in Spain the myth of its inevitable progress would be destroyed. After this one great effort the Fascist nightmare under which Europe lived might disappear.

> Tomorrow for the young the poets exploding like bombs,
> The walks by the lake, the weeks of perfect communion;
> Tomorrow the bicycle races
> Through the suburbs on summer evenings. But today the struggle.[1]

Men from all over the globe volunteered to fight for the Spanish republic. One of the most efficient of the republican military units was the International Brigade, in which Communists, socialists, and liberals served. Writers of many nationalities—George Orwell, who was British; Ernest Hemingway, an American; André Malraux, of France; Arthur Koestler, a Hungarian—came to Spain, fought with the republicans, and advocated their cause in their writings. Their hour of triumph was the heroic defense of Madrid. But they also experienced the dissension which broke out with

[1] W. H. Auden, "Spain 1937," quoted by Hugh Thomas, *The Spanish Civil War* (New York, 1961), p. 221.

Guernica. *Mural by Pablo Picasso, 1937, on extended loan from the artist to the Museum of Modern Art, New York.*

the approach of defeat—particularly a bitter struggle between Communists and anarchists in which many sincere fighters against Fascism were brutally killed.

In the years of appeasement that followed, those who had served in defense of the Spanish republic had a hard time. The governments of the western democracies looked with disfavor on these freedom fighters— "premature anti-Fascists," they were later termed by American officials. In Russia, after Stalin had turned away from the idea of a Communist-democratic alliance against Fascism, many of the participants in the Spanish Civil War were treated as criminals. However, some of the fighters for the Spanish republic survived, and were able to begin new political careers after the Second World War. Among the Communists, Ernö Gerö became one of the political leaders of Hungary. Palmiro Togliatti and Luigi Longo gained prominence in the Communist party in Italy. Of the non-Communists Pietro Nenni and Randolfo Pacciardi became ministers in Italy; André Malraux, in France. But in the years immediately following the Spanish Civil War the spirit of the fight against Fascism in Spain seemed to remain alive only in works of art; the painting "Guernica" (1937) by Pablo Picasso and Ernest Hemingway's novel *For Whom the Bell Tolls* (1940) expressed the tragic hopelessness of man's struggle against inhuman forces.

Anschluss *and the Invasion of Czechoslovakia*

The weakness which the western democracies had shown—first in the Rhineland crisis and then in the Spanish Civil War—gave Hitler the green light to proceed with his aggressive and expansionist foreign policy. In a meeting with his chief military and civilian advisers in November, 1937, he announced that Germany needed more living space, which could be secured only through war; such a war ought to take place in the early 1940's because German rearmament would then reach its peak. Preconditions for a successful war were the elimination of Czechoslovakia and the achievement of the *Anschluss*. Hitler also intimated that the situation which had developed in the Mediterranean as a result of the Spanish Civil War might afford an opportunity for quick action. Although subsequently he adjusted his tactics to changing circumstances, and the actual sequence of events was different from the one envisaged at this meeting, this speech did reveal his fundamental aims. When his chief military advisers expressed some reservations and doubts, they paid for their hesitation with loss of their positions. One of them, Werner von Fritsch, was charged with homosexuality; by the time the groundlessness of this accusation was proved it was too late to reinstate him. The other, Werner von Blomberg, the minister of war, was declared to have violated the officers' code of honor by marrying a former prostitute, even though Hitler had approved of the marriage and attended the wedding. The dismissal of these two generals demonstrated that the army had lost its independence. At the same time the foreign minister, Konstantin von Neurath (1873–1956), a professional diplomat who had been a compliant servant of the Nazis but was somewhat too cautious in Hitler's views, was replaced by a Nazi, Joachim von Ribbentrop (1893–1946). All obstacles to action had been removed.

Hitler's first victim was Austria. Stepped-up Nazi propaganda in Austria for *Anschluss* with Germany had led to increased measures of suppression by the Austrian government. In an interview with Chancellor Schuschnigg on February 4, 1938, Hitler demanded that these measures be lifted and that some of the Austrian Nazis be included in the government. Intimidated by Hitler's vehemence and by the threat of German troop movements toward the Austrian border, Schuschnigg gave in. But he soon realized that once the Nazis had entered the government they would take complete control. On March 9, in desperation, he announced a plebiscite in which the people were asked to vote on whether they wanted to keep Austrian independence. On March 11, Hitler sent an ultimatum demanding postponement of the plebiscite, and on March 12, dispatched his troops into Austria under the pretext that Schuschnigg's government was unable to maintain order. On March 14, 1938, Vienna, where Hitler in his youth had lived in utter misery, saw him return in triumph: the *Anschluss* creating a greater Germany had been achieved. The western powers did nothing except protest feebly on paper; Mussolini, who in 1934, when the first Nazi putsch took place in Austria, had moved his troops to the Brenner frontier, now declared that he was uninterested in the fate of Austria; he had gone too far to deviate from his pro-German course. Overjoyed, Hitler told Mussolini that he would never forget what he had done for him.

The next victim was Czechoslovakia. Hitler wanted the incorporation into Germany of the Sudeten region, a broad stretch of northern Czechoslovakia populated chiefly by Germans. Because this area was south of the mountains separating Germany from Czechoslovakia and included the Czechoslovakian line of fortifications, its loss would mean the end of Czechoslovakia as an independent factor in European power politics. Here again, the western powers put up only weak resistance against Hitler's expansionist policy. The crisis first erupted in the spring of 1938, and several times in the months that followed Europe seemed to be on the brink of war. Although the British government of Neville Chamberlain was little concerned about the fate of the Sudeten Germans and of Czechoslovakia—the affair being, in Chamberlain's words, "a quarrel in a faraway country between people of whom we know nothing"—the British were aware that they could not remain on the sidelines of a European conflict developing from Hitler's demands on Czechoslovakia. This danger was great, for since 1924 France had been tied to Czechoslovakia through a clear and definite defensive alliance, and Soviet Russia was obligated to support France and Czechoslovakia if they had to defend themselves against German aggression. Hence, the British government's main concern was to prevent a clash by force which would make fulfillment of the alliance commitments by France and Russia an automatic consequence. The British tried to persuade Hitler to be content with autonomy for the Sudeten Germans within the Czechoslovak state, and pressed Czechoslovakia to agree to this concession. But Hitler spurred the Nazis in the Sudeten area to demonstrations which led to clashes with the police; he then declared that Czechoslovakian brutality made further existence of the Sudeten Germans under Czechoslovak rule impossible and demanded complete separation of this region from Czechoslovakia, threatening to back his demand by military action.

At this critical moment Chamberlain decided to fly to Berchtesgaden, where he met Hitler on September 15, 1938. There Chamberlain gave Hitler what he wanted, the Sudeten area, in return for a promise that Germany would refrain from immediate military action. The British and French governments forced the Czechs to accept this solution by threatening to withdraw all support if they refused. But Hitler was still not satisfied; in a second meeting between Hitler and Chamberlain, in Bad Godesberg on September 22, Hitler declared that the procedure envisaged at Berchtesgaden for the German take-over was too slow. The transfer would have to be completed by October 1—if necessary, by military invasion. The deadlock seemed complete, and Chamberlain returned to London with little hope that peace could be maintained. But Mussolini, anxious to avoid war and eager to increase his prestige by appearing as Europe's arbiter, intervened, persuading Hitler to convene a conference at Munich on September 29.

The Munich Conference was a shocking demonstration of the extent to which the methods of international politics had deviated from those envisioned for the new world order at the end of the First World War.

The Munich Conference. *In the front row, Neville Chamberlain, Daladier, Hitler, Mussolini, and Ciano, Mussolini's son-in-law and Italian foreign minister; in the second row, Bonnet, French foreign minister (between Chamberlain and Daladier), Ribbentropp (between Hitler and Mussolini), Alexis Leger, general secretary in the French Foreign Office (between Mussolini and Ciano); as poet Leger is known under the name St.-John Perse.*

Then, the expectation had been that the great and the small nations would have an equal voice. But at Munich, the leaders of the four great European powers—Hitler, Mussolini, Daladier, and Chamberlain—conferred alone; only after all decisions had been made were the representatives of Czechoslovakia, the state most concerned, informed of the agreement by a yawning Chamberlain and a nervous Daladier. Hitler had made one concession; the deadline for the complete occupation of the Sudeten area was postponed to October 10. One may wonder what would have happened if the Czechoslovaks had rejected the Munich agreement and fought, whether then public opinion in Britain and France might have forced these powers to come to the rescue. But the Czechoslovaks and their president, Benes exhausted from endless negotiations and broken promises, felt that they could not risk such a gamble. They gave in; Benes abdicated, leaving the government of the country to men he believed might get along better with the triumphant Nazis.

In an eloquent attack on British foreign policy in the House of Commons, Winston Churchill characterized the Munich Conference as "a disaster of the first magnitude." But his was a lonely voice. Returning from Munich, Chamberlain was received like a victorious conquerer. To the enthusiastic crowds he said, "This is the second time in our history that there has come back from Germany to Downing Street, peace with honour. I believe it is peace for our time." Perhaps no remark shows more clearly the erroneous assumptions of Chamberlain's appeasement policy. Later he tried to defend the Munich agreement by explaining that it gave Great Britain and France time to rearm. But this justification was palpably false. In the year between Munich and the outbreak of the Second World War the gap in armed strength between Germany and the western powers did not narrow; it widened. The elimination of Czechoslovakia freed numerous German forces for service elsewhere, and the substantial military equipment installed in the fortifications of the Sudeten area now fell into German hands. Chamberlain did not put enough energy into the drive for British rearmament to compensate for this increase in German military strength. He regarded Hitler as a great German patriot who wanted only to complete Bismarck's work by uniting all Germans in one national state and would then rule happily and peacefully ever after. Defending the Munich settlement in the House of Commons, Chamberlain said, "There is sincerity and goodwill on both sides."

During the winter of 1938–1939 European politicians were in a euphoric mood. The French signed a pact which provided for consultation in all questions of dispute with Germany and indicated that the Germans could have a free hand in southeastern Europe. The British also expressed their willingness to regard southeastern Europe as a German sphere of interest. The harmony between the western democracies and the Axis powers was somewhat disturbed by Mussolini, who suddenly made loud claims for Nice, Savoy, and Tunisia, but the British recognized the Italian conquest of Ethiopia and hoped to act as mediators between the French and the Italians.

None of the men in control in France and Great Britain was very much bothered by events in Germany showing that Nazi brutality had not abated; in one night all the synagogues were burned and destroyed; the Jews were eliminated from German economic life and deprived of their property. At the beginning of 1939 the British government was convinced that political appeasement could now be strengthened by close economic cooperation between Germany and Great Britain. Chamberlain stated on March 10 that Europe was settling down to a period of tranquillity. Six months later Great Britain and France were at war with Germany.

The End of Appeasement

The event which changed British policy from appeasement to resistance was the incorporation of what had been left of Czechoslovakia into Greater Germany. The Nazis stimulated agitation for independence of the Slovak-ian region of the Czechoslovak state, and when the Czechoslovakian government took measures to suppress this movement Hitler ordered Emil Hácha (1872–1945), as Benes' successor as president of the republic, to Berlin and forced him to recognize a German protectorate over Czechoslo-vakia. The next morning, on March 16, 1939, German troops poured over the borders and Hitler entered Prague.

Suddenly British public opinion turned against Germany. This abrupt

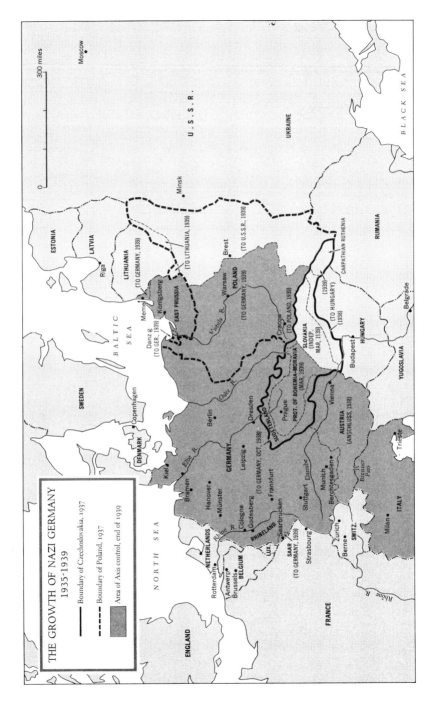

THE GROWTH OF NAZI GERMANY
1935-1939

—— Boundary of Czechoslovakia, 1937

- - - Boundary of Poland, 1937

▨ Area of Axis control, end of 1939

300 miles

Moscow

U.S.S.R.

BLACK SEA

ESTONIA

LATVIA

Riga

LITHUANIA
(TO GERMANY, 1939)

(TO LITHUANIA, 1939)

Minsk

Memel

Königsberg

Danzig
(TO GER., 1939)

EAST PRUSSIA

BALTIC
SEA

SWEDEN

Copenhagen

DENMARK

Warsaw

Brest

POLAND
(TO GERMANY, 1939)

(TO U.S.S.R., 1939)

Vistula R.

Cracow

(TO POLAND, 1939)

UKRAINE

CARPATHIAN RUTHENIA

RUMANIA

(1939)
(TO HUNGARY)
(1938)

SLOVAKIA
(INDEP.
MAR., 1939)

HUNGARY

Budapest

Belgrade

YUGOSLAVIA

Oder R.

Berlin

Dresden

Leipzig

Prague

PROT. OF BOHEMIA-MORAVIA
(MAR. 1939)

SUDETENLAND
(TO GERMANY, OCT. 1938)

Vienna

AUSTRIA
(ANSCHLUSS, 1938)

Danube

GERMANY

Kiel

Elbe R.

Bremen

Hanover

Münster

Cologne

Godesberg

Frankfurt

Saarbrücken

SAAR
(TO GERMANY, 1939)

RHINELAND

Rhine R.

Rotterdam

Antwerp

Brussels

BELGIUM

NETHERLANDS

LUX.

Strasbourg

Stuttgart

Munich

Berchtesgaden

Brenner
Pass

Zurich

Berne

SWITZ.

Milan

ITALY

Trieste

Rhone R.

FRANCE

ENGLAND

NORTH
SEA

German troops entering Prague in 1939.

explosion of British anger—after so many retreats—is difficult to understand. It has been said that British indignation was aroused because with
this action Hitler demonstrated that he was not content with uniting
Germans under his rule, and showed that his previous appeals for national
self-determination had been hollow pretense disguising a brutal policy of
expansion. It is true that the occupation of Czechoslovakia showed up the
misconception of those who had presented Hitler as a great German
patriot. It is more likely, however, that many people in Great Britain were
simply tired of being faced by one crisis after the other, of being bullied.
And it appeared unlikely that a Hitler dominating Europe would leave the
British empire undisturbed.

Chamberlain now reversed his policy, but because of the pressure of
public opinion rather than because he had changed his mind. Indeed, he
tried until the last moment to renew contacts with Hitler. Publicly,
however, he gave the impression of having abandoned appeasement, and
dramatized this shift with a spectacular diplomatic move. His government
gave guarantees to the two states which were now most directly in the way
of further German expansion and therefore most immediately threatened—Poland and Rumania. Many Frenchmen might have preferred to
evade their obligations to Poland, behaving as they had toward Czechoslovakia, but the British support of Poland meant that French retreat was
impossible. When Hitler marched his troops into Poland, on the pretext
that the Poles had not accepted his demands for restoration to the Reich
of Danzig and the Polish Corridor, Great Britain and then France declared
war on Germany, on September 3, 1939.

Hitler does not seem to have expected that his action against Poland
would result in war with Great Britain and France. Lacking all sense of

The signing of the German-Soviet Pact in 1939. *Behind Ribbentrop, Molotov and Stalin.*

moral values he had no appreciation of the revulsion which his march into Prague had aroused, nor did he understand why powers which had refused to fight for strategically important and relatively accessible Czechoslovakia would undertake war for distant and indefensible Poland. On the other hand, it appears that in his quarrel with Poland, Hitler was not willing to agree to another peaceful settlement. Hitler was convinced that to restore German prestige, damaged by the defeat in the First World War, a successful military campaign was needed. Instead of being exhilarated by the results of the Munich Conference, he had been depressed. He had felt that in yielding to Mussolini's demands for a conference he had let slip the opportunity for a victorious war. Nevertheless, although he did not fear war if his actions against Poland involved him in a conflict with Great Britain and France, he would have preferred these powers to remain neutral, so that the campaign against Poland could be kept localized. He had a trump card which in his opinion would secure British and French neutrality. On August 23, 1939, a week before the attack on Poland, Germany had signed a nonaggression pact with Soviet Russia.

In all the calculations of the policy makers the insuperability of the contrast between Nazi Germany and Communist Russia had been taken for granted. When after the German march into Prague, Great Britain gave guarantees to Poland and Rumania, the British and French governments believed that they would be able to gain Soviet Russia's help in stemming further German expansion. British and French missions were sent to Moscow, but after a period of fruitless negotiations they heard the news that instead of tying Russia to the western powers, Stalin had made a pact with Nazi Germany.

SOVIET RUSSIA DURING THE INTERWAR YEARS

It is a strange reversal of fortunes that in the weeks preceding the outbreak of the Second World War, Soviet Russia's friendship and assistance were eagerly sought by the great European powers. History seemed to have turned full circle. Twenty years before, the statesmen arranging in Paris the future of Europe and of the world had been anxious to move Russia out of Europe. And indeed, during most of the interwar years Russia had remained on the periphery of international events. In the 1930's, with Hitler gaining increasing power, Russia gradually took a more active role in European affairs; but still in 1938 it had been allowed no voice in the arrangements for settling the Czech crisis.

If now in 1939 Russia's support was eagerly sought by both of the antagonistic groups, this was proof of the breakdown of the principles on which the settlements reached at the Paris Peace Conference had been based: the notion that the exercise of democracy, and obedience to international law were requisites for acceptance as an equal partner in international life. Statesmen were aware that in the emergencies of wartime Russia's wealth in natural resources—in foodstuffs and minerals—could become decisive, but the courting of Russia was also an indication that people recognized that the Bolshevik rule there was securely established. During the interwar years European intellectual and scholarly circles had never lacked an interest in the developments in Russia, and the chances of success or failure of the Soviet experiment had been the object of vehement, rather partisan, discussion. But an appreciation of the system in its entirety began only when Russia emerged as a necessary, almost crucial, factor in the European balance of power. Only then did people in the other parts of Europe begin really to grasp what had happened within the Soviet borders and to realize that in the preceding twenty years a new Russia had been formed.

The Rise of Stalin

The developments which led to this situation were inextricably tied up with the fortunes of Joseph Stalin (1879–1953). The 1920's were dominated by the fight for Lenin's successorship, which ended in Stalin's victory; and the 1930's saw the economic and political reorganization of Russia, which

A characteristic product of pro-Stalinist propaganda. A *painting intended to show the close collaboration between Lenin and the young Stalin.*

was accompanied by the purges in which all possible rivals of Stalin were eliminated.

Stalin's rise to supreme power in Soviet Russia owed much to luck. In May, 1922, Lenin suffered a stroke, and from that time until his death on January 21, 1924, he was able to work only intermittently. In his last years Lenin clashed with Stalin but was no longer able to follow up the orders by which he tried to curb him. He inserted in his last will a statement that Stalin was too ruthless and should be removed from office. But Lenin's suggestion was not carried out; many of the Bolshevik leaders were more in fear of Trotsky than of Stalin. They prefered to ally themselves with the solid and plodding Stalin against the brilliant but erratic Trotsky, whom they regarded as an unstable intellectual. Thus, when Lenin's will was read in a meeting of the Central Committee of the Communist party, a great majority—forty against ten—voted to suppress publication of the passage directed against Stalin.

In the early years of Bolshevik rule Stalin held a number of positions, highest in the official hierarchy being that of the people's commissar of nationalities. In this office he was instrumental in effecting the transformation of Russia into the federal Union of Soviet Socialist Republics; in 1922 the members of the Union were Russia, Byelorussia, the Ukraine, and Transcaucasia; to these, subsequently the Uzbek and Turkmen republics were added. The major fields of governmental activity—foreign policy, international trade, defense, economic planning, the organization of justice and education—were under federal control, but within this framework the governments of the various Soviet republics could adjust the school system, the administration of justice, the organization of agriculture, to the particular needs and demands of their regions and citizens.

Stalin was also the general secretary of the Central Committee of the Communist party; it was about this position that Lenin was primarily concerned, because Stalin's ruthlessness seemed to him to endanger the Communist party's coherence and enthusiasm. As general secretary of the Central Committee, Stalin, as Lenin wrote, "concentrated an enormous power in his hands." Understanding of the key role played by the general secretary of the Central Committee of the Communist party requires some acquaintance with the constitutional structure of Soviet Russia. The basic elements of the Bolshevik government were the Councils of the Workers and Peasants. Such councils existed on local, provincial, and regional levels, the higher councils consisting of members deputized by the lower councils. Every two years an all-union congress of councils elected a Central Executive Committee composed of two chambers, one representing the people, the other the governments of the member republics of the Soviet Union. This Central Executive Committee met every year, roughly fulfilling the role of a European parliament. It appointed the Council of People's Commissars, which exercised the highest executive power. The government thus appeared to be a pyramidal structure, rising from a broad base to a small peak. But the twelve people's commissars who directed policy were almost independent of the elected body which had appointed them. One reason was that the infrequent and relatively short meetings of the all-union congress of councils and the Central Executive Committee did not allow true supervision of the people's commissars, who had to make important decisions daily. Another reason was that the people's commissars drew their strength from their prominent position in the Communist party, for it was the party that was the controlling element within the Soviet structure. Legally, every man in the Soviet Union earning his livelihood through productive labor had the right to vote. But the lists of council candidates for whom the people could vote were assembled by the Communist party.

The Communist party was relatively small, comprising not more than 1 per cent of the population; in 1930 the party had 1,192,000 members. In sharp contrast to the pyramidal structure of the council system, the party was directed from above, by a Central Committee of about twenty of the most prominent Communists. While the most brilliant and active of these concentrated on work in a special committee—the Politburo—which laid down the general lines of Russian and Communist policy, Stalin immersed himself in the drudgery of party administration. As general secretary of the Central Committee of the Communist Party Stalin had a decisive voice in determining admission to the party and promotion within its ranks. Since the party determined who could be council candidates, he thus exerted control over personnel throughout the government. The result was that he knew intimately the rank-and-file Communists, and they, being dependent on him for promotion, were willing to accept his leadership.

The firm hold over the party organization represented Stalin's main strength in the struggle to succeed Lenin. His rivals—particularly Trotsky, the hero of the civil war—were much better known. The struggle is generally described as a conflict between adherents of the "idea of permanent revolution," grouped around Trotsky, and advocates of "socialism in one country," who followed Stalin. The conflict between the Trotskyites and the Stalinists intensified in 1923, when the end of inflation in Germany terminated the revolutionary ferment in central Europe. Any hopes that the revolution might spread beyond the Russian borders were crushed. To most Bolsheviks it was almost unthinkable that the Russian Revolution would not spark an international revolution. To maintain an isolated socialist state within a capitalist world seemed impossible. At first Stalin accepted this view. But when—after some hesitation—he had convinced himself of the solidity of the capitalist regimes in the face of Communist attacks, he set his course firmly toward the construction of a new Russian society able to stand on its own. During the Fourteenth Communist Party Congress, in March, 1925, Stalin obtained official approval of the doctrine of "socialism in one country."

Other Bolshevik leaders found abandonment of the idea of world revolution more difficult. Many of them, during long years in exile, had established close relations with extremists in other countries. Stalin had been outside of Russia just once—and then for a few weeks—and had no real acquaintance with social and industrial developments in other countries. Moreover, some of the Bolshevik leaders, such as Grigori Zinoviev, the head of the Communist International, and Karl Radek were motivated by ideological considerations in contrast to the empirical Stalin, who was aware that concentration on an economic transformation in Russia would strengthen his own position since an increasing number of party officials would be needed to direct and control the process.

Opposition to Stalin's policy of "socialism in one country" became pronounced only after it was evident that it resulted in the creation of an immense new bureaucracy. Trotsky, for instance, attacked Stalin because instead of leading to the disappearance of the state, in accordance with Marxist theory, his course of action resulted in an aggrandized bureaucratic machinery. But Stalin's views had become the accepted "line" of the Communist party, and Stalin stamped Trotsky's opposition as antirevolutionary and subversive. In 1927 Trotsky was divested of all his functions and expelled from the party, with seventy-five other leading members of the opposition. Exiled to Siberia, he continued his agitation there. In 1929 he was expelled from Russia, and found refuge in Mexico. Eleven years later he was assassinated by a man unquestionably acting on Stalin's orders.

The defeated in the struggle for Lenin's succession. *Trotsky in exile.*

"Socialism in One Country"

Pursuit of the policy of "socialism in one country" resulted in a major social upheaval accompanied by economic hardship and suffering. The golden age which theoretically was supposed to follow the defeat of capitalism seemed still far away, and the Bolshevik leaders were anxious to emphasize that a truly communist society could become reality only after the capitalist system had been overthrown all over the world; at the moment they were at work to create a system of transition, a socialist society.

The underlying aim of "socialism in one country" was to transform Russia into a highly industrialized state, able to compete with more advanced countries, such as Great Britain and the United States, and capable of putting up a good fight against aggression by capitalist nations. In Russia industrialization also involved a transformation of agriculture, which had to be made more efficient, so that the increasing number of industrial workers in the cities could be fed and a surplus could be produced for export, which alone could provide needed foreign currency. The vast changes had to be accomplished without impairment of the fundamental principle of a socialist regime—control of the state over economic life—and without the help of private or foreign capital. To achieve these aims the Russians devised a method that was entirely novel: the drafting of an economic plan which encompassed all fields of economic activity in all parts of the country. Thus, in the following years Russian life was dominated by the efforts to achieve the goals which were set in two Five-Year

Plans. The first was initiated in 1928, but as the Russian leadership proudly proclaimed, it was carried out in four years, so the second Five-Year Plan could begin in 1932.

During the Second World War, Winston Churchill once asked Stalin whether he had found the stresses of the war as bad as those arising from carrying through the policy of the collective farms. " 'Oh, no,' he said, 'the Collective Farm policy was a terrible struggle.' "[2] The Russian economic planners ordered collectivization of agriculture primarily because it would facilitate the use of modern methods and machines which would increase production. But collectivization was expected also to strengthen the grip of the government over rural life. The somewhat wealthier peasants, the kulaks, who had been favored by Stolypin's reforms and later had flourished under the New Economic Policy, became disenchanted with the Bolshevik regime in the course of the 1920's. Because rationing and fixed food prices made agricultural production unremunerative, many peasants refused to deliver their produce to the cities and limited production to their own personal needs. When the government decided on collectivization, the kulaks regarded this policy as a direct attack on their property rights and on their very existence, and they resisted in all possible ways. They burned collective farms, they destroyed tractors and other agricultural machinery, and when integration into the collective-farm system finally became unavoidable, they slaughtered their animals; almost three million horses and cattle—nearly half of their entire stock—were killed. The government then decided to eliminate the kulaks as a class, and incited the poorer peasants against them, assisting this class warfare with police and military forces. The land owned by kulaks was confiscated; their houses were transformed into clubs or schools, and an estimated two million were deported to remote areas, where they were used as forced labor.

The requirements for modernizing agriculture were important in determining the plans set up for industry. For example, the annual production of tractors increased from 6,000 at the beginning of the first Five-Year Plan to 150,000 at its end. Next to the needs of agriculture those of defense were most influential in shaping the industrialization program. The emphasis was on heavy industry. Large new cities sprang up in the vicinity of coal and iron mines; Magnitogorsk, in the midst of rich mineral deposits in the southern Urals, owed its existence to the Five-Year Plans; at the end of the first Five-Year Plan it had about 65,000 inhabitants; seven years later the population had grown to more than 150,000. The concentration on heavy industry necessarily limited the production of consumer goods; for instance, the Five-Year Plan envisaged a shoe industry which would give each person two new pairs every three years. This paucity of consumer goods meant that

[2] Winston S. Churchill, *The Second World War*, Vol. IV, *The Hinge of Fate* (Boston, 1950), p. 498.

wages could be kept down and that the general standard of living remained low. From the point of view of the planners, the shortage in consumer goods had the advantage that workers were unable to spend all their wages and would place some of their earnings in the state bonds which helped to finance industrialization. The Five-Year Plans were also financed by the profits of the state stores and by taxes, notably a turnover tax, a form of sales tax.

Although Russian pronouncements and statistics tended to paint an exaggerated picture of the sucess of the Five-Year Plans, the main goals were undoubtedly achieved. Russia was transformed from an agrarian into an industrial country. In 1932, 70.7 per cent of the Russian national product came from industry. In addition, as a consequence of the centralized organization of Russian economic life, private enterprise disappeared almost completely.

The Soviet rulers, as firm believers in the theories of Marx, regarded intellectual achievements as a superstructure resting on the economic system; they attached great importance to intellectuals and their training. They were aware that an industrial society required a large corps of trained personnel—technicians, engineers, doctors, economists, teachers—and that the great bulk of the people ought to have an education which would enable them to handle modern machinery. Hence the Bolshevik regime established schools all over the country to eliminate illiteracy, which at the time of the revolution was widespread; in 1923, 27,000,000 people in Russia still could neither write nor read.

Workers took evening courses to prepare for university study; universities proliferated, emphasizing technical subjects and the natural sciences. With the reduction of illiteracy, publishing activities grew in extent and importance; newspapers and periodicals dispensed knowledge useful for increasing industrial and agricultural productivity, and they also spread propaganda. The Russian rulers recognized that the work the masses were forced to do and the privations they were asked to undergo were made bearable only by the conviction that the end result would be a life safer and better than ever before. The Russian people had to be sure, however, that their leaders were steering toward this goal with utmost speed on the only possible route. Confidence in the state's leaders was emphasized; Stalin was shown to be omniscient and farseeing. What was later called the "personality cult" began to develop.

The years of the transformation into an industrial society have been called Russia's "iron age." In this period life in Russia was very different in spirit from what it had been for a brief time after the Bolsheviks came to power. Daring revolutionary intellectuals like Trotsky and Radek were now replaced by careful bureaucrats and technical experts. The experiments in avant-garde art and literature which had been promoted by Anatoli Lunacharski, commissar for education under Lenin, were now abandoned, and the government required artists to provide easily understandable, realistic representations of the achievements of the Five-Year Plans and of other events showing Russia's progress under Bolshevism. The fight of the militant atheists against religion was continued because the influence of the church formed an obstacle to the modernization of rural life. Free love and divorce, however, were no longer encouraged, as they had been in the first years of Bolshevik rule, and abortions were once again prohibited. It was hoped, however, that after the successful completion of the two Five-Year Plans, the production of consumer goods would be increased and the disciplined monotony which had become customary would gradually give way to an easier and more varied life. Furthermore, on June 12, 1936, there appeared in *Pravda* ("Truth"), the most widely distributed official newspaper, the draft of a new constitution, which seemed to indicate the beginning of a period in which the Soviet citizens would possess enlarged, well-defined rights.

The Purge Trials

The hope that Soviet Russia was entering a period of liberalization was soon destroyed by Stalin's purges, which made him a dreaded absolute ruler, with the secret police his most important and most feared instrument of government. The number of people who became victims of these purges—who were imprisoned, exiled, or executed—runs into the millions. The most prominent among them were condemned in "show trials," the first of which took place in August, 1936, two months after the publication of the new constitution. Best known among the sixteen defendants in this trial were Grigori Zinoviev and Lev B. Kamenev, both former members of the Politburo. The second great trial was staged in 1937. Among the seventeen defendants was Karl Radek, Soviet Russia's leading political writer. Between the second and the third trials there occurred a secret purge of the Russian general staff; its victims included Mikhail Tukhachevski, a hero of the civil war and the Russo-Polish War, and a number of generals. The third and last trial, in March, 1938, was the most sensational; among its twenty-one defendants were Nikolai Bukharin, who had edited the newspaper *Izvestia* ("News") and was recognized as a leading Bolshevik theoretician; Aleksei Rykov, who had been chairman of the Council of People's Commissars, H. G. Yagoda, a former head of the secret police, N. M. Krestinski, a deputy commissar for foreign affairs, and a number of high diplomats. At all these trials the defendants made "confessions," perhaps obtained through pressure. Most of the defendants were condemned to death and executed, and even those, like Radek, who received only prison sentences never reappeared in public life.

In the light of revelations made after the death of Stalin, the purges have

Zinoviev before the purge trials.

usually been ascribed to his abnormal psychology. Undoubtedly Stalin's pathological distrust and suspicion did play a role in the organization of these trials and the cruelty of the punishments meted out to the defendants. Before 1936, and then again after Stalin's death, Bolshevik leaders who recommended a line of policy which the majority rejected were demoted or removed from power; but they were not killed. The use of the death penalty for political opposition was limited to the time of Stalin's reign. Although the manner of procedure against the defendants in the purge trials was determined by Stalin's abnormal mentality, he did have rational cause to fear the influence of these men. Most of them had been prominent under Lenin in the early years of Bolshevik rule. As "old Bolsheviks" they enjoyed prestige. Some of them, like Bukharin, had opposed Stalin's agrarian policy and maintained that agricultural production could have been increased more effectively by working with the kulaks than by eliminating them. These men were probably more popular than the strict bureaucrats and experts—Stalin's loyal followers—who imposed the hardships of the Five-Year Plans.

Most of those who doubted or opposed Stalin's economic policy recommended a change toward greater production of consumer goods, and the occurrence of such a change might have been expected to promote their chances for a successful political comeback. Stalin was unwilling to permit any loosening of controls or any alterations in economic policy, anticipating that the result would be a threat to his position; at the same time, he believed that continued emphasis on heavy industry was made necessary by the international situation. With the rise of the Nazis in Germany, the possibility of war had been greatly increased. Armament production had to be augmented and accelerated, not slowed down. Every possible obstacle to a uniform direction of policy, appropriate to the dangerous situation, had to be removed. This consideration was probably a motive in the execution of Tukhachevski and the other military leaders. Under Tukhachevski the army had developed into an almost independent power factor and Stalin may have wondered to what extent he would be able to rely on the army if his policy was contradictory to the views of the military leaders. Stalin's distrust of Tukhachevski seems to have been fomented by the Nazis, who expected that Tukhachevski's fall would weaken the Russian military organization. Through Eduard Benes, the president of Czechoslovakia, they succeeded in placing before Stalin cleverly falsified documents compromising Tukhachevski. Significantly, the elimination of Tukhachevski and his followers was accompanied by the reintroduction of political commissars into the army.

Stalin's Foreign Policy

In the threatening atmosphere of the middle 1930's, continued economic austerity and a tightening of the reins of government seemed appropriate. But the ruthlessness with which these policies were pursued had a dubious effect on Russia's relations with other powers.

When the Russian leaders had embarked on a policy of "socialism in one country" they were naturally anxious to remain undisturbed by the outside world. They had normalized diplomatic relations with their neighbors in the west and participated in international efforts toward securing peace, including the Kellogg-Briand pact and the Disarmament Conference. Because of Hitler's emphatically pronounced anti-Communism, his rise to power was disquieting to the rulers of Soviet Russia and they began to seek closer ties with countries that might be equally interested in checking Nazi expansionism. After Russia joined the League of Nations in September, 1934, the Soviet foreign minister, Maxim Litvinov (1876–1952), became a chief advocate of strict sanctions against aggressors. In 1935 Soviet Russia concluded with France and Czechoslovakia agreements promising mutual assistance in case of unprovoked aggression. Correspondingly, on orders from Moscow the policies of the Communist parties in western Europe began to change. At the Seventh Congress of the Comintern, in the summer of 1935, the formula was proclaimed which initiated the new policy of the Popular Front: Communists were now willing to cooperate with the leaders of any group—socialist or rightist—which took a line of resistance to the Nazis.

Just when these broad movements of opposition to Nazism and Fascism seemed to be gaining impetus and the Popular Front obtained electoral victories in Spain and France, the occurrence of the Russian purges resulted in renewed doubts among the democratic forces about the possibility of cooperation with the Bolsheviks. The Russians even extended the purges to the various Communist parties outside of the Soviet Union, attempting to eliminate from power those whom they considered allies of the purge victims and to establish as leaders of the Communist parties men of proven loyalty to Stalin. Russia intervened in the Spanish Civil War not only to defeat Franco but also to eliminate the leaders of the left who were not Stalinists. Such developments strengthened the hands of those politicians in Great Britain and France who from the outset—for ideological and economic reasons—had opposed cooperation with the Soviet Union. It was said that a regime which had to take recourse to terroristic measures could hardly be regarded as a stable and reliable ally, and the question was raised of whether the Russian government was any more humane or civilized than the Nazi and Fascist dictatorships. In the negotiations on the Czechoslovakian crisis during the summer of 1938 Great Britain and France cold-shouldered Russia as they steered openly toward appeasement with Nazi Germany.

We do not know whether Stalin ever had much interest or confidence in an alliance with the western democracies. It is certain, however, that the Munich Conference and the appeasement policy of the western powers increased his fear that these states might come to an agreement with Germany at the expense of the Soviet Union, perhaps giving Hitler a free hand to attack Russia. Moreover, Stalin was enough of a Marxist to regard as negligible the difference between capitalist Nazi Germany and the capitalist democracies of the west. Thus, when in the summer of 1939 British and French missions appeared in Moscow, and at the same time the Nazis expressed eager interest in a pact with Russia, Stalin's main interest was to make sure that these various powers did not unite against the Soviet Union. An agreement with Nazi Germany had the advantage that the Nazis were willing to hand over to Russia the Baltic states and parts of Poland, which Britain and France refused to do. Stalin may also have found the single-minded, ruthless Hitler more attractive than the vacillating western statesmen, who until recently had embraced appeasement. Everything points to the conclusion that Stalin favored an agreement with Hitler. If he continued the negotiations with Great Britain and France, the chief reason was that otherwise the western powers, despairing of Russian support, might drop Poland; Russia would then be faced alone by a Nazi Germany strengthened by victory over Poland. In short, the purpose of Stalin's diplomacy was to bring about war between Germany and the West.

Like all the other statesmen of the time, Stalin miscalculated. If Great Britain and France were slow and not very forthright in their approach to Russia the reason was that they believed erroneously that Soviet Russia and Nazi Germany could never come to an understanding. Meanwhile, Hitler had been persuaded by his foreign minister, Ribbentrop, that a German agreement with Russia would intimidate Great Britain and France into

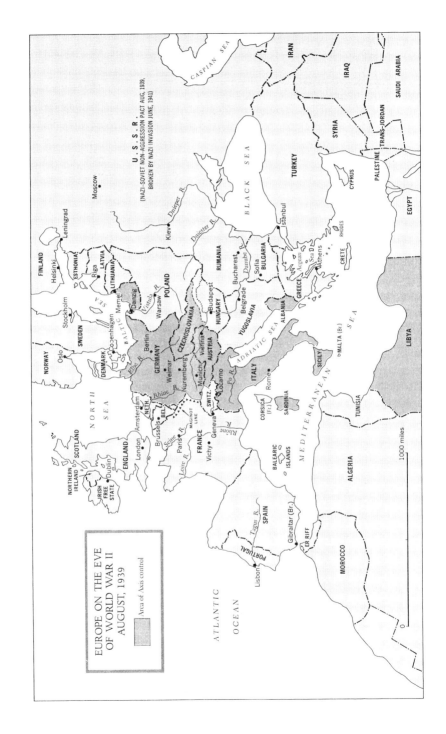

EUROPE ON THE EVE
OF WORLD WAR II
AUGUST, 1939

Area of Axis control

abandoning Poland, so that his forces would have a quick and easy victory. And Stalin believed that the western democracies and Nazi Germany were almost equal in strength and would exhaust themselves in a long and bitter war; Russia—remaining at peace—would emerge as the strongest power on the European continent. The tragedy of the Second World War began with a comedy of errors.

If the war had not broken out over Poland in the summer of 1939, it probably would have been triggered by some other issue. Hitler was straining for control of the continent, and from 1933 on, Europe had been disturbed by crisis after crisis, each more serious than the one before. With everyone living under the threat of an imminent war, the situation had become almost unbearable. Yet when hostilities finally erupted over the German invasion of Poland on September 1, 1939, the public reaction was very different from what it had been at the outbreak of the First World War twenty-five years before. In 1939 there was no enthusiasm, no feeling of liberation. The dreary procession of democratic retreats and defeats, the demonstrated inability to subordinate social conflicts and divergent class interests to the common aim of preserving the basis of freedom had weakened confidence in the strength of the western powers. There seemed validity in the claim of the totalitarian states that they were the wave of the future. Behind the acceptance of the necessity of the war by the people in democratic countries there was a feeling of doom. In the face of terrible defeats, it would require the awakening of a primitive feeling of national pride to shake off this fatalism and to restore hope and confidence.

CHAPTER 7

The Second World War

Winston Churchill entitled the fourth volume of his history of the Second World War, which describes developments from January, 1942, to the spring of 1943, *The Hinge of Fate,* for Churchill saw this period as "the turning point" of the war.[1] Until the end of the summer of 1942 Germany attacked and advanced. Thereafter, the initiative was held by the opponents of Fascism.

Within this general trend of events—the Fascists first on the offensive, then on the defensive—there were movements and countermovements. Thus although the Fascists seemed overwhelmingly superior in the first half of the war, even then their power did receive certain checks, without which the subsequent attack against them could not have been mounted.

THE GERMANS ON THE OFFENSIVE

Until the autumn of 1940 the Germans marched from triumph to triumph. Poland, whose resistance to Hitler's demands had ended the period of appeasement, was eliminated in a campaign of just one month, which provided the first glimpse of the military weapons and tactics which would dominate the conduct of the war. The Germans used their tremendous air superiority to destroy the Polish air force on the ground and then to bomb roads and railroads and interrupt communications so that the Polish troops lost any possibility of movement. There was no such thing as a relatively safe rear. By concentrating an overwhelming force of tanks at certain points the Germans broke through the Polish lines; they then secured their flanks at the breakthrough points and sent the tanks, followed by motorized infantry, streaming into the open countryside, where they turned to the right or left, dividing the enemy forces into isolated segments which were encircled and annihilated one after the other. In the confusion

[1] Winston S. Churchill, *The Second World War,* Vol. IV, *The Hinge of Fate* (Boston, 1950), p. 830.

The beginning of the Second World War. *German motorized troops driving into Poland. Note the boundary sign with the Polish eagle which the Germans removed and took along.*

created by this lightning attack, or *Blitzkrieg,* only the big cities maintained organized resistance. Warsaw was heroically defended, the German answer was a bombardment from the air which reduced it to ruins—the first example of the destruction of a large city by air attack.

On September 27, hardly four weeks after the outbreak of the war, Polish resistance was at an end; and Poland was partitioned between Germany and Soviet Russia. The Russians quickly occupied the eastern half of Poland, which had been promised to them in the German-Soviet treaty, and they also advanced into the Baltic states—Lithuania, Estonia, and Latvia. Thus they gained control of a long stretch of the southern coast of the Baltic Sea. The Germans annexed a large part of Poland and for the remainder created a Polish protectorate ruled by a German government. The delimitation of the German and Russian spheres was settled in Moscow on September 28 in what was called the German-Soviet Boundary and Friendship Treaty.

The "Phony War"

French and British military leaders were slow to learn the lessons of the Polish campaign. They believed that the *Blitzkrieg* tactics had been effective only because of Poland's military weakness and could not be applied against armies of greater power. Although German strength in the west was limited, the British and French had not supported the Poles by an attack on Germany, being satisfied to gain time for building up their forces.

What followed was the period of the "phony war." In the west the

French troops manning the Maginot Line.

enemies confronted each other without engaging in serious fighting. German inactivity lulled the French and British into false security. They placed unjustifiably high hopes on the effects of economic warfare; from the outset they set up a tight blockade to prevent Germany from getting goods from abroad. Because they doubted that the Germans would dare to attack in the west, their measures for strengthening the defenses in France lacked the necessary energy. The Maginot Line was not extended along the Belgian frontier to the coast. The French and British governments felt so secure in the west that their attention focused on other areas. When the Russians invaded Finland in November, 1939, in order to improve their military defense line in the north, the French and British decided to assemble an expeditionary force to aid the Finns. But before this assistance could be sent, the war ended, in March, 1940, with the Finns conceding to the Russians the demanded frontier revision.

Concerned by the British and French interest in this northern area Hitler decided to eliminate the possibility of military action by the western Allies from the north. On April 9 German troops drove over the Danish frontier and occupied Denmark; at the same time they attacked Norway. The Norwegians resisted but were overwhelmed. The German success was due to a brilliantly executed combination of action by naval and air forces and paratroops. The British and French countermeasures were fumbling; troops were thrown in without antiaircraft protection and artillery and were quickly destroyed by the Germans.

From the British point of view the Norwegian defeat had one favorable consequence. A dramatic session of the House of Commons showed that Neville Chamberlain had lost the confidence of his countrymen. He resigned on May 10 and was succeeded by Winston Churchill, who formed a government in which all three parties—Conservative, Liberal, and Labor —participated. Churchill writes that he went to bed that night with "a profound sense of relief. At last I had the authority to give directions over the whole scene. I felt as if I were walking with Destiny, and that all my past life had been but a preparation for this hour and for this trial."[2]

The Opening of the Western Offensive

On the very day this change of government took place, the German offensive in the west began. While the Maginot Line remained quiet, the northern wing of the German armies advanced on a broad front, invading the Netherlands and Belgium. German paratroops seized the Dutch airfields and bridges and made an orderly defense of the country impossible. An air raid on Rotterdam obliterated the center of the city, and on May 14 the Dutch army capitulated after Queen Wilhelmina (ruled 1890–1948) and the government had succeeded in escaping to England. Belgian resistance lasted longer, thanks to British and French support. But the Germans, utilizing the same tactics as in Poland, achieved a breakthrough in the Ardennes and their tanks raced ahead into France, toward Amiens and Abbeville, splitting the defending forces into two parts. The northern part, including the entire Belgian army, most of the British troops in France, and a portion of the French army, was then enclosed in a steadily contracting ring. On May 27 the Belgian King Leopold III (ruled 1934–1951) capitulated with his army. British and French troops were pushed back to the beaches of Dunkerque and evacuated from there. Waiting on the beaches, the Allied forces were subjected to steady bombing from the air. A German tank attack probably would have been disastrous, but Hitler evidently believed that the destruction of the exposed troops could be left to the air force, and kept his tanks back. Nevertheless, the saving of these forces required an immense effort; the miracle of Dunkerque was made possible by the strength of the British navy, under whose protection an endless number of small craft brought the soldiers over the Channel. Between May 27 and June 4, 338,226 men reached England.

The tanks which Hitler did not employ at Dunkerque were used in the attack against the other half of the Allied forces, consisting of the bulk of the French army, which had formed a front along the Somme. Again, the German tanks succeeded in breaking through the defenders' lines. Roads were clogged with refugees; German airplanes strafed people scurrying along, creating panic and confusion. The collapse of communications prevented French airplanes and antitank guns from reaching the front, and the enemy was able to advance rapidly.

On June 14 the Germans entered Paris. The French government had fled southward. In hurried visits, Churchill tried to persuade the French to remain in the war. Prime Minister Paul Reynaud (1878–1966) was willing

[2] *Ibid*, Vol. I, *The Gathering Storm* (Boston, 1948), p. 667.

After the Nazi triumph in France. *Hitler with his generals in Compiègne.*

to do so. But with Germans advancing over the Loire and attacking from the rear the Maginot Line, where the last well-organized French military force was stationed, the military leaders declared all further resistance useless and demanded that the government end the war. Reynaud resigned and was succeeded by Marshall Pétain, who on June 17 asked for an armistice. Most of the country was occupied by the Germans; only southeastern France and North Africa remained under French control. In the unoccupied part of France, with Vichy as capital, a French government under Pétain as head of state was established; in the later parts of the war, starting in April, 1942, the directing spirit of this government was Pierre Laval, who expected a German victory and regarded close cooperation with the Nazis as the only possible French policy.

North Africa's freedom from German occupation subsequently proved of great value to the Allied forces, but in the spring and summer of 1940 the French surrender appeared an unmitigated disaster. This impression was reinforced by the establishment under Pétain of a new authoritarian government in Vichy, so that even unoccupied France was absorbed into the antidemocratic camp. There is no doubt that in the shock of defeat many Frenchman shared Pétain's belief that an abondonment of the ideas of the Third Republic, and a new hierarchical organization of society, were desirable. Few remained convinced, with Charles de Gaulle, that France had lost a battle but not the war. "The outcome of the struggle has not been decided by the Battle of France. This is a world war."[3] This statement was part of de Gaulle's first appeal from London, in June, 1940, to form a

[3] Quoted in *The Complete War Memoirs of Charles de Gaulle*, Vol. I, *The Call to Honour*, trans. by Jonathan Griffins (New York, 1955), p. 84.

movement for the liberation of France. De Gaulle had made a name for himself through writings in which he had stressed the importance of tanks and motorized forces in future wars. In the campaign of 1940 he had proved himself as a tank commander against the Germans; he was named under secretary of war by Reynaud on June 6 because he could be relied on to support the prime minister's efforts to keep France in the war. When these proved abortive, De Gaulle escaped in a British plane to London. There he organized the Free French movement, insisting that he alone spoke for France and that France was still a great power. He kept a proud distance from the various governments-in-exile which, after the German occupation of their countries, were set up in London.

The Battle of Britain

On June 10, before the French campaign had ended, Italy entered the war. The Italians had been resentful that Hitler had gone ahead even though they had told him that Italy was not ready for war in 1939. As long as the "phony war" lasted, neutrality seemed appropriate, since it might give Italy a chance to act as a mediator. But as Germany progressed unchecked, Mussolini became increasingly restless. His proud claims of having created a new disciplined and powerful state would seem idle boasts if Italy remained outside the war. For the outcome of the campaign in France, Italy's entry into the conflict was irrelevant. But it presented a serious threat to British communication through the Mediterranean and to the British position in the Near East.

Great Britain was dangerously alone. The German high command was sure that "the final German victory over England is only a question of time,"[4] and plans were made for invading England. But German strategy had always centered on land warfare and the military leaders, including Hitler, felt insecure in planning for a campaign combining naval and land operations. According to the German military leaders a successful invasion first required air attacks to eliminate all serious British resistance. And Göring, the commander of the German air force, gave assurances that his bombers and fighter planes could force Great Britain to its knees.

The German air fleet was superior to the British, although antiaircraft artillery and the concentration of air squadrons in southern England compensated somewhat for the difference in numbers. The Germans began in July with an attack on airfields and military installations, forcing the British into air battles in order to destroy the Royal Air Force. And indeed the R.A.F. did lose continuously in strength. Then, at the beginning of September—in a change which is generally considered to have been a crucial mistake—the Germans switched to bombing attacks on London. The decisive days of the "Battle of Britain" were in the middle of

[4] From entry dated June 30, 1940, *War Diary of General Jodl.*

After the air raids in London.
*Tumbling ruins with St. Paul
Cathedral in the background.*

September, when the British had to put their reserves into the defense of
London. The British inflicted heavy losses on the German air fleet; on
September 16 alone they destroyed 185 German planes. These blows made
the Germans aware that full air protection for a landing operation was
unobtainable, and they abandoned their invasion plans. However, they
continued night raids on London until November, averaging two hundred
bombers on each mission. These had no direct strategic purpose; they were
intended to weaken British morale and will to resist. The *Blitz* on
London was followed by attacks on other cities; the most devastating being
the raid on Coventry on November 14, in which four hundred people were
killed and the center of the city, including its historic cathedral, was
completely destroyed. At the end of the year London again became the
target of an air attack; incendiary bombs were used and many of the
city's most ancient monuments, including Guildhall and numerous churches designed by Sir Christopher Wren, were badly damaged or destroyed.
But the morale of the people was not broken nor was the production of war
materials interrupted. Britain actually managed to produce more airplanes
than Germany in 1940. In the Battle of Britain, Hitler had received his first
check; he was forced to abandon the plan to achieve quick victory through a
direct attack on Great Britain. As Churchill said of the British pilots who

were instrumental in this triumph: "Never in the field of human conflict was so much owed by so many to so few."

The Opening of the Eastern Offensive

After the failure to achieve a quick decision against Great Britain, Hitler had to decide on his next move. It was then that the plan of a campaign against Russia began to take definite form. German expansion toward the east had always been Hitler's aim, but he had intended to postpone this enterprise until the western nations had been defeated. However, after the victory in France, Great Britain's aggressive potential seemed negligible, and Hitler concluded that the subjection of Russia could be achieved while the war against Great Britain continued. His hostility toward Russia had been reinforced by the energy with which the Bolshevik leaders had acted after the defeat of Poland, taking immediate possession of those areas which had been defined in the German-Soviet treaty as belonging to the Russian sphere of interest. In a visit to Berlin in November, 1940, the Soviet foreign minister, Vyacheslav Molotov (born 1890), showed that the Russians were by no means willing to give the Germans a free hand in the Balkans. Even earlier, Hitler had ordered the German general staff to work out plans for an attack against Russia; after Molotov's visit he decided to carry out these plans in 1941.

Action against Russia was delayed, however, because in the first part of 1941 Germany was drawn into military campaigns started by the Italians in the Balkans and the eastern Mediterranean. Dissatisfied with the minor role which his country was playing in the European conflict, Mussolini had decided to gain military laurels by attacking Greece. But the Italian troops which moved from Albania toward Greece were not prepared for the valiant resistance they encountered. Instead of the Italians occupying Greece, the Greeks conquered a fourth of Italian-controlled Albania.

The Italian plight in the winter of 1940–1941 was made even worse by defeats inflicted by the British in North Africa, where Hitler finally felt that he had to come to the assistance of his fellow dictator by sending German tanks, under one of the best German tank commanders, Erwin Rommel. But Hitler's main attention was directed toward the Balkans. The Italian difficulties gave him the opportunity to extend German control over this area. He forced Hungary, Rumania, and Bulgaria into alliances with the Axis, and when Yugoslavia refused a similar arrangement, he overwhelmed the country in a quick campaign which he continued into Greece. The Greeks were unable to hold off the Germans, and their country was occupied in a few weeks. Finally, through the daring use of paratroops, even Crete was conquered and in German hands by May 31, 1941. In vain had the British sent support to Greece from Africa.

The resultant weakening of their forces in Africa left the British unable

The Nazi invasion of Russia. *After the Germans had passed.*

to resist Rommel, who drove them back to the Egyptian frontier. The entire area seemed helpless and open to a German onslaught, and it is difficult to imagine what would have happened if Hitler had moved into Egypt, Turkey, and other states of the Near East. But Hitler's target was the Soviet Union. Despite delays caused by the Balkan campaign, he gave orders to carry out the plans for an attack, and on June 22, 1941, German troops marched over the borders of Russia. At the same time the Finns resumed military operations against Russia.

The Soviet rulers had received warnings of what was coming, but up to the last moment they made desperate attempts to avoid a break with Germany. They had no illusions about how precarious their situation would be in case of war with Germany.

At first, the campaign against Russia seemed to lead to a quick and complete triumph, even discounting Nazi exaggeration of the number of Russian prisoners of war taken in the early weeks of the campaign. The Russians conceded after the war that "Soviet strategic theory as propounded by the Draft Field Regulations of 1939 and other documents did not prove to be entirely realistic. For one thing, they denied the effectiveness of the *Blitzkrieg* which tended to be dismissed as a lopsided bourgeois theory."[5] The Russians were surprised by the German use of tank formations for breakthroughs and encirclement. The Germans' air superiority enabled their

[5] This citation is from the Russian official *History of the War* (1960). Quoted by Alexander Werth, *Russia at War, 1941–1945* (New York, 1964), p. 133.

air force to attack Russian airfields and destroy Russian planes on the ground. The Russian debacle was magnified by orders ascribed to Stalin to hold out in advance positions, causing the troops to miss opportunities to retreat before the ring of encirclement was closed. At Kiev, in one such encirclement of Russian forces, the Germans took 175,000 prisoners of war.

By October the Germans were before Moscow and Leningrad, and in a speech on October 2 Hitler announced a "final drive" against Moscow. People began to flee the city. Trains were packed; officials set out in their cars; and although some factories worked day and night to produce anti-tank defenses, or "hedgehogs," which were immediately placed in the roads around Moscow, other factories were evacuated. Doubts grew that the capital could be held.

The official will to defend the city was underlined by an announcement that Stalin was in Moscow. His firmness in this desperate situation muted all criticism and established him in undisputed authority as the supreme military leader. He began to be presented as a second Peter the Great. In newspapers and literature there was a deliberate stimulation of interest in the Russian past, even in tsarist history, and the war came to be called the "Great Patriot War." The Bolshevik leaders wanted the struggle to be seen as an event which concerned not only Communists, but all the Russian people. At the beginning of November, in two great speeches, Stalin invoked Russian nationalism as the inspiration for resistance to the hordes of invading barbarians. By then, the German offensive had lost its impetus, probably less because of the strength of the Russian stand than because of logistical difficulties: the necessary supplies for the tanks, artillery, and men had not kept up with the rapid advance. When the Germans started a second push in November, the Russians were prepared; their embittered resistance, together with an early onset of winter, which severely hurt the insufficiently clad German troops, caused this second offensive against Moscow to fail.

Nevertheless, the Russian situation remained serious. By the end of the campaign of 1941 the Germans had conquered most of the Ukraine, were close to Moscow, and had surrounded Leningrad, which remained under siege for eighteen months. These advances had been bought with very heavy losses—between 700,000 and 800,000 men. The Russians were quick to learn from their defeats. Generals who had been promoted because of their political merits were replaced by brilliant professionals, such as Georgi Zhukov, Semion Timoshenko, and Boris Shaposhnikov. The Russians showed great ingenuity in transporting factories from threatened areas into the safe hinterland of the Urals and Siberia. They were able to accelerate the production of tanks, airplanes, and artillery; and the Russian heavy artillery proved to be superior to that of the Germans. Moreover, supplies from Great Britain and the United States began to arrive on convoys that

AXIS EXPANSION IN THE WEST
1942

Greatest extent of Axis occupation
or control

Areas controlled by Vichy France

ARCTIC   OCEAN

Petsamo

FINLAND

NORWAY   Helsinki

Oslo   Stockholm   ESTONIA

SWEDEN   LATVIA

SCOTLAND   LITHUANIA

NORTH   EAST
SEA   DENMARK Copenhagen   PRUSSIA

IRELAND

ENGLAND   Hamburg   Warsaw
       Coventry   Berlin
London   Rotterdam   GERMANY   POLAND
          NETH.
Abbeville   Brussels
          BEL.   Lidice Prague
Amiens   LUX.   CZECHOSLOVAKIA
ATLANTIC   Munich Vienna   Budapest
       Loire R. Paris   AUSTRIA HUNGARY
OCEAN   FRANCE   RUMANIA
Oradour-sur-Glane Vichy   SWITZ.
       Bordeaux   Belgrade
                        ITALY   YUGOSLAVIA   BULGARIA
             Marseilles
                                          ADRIATIC SEA
       CORSICA   Rome   ALBANIA
Madrid   Naples   GREECE
   Barcelona
Lisbon PORTUGAL SPAIN   SARDINIA

Seville   MEDITERRANEAN   SICILY

ER RIFF   MALTA
                                 (Br.)   SEA
Casablanca
       MOROCCO   TUNISIA
IFNI   ALGERIA

                                 LIBYA

0   500 miles

traveled on hazardous sea lanes to Murmansk. These supplies filled the gaps in production that occurred while factories were being moved to safe areas. In contrast to what had happened in Poland, France, and the Balkans, victory in one quick campaign escaped the Germans in Russia.

THE WAR AT ITS HEIGHT

The Global War

At the beginning of 1942 the entire war changed in character. It stopped being a purely European conflict, and became global. To Japanese advocates of expansionism the European struggle seemed to offer a unique opportunity for establishing a Japanese empire in the Far East. Great Britain was unable to intervene, and the German occupation of the Netherlands and France made the Far Eastern possessions of these countries an easy prey. From French Indochina, which they occupied in 1940, the Japanese prepared to move against Burma, the East Indies, and Singapore. The United States, which wanted to help Britain, and in addition had a vital interest in preventing the domination of this area by a single power, opposed these Japanese moves by diplomatic representations and economic pressures. Negotiations conducted in Washington between the two states were unsuccessful, however, and were near collapse when, on December 7, 1941, the Japanese made a surprise attack on the United States fleet in Pearl Harbor, sinking three battleships and severely damaging five others. The next day the United States formally declared war on Japan.

The outbreak of hostilities between Japan and the United States was followed on December 11, by declarations of war on the United States by Germany and Italy. The Axis powers were bound by a treaty concluded in 1940 to assist Japan in case of attack by a state not involved in the European war; it remains strange, however, that Hitler, who had few inclinations to honor treaty obligations, believed that he had to fulfill this one. To declare war on the United States was his personal decision, and his hatred of President Roosevelt, the protagonist of the democratic world, was probably a prime motive. Most of all, Hitler's decision showed that despite the setbacks in Russia he felt supremely confident. His lack of knowledge of American politics also played its role. He seems never to have considered that without this declaration of war, American military action might have focused on the Far East rather than Europe.

Ever since the outbreak of the war in Europe, President Roosevelt had left no doubt that the sympathies of the United States were with those who resisted the onslaught of Nazism and Fascism. In November, 1939, American neutrality legislation had been modified to permit belligerents to buy war materials in the United States, provided they paid cash and carried their purchases back in their own ships. The fall of France in the summer of

1940 stimulated American preparedness; the military budget was raised and conscription was introduced. Moreover, in the same summer Roosevelt gave direct encouragement to British resistance by an arrangement in which, in return for granting the United States a 99-year lease of certain of their bases in the western hemisphere, the British received a number of American destroyers. In a broadcast on December 29, 1940, Roosevelt declared formally that it was the task of the United States to serve as "the arsenal of democracy," and Congress responded by passing in March, 1941, the Lend-Lease Act, which permitted the president to provide war materials to those states whose survival was vital to the security of the United States; after the Nazi invasion of Russia this act was applied also to Soviet Russia. The identity of American and British interests was publicly announced in the Atlantic Charter, a document issued after a meeting between Roosevelt and Churchill on a warship off the coast of Newfoundland in August, 1941. In the Atlantic Charter, the two leaders emphasized that the war must result in freedom, independence, and an improvement in living standards for all peoples. Thus, even before the German and Italian declarations of war on the United States a firm bond tied the United States to Great Britain. On December 22, Churchill and a number of his military advisors arrived in Washington, and except for a trip to Canada he stayed in the United States until January 14, 1942. In the meetings in Washington two important decisions were made, one strategical, the other organizational. It was agreed that a defeat of Hitler was the first goal; the European theater of war was given precedence over the Far East. In addition, a unified command was created: within each of the various theaters of war the British and American troops were placed under a single commander, either British or American. The direction of the strategy of the war was entrusted to a committee, the Combined Chiefs of Staff, in which the outstanding figures were General George C. Marshall (1880–1959), the chief of staff of the army on the American side, and Sir John Dill (1881–1944) on the British side.

There was never close cooperation in military planning between the Combined Chiefs of Staff and the Russian general staff. On the contrary, the Russians were most reluctant to give information to the British and American military representatives in Moscow. The organizational unification of British and American military effort helped to prevent the delays, frictions, and disorders which usually occur in the conduct of a coalition war; even so, some decisions were reached only after long debates. It was the bond of friendship and respect which existed between Roosevelt and Churchill— together with their interest in and understanding of military affairs—that served to smooth out the difficulties which arose from differences among the generals.

The main issue under dispute throughout the war years was the timing of the invasion of France. The Americans were eager to embark on this enterprise in 1942, the British were probably right in considering such an undertaking premature at a time when the Germans were at the height of their power and the American troops were inexperienced. The British idea of abandoning the plan of a continental invasion in 1942 and substituting a landing in North Africa was appropriate, just as at a later stage the Americans were probably justified in opposing British plans to extend operation in the Mediterranean area by an attack through the Balkan Peninsula—the "soft underbelly of the Axis"—and in insisting instead on invasion of France across the English Channel.

The Turning Point

Although the entry of the United States into the war provided the anti-Fascist powers with a productive capacity which would assure them material superiority, the situation in 1942 was still precarious. It was by no means clear that the American industrial potential could be mobilized before the Fascist states had placed themselves in an almost invincible position—before Japan had gained full control in the Far East and the Axis powers in Europe had driven the British from the Mediterranean and knocked Russia out of the war.

In the first months of 1942, the advance of the Japanese in the Far East was awesome. They took the Philippines from the Americans; they conquered British forces on the Malay Peninsula and by February 15 were in Singapore, where they took sixty-thousand prisoners. In combined land and sea operations they overran the Netherlands East Indies, reaching Batavia in March. They occupied Burma, and took Mandalay on May 2. The road to India seemed open to them, and the barriers against their advance into Australia appeared to have fallen.

In Europe the campaigns of 1942 were of crucial importance. Hitler counted on accomplishing in a second Russian campaign what he had not succeeded in doing in 1941. The reserves which he could put into this fight were formidable. For almost a year he had been in control of the entire European continent except for the Iberian Peninsula, and during this period he had organized the continent according to Nazi aims. In the occupied territories of the East the Germans acted as if they were permanent rulers. Many of the inhabitants were removed and resettled, and large landed estates were given to German generals and Nazi leaders. Yugoslavia was divided, with one part forming the kingdom of Croatia, ruled by an Italian prince, and the rest remaining under direct German administration. Bulgaria, Rumania, and Hungary, being Nazi allies, retained their old rulers but were dominated by German-supported parties patterned after the Nazis.

AXIS EXPANSION IN THE EAST
1942

Greatest extent of Axis control

Norway, the Netherlands, Belgium, and part of France were under German occupation. Puppet governments were installed, which came to be known as Quisling governments, after the Norwegian Nazi leader, Vidkun Quisling.

The conquered countries were forced to place their economic resources at the service of the German war effort and to accept the Nazi ideology. Their cooperation was required in the execution of anti-Semitic measures. This was the time when the "final solution" of the Jewish question was undertaken. Jews from all parts of Europe were taken into custody and shipped like cattle in crowded freight trains to concentration camps, where they met their death in gas chambers. The number of those who were killed —about six million—is almost beyond imagination. And one must add that the policy of the "final solution" was carried out with a ruthlessness and brutality which afflicted its victims before their death with the most terrible sufferings and torture.

Strict controls over the economic life of the occupied countries made it possible to maintain a fairly high standard of living in Germany. Men of the subject countries were conscripted and transported to work in German factories and labor battalions. The propaganda intended to justify these measures emphasized that German arms were defending Europe against Communism and that German domination would usher in a new period in which Europe would be unified. In all the subject countries parties organized in the pattern of the German Nazi party were established, and military units were formed to join in the fight against Communism. Thus when the offensive against Russia started in 1942 Rumanian, Hungarian, and Italian armies, as well as legions of volunteers from all over Europe— even from Spain—fought under the German command.

With the tightening of German controls over Europe, resistance movements arose in almost all of the occupied countries. Originally these movements consisted of isolated groups, such as the remnants of the former political parties, among which the Socialists and Communists had particularly kept some cohesion, or of groups of nationalists, Catholics, and Protestants, who felt that they dishonored themselves if they allowed the brutal and un-Christian behavior of the Nazis to go on without taking some action. In the course of time these various units began to cooperate with one another and combine into coordinated resistance organizations. All these movements worked underground; for several years their activities consisted mainly of giving help and protection to those who, for political or racial reasons, were persecuted by the Nazis; *Anne Frank: The Diary of a Young Girl* (1947) gives a moving portrayal of the existence of a Jewish family hidden by Dutch friends, but in the end found by the Nazis.

Another function of the resistance was the transmission of intelligence, particularly about German military movements; the French were able to maintain secret contacts with Great Britain, and the headquarters of De

Gaulle's Free French movement in London were extremely well informed about developments in France. The various resistance groups kept in contact through secretly printed newspapers, many of a very high intellectual level. They contained not only uncensored news but also lively debates on what the political structure of the occupied countries should be after liberation. The generally accepted aim was a thorough reorganization of political and social life. This demand for radical changes was only partly the result of the importance of Socialists and Communists in the resistance; repudiation of the prewar ruling groups, whose policies had led to defeat and occupation, was general, and contempt for the men of the former ruling circles was intensified by the willingness of many financial and industrial leaders to collaborate with the Germans.

Throughout the occupation, the men of the resistance undertook single acts of sabotage, but the introduction of more elaborate guerilla operations depended on circumstances. The Germans never succeeded in completely controlling the wild and inaccessible mountain regions of Yugoslavia; Yugoslav military organizations—the Communists under Marshal Tito (born 1892), the royalists under Draza Mihajlovic—remained active, usually fighting the Germans but sometimes fighting each other. In the wide forests and swamps of Russia, units composed of peasants and of soldiers who had escaped German encirclements operated behind the front, substantially damaging the German lines of communications. Resistance armies in Italy and France went into action when the invasion by American and British forces was imminent, contributing considerably to the collapse of German rule in the occupied areas.

Those participating in the resistance constituted a relatively small part of the populations, and they were exposed to great danger up to the end. The German secret police ruthlessly tortured people believed to possess information about underground activities, and the German troops, particularly the fanatic members of the S.S., tried to stamp out sabotage and resistance by brute force. They made arrests in the middle of the night, took hostages and killed them on the smallest provocation, and shot people for the slightest suspicious moves.

The names of Lidice and Oradour are testimonies of Nazi terrorism. In revenge for the assassination of the Gestapo leader Reinhard Heydrich in 1942, the Czech village of Lidice was destroyed; its entire adult male population was killed, the women were placed in camps, and the children, separated from their families and nameless, were dispersed. In the French town of Oradour, in punishment for presumed support of partisans, the men were shot and the women and the children were herded into the church and burned. Because the conqueror's controls were so thorough and brutal, the resistance movement could exert effective pressure on the Nazis only when their reserves became strained and their grip started to loosen.

THE ALLIES ON THE OFFENSIVE

The Reversal of Fortune

Hitler's campaign against Russia in the summer of 1942 seemed to offer the Germans their last opportunity for victory. It was undertaken before the United States could effectively intervene in the war, and at a time when, despite the failure before Moscow, German power was still at its peak. The offensive began in June. It was mainly directed toward the southern half of the Russian front, its purpose being to deprive the Russians of the agricultural areas of the Ukraine, the industrial areas of the Donets Basin, and the oil fields of the Caucasus. The Nazis expected that Moscow and Leningrad, cut off from supplies, would be taken from the rear by encircling movements. The German armies succeeded in penetrating into the Caucasus, but their advance to the Volga was stopped at Stalingrad, and the battle for Stalingrad developed into one of the decisive battles of the war. Stalingrad was strategically important because its conquest would have cut communications between Moscow and the south. Moreover, the name had great symbolic value to both Germans and Russians.

At the beginning of the winter, except for a few buildings on the right bank of the Volga, all of Stalingrad had been taken, and Hitler announced on November 9 that the city was "firmly in German hands." But the Russians resisted obstinately, using heavy artillery from the other side of the

The battle for Stalingrad. *One of the last German airplanes to take off from Paulus' encircled army.*

river. Then they succeeded in breaking through the front north and south of Stalingrad, and by the end of November the Germans, led by General Friedrich Paulus, were no longer attacking the Russians but defending themselves; the army before Stalingrad, 300,000 men strong, was encircled. Hitler forbade any attempt at withdrawal by a breakthrough toward the west, assuring Paulus of provisions by air. But this proved impossible, and slowly but steadily the ring around Paulus' army was drawn closer, until the German forces were reduced to a few isolated groups. On January 31, 1943, Paulus surrendered, with the 123,000 men who were left of his army. Hitler's reaction was an emotional outburst of reproach that Paulus had not committed suicide.

The hole torn in the German front through the encirclement of the army before Stalingrad made the Germans' situation in southern Russia untenable and forced them to draw back. By the spring of 1943 the lines on the eastern front were roughly the same as they had been one year earlier.

In the fall of 1942, while the German military situation was deteriorating in Russia, there was a reversal of fortune in the Mediterranean area as well. In the winter of 1941–1942 the British had succeeded in forcing their opponents back from the Egyptian frontier, but in 1942 Rommel, commander of the German-Italian forces, had pushed the British back into Egypt, where overextended supply lines forced him to a halt. A lull permitted the British to strengthen their position through reinforcements sent by sea around Africa; at the end of October the British Eighth Army under a new commander, Bernard Montgomery, was able to take the offensive. The Battle of El Alamein became the first victory of British troops over a German army in the Second World War. The fighting began on October 23, 1942, with a heavy artillery barrage which opened some holes in the German lines; British tanks penetrated these gaps and forced the Germans to withdraw. The front was small, consisting of hardly forty miles between sea and desert; because of British air superiority and control of the sea, the German supply lines, which ran along this narrow stretch between sea and desert, became unusable, and Rommel's troops were forced back from one position to another, finally from Libya into Tunisia.

While the British were exploiting their victory at El Alamein, a combined force of British and American troops under General Dwight D. Eisenhower landed in French North Africa on November 8. The Americans had yielded to the British insistence that an invasion of the European continent was not feasible in 1942, but some action which would divert German forces from the Russian front seemed necessary, and North Africa was chosen as the site for a surprise invasion. The operation was entirely successful. The French in Morocco offered only token resistance and then transferred their support to the British and Americans. The Germans in Tunisia had to fight not only Montgomery's Eighth Army coming from the south but also the British-American forces coming from the west. Encircled, the German beachhead in Tunisia was eliminated by the middle of May, 1943.

During this same period, the summer of 1943, the Allies were also beginning to make gains in the Pacific theater. In three great sea and air battles—of the Coral Sea in May, of Midway in June, and of the Solomon Islands in August—the Japanese fleet was crippled, and further advances toward the south were checked. The British succeeded in bolstering the defenses of India, and Chinese resistance on the Asian mainland remained alive. Despite amazing conquests, Japan was still enclosed in a ring of hostile forces. By the end of the summer the offensives of Japan and the Axis forces had been halted and the initiative was held by the anti-Fascist coalition.

Germany Before Surrender

Now the outcome of the war was inevitable. The American industrial machine was in full gear and was producing planes, ships, and tanks at a rate which would have seemed impossible at the beginning of the war. The Russian factories which had been transported into the Urals and Siberia were working to capacity. British war production increased steadily because air superiority gained with American help meant protection from sustained German air attacks. Now it was Germany that suffered from steady bombings; by the end of the war most of the larger German cities were in ruins. Clearly the decisive factor in warfare had become superiority in weapons and equipment, based on industrial mass production. Even Hitler recognized this fact and in the final stages of the war expected a favorable outcome only from new miracle weapons. But the guided missiles, the V-1 and the V-2 rockets which Germany was able to put into use in 1944, were of limited effectiveness, and work on jet engines had not been completed when the war ended.

For the Germans, the sole rational hope for victory lay in the possibility of breaking up the coalition which was closing in on them from all sides. The relations of the United States and Great Britain with their Russian ally had been troubled from the start. When the Germans invaded Russia in 1941, Britain and the United States promised to give the Soviet Union all possible support, and indeed the supplies sent there were of crucial importance in maintaining Russian resistance in the critical first years of the German-Russian struggle. But the Russian leaders did little to publicize this outside help among their people; in their public statements about their allies they blew hot and cold. Their main interest was to promote a "second front," an Allied invasion of western Europe. Sometimes the Russians accused Britain and the United States of timidity and lack of energy in their pursuit of the anti-Fascist war; sometimes they praised them—depending

The Yalta Conference. *Churchill, Roosevelt and Stalin with their foreign ministers—Eden, Stettinius, Molotov—behind them.*

on what approach seemed more likely at the moment to accelerate the opening of this second front.

Relations were further troubled because the Russians were unwilling to recognize the governments-in-exile, particularly the Polish government. They wanted to avoid any commitments which might affect the settlement of frontiers after the war. In eastern Europe they supported only the resistance movements led by Communists. When in January, 1943, after the successful landing in North Africa, Churchill and Roosevelt met in Casablanca, one of their purposes in demanding from Germany "unconditional surrender" was to dispel Russian fears that the western powers might make a "deal" with Nazi Germany at the expense of the Soviet Union. At the meetings of Roosevelt and Churchill with Stalin in December, 1943, in Tehran and in February, 1945, in Yalta, the discussion was largely confined to problems of strategy; statements about postwar boundaries and peace plans were so vague that the lack of any definite agreement on these issues between Russia and the western powers was obvious.

Nevertheless, there was no real reason for the Nazis to hope that the anti-Fascist coalition could be broken up before Germany was completely defeated. Neither the Russians nor the western powers were willing to negotiate as long as Hitler was in power. Germans with political insight believed that better peace terms or a separate settlement with either the West or the East might be obtained if Hitler was removed. The result was a conspiracy by socialists and liberals, high civil servants and generals, which culminated on July 20, 1944, in an attempt on Hitler's life. But the attempt failed; just a moment too soon, Hitler moved away from the place where a bomb exploded. The war was thus destined to last for almost another year.

Why did the German people go on fighting though their situation was clearly hopeless? Obviously the Allies were unwilling to negotiate with Hitler and the men around him, so for the Nazi leaders there was no alternative to struggling on. German troops on the eastern front fought willingly and obstinately until the surrender because Nazi propaganda had drummed into them a passionate hatred of Bolshevism, and they feared the retribution which might be exacted for what had been done to the Russian people; a Russian invasion and occupation of German soil seemed worse than death.

Although the decline in the German fortunes after 1942 weakened the hold of Hitler and of Nazism over the minds of the German people, a corps of loyal Nazis survived until the end. Members of the S.S. particularly stayed firmly tied to the Nazi regime and their military units remained a valuable fighting force, which was thrown into combat at critical points until the final weeks of the war. Moreover, many of the teen-age members of the Nazi youth organization, who were conscripted in the last winter of the war, continued to regard Hitler as a man of destiny. The fanaticism of the S.S. guaranteed to the Nazi rulers an instrument for control by terror, and toward the end it was primarily fear and terror that kept the German people in the war. Himmler and his police imprisoned and tortured everyone suspected of holding anti-Nazi opinions or defeatist views. Such crimes—judged in Nazi-staffed People's Courts from which there was no appeal—were punished by death. The ruthlessness of the S.S. police increased after the attempt on Hitler's life. Entire families of persons suspected of political crimes were placed in custody. There was a grisly report in the last days of the war about corpses of soldiers by the hundreds dangling from the trees of one of Berlin's streets because they had absented themselves from their military units.

Organization of resistance to the Nazi rule was impeded only by the thoroughness and the terror methods of the police but ironically also by Allied bombing attacks. The saturation bombing of German cities disrupted communications and thereby strengthened the control of the Nazi rulers, who had priority use of roads, railroads, telegraph, and telephone. In coping with civil disasters, the Nazis made certain that water and food were given only to those who had appropriate identification papers. The Nazis were in charge of evacuating people from bombed quarters, and for weeks the whereabouts of the evacuees might be unknown even to close relatives and friends. The Nazi leaders and the Nazi apparatus alone maintained awareness of the situation as a whole; for the rest of the population life became atomized.

Even though the end seemed in sight in the spring of 1943, after the victories at Stalingrad and in North Africa, the military operations of the last two years of the Second World War were bitterly fought. Severely mauled, the German war machine was still formidable, and the Japanese still controlled a vast area of great natural resources and great defensive strength. A serious Allied defeat might have raised a cry for negotiations with the enemy, which would inevitably have been accompanied by all the difficulties involved in gaining cooperation among members of a coalition.

The Overthrow of Mussolini

The first of the Axis powers to collapse was Italy. After the defeat of the Germans in Tunisia the American-British forces, now in control of air and sea in the Mediterranean, landed in Sicily, and soon conquered the island. During the Sicilian invasion, on July 25, 1943, Mussolini was overthrown by a group which included leaders of the anti-Fascist underground, some prominent Fascists, and the military high command. Although the new government under Pietro Badoglio (1871–1956), a military man, officially declared it would continue the war, secret negotiations for an armistice were started immediately. The Nazi leaders were prepared for such an event. When the armistice was announced on September 8, German tank divisions closed in on Rome and plans for an Allied landing on the beaches near Rome had to be abandoned as too risky. During the winter the fronts stabilized between Rome and Naples; even the landing of Allied troops in Anzio did not lead beyond the formation of a beachhead. Central and northern Italy remained under Axis control.

After being overthrown Mussolini had been imprisoned, but German paratroopers succeeded in liberating him. He was induced by the Germans to establish a Fascist government in northern Italy, where he proclaimed that, free from conservative and monarchist restraints, he could now pursue the original Fascist ideas of social reform. But actually his government called the Republic of Salò after the small town where some of its offices were installed, was controlled by the Germans. It was the Germans who insisted on holding trials at Verona for six Fascist leaders who had participated in the overthrow of Mussolini, among them his son-in-law Count Ciano. They were condemned to death and executed.

The End of the War in Europe

The collapse of Fascism did not end the fighting in Italy, but it had a great moral effect, spurring anti-German activities all over Europe, and in addition was of military significance for all the theaters of war. The Allies could give more effective support to the partisans fighting in Yugoslavia; German manpower resources became severely strained because the

Derailment of a train. *The work of the French resistance.*

Italian occupation troops in the Balkans now had to be replaced by German forces. Moreover, the necessity of sending German tank divisions from the Russian front to Italy in July, at the time of the overthrow of the Fascist regime, had its impact on the eastern theater. The Germans were then undertaking another offensive, their last, in the east, in the center of the Russian front. But the Russians, in a counteroffensive, forced them back on a broad front, reaching the Dnieper and reconquering Kiev in November, 1943.

From this time on, the Allies held the initiative entirely, and in 1944 they advanced everywhere. The Russians continued to attack throughout the winter and by the beginning of the summer of 1944 were driving on to the borders of Poland and Rumania. By the end of the summer they had reached East Prussia, forced Finland out of the war, and shifted the chief weight of their attack to the southern part of the front, where they brought about the surrender of Rumania and Bulgaria. The Russian armies thus were approaching the frontiers of Nazi Germany from the southeast as well as from the east, their advances facilitated by the increasing pressure which Great Britain and the United States were able to exert.

The stalemate on the Italian front was broken; Rome and Florence were taken, so only northern Italy remained in German hands. And Greece was liberated.

The decisive accomplishment, however, of the United States and Great Britain in 1944 was the invasion of western Europe. On June 6, 1944, American and British forces crossed the English Channel and established beachheads on the Normandy coast. The success of this daring operation was primarily due to the complete Allied domination of the air, which largely

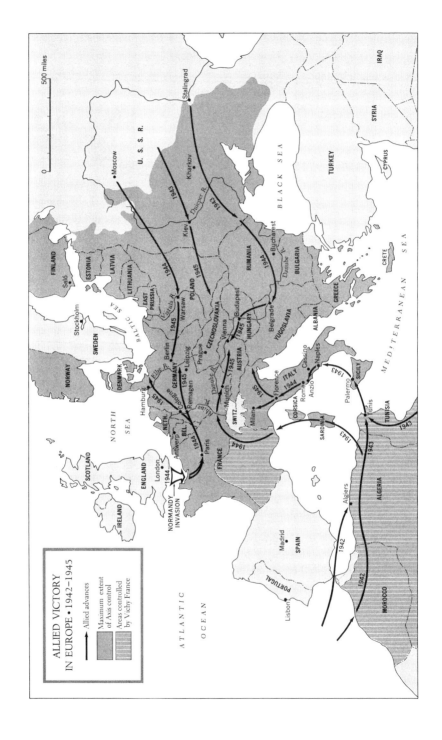

ALLIED VICTORY
IN EUROPE • 1942–1945

Allied advances

Maximum extent
of Axis control

Areas controlled
by Vichy France

frustrated German efforts to reinforce and supply their front lines. Moreover, the landings were protected by the heavy guns of the British and American ships, their fire directed in accordance with the excellent information about the German positions provided by the French underground. Artificial harbors brought over from England solved the problem of establishing a continuous stream of supplies for the invading troops—a problem which had appeared to stand in the way of any landing on a great scale. Nevertheless, it was a difficult operation which had been meticulously planned and brilliantly executed under the supreme command of General Eisenhower, with the British General Montgomery and the American General Omar Bradley as field commanders.

The hours after the initial waves of American and British troops had landed on the beaches were critical. But the German military leadership proved to be uncertain and faulty. The German generals could not agree on whether to defend the entire coastline or to permit the Allies to move into the interior and draw them into a battle while they were still relatively weak. Moreover, at the crucial moment Hitler refused to allow the employment of the German tank reserves because he was convinced that the landing in Normandy was a feint and that a stronger force would attack elsewhere on the coast. Once landed in strength, the Allies were able to effect a breakthrough with their tanks and to fan out in the rear, driving the Germans to retreat. By September, the liberation of France and Belgium was nearing completion, and the Allied armies were establishing themselves along the former German frontiers, where they were forced to stop because supplies were running short. A question which has been raised but can never be answered is whether the war might have been ended in 1944, if the Allies, instead of advancing on a broad front had kept their northern wing back and given all their supplies to the advancing tank forces of Patton on their southern wing, which then might have crossed the Rhine and penetrated into southern Germany.

As it was, a further campaign in 1945 was needed. Before the Allies could resume their advance in the west, Hitler ordered a last German offensive, with troops and tanks brought together from all parts of the front. In December, 1944, the Germans attempted to break through the center of the American-British line in the Ardennes. On the first two days of their attack the Germans advanced quickly and inflicted heavy losses upon the Americans. Moreover, the initial German success shook Anglo-American morale because it seemed to demonstrate the illusory nature of the assumption that the war was almost over; the alliance with Russia rose in value. But after moving forward two days the Germans were halted; the western allies were able to regain the initiative, and in two weeks of fighting the German armies were pushed back to the line from which they had started. German losses in men and particularly in tanks were so severe that

Germany in defeat. *Tanks entering Magdeburg near the Elbe where Russian and American troops met.*

probably the effect of the "Battle of the Bulge" was to shorten the war. To relieve the pressure on the Allies on the western front, the Russians resumed the offensive in Poland early in January, and by the end of February they had driven the Germans out of Poland and were within fifty miles of Berlin. The British and American forces were able to mount an offensive in February, and on March 8 the American First Army crossed the Rhine at Remagen, south of Bonn. While the Germans were still fighting desperately in the east, the Allies in the west were mainly conducting mopping-up operations. On April 26 Russian and Allied forces met at the Elbe River. Three days later the German troops in Italy surrendered. On April 30, with Russian troops converging on Berlin from all sides, Hitler committed suicide in his bunker in the center of the city. With Hitler's death, German resistance ended. The German military commanders surrendered unconditionally on May 7 in Rheims to Eisenhower and one day later in Berlin to Zhukov, the Russian conqueror of Berlin.

The complete defeat of the German military forces after their series of stunning victories has raised many questions about the nature of Hitler's military talents and leadership. German generals, anxious to maintain the prestige of the German general staff, have claimed for themselves the credit for all the successes, while putting the blame for the defeats on Hitler. Their explanation is too simple. Hitler rightly emphasized, contrary to traditional military thought, the importance of tanks and airplanes in modern warfare. He made certain that due attention was given to the construction of these weapons and to training in their use. Unlike many of his generals, Hitler was aware of the daring ways in which these new weapons could be employed, and he took an active part in the planning of the successful Norwegian and French campaigns of 1940, which showed the possibilities of the modern *Blitzkrieg*. And Hitler's strategic judgment was not much worse than that of his generals. He was undoubtedly right when, against their advice, he insisted on defending an advanced front line in Russia during the winter of 1941–1942; retreat would have brought certain disaster. But Hitler lacked technical training and the patience for logistic details; he was inclined to plan and order operations without taking such factors as supplies and communications fully into account. He relied on his intuition, particularly after the early successes of the German army had confirmed his own and his followers' faith in his supreme military talents. His intuition, however, played him false at two critical moments: in 1940, when he refused to use his tanks against the encircled British army at Dunkerque; and in 1944, when he believed that the invasion in Normandy was a feint and reserves had to be kept back to repulse a landing elsewhere. But there were other signs of deterioration in Hitler's military leadership during the last three years of the war. Confident of his intuition and unable to grasp fully the technical difficulties involved in fighting in Russia or in the desert, he regarded each reverse as the fault of cowardly or treasonous subordinates; he denied his generals any freedom of action and reserved all decisions, even at the local level, for himself. By prohibiting withdrawals he sacrificed troops which could have been saved. He lived shut off in his headquarters, avoiding all encounters which might deter him from indulging in his strategic daydreams. Because he seldom visited the front and the bombed German cities, he lost contact with the crude reality of totalitarian war. In the final months he gave orders to armies which did not exist or existed only on paper. It seems that not until April 22, when he was informed of the failure of S.S. troops to attack the Russians, did he realize the hopelessness of the situation and decide to stay in Berlin to the end.

One of the last scraps of news Hitler received was of the end of his

The commanders of the British, American, Russian, and French armies. *Montgomery, Eisenhower, Zhukov, Lattré de Tassigny in Berlin after the Allied victory.*

fellow dictator, Mussolini, on April 28. When the German army in Italy surrendered, Mussolini and his mistress had tried to escape to Switzerland, but at Lake Como, near the Swiss border, Italian resistance fighters caught and shot them. Then their bodies were brought to Milan, and hung head downward in the Piazza Loreto. The news of Mussolini's death confirmed Hitler in his decision to commit suicide. At this last moment he married his mistress, Eva Braun, and then dictated a long verbose testament which repeated the usual accusations against "international Jewry"; having poisoned his favorite dog so that it would not have to live with another master, he shot himself and together with Eva Braun, who had taken poison, was burned. The facts of Hitler's melodramatic end are well proven.

The Fall of Japan

The German surrender made it possible for the British and Americans to concentrate their final effort on the Far East. In May, 1945, when the war in Europe ended, Japan found itself in roughly the same position in which Germany had been five months before. By the beginning of May, just before the monsoon season would have forced a halt in military operations, British, Indian, and Chinese troops under the command of Lord Louis Mountbatten, reconquered Burma in a difficult and risky operation; most of the supplies had to be brought in by air, and more than 200,000 engineers and laborers were employed in building the airfields and roads needed to maintain the impetus of the advance.

A similar success was registered by the Americans in the Philippines. Their operations to recover these islands had started in October, 1944. In a brilliant strategic stroke the Americans passed up the most southern Philippine island, Mindanao and began their offensive with an operation against the central Philippine island of Leyte. The landing there on October 20 was made possible by a naval victory in Leyte Gulf, which severely crippled the Japanese air force and eliminated the Japanese fleet as a factor of military importance. The battle was of great significance for naval history, demonstrating that the time had passed when victory at sea could be decided by encounters among heavy battleships. At Leyte Gulf aircraft carriers, airplanes, destroyers, and torpedo boats were the chief instruments of destruction. The defeat of their navy prevented the Japanese from getting supplies to their troops in the Philippines, and the American forces under General Douglas MacArthur (1880–1964) proceeded without setback to victory in the islands.

Having gained control of the Philippines, the Americans could advance to Iwo Jima and Okinawa, islands closer to Japan, which might serve as bases for a direct attack on the Japanese mainland. Well aware of the strategic importance of these two islands, which formed their homeland's outer line of defense, the Japanese resisted tenaciously, and the fighting was sharp and bloody. However, in the middle of March, Iwo Jima was conquered, and on May 21, two weeks after the surrender of Germany, Sugar Loaf Hill, the key to the Japanese position on Okinawa, was taken.

Japan was now subjected to continuous intensive bombing by American planes. The loss of shipping resulting from these air attacks was fatal to the Japanese war effort, for Japan was dependent on imported coal, oil, and food. Recognizing that their situation was hopeless, the Japanese were ready to surrender; their decision was accelerated on August 6 and 8 by the dropping of two atomic bombs, one on Hiroshima and one on Nagasaki, which burned out more than half of these cities, killed 130,000 people, and injured an equal number. Japan accepted the Allied terms of surrender on August 14. On September 2, 1945, the Second World War officially came to an end on the deck of the battleship *Missouri* in Tokyo Bay, as the Japanese signed the articles of surrender in the presence of General MacArthur.

The decision to drop the atomic bomb aroused a dispute which is still going on. Scientists had counseled against its use because of its terrifying destructive power. An initial explosion of the bomb on a deserted island, which would have demonstrated its efficacy to the Japanese, would have been more in line with American ideas about morality and law in international relations. Yet, when the decision was made American leaders were not aware of how near Japan was to surrender, and believed that heavy fighting was still ahead. It is perhaps instructive that the last military action in the Second World War demonstrated that, as devastating as the war had been, the limits of destruction which modern technology could achieve had not yet been reached.

CHAPTER 8

The New Setting of Political Life

THE SECOND WORLD WAR, which began in September, 1939, with the invasion of Poland by German forces, had been brought to a close nearly six years later when an American airplane dropped an atomic bomb on a Japanese city. The way the war ended clearly demonstrated that Europe had been absorbed into a much more extended political system, embracing the entire globe, and that science and technology had become dominant in the development of human affairs. These two phenomena—the evolution of a global political system and the attainment of scientific achievements of a revolutionary character—were intimately linked. A close interconnection of the nations of the world could never have been reached without the technical innovations based on the discoveries of the scientists. Science and technology had created an entirely new setting for the forms of political life and the conduct of political affairs.

THE SECOND INDUSTRIAL REVOLUTION

The proper position of a scientific discovery in a chronological historical account is often difficult to determine. The time at which the scientist makes his discovery may be distant from the period in which its full significance for the structure of the scientific world view becomes evident and still more remote from the point where a realization occurs of the practical application which industry can make of such a discovery. But modern warfare has shortened the distance between scientific discoveries and their practical applications; money, manpower, and raw materials are made available for any experiment which may be of some use in a war effort. Hence, the two world wars became powerful engines accelerating the transformation of the external conditions of life.

That such a transformation was underway was obvious before 1914. In the nineteenth century the decisive steps had been taken for the production and harnessing of new sources of energy: research on the nature of electricity, the realization of the usefulness of gas and oil as fuel, and invention of the turbine and the internal-combustion engine.

Thus, scientific discoveries and technological innovations led to the creation of vast new industries centering on electricity and on chemicals. In the later part of the nineteenth and the first decade of the twentieth century, these industries transformed in a startling way both everyday life and the structure of the European economy. Houses and streets were illuminated by electric lights; advertising made use of brilliantly lighted billboards that often towered over the cities. Chemical fertilizers increased the yields from soil which had lost much of its richness over centuries of planting and re-planting. New medicines and new vaccines began to limit the spread of dread diseases such as syphilis, smallpox, and rabies.

The First World War accelerated research and development in the chemical industry. The most important consequence of wartime needs was probably the discovery that atmospheric nitrogen could be made into ammonia, which is an essential ingredient both for the manufacture of explosives and for fertilizers. Their production was no longer dependent on imports from those countries—primarily Chile—which possessed deposits of natural sodium nitrates. Actually, without the industrial production of sodium nitrates, Germany could not have carried on the war for a great length of time. The chemical industry also benefited from the challenge to create substitutes for goods which could not be produced during wartime because of difficulties in obtaining raw materials; the manufacture of plastics and artificial yarns steadily expanded after the war.

The First World War also exerted a great impetus in the areas of transportation and communication. A revolutionary change already had begun to take place in the decades before the First World War. Although, technically, ocean travel remained much as it had been for a century, the luxury offered to first-class passengers in the period before 1914 reached a high point. A glimpse of the opulent life on the great ocean-going liners can be gained from descriptions of the sinking of the *Titanic* which, on its maiden voyage in 1912, raced to obtain the blue ribbon for the speediest Atlantic

The first flight of an airplane. *The Wright brothers near Kitty Hawk in 1903.*

Marconi in 1901 with instruments for wireless reception.

crossing and crashed into an iceberg. The two inventions which were starting a revolution in transportation before the First World War were the
automobile and the airplane. Before 1914, automobiles were not yet in
wide use, but they had become the preferred mode of transportation of the
rich and powerful and could be seen on the roads. Airplanes were still in
a developmental stage, although great strides had been made since 1903,
when the brothers Orville and Wilbur Wright had been able to keep their
flying machine in the air for 59 seconds at Kitty Hawk, North Carolina.
The potential of aircraft was strikingly demonstrated by the flight of the
Frenchman Louis Blériot over the English Channel in 1909. In the field
of communication, telegraph and telephone, of course, had been in use
since the second half of the nineteenth century, but new developments
were ushered in by Marconi's successful experiments in wireless telegraphy
in 1895.

The impact of the First World War on developments in the fields of
transportation and communication differed. Warfare was not yet motorized; tanks made their first appearance only in the final phase of the
conflict. Larger military units, if not on foot, were transported by railroad;
smaller groups, however, particularly officers, moved around in automobiles;
the resulting increase in automobile construction prepared the postwar
expansion of the auto industry. In the case of the airplane and the radio,
the war was of decisive importance in effecting a quick transition from the
experimental stage to general use. Because of its role in the war the great
possibilities of airplane transportation became recognized. Passenger service
was installed between London and Paris in 1919, and between Amsterdam
and London a year later. Soon all larger European cities had airfields and
were connected by scheduled commercial flights. Nevertheless, in the public
mind there remained something dangerous and romantic about fliers and

flying, and no other event in the 1920's caught the imagination of the world as did the daring and lonely flight to Paris of Charles Lindbergh in May, 1927—the first crossing of the Atlantic by air in an eastward direction. While Lindbergh's achievement dramatized the possibilities of air travel, the beginning of regular transatlantic air service was delayed until more than ten years later, to the eve of the outbreak of the Second World War.

Once the First World War had proved the varied applicability of wireless communications, first amateurs and then experts began to experiment in this field and financiers invested heavily, leading to the development in the 1920's of a radio industry. Sensitive receiving instruments replaced primitive earphones; radio stations presented programs lasting throughout the day. Every European state had a broadcasting company working under government control, and international conventions established the wavelengths which each country was entitled to use. In 1927 wireless-telephone service between England and America was inaugurated.

The new means of communication diminished the distance which in the previous century had separated private life and the world of politics and business. With voices from radio present in the home the individual was subjected to constant demands from the outside world. Powerful propaganda efforts had been exerted during the First World War to keep spirits from sagging on the home front—wherever he went the citizen encountered posters urging service in the army or the buying of war bonds, or warning about enemy spies. After the war the technical devices of propaganda were taken up by advertisers in print, on billboards, in the cinema, and on the radio.

The war had revealed that the human mind could be influenced and patterned; it had undermined the previously prevalent view that feeling and action are controlled by reason, and had shown the strength of appeals to the emotions and basic drives. These insights and observations stimulated an increasing concern with psychology, which developed on two levels after the First World War. At one level was a sophisticated interest in the views and theories which psychology and medical science had developed. Characteristic was the rise to fame of Sigmund Freud, who had made his discoveries about the power of the unconscious at the beginning of the century in Vienna. In the 1920's his views—and those of his pupils (subsequently his adversaries), Alfred Adler and Carl Gustav Jung—were widely discussed, and permeated the views of man presented in novels and plays. At the other level was a practical concern with psychology which inquired into man's reactions to external stimuli and the possibility of conditioning human behavior, as investigators tried to find the psychologically most effective means of mass control.

The changes in man's surroundings brought about by science, technology, and industry created new possibilities in the conduct of public affairs. But

The first television camera in 1929.

to what extent they were realized depended on the particular situation in each country, especially on the strength of its political tradition. Although the technique of radio "fireside chats" contributed to the popularity of Franklin Delano Roosevelt, its imitation by Doumergue in France was regarded as a sign of arrogance and authoritarianism and played a role in the overthrow of the Doumergue government. It was natural that those political movements which arose in opposition to the established political structure were most ready to use new political techniques. Mussolini and Hitler both stressed that they were leaders of modern movements. Mussolini liked to be photographed piloting an airplane; Hitler was seen frequently in his Mercedes Benz. In the western democracies there was much admiration for the courage of Neville Chamberlain when in September, 1938—in order to meet Hitler in Berchtesgaden—he entered an airplane for the first time in his life, with an umbrella on his arm. But the Nazis and Fascists considered Chamberlain's reluctance to use modern means of transportation contemptible—a sign of the backwardness of the democracies.

Without the existence of modern techniques Hitler's rise to power would hardly have been possible. His appearance during election campaigns in every part of Germany, in big cities, small towns, and villages, could be accomplished only by means of airplanes and motorcars, and his ubiquitousness served as proof that the new Nazi party had greater vitality and strength than the other old parties because it was directed by the will of one man. After he came to power Hitler quickly made use of the opportunities provided by modern technology. In the propaganda methods of the Nazi government, broadcasting was of central importance. The German people were cut off from all information which did not originate from official Nazi sources and they were ordered to turn on the radio when Hitler spoke, so that they would absorb his interpretation of events. When

Hitler made an aggressive move, such as ordering the German troops into the Rhineland, he accompanied this action with a broadcasted speech in which he emphasized his wish for peace and made proposals for negotiations. Such speeches were quite effective in preventing counteractions because enough people in other countries, particularly in Great Britain, preferred to believe his words and to overlook his deeds.

Hitler's enthusiasm for technical innovations was a strength of his regime. In German rearmament he placed the emphasis strongly on modern weapons. He took a great interest in the construction of a network of roads (*Autobahnen*) which not only would help the development of the German motorcar industry but in wartime would permit the motorized transportation of troops and the quick movement of tanks. Shoddy as their ideas were, the leaders of the Nazi movement had grasped early the use to which modern technology could be put in establishing political control and building up military strength.

The Second World War transformed the external conditions of life even more thoroughly and radically than the First World War had done, and many of the implements of war were later converted to peacetime uses. On land and sea, for bombing the hinterland or for the support of soldiers in combat, for the transportation of men and of materials, the airplane was decisive in the Second World War. The gigantic bombers which had been built in response to wartime emergencies prepared the way for the transoceanic passenger air travel which developed after the war. The jet engine was invented during the war and nearly perfected by its end. Rockets, used as weapons by the Germans in the last year of the war, thereafter became important parts of the military equipment of all modern armies, but their most spectacular employment was in space exploration. The theoretical problems of constructing a device which would permit the location and detection of objects at distances not visible to the eye had been solved previously, but radar was fully developed only during the war years.

The creating of substitute (*Ersatz*) materials was almost more important in the Second World War than in the First. The extension of the war to the Far East led to an acute shortage of raw materials. For example, the Japanese occupation of Indonesia cut off the United States and Great Britain from a major source of natural rubber; as a substitute, a durable synthetic rubber was developed. The conduct of war in hot and humid climates and in areas afflicted by dangerous epidemics necessitated special attention to the problems of health and sanitation. Food refrigeration was improved. Under pressure of war new methods of immunization against contagious diseases were developed. The first antibiotic, penicillin, had been discovered in 1929 but its effectiveness against infections was established only during the war, and then its large-scale production was started in the United States. The invention of a process to extract plasma from the blood helped to reduce mortality from wounds. The damages and sufferings of the Second World War were very different from what the experiences of previous wars might have suggested.

THE NUCLEAR AGE

The greatest impact which the Second World War had on the conditions of life, however, was connected with its final event: the dropping of the atomic bomb, which ushered in the nuclear age. The atomic bomb was awesome proof that modern physics had unlocked a new source of power with almost unlimited potential for destruction, or—if applied to peacetime pursuits—for the good of man. This new weapon was developed under wartime conditions, but the scientific discoveries that made it possible had begun nearly a half century earlier.

The "understanding of atomic physics ... had its origins at the turn of the century and its great synthesis and resolutions in the nineteen twenties."[5] Thus did J. Robert Oppenheimer, one of the principals in this scientific revolution, characterize the main stages of its development. Its great events at the turn of the century were Max Planck's publication in 1900 of "On the Theory of the Law of Energy Distribution in a Normal Spectrum," which presented the thesis of the quantum theory, and Albert Einstein's publication in 1905 of the papers which set forth the special theory of relativity. By 1903 the need for a new theoretical outlook had been confirmed by experiments in the course of which Pierre and Marie Curie isolated radium and Antoine Henri Becquerel recognized the extent of radioactivity. After the First World War, the implications of these theories and discoveries were explored by a score of young scientists. The great centers of this absorbing intellectual adventure were Copenhagen, where Niels Bohr, the guiding spirit of the entire field of atomic reasearch, worked; Göttingen, where Max Born, James Franck, and David Hilbert maintained the tradition of this university as a center of mathematics and natural science; and Cambridge, where Ernest Rutherford continued his study of radioactivity and then, together with Sir James Chadwick, turned to the investigation of the composition of the atom. There was a lively exchange among all these groups, and the genesis of a new physical world view which, although it did not invalidate the classical Newtonian physics, limited its applicability, was the common achievement of scientists from many countries.

The creative excitement of these decades was caused by the necessity of revising the basic assumptions of classical physics, notably the supposition that through observation and experiments it is possible to establish the laws

[5] J. Robert Oppenheimer, *Science and the Common Understanding* (New York, 1953), p. 35.

Meeting of physicists in Göttingen in 1921. *Sitting, Max Born; standing from left to right: Wilhelm Oseen, Niels Bohr, James Franck, Oscar Klein.*

which demonstrate the causal connection determining the processes of nature. When Planck showed that certain incongruities in the radiation of energy is probable but it is not predetermined. Similarly, Einstein's demon-continuous waves but in flashes, like a stream of bullets of fixed size ("quantum"), his theory suggested that the assumption of complete continuity in the process of nature was untenable. Nature is discontinuous; that a certain sequence of events will result from the release of a quantum of energy is probable but it is not predetermined. Similarly, Einstein's demonstration in his theory of relativity of the bonds between the dimensions of space and of time forced a reexamination of the value of the material provided by observation. It was found that when measurements of a small elementary particle like the electron focus on speed, those of its precise position become uncertain, while measurements of position reduce precision in the measurement of speed. The conclusion was that in the description of nature there remains an element of uncertainty.

The disclosure that discontinuity and uncertainty are inherent in nature nullified the expectation of earlier scientists that immutable laws would someday be discovered which could explain all known phenomena. The work of the physicist became limited to the exploration of relations among the phenomena. But this limitation actually gave the investigator scope for greater creative efforts.

The basis for this change in theoretical assumptions which was worked out in the 1920's and 1930's was concrete investigation; the intellectual speculations were accompaniments of the discoveries resulting from a study of the atom. Already in the nineteenth century there had been some research which showed that the atom did not form an indivisible basic unit of matter, as had been assumed. The investigations of the twentieth century gradually revealed that the atom is composed of a very small nucleus (usually consisting of positively charged protons and electrically neutral neutrons) which is surrounded by negatively charged electrons. The problem was that, despite the radioactivity of certain elements, which ought to have led to a loss of energy, their atoms remained stable. And the explanation of this fact with the help of the new theoretical insights led to the discovery of nuclear energy. The freeing of this energy through the splitting of the atom—the result of bombarding uranium with neutrons—was first achieved in January, 1939, by Otto Hahn and Fritz Strassmann in Germany.

By then the United States had become the chief center of modern physical research, partly because laboratories equipped for such research on a major scale had been developed in places like Berkeley and Pasadena, partly because the totalitarian regimes had forced many of the leading Italian and German physicists to seek sanctuary in the United States. When information arrived that the Nazis might use the achievement of nuclear fission for the construction of a bomb, the activity of many of the physicists in the United States became concentrated on the problem of producing such a weapon before the Nazis could do so. The obstacles to such an enterprise were immense. The development of an atomic bomb required the cooperation of investigators from virtually all the fields of science. A by-product of this undertaking was the construction of a computer to accomplish the needed complicated mathematical calculations. The expenses were immense; the outlay for the Manhattan Project, as it was called, amounted to two billion dollars. Moreover, because complete secrecy had to be maintained, the teams of scientists and technicians, under the direction of J. Robert Oppenheimer and the military control of General Leslie Groves, lived and worked entirely cut off from the outside world. Without the pressure of the war emergency these difficulties could not have been overcome. But after two years of work, on July 16, 1945, the first atomic explosion was successfully achieved in New Mexico, filling those who could appreciate the possibilities and the dangers of the harnessing of nuclear energy with "terror as well as exultation."

"ONE WORLD" AND THE ESTABLISHMENT OF PEACE

The Second World War and the technical innovations connected with it gave rise to a new international outlook. The world had really become "one world." During the war powers like the United States, Great Britain, and Russia were involved in military action on a global scale. Technological advances in the postwar period have reinforced the interconnection among all parts of the world. Troops can be transported to distant areas in a matter of hours; missiles can be directed to remote targets; and nuclear rockets can be fired by nuclear submarines suddenly emerging at distant coasts. There is now a global balance of power which can be affected by events at almost any place.

The leaders of the wartime coalition were aware of the extent to which the world had been drawn together. The first conference at which Roosevelt, Churchill, and Stalin met was held at Teheran in November, 1943. Although discussions were chiefly concerned with military planning, and particularly with the establishment of a second front in the West, postwar developments were adumbrated in general terms. A second Big Three conference took place at Yalta, in the Crimea, in February, 1945. Again military questions stood in the forefront. But the approaching end of the war made the consideration of the postwar settlement a necessity, although the decisions remained rather vague and general. The liberated and the defeated countries were to become democracies. Germany and Austria were to be occupied, with each of the victorious powers receiving a zone of occupation, although in the capitals—Berlin and Vienna—a central administration assuring uniformity of occupation policies was to be established. But the American government was also urging the creation of an international organization to guarantee the maintenance of peace in the future; hence the American delegation regarded as valuable the Russian agreement, obtained at the Yalta meeting, to the establishment of such an organization. On April 25, 1945, a conference opened in San Francisco attended by all nations which had declared war on Germany and Japan; it ended on June 26 with the signing of the United Nations Charter.

From the start the most important members of the United Nations were two powers which after the First World War had remained outside the League of Nations: the United States and Russia. The League of Nations, though aimed to embrace the entire world, had always remained Europe-centered; the United Nations can claim to be global. Its headquarters were established not in Europe but in New York. The first two heads of its permanent international staff—Trygve Lie and Dag Hammarskjöld—came from the Scandinavian countries, but in 1962 a Burmese statesman—U Thant—became secretary-general.

The Economic and Social Council, one of its important organs, and the various specialized agencies working with and under the United Nations, make significant contributions by studying such problems as nutrition, overpopulation, and disease in what are regarded as the underdeveloped areas of Asia and Africa, by indicating the remedies which modern technology can provide, and by directing attention to the need for action. The International Bank for Reconstruction and Development, which is also connected with the Economic and Social Council, can provide these countries some of the requisite financial assistance.

In the political area the United Nations, with more members than the League of Nations ever had, appears much more egalitarian than the League because in the annual meetings of the General Assembly each of the numerous members has just one vote. Nevertheless, the greater powers exert a dominating influence. The Security Council, which is the crucial organ in decisions regarding critical political problems, has the United States, Great Britain, Russia, France, and China as permanent members; in addition six other members are elected by the Assembly for two-year terms, and these elections usually assure wide geographical representation. Since concurrence of all the permanent members is necessary for any decision of the Security Council which is not purely procedural, the permanent members have the power of veto.

But the actual power relationship existing in the present world is not fully reflected in the organization of the United Nations. In addition to the circle of states distinguished by membership in the Security Council, there is another exclusive circle, consisting of those possessing nuclear bombs: the United States (since 1945), Russia (since 1949), Great Britan (since 1952), Communist China, which is not a member of the United Nations (since 1964), and France (since 1966). Of these states, the United States and Russia have the largest number of nuclear weapons and are most advanced in the scientific exploration of the field. Their great natural and financial resources constitute an advantage which in the course of time will increase the distance which exists between these two and the other members of the nuclear club. Thus, science and technology have created two superpowers which can force all other nations to their will. The role which other states play in the United Nations is limited; they can take the initiative and shape policy only as long as the two superpowers neither clash nor combine.

The United Nations and the Maintenance of Peace

After attempts to establish international control of nuclear weapons failed, and Russia and the United States became involved in a competition for nuclear superiority, the United Nations was clearly divided between adherents of Russia and adherents of the United States. This division dominated the organization in the first decade after the end of the Second World War. These were years of crisis and tension because the problems of the postwar settlements and the rise of the peoples of Asia and Africa against their European rulers created continuously dangerous situations which led to confrontations between Russia and the United States. But when in the 1950's some nuclear balance between the superpowers was achieved, an increasing number of members of the United Nations began to feel able to move into an uncommitted position.

Has the United Nations been effective in guaranteeing peace; has it played its role in preventing the crises of the postwar epoch from developing into war? This is a difficult question to answer. The formal meetings of the General Assembly and of the Security Council have hardly contributed to lowering the temperature in critical situations. The various delegates attack one another's speeches acidly. Each accuses his opponent of distortions and lies, and criticizes him as representing an aggressive and oppressive power. The debates rigidify the antagonistic positions of the adversaries and serve self-justification and propaganda rather than defining a middle ground for negotiations. On the other hand, with modern means of communication statesmen can assemble from the most different parts of the earth within hours and the Security Council provides a recognized meeting place in critical situations. The speeches may serve to let off steam and to give the people at home the impression that their government is taking a resolute stand for its righteous cause, so that, freed from the pressure of excited public opinion, serious negotiations can begin. The United Nations fulfills the important function of bringing antagonists together behind closed doors, behind the façade of the public meetings. For instance, it provided the opportunities for initiating the secret negotiations which ended the crisis of the Berlin blockade in 1949. Perhaps instead of regarding the United Nations as a supranational government entrusted with preserving peace and order, one should view it as an instrument created to adjust diplomatic machinery to the requirements of the twentieth century. The niceties of traditional diplomatic language may not be appropriate to the more robust age of mass participation in public affairs. But the new roughness in the forms of diplomacy is counterbalanced by a willingness to make use of all available means for discussing differences in personal meetings which in earlier times frequently were not possible or were rejected because of considerations of prestige.

Although the United Nations provides diplomatic machinery appropriate to the modern age, the final decisions on war and peace are still left to the statesmen of the leading powers. It is the utter terror of the weapons which modern science and technology has created, rather than the moral force of an international organization, that—fortunately—has weighted the scale on the side of increasing restraint.

CHAPTER 9

Between Surrender and Cold War

EUROPE AFTER THE ALLIED VICTORY

THE COMPLETENESS of the Allied triumph, signified in the acceptance of "unconditional surrender," meant that the victors had to assume responsibility for life in the defeated nations. This awesome task was complicated by the misery and devastation which prevailed not just in Germany and Italy but in Europe as a whole.

The Legacy of Total War

The most visible imprint left by the Second World War was the physical destruction in the urban areas. Except for the university towns of Oxford, Cambridge, and Heidelberg, which out of consideration for cultural values had been left intact, all the larger towns of England and Germany had suffered extensive damage, with many areas, particularly in their centers, completely razed. Warsaw, Vienna, Budapest, Rotterdam were in ruins. In France most of the harbors along the channel coast had been hit severely.

In contrast, the European countryside, except where it had been the site of military operations, was untouched. But communications between rural and urban areas had been severed, and the various parts of a country existed almost in isolation. Roads, bridges, and railroad lines had been demolished or damaged. Locomotives and railroad equipment had been broken or stalled at the military fronts or had so deteriorated that they were almost unusable. The factories which produced the equipment needed for reconstruction had been wrecked, and manpower was not immediately available.

The Germans had been adequately fed during most of the war, but they had been supplied at the expense of the Nazi-occupied countries. Hence, in most of Europe people were near starvation and their capacity for work was small: The male inhabitants of the Nazi-occupied countries, having served as forced laborers, were dispersed in labor camps all over Europe. Moreover, during the war the populations of entire regions had been moved; thus the Nazis had transferred the inhabitants out of parts of Poland and the

After the war. *Displaced people returning to their former homes.*

Ukraine so that Germans could be settled there. At the end of the war an analogous policy was carried out by Hungarians, Serbs, and Czechs who were unwilling to tolerate troublesome German minorities within their borders. In addition, Germans of East Prussia and Silesia, in fear of the approaching Russian armies, fled toward the west. Roads were clogged with people trying either to return to their own countries or to find new homes. To those who saw the European continent in the spring and early summer of 1945 it seemed incredible that within a few years life might again become normal.

Impoverishment and economic and social disorder were not confined to Germany, Austria, and Italy. The plight of the liberated countries was equally serious. Life in the whole of Europe had to be reorganized and brought back to health. Initially this task fell upon the victors. Their troops were stationed all over Europe, since military occupation of the defeated countries required secure lines of communications through the adjacent areas. The control which the victors exerted by military means was reinforced by the fact that only they could supply the food and the basic resources needed by the European countries for reconstruction.

The task of providing for military requirements and economic assistance involved a certain amount of political interference even in areas where the victors did not possess exclusive control, as they did in Germany and Austria. In most of the liberated countries the political situation was tense, almost revolutionary. The leading politicians of the prewar era, who had withdrawn or gone into exile during the period of Nazi rule, came forward in the expectation that they again would play a leading role. Their aim was restoration of the prewar situation in their respective states. But they were confronted by new leaders, who had come to prominence through their activities in the resistance movements and now wanted social and political changes which would weaken the influence of the previously ruling circles.

After the war. *The Krupp works in ruins.*

The victors could not permit their troops to live among the starving and despairing population and under the threat of civil war. Hence, all over Europe the Americans, the British, and the Russians became involved in the revival of political and social life. Almost unavoidably the political ideas and traditions of each of these powers patterned the political revival in the areas in which it maintained a strong military posture.

Wartime negotiations and conferences, and particularly the conference at Yalta, had established only general and somewhat vague principles concerning the treatment of the Germans after surrender. It had been agreed, however, that Austria would again be separated from Germany, that both Germany and Austria would be entirely occupied, and that each of the victorious powers—Russia, Great Britain, and the United States—would receive a zone of occupation in Germany and in Austria. France was later added to the three victors and was given occupation zones cut out of those originally assigned to Great Britain and the United States. The capitals—Berlin and Vienna—were to be placed under the common administration of all the victors; it was envisaged that these cities would serve again as national capitals, each housing a central administration subject to the control of the occupying powers.

The rest of Europe was clearly divided into two different spheres of influence. Eastern Europe and the Balkans had been freed from Nazi rule by Russian armies and these forces remained stationed there ostensibly to maintain communication with the Russian-occupied zones of central Europe. But the Russians soon impressed their political patterns on the countries in these regions. Northern and western Europe—Norway, Denmark, the Netherlands, Belgium, France, and in the south, Italy and Greece—had been liberated by American and British troops, and those parts of Europe were organized in conformity with the concepts of western democracy. Thus, political revival in eastern and western Europe took very different forms, but the road was clearly staked out and the process of reconstruction started quickly.

The Settlement of the Frontiers

The victorious powers took care that within their spheres of influence no serious conflicts about boundaries arose. Readjustments were relatively minor. In the east Rumania had to cede northern Bucovina and Bessarabia to Soviet Russia, and part of Dobruja to Bulgaria. But Rumania received northern Transylvania from Hungary, which also had to relinquish some land to Czechoslovakia. Finland lost to Russia the territory of Petsamo in the north and the Karelian Isthmus in the south. Russia kept the Baltic states and extended its dominance southward along the Baltic Sea by annexing the northern part of what had been East Prussia; Poland recognized the frontiers which Russia had established in 1939 as a result of the Nazi-Soviet pact, but was promised some extension of its frontiers in the west as compensation.

The boundary changes in the areas controlled by the United States and Great Britain were still less significant. It was recognized that the former frontiers of France had to be restored, and after some negotiations it was agreed that the Saar region would be economically attached to France so that France would have priority in the use of Saar coal; the territory itself would remain under German sovereignty. Slight frontier revisions in favor of Belgium and Denmark were arranged at the expense of Germany. Italy ceded some border territory to France, lost all of its overseas possessions, and returned the Dodecanese to Greece.

The determination of frontiers was complicated only along the line where the Russian and western spheres of occupation touched each other; that is, the line which led from the Baltic Sea through the center of Germany along Czechoslovakia and Austria to the region between Yugoslavia and Italy. The final settlement of these boundaries required years of hard negotiations, and in the case of Germany, agreement has not yet been reached.

The course of political reconstruction could differ greatly in the various countries of the Russian and the Anglo-American spheres because during the war no clear and definite agreement about the form of the postwar settlement had been obtained. The Big Three—the United States, Great Britain, and Soviet Russia—had limited themselves to proclaiming that the European countries should be democracies; a precise interpretation of this term, however, had not been given.

Soviet Control of Eastern Europe

The Soviet rulers established "people's democracies" in the countries they controlled, but to the west the forms of government emerging in eastern Europe seemed hardly democratic. For the Communists regarded the workers and peasants as the only sectors of the population with the right to exert control over the government. They alone constituted "the people." Even among the workers and peasants only the politically conscious and active members—those in the Communist parties—deserved to have a voice. As in Soviet Russia, the candidates for the committees and councils which constituted the government and the administration had to be members of the Communist party. And the party was a strictly hierarchical structure directed from above, with its secretary, as in Russia, holding the key position. Thus, the "people's democracies" which the Soviets organized were actually Communist dictatorships.

The achievement of complete Communist rule took some time, and the methods employed by the Russians varied according to the situation in each particular country. Usually, the Russian occupying troops began by forming a coalition government, called a United Front government, in which the Communists were partners and held key positions. From this government the non-Communist members were gradually eliminated by methods in which psychological pressure and propaganda were combined with brute power; the presence of Russian troops made resistance to Russian demands almost impossible. Meanwhile, large parts of the population, workers and peasants in particular, acquired a vested interest in the maintenance of the system; in all the Russian-controlled areas large landed estates were divided among the peasants and the important industrial enterprises were nationalized. Undoubtedly such measures created a certain amount of popular support.

In Bulgaria and Rumania the Communists were dominating in the government by the summer of 1945, although the young monarchs of these countries were deposed only in 1946 and 1947. In Poland the Russians proceeded more circumspectly. They could not disregard the particular interest which Great Britain and the United States took in the fate of Poland; the Second World War had started in order to save the independence of Poland. After its defeat the Polish government had gone into exile in London, and it was recognized by Great Britain and the United States. Nor could Great Britain and the United States have any doubt about the great increase in power which domination over Poland would give to Russia; they were well aware that it would place Soviet might in the center of Europe. But in the end the vehement protests of the United States and Britain against the Communist pressure in Poland only slowed down the Russian abandonment of the pretense of democratic procedure. A Communist monopoly of power was achieved there in

TERRITORIAL CHANGES IN
EASTERN EUROPE TO 1947

— · — · — 1947 boundaries

— — — — 1939 boundaries

• • • • • • Nazi–Soviet boundary, 1939

Territorial changes resulting from
pre- and post-war settlements

0 ——————— 500 miles

Petsamo
(TO U.S.S.R.)
Murmansk

WHITE
SEA

(TO U.S.S.R.)

FINLAND

GULF OF BOTHNIA

Helsinki

KARELIAN ISTHMUS
(TO U.S.S.R.)

Leningrad

NORWAY

Oslo

Stockholm

SWEDEN

ESTONIA
(TO U.S.S.R.)

Moscow

LATVIA
(TO U.S.S.R.)

NORTH
SEA

DENMARK

Copenhagen

BALTIC SEA

LITHUANIA
(TO U.S.S.R.)

(TO U.S.S.R.)

Königsberg

EAST
PRUSSIA
(TO POLAND)

Minsk

Berlin

Danzig
(TO POLAND)

(TO POLAND)

POLAND

Warsaw

EASTERN
POLAND
(TO U.S.S.R.)

U.S.S.R.

Kiev

GERMANY

Prague

Cracow

CZECHOSLOVAKIA

NORTHERN
BUCOVINA
(TO U.S.S.R.)

Vienna

Bratislava

AUSTRIA

Budapest

HUNGARY

SUBCARPATHIAN
RUTHENIA
(TO U.S.S.R.)

(TO U.S.S.R.)

BESSARABIA

Odessa

SWITZ.

Trieste
(FREE CITY)

(TO YUGOSLAVIA)

RUMANIA

BLACK
SEA

ITALY

ADRIATIC SEA

Belgrade

YUGOSLAVIA

Bucharest

DOBRUJA
(TO BULGARIA)

Rome

BULGARIA

Tirana

Sofia

Istanbul

ALBANIA

GREECE

TURKEY

January, 1947. Six months later complete Communist control was attained in Hungary. In Czechoslovakia a coup carried out by Communist-led workers established a purely Communist government in February, 1948. This event was the more shocking because during the interwar years Czechoslovakia had stood out as a democratic western-oriented country, and its leaders had enjoyed a high reputation in the west. Now Benes, the president, resigned and the foreign minister, Jan Masaryk (1886-1948), the son of the founder of the state, died in circumstances which were suspicious enough to raise serious doubts about the official explanation of suicide. With the Communist coup in Czechoslovakia, western political influences and notions disappeared, at least in any visible form, from the regimes under Russian occupation.

The Return to Parliamentary Democracy in the West

In the areas of Europe which had been liberated by the armies of the United States and Great Britain, "democracy" was widely interpreted as parliamentary democracy. Before Fascist and Nazi domination, Italy and France had been parliamentary democracies. The establishment of this form of government in these countries therefore constituted a restoration. But a simple return to a previous situation is never possible, and most of the people who had fought heroically against Fascist and Nazi despotism wanted something new, something better than had existed before. The resistance movements had included men from the entire political spectrum—from nationalists of the right to Communists on the extreme left. They were united in their hatred of Nazi collaborators and in their rejection of the prewar political system.

It was not difficult to settle accounts with individual traitors; in all of the formerly occupied countries trials against Nazi collaborators and war criminals took place. In France members of the Vichy government were brought before a high court. Laval was executed; Pétain was sentenced to prison and died there. Most of the Nazi collaborators and sympathizers in France were tried before special courts; in the first year 40,000 out of 125,000 defendants received more or less severe punishment. But the men of the resistance, or at least most of them, attributed responsibility for the surrender to Fascism and Nazism not only to individuals but to a system which had allowed a determining political influence to industrialists and bankers. Democracy, it was believed, could not flourish where economic power was concentrated in the hands of a few big capitalists. The successful functioning of a parliamentary democracy was thought to be predicated upon social and economic reforms which would strengthen the position of the great masses of the population against the rich upper group. In the last months of the war, and in the liberation period, resistance groups tried in many areas to assume executive power and constitute themselves as governments. They were balked by the military leaders of the victorious American and British armies, who were primarily interested in smoothly functioning supply and communications lines, and feared disorder and chaos. Furthermore, De Gaulle, the acknowledged head of the French resistance, opposed the encroachment of individual groups on what he considered to be the paramount authority of the state.

Yet despite the failure of the resistance to effect changes and reforms during the fluid situation at the war's end, it was generally recognized that neither France nor Italy could just reactivate its former constitution. In France a plebiscite determined that it was necessary, as De Gaulle declared in a broadcast in September, 1945, "to adopt a different system in order to revive the spirit of clarity, justice and efficiency which is the true spirit of the republic." And in both countries constituent assemblies were elected to develop new constitutions—in France on October 21, 1945, and in Italy on June 2, 1946.

The elections for these assemblies saw the rise of two newly powerful parties, a Catholic party at the center of the political spectrum and the Communist party at the extreme left. Italy changed from a monarchy to a republic, but in other respects the constitution adopted by the constituent assembly was very similar to the one which had existed before Fascism. Only the anticlerical emphasis of the nineteenth-century liberal constitution was eliminated, with Mussolini's *concordate* with the pope becoming an integral part of the new constitution. Roman Catholicism remained in Italy "the sole religion of the state." The new French constitution was more democratic than that of the Third Republic had been; a second chamber, an indirectly elected Council of the Republic, replacing the Senate, remained in existence but its functions were insignificant. The National Assembly, replacing the former Chamber of Deputies, was all-powerful, and it was expected that the removal of the conservative counterweight which the Senate had represented in the Third Republic would help to create greater governmental stability in the Fourth Republic.

In the years immediately following the end of the war, both Italy and France were ruled by left-center coalitions composed of the new Catholic party, the socialists, and the Communists. Despite continuous friction between the Catholic and Communist parties, a working collaboration was maintained among all three groups, based on the lesson, drawn from the years of Fascist rule, that the power of the great capitalists had to be curbed if democracy was to work. In Italy, the state retained the share which, under Fascism, it had acquired in many of the more important industrial enterprises; but wheras under Mussolini, the influence which control of industries gave to the government had been used in favor of big business, the governments of democratic Italy were expected to use this power to restrain this group. In France indignation about the "rule of the two hundred families," which before the war had exploded in the Popular Front election of 1936, had only been deepened by the events under the Nazis and the Vichy regime. And the parties in the government had no difficulty in agreeing on a wide program of economic and social reforms. They embarked on a policy of nationalization which included the credit system (banks and insurance companies), the fuel and power industries (coal, gas, and electricity), strategically important enterprises (airlines, the merchant marine), and a number of large industrial concerns which had been working for the Germans, the best known being the Renault automobile works. The economic situation of the workers was improved by the introduction of a comprehensive social-security scheme. Also, employees could form works committees, with an advisory function in the running of the factories. Finally, the role of the trade unions in collective bargaining was strengthened.

By the end of 1946 French and Italian political life had been set on its new course. At that time the contrast between western and eastern Europe—the states of the one forming their political decisions by means of parliaments and a multiparty system, those of the other having their policy directed and controlled by the leadership of one party—had not yet been fully developed, and the differences did not seem as definite and as unbridgeable as they now appear: with members of socialist and bourgeois parties participating in the governments of Poland, Hungary, and Czechoslovakia, and with Communists in the French and Italian coalition governments, the situation in the first two postwar years still seemed rather fluid. Moreover, after difficult negotiations which extended through a series of conferences—in London in September, 1945, in Moscow in December, 1945, and in Paris during the spring and summer of 1946—the situation which had developed in the defeated countries was given recognition through peace treaties, with Italy, Bulgaria, Rumania, Finland, and Poland. Yet, appearances that a trend toward stabilization was setting in and that a halfway meeting between East and West might be possible were deceptive. On the question of Germany, the most important issue in the settlement of European affairs, no understanding between East and West was reached. On the contrary, the negotiations about the treatment of Germany which had taken place since the end of hostilities had steadily widened the gap between East and West.

The Pivotal Question of Germany

It was natural that the question of Germany's future should become decisive in breaking up the wartime alliance and in dividing West and East. Germany's position in the center of Europe, and its wealth in mineral resources, made it a critical area even in defeat.

During the war the Allies had outlined only a very general framework for

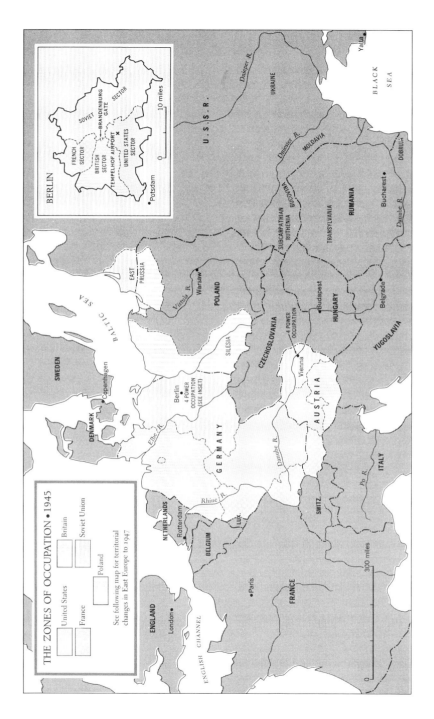

BERLIN

SOVIET SECTOR

BRANDENBURG GATE

FRENCH SECTOR

BRITISH SECTOR

UNITED STATES SECTOR

TEMPELHOF AIRPORT

0   10 miles

• Potsdam

THE ZONES OF OCCUPATION • 1945

United States

Britain

France

Soviet Union

Poland

See following map for territorial changes in East Europe to 1947

ENGLAND

London •

ENGLISH CHANNEL

NETHERLANDS

Rotterdam •

BELGIUM

LUX.

FRANCE

• Paris

SWEDEN

Copenhagen •

DENMARK

BALTIC SEA

GERMANY

Berlin 4 POWER OCCUPATION (SEE INSET)

Elbe R.

Rhine R.

SWITZ.

Danube R.

Po R.

ITALY

EAST PRUSSIA

Vistula R.

Warsaw •

POLAND

SILESIA

CZECHOSLOVAKIA

AUSTRIA

Vienna

4 POWER OCCUPATION

HUNGARY

Budapest •

YUGOSLAVIA

Belgrade •

U. S. S. R.

UKRAINE

Dnieper R.

Dniester R.

SUBCARPATHIAN RUTHENIA

BUCOVINA

MOLDAVIA

TRANSYLVANIA

RUMANIA

Bucharest •

Danube R.

DOBRUJA

BLACK SEA

Yalta •

0   300 miles

the treatment of Germany. They had agreed on occupation zones, and now these were set up. The Russian and American zones were roughly equal in size, and each had about 7.25 million inhabitants. The British zone was smaller but had 5 million more people because it included the densely populated Ruhr area. The French zone was the smallest in extent and in population (5 million). The main aim of the victors, as stated in a communiqué issued after the Yalta Conference, was to prevent future military aggression by Germany: "To insure that Germany will never again be able to disturb the peace of the world." Hence the powers agreed that Nazis ought to be punished and that German society ought to be changed so that militarism could no longer prosper. Germany was to be demilitarized; production was to be kept down to a level which would prevent industrial expansion and shift the balance in economic life toward agriculture. Living conditions in Germany were not to be better than those of the neighboring countries. Germany was to compensate for the damages caused in the Second World War, but in an attempt to avoid the mistakes made after the First World War it was specified that payments were not to be made in gold. Implementation of these principles was to be worked out in a peace treaty, which would also define Germany's frontiers. One important territorial change was envisaged. Because Poland's eastern borders had been modified in favor of Russia, the German-Polish frontier would be along the Oder and Neisse rivers. Until the final peace treaty was concluded the Poles would exert control as an occupying power in the areas assigned to them.

The principles established by the Allies for the treatment of Germany proved to be insufficient. First of all, they envisaged a situation very different from the one actually found by the occupying armies. Germany was crowded with refugees from East Prussia, West Prussia, Pomerania, Poznań, and Silesia, people without means and without employment. Destruction through bombing had caused a severe lack of housing. The breakdown of transportation created food shortages in the towns. The occupation forces were not staffed to deal with this emergency situation. The establishment of indigenous authorities, the promotion of industrial activities for reconstruction and for employment were much more urgent than had been assumed.

But the principles for the treatment of Germany on which the Allies had agreed were deficient also because they permitted varying interpretations and consequently were applied in different ways in the several zones of occupation. Indeed, there was only one area in which successful cooperation of the coalition partners continued: the punishment of the major war crimes. A trial before an international tribunal at Nuremberg between November, 1945, and October, 1946, resulted in the death sentence, and subsequent hanging, of ten Nazi leaders, among them Foreign Minister

The Nuremberg Trials. *Among the Nazi leaders in the front row are Göring (at the extreme left), Hess (second from left), Ribbentrop (third from left), and Schacht (at the extreme right). In the second row Papen is third from left and Speer third from right.*

Joachim von Ribbentropp, Hitler's military advisers Wilhelm Keitel and Alfred Jodl, Minister of the Interior Wilhelm Frick, and the Jew-baiter Julius Streicher. Göring committed suicide in prison. Himmler had killed himself after capture. Perhaps never before was a group of men, who five years earlier had strutted around as rulers of an entire continent and had ruthlessly sealed the fate of millions, so quickly eliminated.

Most of the other issues, however, were handled by the wartime partners in accordance with their particular political traditions and customs, and the cleavages which developed in consequence were particularly deep between the Russian and the western zones. For instance, all the occupying powers were obligated to eradicate Nazism from German life. But east and west had entirely different approaches to the problem of denazification. To the Russians denazification meant the destruction of the system—bourgeois capitalism—which had permitted the rise of Nazism, and denazification would be considered accomplished when the laboring classes were firmly established in power. Thus, the Russians in their zone of occupation terminated private ownership of big industrial and financial enterprises and divided up the large landed estates in the areas east of the Elbe. They quickly revived political life and created for their zone a German government dominated by an anticapitalist Socialist Unity party, although for some years participation of a left-wing bourgeois party in the government was tolerated. With the establishment of a new ruling class of workers and peasants, the Russians considered denazification successfully completed.

In the west, denazification was taken to mean that those who had been active in the Nazi regime were to be deprived of participation in politics and economic life. Denazification was directed against individuals; it did not imply a change in the German social structure. The denazification proceedings in the west had the disadvantage of being slow and bureaucratic; every German had to fill out a long questionnaire about his activities during the Nazi period, and the paper work became so unmanageable that sweeping amnesties had to be granted.

The two approaches to denazification typify the fundamental differences between the political and social concepts which determined occupation policies in the eastern and in the western zones.

With the emergence of widely differentiated social structures in the two halves of Germany, the conclusion of a peace treaty which would encompass the nation as a whole became increasingly complicated. Aware of the danger of such a development, the wartime leaders had agreed to establish in Berlin a central German administration which would act under the supervision of an Allied Control Council. Berlin, in the midst of the Russian zone, was placed under direct four-power control, with each power—the Americans, the British, the French, and the Russians—quartered in a different part of the city.

It is not clear whether the Russians were ever willing to permit the formation of a central German administration not dominated by Communists. The regime which they had set up in their zone was rather shaky, and they must have feared that it might not survive if the establishment of a central administration should open the door to the West. Thus acceptance of a single government for all of Germany might cost them their grip over even the eastern part of the country. A continued division of Germany into various zones might have appeared to them preferable to the establishment of a unified state in which the Communists had no control.

The issue which ended all plans for a central German administration and actually terminated the effective functioning of the Allied Control Council was the matter of reparations.

Here again the devastation which the victors found in Germany made previously conceived plans unrealizable. It had been agreed that in compensation for the immense damage caused by the German invaders, the Russians would have the right to transfer German industrial installations to the Soviet Union and to receive as reparations a proportion of the goods currently produced by German industry; they were expected in return to deliver food stocks to the western zones of Germany from the agricultural areas which they were occupying. The presupposition of this plan was that the whole of Germany would be treated as an economic unit. However, the scarcities in the eastern zone, which were the result of war devastation but were aggravated by Russian exploitation of the zone, made delivery of food to the western zones impossible; therefore, the United States and Great Britain had to export food at their own expense to western Germany in order to feed their troops and to keep the German working population at least on a subsistence minimum. This meant that deliveries from the western zones to the Russians would be financed by the United States and Great Britain—that the reparations which the Germans were to make to the Russians would actually be paid by the western powers. As a result, no deliveries to Russia of industrial products from the western zones ever took place, and the conflict on this issue totally disrupted the work of the Allied Control Council; thereafter the western occupying powers and Russia handled economic affairs in their zones independently. Attempts to overcome the deadlock on the level of foreign ministers' conferences were unsuccessful. On the contrary, such a conference in Moscow in April, 1947, not only lacked positive results but even widened the gap between Russia and the West.

The Marshall Plan

Two years after the German surrender all of Europe still suffered from the destruction of the war, from the interruption of communications and commerce, from a lack of capital to stimulate industrial productivity. After the high expectations of victory, many people were disappointed and dissatisfied. Russian intransigence was probably heightened by the expectation that Communism would gain in strength if Europe remained in this unsettled state. In this situation the American secretary of state, George C. Marshall, who had been deeply disturbed by the failure of the foreign ministers' conference in Moscow, on June 5, 1947, made a speech at Harvard University in which he promised American support if the European powers would work out plans for economic reconstruction. The result was the European Recovery Program, usually called the Marshall Plan. Over the next years—until 1952, when the plan officially ended—12.4 billion dollars were given as economic aid to the participating countries: Austria, Belgium, Denmark, France, Great Britain, Greece, Iceland, Ireland, Italy, Luxemburg, the Netherlands, Norway, Portugal, Sweden, Switzerland, and Turkey. Economic recovery set in rapidly and the outlook in western Europe changed.

Originally the assistance of the recovery program was also made available to the various countries under Russian control, and Czechoslovakia accepted the offer, but under the pressure of Molotov, the Russian foreign minister, the Czechs withdrew. No country in the Russian sphere of interest participated in the program. In March, 1946, Winston Churchill had warned that "from Stettin in the Baltic to Trieste in the Adriatic, an iron curtain has descended across the continent." By the time another year had passed, eastern and western Europe really were separated; the next event was a direct confrontation in a "Cold War."

THE FAR EAST AFTER THE JAPANESE SURRENDER

Since the Second World War had been a global conflict, the European developments after the end of the war cannot be understood apart from events in other parts of the world. The unwillingness of Russia and the United States to make concessions on the question of Germany, the rapidity with which wartime cooperation changed into tension and conflict, can be comprehended only if we realize that during the same period a clash between Russian and the American interests developed in the Far East.

When Japan surrendered on August 14, 1945, friction between Russia and the West in this area seemed unlikely. During the war Russia had been anxious to concentrate all its military efforts upon Germany and had carefully avoided embroilment with Japan. However, at the Yalta Conference, Stalin had promised that his nation would enter the war against Japan after the termination of military operations in Europe. Accordingly, Russian forces were assembled near the Manchurian border and Russia declared war on Japan on August 8. Since the Japanese military situation had become hopeless by then, and the atomic bomb dropped on Hiroshima on August 6 had broken the Japanese will to resist, Russia's entry into the war played no part in the Japanese defeat. The procedures followed by the Americans in negotiating and accepting the Japanese surrender showed clearly that they regarded the settlement with Japan exclusively as their own. And during the following years, the United States remained the only outside force to exert control and influence over the reconstruction of Japan as a political power.

But Japanese troops had penetrated far into China and had occupied most of southeast Asia. The Japanese surrender had wide repercussions in these regions. In these areas not only the United States but also China and Great Britain had fought, and America's allies were unprepared for Japan's sudden collapse.

The size of the area, the number of inhabitants, the variety of peoples, made the handling of the problems of southeast Asia a complex task. These inherent difficulties were aggravated by revolutionary ferment resulting from Japanese rule and occupation.

Japan had treated the nations of southeast Asia in various ways. For instance, Thailand had been considered an ally, and had been permitted to enlarge its frontiers at the expense of its neighbor, French Indochina. In other areas, in Malaya and in the islands of Indonesia—Java, Sumatra, Borneo, Celebes—the Japanese had ruled through military administrations. In China, in the Philippines, and in Burma they had established puppet governments. French Indochina was a special case. As long as France was in the Nazi orbit, the French administrators of Indochina had collaborated with Japan. But after the liberation of France, the French turned against Japan and the Japanese established a puppet government.

Japan exploited all these areas brutally. Yet the Japanese occupation had revolutionary and lasting consequences. The Japanese invasion of this area demonstrated that Asian people were able to shake off the yoke of European rulers; nationalism had received a powerful impetus. The attitude of the nationalist leaders of these peoples to the Japanese rule was rather ambiguous. Some regarded the formation of a national government, even if limited in its freedom of action by Japanese power, as a first step toward independence, and were willing to cooperate with the Japanese in setting up the puppet regimes. Others considered Japanese rule to be quite as oppressive as that of the western powers, and organized resistance movements. In the course of these developments indigenous leaders gained a strong hold over the masses. The nationalist leader in Indochina, Ho Chi Minh (1890–1969), fought against the Japanese; in Indonesia, Achmed Sukarno (born 1901) cooperated with the Japanese, but held out against their plans to divide the region into independent units, championing a united Indonesia.

The Retreat from Colonialism

Since the Allied forces in southeast Asia were under British command during the war, the British took charge of the area after hostilities ended. The first task of the British was to organize the surrender of the Japanese forces which were stationed in this area and burdened its economy. The presence of large armies, the disturbances of war, the flight of people from their homes, and the interruption of communications had restricted cultivation of the land, and in many regions people were starving Therefore, a foremost concern of the British authorities was to increase the production of food, particularly rice, and to arrange for its distribution. In attempting to accomplish this task the British were confronted with an unpleasant political dilemma. Undoubtedly cooperation with the indigenous governments and forces would have been most effective. But this would have strengthened the governments which the French and the Dutch, who had formerly been the rulers in these regions and were anxious to resume control, wanted to eliminate. The French and the Dutch were Britain's allies and Britain itself had colonies in southeast Asia. This contradiction between short-range and long-range interests prevented the development of a uniform policy for the entire area. Settlements were difficult to arrive at, and they varied from one region to the other. The Dutch were unable to reinstate themselves and were forced to recognize the independent Republic of Indonesia in 1946. The French reestablished their rule in Indochina, but fighting against them never ceased and after long and costly campaigns, climaxed by the defeat at Dien Bien Phu in 1954, the French withdrew and left three independent states: Laos, Cambodia, and Vietnam. The British returned to Malaya and Singapore and promoted a political evolution through which Malaya became independent but remained part of the British empire. In southeast Asia the Japanese defeat started a process of revolution which has not yet been completed.

The first manifestoes of the Communist International had stated that the liberation of the peoples of Asia and Africa from colonial rule formed an integral part of the Communist fight against capitalism. Thus, the Russians, although not directly involved in the struggle in southeast Asia, clearly favored nationalist movements in this region, and they had close contacts with some of the nationalist leaders. For instance, Ho Chi Minh was trained in Moscow and worked in the Communist movements in Europe before returning to his native Indochina.

Since American foreign policy too had an anticolonial tradition, the rise of nationalist movements in southeast Asia did not necessarily place Russia and America on opposite sides. However, the United States acted in close cooperation with Great Britain and France in Europe, and there was danger, therefore, that the United States would be stamped as an ally of traditional European imperialism. This actually did happen in China, the nation which presented the most difficult problems of the Asian postwar situation.

The Struggle in China

That China would be a source of conflict between Russia and the United States was not apparent at the end of the war. Here again the most urgent task was to effect the disarmament and withdrawal of the Japanese armies, stationed in the vast regions along the Yangtze and the Yellow rivers. The fact that much time had to be spent arranging the removal of these troops proved to be a disadvantage to the Chinese Nationalist government under Chiang Kai-shek. In the interim period the Communist armies of Mao Tse-tung in the north had the opportunity to expand their power. In August, 1945, Russia had recognized Chiang Kai-shek's regime as the central government of China, so it seemed justifiable to assume that the Russians were anxious to establish cooperation between the Communists in the north and Chiang Kai-shek's government in the south. The United States had a similar aim. The Chiang Kai-shek government had been frequently criticized in the United States for its lack of energy in pursuing the war against the Japanese, and many Americans hoped and believed that cooperation with the Communists would stimulate the Nationalists and provide an impetus to social and agricultural reform which would be highly desirable for China. But protracted negotiations failed to settle the differences between the Nationalist government of Chiang Kai-shek and Mao Tse-tung's Communist forces. Instead, there developed a sharp contest between the two opposing Chinese governments for the control of Manchuria, and in this conflict the Russians decided to back Mao. At the time of the Japanese surrender, the Russians had occupied Manchuria— temporarily, they declared. In the next months, they made no effort to evacuate the area, but in April, 1946, when the struggle over German reparations became critical, they moved their troops from Manchuria very suddenly, and the rapidity of their retreat gave the Chinese Communists the opportunity to move in.

The American government continued its efforts to establish peace in China, but neither of the warring factions really wanted an agreement, because each believed that it could win over the entire country. When General Marshall, who had been sent to China in December, 1945, abandoned his peace efforts in January, 1947, he assigned responsibility for the failure of his mission to both sides: the "dominant group of reactionaries" in Chiang Kai-shek's government and the "dyed in the wool"[1] Communists in the other camp. The final result was an open confrontation and civil war between Chiang Kai-shek's forces, somewhat reluctantly and halfheartedly backed by the United States, and Mao Tse-tung's Communists, supported by Russia. With conflict between Russia and the United States developing over China, the differences between these two powers concerning settlement in Europe gained in significance and sharpness.

[1] These phrases are from General Marshall's statement on China on February 7, 1947.

CHAPTER 10

The Cold War and its Consequences

THE TERM "COLD WAR" is widely used in discussions of recent history, but it has remained a rather vague and indefinite notion. It is not clear when the Cold War began, nor how long it lasted. Some see its beginning in the famous statement issued on March 12, 1947, by President Harry S. Truman (born 1884) in response to a note from the British declaring that they were no longer able to give assistance to the Greek government in its fight against Communist guerillas; the Truman Doctrine declared that "it must be the foreign policy of the United States to support free peoples who are resisting attempted subjugation by armed minorities or by outside pressures." Some regard the Berlin blockade of 1948–1949, with which the Russians tried to end the four-power rule of Berlin, as the beginning of the Cold War. Others consider the outbreak of the Korean War to be the crucial event.

THE POLARIZATION OF POWER

Like the causes of other wars the origins of the Cold War have been much discussed. Who was responsible for the development of this critical situation? There was actually a certain inevitability in its coming about. After the war, power was largely divided between Soviet Russia and the United States, and polarization of power between two states has almost always led to war. Moreover, in the years since the Bolsheviks gained control, the two nations had come to represent, for their citizens, opposing sets of values: to Americans, Soviet Russia was a country of criminal lawlessness, with no regard for the values of civilization; to Communists, the United States was the embodiment of their chief enemy—capitalism.

These ideological contrasts were solidified by a conflict in economic interests. The traditional policy of the United States was to encourage free trade throughout the world. And Communist Russia's withdrawal from international commerce was considered an important reason for the economic difficulties of the interwar years. The Russians, however, regarded every attempt to force the opening of the commercial barriers and to entangle their nation in the workings of the capitalist system as an aggressive act aimed at undermining the Communist regime. The cooperation of the Russians with the western powers in the Second World War was not sufficient to eradicate reciprocal distrust. In the Russian press, praise of the British-American war effort was mixed with complaints about western slowness in opening a second front. And the Russian masses were quite inadequately informed about the amount of aid which the Soviet Union received through Lend-Lease. In the United States, on the other hand, people were kept in the dark about the great difficulties which western diplomats and military leaders encountered in achieving a minimum of concerted action with their Communist partners. And because many Americans had optimistic illusions about the possibilities of an alliance with Russia, their disappointment was great when cooperation broke down.

In addition, the wartime conferences, particularly the conference at Yalta, had shown divergences in the views of the western and Russian statesmen concerning the postwar settlement. American diplomats were anxious to postpone arrangement of the details of the peace until after the end of hostilities, and they hoped and expected that the foundation of an international organization embracing the entire world would then smooth the path for agreement on particular issues; the American negotiators, therefore, were pleased when, at Yalta, they obtained Russia's agreement to the foundation of the United Nations. Yet the hesitant attitude of the Russians made it clear that they were not willing to concede to the United Nations supranational authority, and it is questionable whether they were ever prepared to grant to it any political function beyond that of providing, in times of crisis, a meeting place where tensions could be aired and

Winston Churchill delivers a famous address. *On March 5, 1946, in a speech delivered in Fulton, Missouri, the former British prime minister warned that an "iron curtain" separated eastern Europe from the rest of the continent. The phrase "iron curtain" was to be often repeated during the Cold War years.*

Scene from the Greek civil war. *Mules carrying munitions into the mountains.*

negotiations could be initiated. But while the Russians' interest in the establishment of the United Nations was limited, they were anxious to gain security against aggression and to expand their territorial frontiers toward the west. They were determined that no foreign power should have any influence in the entire area now considered as lying behind the Iron Curtain.

Churchill at Yalta was ready to accept a division of Europe into spheres of interest. But the United States was not. It was argued in the American delegation that such a plan suggest a revival of the balance of power and of all those concepts of traditional diplomacy which Americans abhor. Nevertheless, it might have been better if an understanding had been achieved about where the several victorious nations were to exert their influence. Certainly, it is impossible to state with any assurance that the Russians would not have tried to create unrest in western Europe if the United States had not attempted to stave off Communist control of Poland. But without any delimitation of spheres of interest, the Russian concern with Italian and French affairs may have appeared to the Russians not very different from the American concern with Polish affairs.

Thus, at the end of hostilities, there had still been no real clarification of the issues between the United States and Russia. Each could only speculate about the intentions of the other and indulge in guesses as to how far the other would go. In the period of the Cold War the generally accepted opinion in the West was that Russia wanted to extend Communist rule as far as possible, and from the events preceding the Cold War an impressive case was built up to show that an aggressive expansionism was the constant and dominating motive of the actions of the Russian leaders. For example, the control achieved by the Communists over the governments of Bulgaria, Rumania, Hungary, and Poland was cited. In addition, it was noted that the Communists did not desist from the attempt to achieve power in Greece, where Communist guerillas supported from the north were able to maintain a civil war until October, 1949. Moreover, while the western powers agreed to the signing of peace treaties with the countries in the Soviet sphere, the Russians raised obstacles to the formal conclusion of peace with Austria and Germany, countries in which the influence of the western powers was strong. In their zone of Germany, the Russians conducted affairs without much regard to the principles previously laid down; they quickly revived political life so that Communist influence would be secured; they reorganized economic life in accordance with Communist ideas; and when the western powers opposed the Russian reparations policy the Russians prevented the formation of a central German administration. Their intervention to stop participation of any of the eastern countries in the Marshall Plan in 1947, and their backing of the Chinese Communists against the Nationalist Chinese under Chiang Kai-shek, were further proof of their unwillingness to come to any accommodation with the West by means of reciprocal concessions. The veto with which in 1947 they killed in the United Nations the American plan for control of atomic weapons strengthened the view that there existed an insuperable antagonism between Russia and the Russian-controlled areas on one side, and the rest of the world, the "free world," on the other.

While the people of the West regarded the Russians as aggressors, they believed the policies of their own governments toward Russia to be purely defensive and motivated by good will. After the tension of the Cold War had lessened, however, the simplistic character of this view became apparent. It was realized that the American government had taken a number of steps which to the Russians might have seemed less than friendly. Lend-Lease was abruptly terminated at the end of the war, and the Russian request for American credit for the purposes of postwar reconstruction, made in August, 1945, was "mislaid" and discovered only seven months later. Moreover, it must be realized that just as the United States regarded the measures of agrarian reform and socialization introduced in the Russian-controlled countries as an attempt to exclude western influence, so the Russians regarded the restoration of free enterprise in the states of western Europe as an attempt to rebuild these countries in a strictly anti-Communist "imperialist" spirit. Some analysts have even maintained that the United States not Russia, was the aggressor in this period—that the explosion of the atomic bomb was addressed to Russia rather than Japan. American policy makers, it has been argued, wanted to bring about a showdown with Russia at a time when American troops were still in Europe and Asia, and America possessed a monopoly in atomic weapons. In this context it is of some significance that, generous as it was, the American plan for the banning of atomic weapons presented to the United Nations in 1946 by Bernard Baruch left the United States in possession of its atomic monopoly until the envisaged inspection and control apparatus could be set in motion. American atomic superiority was to be maintained, at least for a time.

Nevertheless, it seems unlikely that the United States—in 1945, when it had an atomic monopoly and Russia was still weakened as a result of the war—had a considered strategy for forcing a showdown with Russia. It is probably more correct to say that in both the United States and the Soviet Union those in the ruling groups were divided about the policy to be pursued toward the other power; in each country there were proponents of a soft line and of a hard line. In Russia most of the economists were in favor of seeking American aid for reconstruction since the alternative would be to postpone indefinitely once again the production of consumer goods which Russia had been unable to initiate in the emergencies of the 1930's. In the United States some politicians, including a former vice president under Roosevelt, Henry A. Wallace, were perhaps overoptimistic about the chances for cooperation with the Soviet Union, but others too were convinced that a steadily conciliatory attitude, together with agreements on single isolated issues, might slowly effect a softening of Russian antagonism. Yet in both countries, policy came to be dominated by the hard line advocates, who believed that the contrasts between the two were insuperable and that any concession to the other must mean a loss of power for oneself.

In the United States men who must be counted as advocates of a hard line—Secretary of Defense James Forrestal (1892–1949), military men, and members of the State Department—were certainly in a powerful position. In Russia, those who recommended cooperation with the United States had little if any chance. Stalin, who remained the decisive figure, inclined toward a hard line. We have seen how in the 1930's an economic policy which emphasized heavy industry at the expense of consumer goods not only increased Russia's military strength but also made necessary the maintenance of strict controls and thereby served Stalin's aim of concentrating power in his own hands. It is true indeed that the victory in the war had immensely raised Stalin's stature. But the war had created other heroes as well, and the participation of the entire population in the national struggle against the invaders had loosened the dominance of the party. A new period of economic hardship which would demand strict discipline and a tightening of controls would reinforce Stalin's position; if it could be shown that Russia was threatened from the outside, people would be willing to accept the sacrifices required for the restoration of their nation's economic strength without foreign help. Hence Stalin not only rejected continuance of the slight cooperation with the capitalist world which the war had produced, but placed on the United States the responsibility for the burden involved in his country's consequent economic isolation. Andrei Zhdanov (1896–1948), one of Stalin's most trusted lieutenants, explained: "The United States proclaimed a new, frankly predatory and expansionist course. The purpose of this new, frankly expansionist course is to establish the world supremacy of American imperialism." With the Truman Doctrine of March, 1947, and the Zhdanov speech of September, 1947, the fronts were clearly drawn.

Whenever international relations are critically strained, the occurrence of any provocative incident may spark an explosion, and in this sense the period of the Cold War was a dangerous one. Nevertheless, there were reasons why the Cold War did not become hot. In both the United States and Russia considerations of domestic policy helped make it desirable to emphasize the aggressive aims of the adversary. The inconveniences and hardships involved in the maintenance of a strong military posture would be accepted more easily if people felt they were living under a direct threat. But actually neither the United States nor Soviet Russia intended to attack the other. Unwilling to be placed in the position of submitting, each contested any move by the other which might extend its territorial control and upset the balance of power. But each was cautious with respect to areas and issues which the other might consider vital for its existence. Thus, the crises of the Cold War led repeatedly to the brink, but never over the brink.

The Berlin Blockade

The event which might be regarded as ushering in the critical years of the Cold War was the blockade of Berlin. After the collapse of efforts to establish a central administration for the whole of Germany, the powers occupying western Germany—the United States, Great Britain, and France—began to build a common political and economic organization for their three zones. When the first measures for this unified administration were taken, the reaction of the Russians was unexpectedly vehement. On June 24, 1948 by cutting off all land and water communications, the Russians isolated the parts of Berlin under western control. It is not quite clear what they sought to achieve by provoking this test of strength. Perhaps they hoped to force the western powers out of Berlin, so that a clean separation of western and eastern spheres of interest could be effected in Europe. Or they may have expected that the unsettling effect of this Berlin blockade would frustrate the working of the European Recovery Program and give new strength to the Communist movements in western Europe. Whatever their motives, the Russians assumed that the western powers, particularly the British and the French, would be most reluctant to take measures which would involve a risk of war; and they were convinced that if no military clash occurred, the blockade would force Berlin into starvation and surrender. They overlooked the possibility that the two million people of West Berlin might be supplied by air. But that is what happened. An airlift broke the blockade, negotiations were started, and on May 12, 1949,

The Berlin blockade. *An airplane with provisions arriving over the Berlin airfield. The spectators are standing on the rubble of destroyed houses.*

the Russians removed the restrictions on communications between western Germany and West Berlin. After almost a year, the blockade was over.

The Korean War

After the Berlin blockade, Asia became the scene of the Cold War. By the beginning of 1949 the victory of the Chinese Communists under Mao Tse-tung was a certainty, and by the end of the year the Nationalist government under Chiang Kai-shek had withdrawn to Formosa (Taiwan). The United States refused to recognize the Communists as the legitimate rulers of China and continued to give recognition and protection to the Nationalist government. The tension between the United States and Communist China became the crucial element in the next dangerous crisis of the Cold War, that of Korea.

After the Second World War the area of Korea north of latitude 38 had been occupied by the Russians, that south of the thirty-eighth parallel by the Americans. As in Germany, agreement on a common government for the entire country had been impossible to reach. Eventually, the occupying forces were withdrawn, the Russians leaving a Communist regime in North Korea, the Americans a western-oriented democracy in South Korea. On June 25, 1950, North Korean troops began to invade South Korea, attempting to unify their divided nation. American military leaders had gradually become aware that a non-Communist South Korea was indispensable for the defense of Japan, and the United States government ordered American troops into South Korea to support the faltering South Korean government. The matter was brought before the United Nations at a time when the Russians were boycotting the Security Council, and a resolution was passed which condemned the North Korean aggression. A United Nations Command was set up, headed by General Douglas

MacArthur, and although most of the troops were American they were supported by contingents from many other countries. The U.N. military operations were conducted with wavering success. Having succeeded in driving the North Koreans out of the south, the Americans advanced beyond the thirty-eighth parallel, but there they encountered opposition by strong North Korean forces aided by Communist Chinese armies, and were driven back far into South Korea. Finally a front along the thirty-eighth parallel was established and armistice negotiations were initiated. In July, 1953, after almost two years of negotiations, an armistice was concluded which ended the war with the *status quo ante*: Korea remained divided along the thirty-eighth parallel.

War in Indochina

While the Korean War slowly petered out, another dangerous military clash developed on the southern frontier of China. There, a nationalist movement known as the Viet Minh, under the leadership of Ho Chi-Minh, was fighting the French for greater autonomy in that part of Indochina which, after the separation of Laos and Cambodia, was called Vietnam.

The Viet Minh received recognition and aid from Communist China and Soviet Russia, while France and the puppet regime which it had established were supported by Great Britain and the United States. Modern weapons and bombing from the air were unable to destroy the guerilla forces fighting in millet fields and rice paddies, and when the French advanced into the north, a part of their forces was cut off and finally forced to surrender at Dien Bien Phu, in May, 1954; ten thousand French soldiers became prisoners. At this point mediation by Russia, the United States, and Great Britain resulted in an armistice; among its terms were provisions for an election to be held in 1956, to unify Vietnam. Until then Vietnam was to be divided along the seventeenth parallel, with the northern half Communist-controlled and the southern half western-oriented.

The Nuclear Stalemate

With the Korean armistice in 1953, and the settlement of the conflict in Indochina in 1954, the Cold War abated. The next few years were free of military clashes in which Russia and the United States were backing opposite sides or in which, as in the Korean War, one of them was directly involved. Moreover, developments in the field of nuclear weapons helped to reduce tension from 1954 on. After the negotiations about atomic control in the United Nations had failed, the Russians had gone ahead with their own search for nuclear weapons and in August, 1949, had succeeded in producing their first atomic explosion. This event came earlier than had been expected and aroused great concern in the United States. The sharp American reaction stimulated fears in Russia that America might start a preventive war before Russia had accumulated an arsenal of atomic weapons. The Russians therefore pursued their development of nuclear arms with increased energy.

Correspondingly, fearing that the Russians' advances would give them superiority, President Truman, early in 1950, ordered a crash program to develop a hydrogen bomb; the first such device was successfully tested in November, 1952. Nine months later the Russians constructed their own hydrogen bomb. The nuclear armament race between Russia and the United States augmented the nervousness and tension of this period. By 1954, with both Russia and the United States in possession of the hydrogen bomb, the continuation of the nuclear-arms race became meaningless. The incredibly destructive force of this weapon made the leaders of both states realize that in a war the two superpowers could only destroy each other. Neither of them could win.

In the quieter atmosphere of the following years, views about the reasons for the military conflicts of the critical period of the Cold War changed. These wars came to be regarded as having been caused by local conditions or by misunderstandings. For instance, the North Koreans seem not to have expected that their attempt to unify the country by force would encounter strong American opposition, for high American military and diplomatic officials had made pronouncements suggesting that America considered Korea to be of little strategic value. The particular reasons for the conflict in Indochina also became apparent: it was seen to have been a national revolt against foreign rule and a civil war of the suppressed classes against the French-oriented wealthy ruling groups. But at the time, there were very different explanations for the genesis of the struggles in Korea and Indochina. The various conflicts appeared to be integral parts of a grand design—understood by the Americans as a Communist drive for control of the world, and by the Russians as an American attempt to encircle and strangle Communism. But both powers desisted from embarking on actions which would have provoked a direct military struggle between Russia and the United States, and afterwards the grand design appeared less definite and its execution less imminent than it had seemed at the high point of the crisis.

THE FORMATION OF OPPOSING ALLIANCE SYSTEMS

During the Cold War years of highest tension, the emergency seemed so great that each of the opposing powers tried to strengthen its position by uniting in a tight organization the powers which it controlled or with which it was allied. The resulting division of large portions of the world into antagonistic blocs profoundly affected the character of developments in Europe.

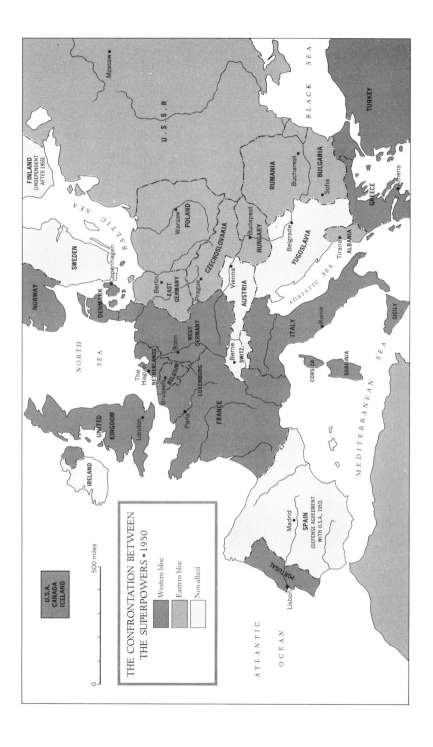

THE CONFRONTATION BETWEEN
THE SUPERPOWERS • 1950

500 miles

Western bloc
Eastern bloc
Non-allied

U.S.A.
CANADA
ICELAND

ATLANTIC

OCEAN

MEDITERRANEAN   SEA

PORTUGAL

Lisbon

Madrid

SPAIN
(DEFENSE AGREEMENT
WITH U.S.A., 1953)

IRELAND

UNITED
KINGDOM

London

Paris

FRANCE

LUXEMBURG

BELGIUM

Brussels

NETHERLANDS

The
Hague

NORTH

SEA

CORSICA

SARDINIA

SICILY

ITALY

Rome

Berne

SWITZ.

WEST
GERMANY

Bonn

Berlin

EAST
GERMANY

Prague

CZECHOSLOVAKIA

Vienna

AUSTRIA

DENMARK

Copenhagen

NORWAY

SWEDEN

BALTIC   SEA

FINLAND
(INDEPENDENT
AFTER 1955)

Moscow

U. S. S. R.

Warsaw

POLAND

Budapest

HUNGARY

YUGOSLAVIA

Belgrade

ALBANIA

Tirana

ADRIATIC   SEA

RUMANIA

Bucharest

BULGARIA

Sofia

BLACK

SEA

GREECE

Athens

TURKEY

The fundamental basis for the pursuit of a common line by the Communist powers was provided by the Communist Information Bureau (Cominform), created in 1947, as a replacement for the Comintern, which, as a concession to the western allies, had been dissolved during the war. The Cominform comprised only representatives of the Communist parties of the European states, and its activities were chiefly propagandistic. In addition, however, Soviet Russia created particular ties with all the Communist-controlled states. During the war Russia had concluded mutual-assistance treaties with the governments-in-exile which guaranteed help in case of future German aggression and provided for close economic, cultural, and political cooperation with Yugoslavia, Czechoslovakia, and Poland. Similar pacts were negotiated in 1948 with Bulgaria, Rumania, Hungary, and Finland, the former Axis satellites. A comparable treaty, assuring assistance against attack by Japan or by powers allied to Japan, was signed with China in 1950. Chinese agreements with North Korea and North Vietnam tied these countries to the Russian bloc. Finally, in 1955 the relation of the Communist states in Europe to one another and to Soviet Russia was redefined by a pact concluded in Warsaw; in addition to the partners of previous mutual-assistance agreements—Soviet Russia, Albania, Bulgaria, Hungary, Poland, Rumania, Czechoslovakia—the treaty included East Germany, which now advanced to full membership in the Soviet alliance system. The Warsaw Pact precluded participation of its members in any other coalition or alliance and assured members of immediate assistance, including the use of armed force, in the event of armed aggression, establishing for this purpose a joint command for the armed forces of the members, as well as a consultative committee to harmonize political action. The stationing of Russian troops in eastern European countries, notably in Rumania, Hungary, Poland, and East Germany, which until then had been justified by the need to maintain communications with the Russian occupation zones in Germany and Austria, was now guaranteed by bilateral treaties.

A similar comprehensive alliance system was established by the United States. One might say that the Russian bloc and the western bloc developed in response to each other. Wartime cooperation had brought the western European states—Belgium, France, Luxemburg, the Netherlands, and Great Britain—close together, and in Brussels in 1948, they embodied this relationship in a treaty in which they committed themselves to a common defense against attack. As a counterweight against the East this alliance was obviously weak and in the following year, a larger system was developed which, with the exception of Spain and Switzerland, encompassed all the countries of northern and western Europe, as well as Italy, and most importantly, included the United States. In the North Atlantic Treaty, concluded on April 4, 1949, the signers stated that "an armed attack against

The signing of the North Atlantic Treaty. *President Truman addresses the assembled delegates on April 4, 1949.*

one or more of them in Europe or North America shall be considered an attack against them all." In the event of such an attack they promised immediately to take whatever action was deemed necessary, including the use of armed force. As a result of this treaty the signers agreed to build up a common military organization—the North Atlantic Treaty Organization, or NATO. In 1952 Greece and Turkey became participants in NATO. Turkey was the easternmost member of this alliance, but the chain was continued by a Middle East Treaty Organization, established in 1955, which included Turkey and Britain (NATO powers) and Pakistan, Iraq (until 1959), and Iran. The last link in this ring around Communism was the Southeast Asia Collective Defense Treaty of 1954, in which Great Britain, the United States, France, Pakistan, Australia, New Zealand, the Philippines, and Thailand participated. Thus, by 1955, when the most critical phase of the Cold War was over, both Russia and the United States had organized firmly tied blocs.

Despite the globe-encircling nature of these alliances both camps were aware that the critical area was Europe. Control over Europe would mean an incontestable superiority over the other side. Hence, each of the superpowers—Russia and the United States—was anxious to firm up its partners in Europe so that they would form a solid unit able to resist attack from the other side. These aims patterned political and social life in both eastern and western Europe.

The Solidification of the Soviet Bloc, 1948–1953

By 1948 the governments of the countries in the Russian orbit were entirely Communist. Through factory and village committees the Communist party exerted its authority on the local level. Its youth organizations, backed by the power of the minister of education, guaranteed the Marxist character and ideological orthodoxy of the education system; a clash with the Catholic Church was therefore unavoidable, and indeed in every satellite country with a strong Roman Catholic population sensational proceedings against the leaders of the Roman Catholic Church were instigated: in 1946 against Archbishop Stepinac in Yugoslavia, in 1949 against Cardinal Mindszenty in Hungary, and in 1951 against Archbishop Beran in Czechoslovakia. Thus, the uniformity of Communist party strategy and tactics tied the various eastern European states to Russia. The Russians also possessed more direct means of exerting authority and control. Russian troops remained in Hungary and Poland and the military forces of these countries were built up under Russian surveillance. Moreover, the secret police in the several eastern European countries formed an almost autonomous body independent of their respective governments; they worked in close contact with the Russian secret police. Ideologically and institutionally Bolshevik Russia deeply interpenetrated the life of eastern Europe.

The all-important aim, of course, was to change the economic structure of the states of the Soviet bloc according to Bolshevik concepts, and doing this involved three tasks: to divert the trade of these countries from the West to the East, to collectivize their agriculture, and to industrialize them. It ought to be said that if one takes an overall view, these goals were attained. By 1951, 92 per cent of Bulgaria's trade was with Soviet Russia. Even Poland's trade with Russia, which before the war amounted to only 7 per cent of the country's foreign trade, had reached 58 per cent by 1951. At the same time, industrial production increased remarkably. By 1952, annual production in Poland and Czechoslovakia, the two most industrialized countries of the bloc, was double its prewar level, and the total steel production in eastern Europe was then roughly equal to that of West Germany, and twice what it had been before the war. The labor force employed in industry in eastern Europe increased about 33 per cent by the early 1950's.

The issue which created the greatest difficulties was the collectivization of agriculture; Russia's insistence on applying the Soviet pattern took little account of the situation existing in eastern Europe. Since agricultural reforms resulting in the dismemberment of the large estates had already taken place, most of the land was divided into small or middle-sized farms, and their owners were reluctant or unwilling to join collectives. Moral and economic pressure and even violence had to be used to attain collectivization. And progress in the various countries was very uneven, rather quick in Bulgaria and Czechoslovakia, but slow in Poland and Hungary.

Tensions arising from a strict application of the Soviet pattern to eastern Europe were exacerbated by Russia's adding to its imposition of overall economic control a policy of direct economic exploitation. Even after Hungary and Rumania had become purely Communist, they continued to pay reparations to Russia. Moreover, the Russians seized all German property in these countries and dismantled all German industrial installations, which they then transferred to Russia. The Russians also participated in a number of joint companies controlling such enterprises as the Rumanian merchant marine and the Hungarian bauxite mines. Thus, a portion of the earnings of these companies went directly to Russia. Moreover, the Russians forced upon these countries agreements to deliver certain goods, such as coal, at extremely low prices.

It is no wonder that the rigid exploitative economic policy pursued by Soviet Russia created dissatisfaction and unrest. Between 1948 and 1954 the eastern bloc underwent some serious crises.

In 1948 peasant resistance to collectivization and a general resentment over Russian interference in Yugoslav affairs led to a break between the rulers in the Kremlin and Marshal Tito, the head of the Yugoslav Communist party. As the military leader of the partisans during the war, Tito had become a national hero, with a very strong hold over the people. Moreover, because the partisans had been able to maintain some organized resistance throughout the entire war the Yugoslavs did not wait to be liberated by the Allied armies; the partisans took over the country when the Nazi power collapsed. Yugoslavia was the only country of eastern Europe which Russian troops never entered. Thus, when Yugoslavia resisted Soviet demands, Russia had no strong levers within the nation.

The Russians were not ready to risk the general war which might result from military intervention, and they evidently expected that exclusion from the Cominform, which implied writing off Yugoslavia as a member of the Communist bloc, would force Tito to submit. But Tito's popularity with his people, together with some economic help from the West, made it possible for him to retain power, and the Russians resigned themselves to this situation although they continued vehement vocal attacks against Tito and maintained an economic blockade of Yugoslavia. Under Tito, Yugoslavia developed a special form of Communism—a mixed economy. There was no overall economic planning for the entire country. In agriculture, collective farms coexisted with privately owned farms. Industry was nationalized, but control was exercised by the workers in the individual factories, and there was a free market for the sale of many consumer goods.

Tito's defection aroused in Stalin and the Russian leaders fears that other eastern European countries might follow the Yugoslav example, with each country forging its own inidvidual type of Communism. Consequently, under pressure from the Russians, widespread purges took place in these states. One aim of the purges was to make the Communist party an absolutely reliable instrument for the execution of directives given from above. In every eastern European country the size of the Communist party had greatly increased as many who had belonged to the dissolved and suppressed non-Communist parties had thought it useful to enter Communist ranks; this influx of incompletely trained and untested members was especially dangerous for the efficiency of the party because even the upper strata contained discordant elements—on the one hand those who had taken refuge in Moscow during the war, and on the other those who had remained in their country, working in the underground. These two groups now competed for control of the party. In danger of becoming unwieldy and divided, the Communist parties in eastern Europe instituted mass purges. Hundreds of thousands were deprived of membership in the party as "alien" or "hostile" elements. Another aim of the purges was to eliminate those Communist leaders who might be inclined to follow the example of Tito, and the consequence was a substantial change in the composition of the Central Committees of the Communist parties in the various states. Leaders who might be inclined toward Titoist deviations were brought before tribunals in sensational procedures patterned after the Russian purge trials of the 1930's, complete with accusations of treason, confessions, and finally the imposition of the death penalty. The most outstanding victims of these trials, starting in 1949, were Traicho Kostov, the vice premier of the Bulgarian government; Laszlo Rajk, the minister of the interior in Hungary; and in Czechoslovakia, Vladimir Clementis, the foreign minister, and Rudolf Slansky, general secretary of the Communist party and deputy prime minister. Wladyslaw Gomulka, the general secretary of the Polish Communist party, was deposed and later imprisoned, but he escaped execution.

The purges and trials of the leadership in the Russian satellite countries continued until 1953, and in the course of time their purposes went beyond those of party discipline and the elimination of Titoists. The motives for the persecution of individuals are frequently obscure. These were the years when Stalin's suspiciousness had clearly become pathological and when anticipation of his approaching death sharpened the conflicts among Russian Communist leaders anxious to eliminate possible rivals. The trials n the satellite countries appear to have been repercussions of the struggles in the Russian leadership group, as is suggested by the fact that some of these trials, like some of those in Russia, had anti-Semitic overtones. In his dealings with the various eastern European nations Stalin preferred to work through one person entirely devoted and obedient to him. And the purges served to concentrate power in each country in the hands of one entirely pro-Stalin Communist leader: Mátyás Rákosi in Hungary; Walter Ulbricht in East Germany; Klement Gottwald in Czechoslovakia; Boleslarv Bierut in Poland. Like Stalin himself, though to a slighter extent, each of these leaders became the center of a cult of personality. By the time Stalin died in 1953, the various means which had been applied to unify the Russian-controlled areas of Europe—ideological uniformity, institutional identity, economic integration, force—appeared to have transformed them into a monolithic bloc ruled and directed by Russia, and most of the member states seemed to be on the way to reaping the fruits of the economic transformation to which they had been submitted. But the tensions produced in these countries by the changes which they had undergone had been suppressed rather than eliminated, as the events of the later 1950's would show.

Integration in the West

The term "free world" is frequently applied to that part of Europe which lies outside the zone of Russian control and influence, and it is indeed true that certain values and institutions regarded as basic for a life in freedom have been maintained in most countries of western Europe. A system of law which gives assurances against arbitrariness in the persecution of crimes, a guarantee of freedom of thought and expression, and a representative government based on a multiparty system—recognition of the paramount importance of these formed the unifying ideological bound in the West. It would be an error, however, to conclude that all the countries of western Europe were able to develop according to their own interests and traditions without outside pressure; in a political constellation dominated by two superpowers, rejection of one meant dependence on the other. The influence of the United States and the needs of the Cold War were crucial in patterning the forms of political development in western Europe.

First of all, cooperation with the United States required removal of the Communists from political power. In West Germany the Communist party was declared unconstitutional and forbidden. In May, 1947, more or less at the time that the Russians were eliminating the non-Communist parties in eastern Europe, governments were formed in France and Italy excluding the Communists, who had hitherto been members of the ruling coalition. Within the Italian and French governments, conflicts between Communists and non-Communists about the course of foreign policy and economic policy had been constant, and the end of the period of cooperation with the Communists was not unexpected. Because Italy and France were parliamentary democracies, however, the elimination of the Communists was not considered accomplished until the people had spoken in the next elections.

Particular importance was attached to the Italian elections of April, 1948, because in contrast to France, where a wide gap separated Communists and socialists, in Italy there was a possibility that the Communists, together with their allies, the left-wing socialists, would gain a majority over supporters of the prime minister, Alcide de Gasperi (1881–1954), a Christian Democrat who enjoyed the active and energetic backing of the Roman Catholic Church. The Marshall Plan, initiated in the previous summer, had begun to demonstrate the advantages of American support, and American diplomats had no reluctance to indicate that a victory of Communism would end this assistance. In addition, the United States, together with Great Britain and France, in a statement issued a few weeks before the election, promised to support the Italian claims to Trieste and its surroundings—an area where the Russian and American zones of influence touched, and a subject of dispute between Italy and Yugoslavia since the end of the war. The direct participation of Catholic priests and foreign diplomats gave these Italian elections an unusual aspect. The disregard of the traditional rule that foreign powers ought not to interfere in the internal affairs of another country showed the supranational nature of the conflict then evolving, and the results justified the extraordinary efforts which had been made to keep the Communists out of power; the Christian Democrats won an absolute majority, with 305 seats out of 574.

But the elimination of the Communists from political power was only the beginning in the process of making western Europe a bulwark against the East in the Cold War. Just as the Russians were securing their position in eastern Europe by economic reorganization and by the development of a unified military command, so the United States set about to stabilize economic life and create an integrated military force in western Europe. The Marshall Plan and NATO represented important first steps toward achieving these aims. But all further progress encountered a difficult obstacle—the peculiar situation of western Germany within the free world. The states which had defeated the Nazis had agreed that Germany ought to be deprived of the means of again becoming an aggressor. It was to be permanently demilitarized, and the great industrial power which it possessed through the rich iron and coal mines of the Ruhr area was to be reduced. However, these notions about a demilitarized and deindustrialized Germany came into conflict with the demands arising from the Cold War: German manpower and German industrial resources were required to maintain and strengthen the military organization of the west, and in all plans for halting an attack from the east the territory of western Germany, abutting the Soviet zone, was crucial. It was hardly possible to envisage military operations among people who felt themselves to be discriminated against, who were dissatisfied and hostile. Nevertheless, Germany's western neighbors regarded a revival of its military and industrial power with great distrust. Western Germany in 1947 had 6 million more inhabitants than France (47.5 million against 41 million). The most appropriate means of overcoming the difficulty posed by the German problem seemed to be integration through the creation of common organizations which would equally limit each nation's freedom of action and weaken traditional national contrasts.

The economic and political unification of the occupation zones in western Germany—first the integration of the American and British zones and then the merger of the French zone with them—had slowly progressed since 1946. A decisive step was the introduction of a new currency in June, 1948, which halted inflation and affirmed the economic unity of western Germany; the next logical measure was the establishment of a unified political organization. On the local and regional level, political activity had been permitted since 1946, with local German administrations working under the control and supervision of the Allied powers. After the establishment of economic unity through currency reform, a parliamentary council consisting of delegates of the various German state governments worked out a constitution for a federal government. The West German Federal Republic came into being in May, 1949.

But the political revival of Germany renewed fears of what Germany might do with its power, and before Germany was resuscitated as a sovereign state, steps were taken to ensure Allied control of its industrial development. In 1948 the Ruhr Statute was concluded; this agreement was signed by the United States, Great Britain, France, Belgium, the Netherlands, and Luxemburg and Germany joined in 1949. It gave the signatory powers authority to limit the output, and allocate the exports, of coal and iron from the Ruhr. The next step was the creation of a European free market for coal and steel. The initiative for this development was taken by the French foreign minister, Robert Schuman (1886–1963). Great Britain stayed aside, but Belgium, the Netherlands, Luxemburg, Italy, and West Germany reacted favorably to the French suggestion, and the European Coal and Steel Community, superseding the arrangements of the Ruhr Statute, was established in 1951. An assembly consisting of representatives elected by the parliaments of the member states was to appoint an executive body, the High Authority, to supervise the functioning of the coal and steel community, with the right to set maximum and minimum prices and even to limit production, if necessary.

With the subordination of the industrial production of the Ruhr area to a European economic program, one of the dangers inherent in the revival of Germany as an independent power was arrested. A similar solution was found for the question of German rearmament, although for some time a positive outcome seemed to be lost in a maze of negotiations. The North Atlantic Treaty had provided for a joint military organization of the member nations. Eisenhower was made supreme commander of the NATO forces in Europe in 1950, and American troops retained bases in western Europe in accordance with NATO planning. When the outbreak of the

Korean War made the United States government fear that its resources might become overstrained, it demanded that Germany be permitted to rearm to strengthen the western military posture in Europe. America's allies, particularly the French, responded with a remarkable lack of enthusiasm to this American eagerness to forget the past. But unable to resist the request of their powerful ally, the French suggested an integrated European army, in which they hoped the German contribution would be kept to a minimum. After lengthy negotiations, a treaty for a European Defense Community was concluded in May, 1952. But most of the signatory powers felt doubtful about the abandonment of sovereignty over their military forces implied in an integrated army. The French themselves in August, 1954, rejected ratification of the treaty, and suddenly a different and much simpler solution was obtained. West Germany became a member of NATO and was recognized as a sovereign state. Foreign troops stationed on German soil could now be regarded not as occupation forces but as allies, present on the basis of NATO membership. The French were reconciled to German rearmament by a British promise to leave several divisions on the Continent; thus, the French felt, if war did break out the British would be immediately involved. Moreover, the French obtained the establishment of a Western European Union which united Belgium, France, Luxemburg, the Netherlands, Great Britain, West Germany, and Italy in defense against attack and committed the participants to a "progressive integration of Europe." The Western European Union was also entrusted with control over the size of the military forces and the armaments of the individual nations; the French had some guarantees, therefore, that Germany's military strength would not go beyond the contribution which NATO assigned to it.

CHAPTER 11

Reconstruction and Change in Western Europe

THE ESTABLISHMENT of close cooperation among the powers of western Europe, and the founding of supranational European institutions—in short, the acceptance of a policy of European unification—was made possible by the significant fact that in France, Italy, and West Germany during the first decade after the end of the Second World War, parties of very similar political aims and outlook were in power, namely, political parties which emphasized Christianity and Roman Catholicism as a common feature. In Italy the party was called *Democrazia Cristiana* (Christian Democracy), and from 1948 to 1953 it had the absolute majority in parliament. In West Germany the name of the party was *Christlich-Demokratische Union* (Christian Democratic Union) and it was the largest German political party ever since the first German parliamentary elections, in 1949; it obtained an absolute majority in 1953. In France the M.R.P. (for *Mouvement Républicain Populaire*), as the Catholic party was called, had its greatest strength immediately after the war and then declined, first slowly, later rather rapidly; in 1946 the M.R.P. received one vote in four; five years later, only one in eight. Nevertheless, no government in France was formed in this period without the participation of the M.R.P.

As Catholic parties their members and leaders were used to view national life embedded in a supranatural organization; the idea of a unified Europe, of building a Christian fortress against the attack of barbarians, had strong historical roots for them. The party leaders followed a policy of close European collaboration not only because it was dictated by the practical needs of the Cold War but also because it corresponded to their aims and convictions. The men chiefly responsible for the European direction of French, Italian, and West German foreign policy in these critical years were Robert Schuman, between 1947 and 1953 first prime minister, then foreign minister, in France; Alcide de Gasperi, Italian prime minister from 1945 to

1953; and Konrad Adenauer, German chancellor from 1949 to 1963.

De Gasperi and Adenauer impressed themselves upon the history of their countries by charting the political course of postwar Italy and Germany. Both leaders were very different from the idealistic statesmen of the early years of the twentieth century, with their passionate commitment to the great causes of social reform or national expansion. Their speeches emphasized concrete points and justified their policies with practical, commonsense reasons. What they wrote or said tended to be monotonous and pedestrian—Adenauer's chief saving grace was a dry wit which revealed his sharp eye for the weaknesses of his fellow men. De Gasperi and Adenauer appeared disinclined to embark on a discussion of broad principles and seemed to consider a good style and beautiful phrases as unnecessary embroidery. They gave the impression of being always in a rush, always exclusively concerned with settling the business at hand. The matter-of-factness of these two may have been rooted in their feeling that they no longer had much time to accomplish what they felt destined to do. De Gasperi had been at the beginning of a promising political career when Fascism came to power in Italy; he spent the next twenty years partly in prison, partly as an employee in the library of the Vatican. He was in his sixties when he reentered politics as a leader of the Italian resistance. Adenauer was close to seventy when, after twelve years in a political wilderness during the Nazi regime, he was reinstituted as lord mayor of Cologne by the occupying American forces and could resume a political career.

THE RECOVERY OF THE DEFEATED POWERS

The situation in Italy and Germany when De Gasperi and Adenauer took over was hardly suited for men of great plans and imagination. In the years right after the Second World War policy in these nations had to be primarily concerned with securing the basic requirements of social existence: with setting economic life again in motion and with reestablishing membership in the society of states. In economic matters De Gasperi and Adenauer had extremely capable helpers: Luigi Einaudi, Italy's leading economist, first as director of the Bank of Italy and then as minister of the budget, balanced the Italian budget by rigorous means; in 1948 he became the first president of the Italian republic. Adenauer's minister of economic affairs, Ludwig Erhard, relied courageously and successfully on the workings of free competition to stimulate production.

As a result of the impulse given by the Marshall Plan, European economic life soon began to recover. Progress was particularly pronounced in the countries of the Coal and Steel Community, and since in the early 1950's some of France's economic resources were still being absorbed by the struggle to preserve its colonial empire, West Germany and Italy, the defeated of the Second World War, were most benefitted by the economic upswing. In both countries economic miracles were achieved. In Germany the average annual rate of economic growth was 6 per cent; in Italy it was even higher. Yet in each of these countries the course of economic recovery showed different features.

Postwar Italy

Thanks to the rapid progress of the Allied armies into the Italian industrial north, and thanks to the activities of the partisans, the damage done by the war to industrial installations was a relatively low 15 per cent. Italy therefore was able quickly to restore industrial production and to export consumer goods to the rest of Europe. But as other countries set their own industrial machinery in motion, the demand for Italian goods decreased. Then the Marshall Plan provided a new stimulus, and the Italian government used the industrial and financial holdings inherited from the Fascist government to provide capital for industrial modernization. The results were startling indeed. The index of industrial production in 1954 was 71 per cent above that of 1938, the last prewar year. And electric-power production—because of Italy's lack of coal, probably the most important of the country's industries—had increased in 1953 by more than 100 per cent over 1938. By 1954 real wages were more than five times what they had been at the end of the war and almost 50 per cent higher than they had been in 1938. Nevertheless, the Italian economic situation still had great weaknesses. The domestic market remained rather undeveloped because of the poverty of the agrarian south. Although in 1954, 40 per cent of the national income came from industrial activities and only 26 per cent from agriculture, 42.4 per cent of the working population were engaged in agriculture. These figures show that the rural population had remained utterly poor, unable to buy any manufactured goods. Many of these people tried to leave the land and find work in the industrial centers of the north, where they swelled the labor market. Although unemployment had decreased, Italy still had more than four million jobless in 1954. This problem could be solved only by land reform in the south which would give more land to the peasants, but would also bring industry into this region. In dealing with this issue, the De Gasperi regime failed. Land reform had been promised at the end of the war, but the government proceeded with this task only slowly and hesitatingly. The industrial revival neither destroyed nor changed the previously existing social structure; the members of the old ruling group—industrialists allied with landowners—remained powerful throughout the early years of reconstruction. They were willing to support the Christian Democratic government because it controlled the financial resources needed by industry; they were willing to raise the wages of the

Alcide de Gasperi addresses a crowd before the 1948 elections.

workers in order to ease industrial recovery; they even accepted the introduction of an income tax, which had not previously existed in Italy—although it should be remarked that the tax law permitted declarations which had only a very remote relation to actuality. But the old ruling group opposed changes—such as land reform—which would fundamentally alter the social structure.

In consequence of the strength of the opposition to any social change, the Communists and their left-socialist allies continued to exercise strong appeal among the lower classes and made gains among the peasants and rural workers in the south. The Christian Democrats themselves split into a right wing which was willing to cooperate even with monarchists and former Fascists to prevent any change in the social structure, and a left wing which believed in the necessity of cooperation with the socialists to effect thorough social reforms. This split, together with discontent about the inertia of the government, resulted in elections in 1953 which denied De Gasperi his desired absolute majority, and he was forced to retire.

West Germany

In West Germany, the break with the past, not only with Nazism but also with the pre-Nazi past, was more thorough than in Italy. The severance of eastern Germany meant the disappearance of the *Junkers*, the owners of large estates east of the Elbe, who had continuously pressed for protective tariffs and government subsidies. And the creation of the Coal and Steel Community kept the industrial barons of the Ruhr in check. Thus the German ruling group was freed of its socially most reactionary and politically most aggressive elements. One result was a change in the composition of the German civil service, since the classes from which its members had been recruited no longer existed; although still a power within the state, the civil service became less authoritarian.

Germany's situation also differed from Italy's in that its cities and industries had been thoroughly destroyed. The huge task of reconstruction required the cooperation of all strata of the population—of government, employers, and employees, of capitalists and workers. At the same time, the scarcity of goods of all kinds made production, once begun, highly profitable; in the first years the Germans themselves eagerly bought all they could produce. Workers were therefore in great demand, and unemployment disappeared almost completely. The economy of West Germany was able to absorb the refugees from the eastern part of Germany; they turned out to be less of a discontented nationalist pressure group than had been expected and feared. The shortage of workers made employers willing to accept improvements in the status of labor. Maintenance of full employment and social security were recognized as legitimate government functions, and "codetermination," which gave the workers a share in the management of industry, was established by law. After the dictatorial handling of social questions by the Nazis, such government intervention in labor relations was considered entirely compatible with the principles of the "free market policy" advocated by Erhard, Adenauer's minister of economic affairs. If employers shared a willingness to improve the status of labor, the workers too were in a cooperative mood. They were anxious to work, so that with their earnings, they could begin to obtain the necessities of life. Thus although wages at the outset were low, the attitude of the trade unions in wage negotiations was conciliatory and no strikes of significance occurred in Germany in the first years after the war. Consequently German goods quickly reconquered a position on foreign markets.

The prevailing eagerness to prevent conflicts which might delay reconstruction and economic recovery goes far to explain the popularity of the majority party, the Christian Democratic Union, in Germany. Another reason, of course, was that the loss of the eastern part of Germany meant a great increase in the percentage of Catholics in the population, since the south and west of Germany had always been predominantly Catholic (in 1933 Catholics constituted 32.5 per cent of the German population; in West Germany in 1950 the figure was 43.8 per cent). However, the Christian Democratic Union was strong even in the northern, predominantly Protestant areas. The predecessor of the Christian Democratic Union, the old Center party, had always included a variety of social groups, ranging from the workers in the Catholic trade unions to industrialists and landowners. After the Nazi collapse, when external circumstances as well as emotional needs required a new beginning through common action, the appeal of a party which could be regarded as a microcosm of the entire population was obviously great; in contrast to Christian Democracy in Italy, which achieved

Konrad Adenauer on the day of his election. *The chancellor of the German Federal Republic signs autographs in the Bonn parliament building, September 15, 1949.*

its majority by mobilizing one part of society against the other, the German Democratic Union could be characterized as an organized consensus.

The position of Chancellor Adenauer, the leader of the Christian Democratic Union, was strong also for constitutional reasons. In an effort to avoid the instability characteristic of the Weimar Republic, the constitution of West Germany had sharply restricted the rights of parliament. Once a chancellor had been appointed and had received a vote of confidence, the vote of a majority against him could force him to resign only if his opponents had agreed on who would replace him. The only two other parties were a small bourgeois party on the right of the Christian Democratic Union and a Socialist party on the left, and it seemed most unlikely that these two extremes would come together and agree on a candidate for the chancellorship.

The opposition was ineffective also because it had no clear alternative policy to offer. The socialist demand for socialization of key industries aroused little enthusiasm even among the workers—partly because the swollen bureaucracy of the Nazi dictatorship had produced a deep dislike of the red tape connected with all government-controlled enterprises, partly because the trade unions were concentrating on the immediate problem of getting the economy moving again, and were not bothering about an ideal society in a distant future. Moreover, West Germany had retained a federal structure, and in some of the states composing the Federal Republic the Socialists ruled in coalition with the Christian Democratic Union. As long as the concrete, practical tasks of reconstruction were urgent and in the foreground of interest, the differences between Socialists and the Christian Democratic Union were of little significance in domestic affairs.

For the Socialists the chief target of criticism was Adenauer's foreign policy. The chancellor was said to toe the American line, destroying all possibilities for agreement with the east and all chances for German reunification by adopting an anti-Russian course. Yet, to the majority of the German people these objections against the foreign policy of Adenauer's government seemed rather theoretical. Still numbed by defeat and conscious of the immense military strength of the two superpowers, the German people in these early years had little interest in resuming a role in international affairs. They were content to devote themselves, under American protection, to the tasks of material improvement.

It is ironical that as a result of the Cold War, which made the economic and military strengthening of western Europe an urgent necessity, the two European countries which most quickly returned to prosperity were those which had lost the war. Germany and Italy were able to draw strength out of weakness. And their lack of colonial possessions was an advantage in that they were not involved in the expensive efforts to subdue non-European peoples revolting against European rule.

THE DECLINE OF THE EMPIRES

At the end of the Second World War four European powers still retained empires; the Netherlands, Great Britain, France, and Belgium. The breakup of the British and French empires were the decisive historical events, but the Dutch loss of Indonesia was a prelude of some significance for it revealed that the revolt of the colonial peoples was linked to the Cold War.

After the Second World War, Dutch officials were able to return to Indonesia only after their government had declared its willingness to recognize the native government formed under the Japanese and to establish a Netherlands-Indonesian union. But conflict soon developed over the division of functions between the Dutch and the Indonesians and led to military action in which the Dutch supported separatist movements against the republican government. Finally, in 1949, the Dutch recognized the sovereignty and independence of the Republic of Indonesia. The abdication of the Netherlands as a colonial power was to a large extent a result of the Cold War. In negotiations in the United Nations, Indonesia had been strongly supported by Russia; and with the exception of France, which took the Dutch side because of its own colonial interests in this area, no power—not even Great Britain or the United States—was willing to back the Dutch fully, because of the danger of driving the Asian nations into Russia's arms. The Dutch defeat was a clear indication of the strength

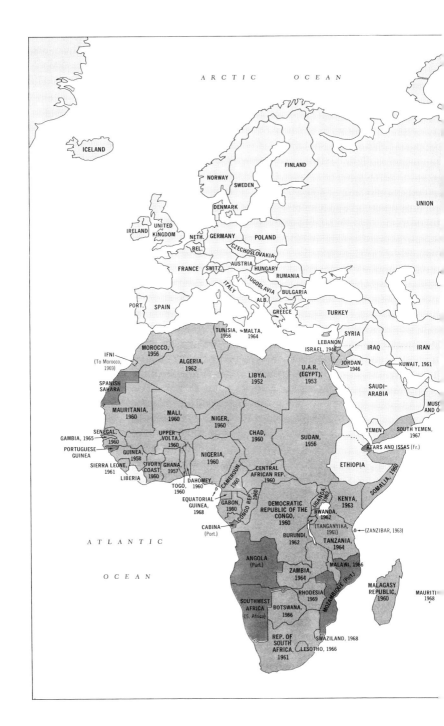

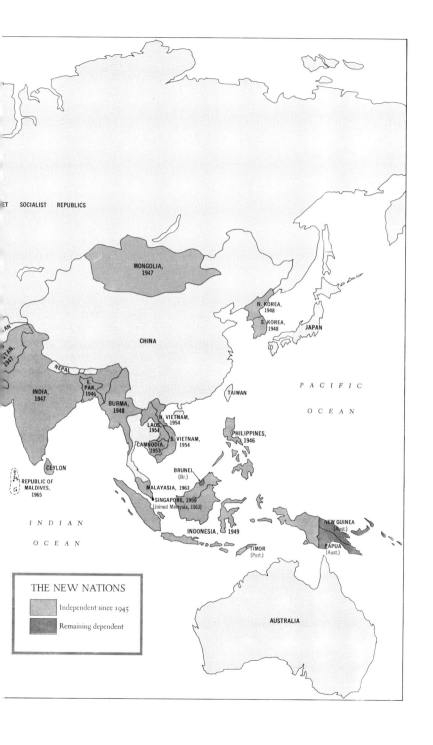

ET SOCIALIST REPUBLICS

MONGOLIA,
1947

N. KOREA,
1948

S. KOREA,
1948

JAPAN

CHINA

TAIWAN

PACIFIC

OCEAN

AN

TAN,
1947

NEPAL

INDIA,
1947

E.
PAK.
1946

BURMA,
1948

N. VIETNAM,
1954

LAOS,
1954

S. VIETNAM,
1954

CAMBODIA,
1953

PHILIPPINES,
1946

CEYLON

REPUBLIC OF
MALDIVES,
1965

BRUNEI
(Br.)

MALAYASIA, 1963

SINGAPORE, 1959
(Joined Malaysia, 1963)

INDONESIA, 1949

NEW GUINEA
(Aust.)

PAPUA
(Aust.)

INDIAN

OCEAN

TIMOR
(Port.)

THE NEW NATIONS

Independent since 1945

Remaining dependent

AUSTRALIA

which the revolt of the colonial people's had acquired as a result of the clash between Russia and the United States.

Postwar Britain: Imperial Decline and Internal Reform

All the European colonial powers faced this situation in which resistance in their possessions was interlinked with the Cold War. It was particularly difficult for Great Britain, which after six years of intense Nazi attacks needed time to recover and to rebuild, but as a wide-flung imperial power with the claim of being equal to Russia and the United States was expected to hold the line against the Communist advance.

The longing of the British people for an escape from the dark and anxious years of the war, and for a new and better life, revealed itself almost immediately. Even before Japan's surrender, the British electorate overthrew Churchill. The Labor party received just 100,000 more votes than the other parties, but they were so distributed that Labor emerged with a majority of 250 over the Conservatives and Liberals in the House of Commons. There were several reasons for this change in government. The Conservatives had been in power since 1931, and if elections had not been postponed because of the war, the usual swing away from the party in power would probably have occurred five years earlier. The credit which Churchill's war leadership had gained could not be transferred to the Conservative party. The slowness with which the Conservatives had enacted measures to overcome depression before the war, the failure of Chamberlain's appeasement policy, the lack of energy in pursuing rearmament, which had left Great Britain open to Nazi aggression—all these were still in the minds of the people. Greater enthusiasm and greater effort for social reform could be expected from Labor than from the Conservatives. Finally, Labor had been a coalition partner in the Churchill government, and some of Labor's leaders—Clement Attlee, Ernest Bevin, Sir Stafford Cripps—had played distinguished roles in the war.

The government now formed by Clement Attlee (1883–1967) became one of Britain's great reform ministries. Building on the foundation laid by Asquith's Liberal government before the First World War, Labor established the "welfare state." The National Insurance Act, which became law in 1946, provided for almost complete coverage in cases of sickness, old age, and unemployment. It is characteristic of the connection between Labor and the pre-1914 Liberals that this act grew out of a report by the Liberal economist William Beveridge. The National Insurance Act was complemented by a National Health Service Act which assured complete medical care to all residents of Britain; it aroused the bitter resistance of physicians and was carried through by the energy of Aneurin Bevan (1897–1960), probably the one Labor leader who somewhat resembled Churchill in imagination, charm, and rhetorical power. Like the Liberals before the

First World War, the Labor party encountered resistance in the House of Lords. The result was further curtailment of the power of the upper chamber with respect to legislation; henceforth it could only impose a veto effecting a brief delay.

In economic policy Labor went far beyond anything the Liberals had ever envisaged, undertaking to create a socialist society, although the term used was "nationalization" rather than "socialization." The Bank of England, the road-transport system, coal mines, civil aviation, canals and docks, the electrical supply industry, and the iron industry were placed under state control and managed by government-appointed boards. The previous owners received compensation.

Through such measures Labor expected to provide a new impetus to British economic life and increased opportunity to the masses. However, these reforms did not provide the expected stimulus to society because the British people were exhausted after the tensions of the long war. Moreover, the beneficial effects of these reforms were counteracted by their coincidence with a severe economic crisis.

The developments of the Second World War had aggravated the long-standing difficulties of British economic life, particularly the problem of its unfavorable balance of trade. British foreign assets had disappeared and foreign debts had increased. Some temporary relief and some improvement in the competitive position of British goods on foreign markets was achieved through loans from the United States and a devaluation of the currency in September, 1949. But a lasting remedy could come only from a limitation of imports and an increase in exports—restriction of the production of consumer goods for the home market and forced production of goods for foreign markets. The Labor government, whose socialist ideology justified a controlled economy, continued rationing of food, fuel, and clothing, and restricted the amount of currency which a traveler might take out of the country. The architect of this austerity policy was Sir Stafford Cripps (1889–1952), a brilliant technician, ascetic, and little inclined to acknowledge the need for human amenities. The time of Labor rule was constraining rather than liberating, gloomy rather than exhilarating.

In this economically precarious situation, the question of whether possession of an empire was more an advantage than a disadvantage became a subject for sharp dispute. Colonies facilitated access to raw materials such as oil, rubber, and cotton and to foodstuffs such as coffee, tea, and rice. But they also burdened the mother country with the need to maintain a strong military posture all over the globe. Indeed, of the many justifications for colonial rule produced by the Victorians, the one which still had some validity was that only a modern industrial power could adequately defend a colony against attack. The preservation of an empire required an extended

Fuel shortage in Great Britain. *During the bitterly cold winter of 1948, the British people stood in long queues to draw their meager coal rations.*

military establishment, with all the expenses necessary for the equipment of a modern army, navy, and air force. And in a time of shrinking distances successful military protection also involved participation in the politics of the entire area in which the colonial territory was situated. Indeed, at the end of the war British troops were distributed all over the world; they were to be found in Germany, Italy, and Greece; in the Near East, Egypt, and Africa; and in the extended regions of southeast Asia. There was no conflict on the globe in which Britain was not involved. Unquestionably the occupation forces in Germany, expensive as they were, had to be maintained if Great Britain was to continue to play a role in Europe. But in the nation's straitened economic circumstances, an increase of the working force at home and a reduction in military expenses were evidently desirable, and the Labor government became anxious to decrease non-European military obligations as far as possible.

Abandonment of Britain's colonies was entirely compatible with Labor's fundamental principles. The party had always opposed imperialism and its concomitant, power politics. Although in the wartime conferences Churchill had emphasized the special interest of Great Britain in the eastern Mediterranean, the Labor government in 1948 declared itself unable to defend Greece and Turkey against Communism and left this task to the United States. The result was the Truman Doctrine (see p. 344). Moreover, the Labor government was anxious to give independence to those British colonies and dependencies which had fully developed political institutions and to introduce self-government for those which were still ruled by British governors because they were believed to be unready for independence. The most spectacular result of this policy was the granting of independence to India. The Labor government offered full freedom to India in March, 1946, but implementation was delayed by difficulties chiefly of an internal nature, caused by the differences between Hindus and Moslems. After long negotiations, the only feasible solution appeared to be the establishment of two states, one Hindu and one Moslem. The creation of India and Pakistan involved an exchange of population, the moving of millions of refugees, accompanied by terrible hardships. Moreover, the delineation of the frontiers did not cleanly separate Hindus from Moslems, and some controversies, such as the dispute over the control of Kashmir, led to bitter and long-lasting tension between the two states. The most distinguished victim of the hatred aroused by the division of India was Gandhi, the founder of the modern Indian nationalist movement; in 1948 he was assassinated by a fanatic Hindu who resented his agreement to the establishment of two states. Nevertheless, the creation of an independent India and Pakistan ended an explosive situation which had troubled the British empire for decades, and Labor had the added satisfaction that India decided to remain a member of the British Commonwealth. The granting of independence to India led unavoidably to the same change in status for the other states of this area. Burma became independent on January 4, 1948, the day and the time for the celebration of this event having been carefully chosen by astrologers. Burma left the Commonwealth; however, Ceylon, which gained sovereignty the same year, remained within the Commonwealth. The rapidity with which these changes took place reflected Communist pressure. The hope was that achievement of independence would diminish the attraction of Communism for nationalist groups. Nevertheless, Burma's emancipation was followed by a long civil war against Communist-inspired factions, and fighting between Communist-directed Chinese in Malaya and anti-Communist Malayans delayed until 1963 the establishment of the Federation of Malaysia. After a short time as a member of this federation, Singapore became independent, though remaining in the British Commonwealth.

Labor envisaged similar developments for Britain's colonies in Africa, but was convinced that further preparations were needed for the granting of independence there. The government accordingly established legislative assemblies in the Gold Coast and Nigeria and increased the number of nonwhite members in the legislative council of Kenya. The goal was the formation of independent states in which the natives would enjoy full citizenship.

The Conservatives regarded Labor's dissolution of the British imperial position with a critical eye. At the same time, the continued restrictions on economic life were diminishing the government's popularity, and Labor began to lose ground. Elections in 1950 resulted in a Labor majority so small that it was almost unmanageable. In October, 1951, the Conservatives were returned to power and Churchill again became prime minister. Some Labor measures—the nationalization of the iron and steel industries and of road transport—were revoked. But the Conservatives were aware that they had received no mandate to eliminate the main features of the welfare state. Moreover, the possibilities for initiating a new economic policy were limited because payments of pensions, compensation for war damage, expenses for the welfare state, and interest on public loans formed large, irremovable items in the budget. Nor were the Conservatives able to solve the basic problem of the deficit in the balance of trade. Yet life in Britain did become less constricted. The Conservatives were helped by the general prosperity of the 1950's; they succeeded in cutting red tape and in accelerating housing construction. But the Conservatives only improved upon the domestic policy of the Labor government; they did not alter it.

On the other hand, the Conservative government was less inclined than Labor to abandon Britain's imperial aspirations. The Labor ministry had not been able to resolve the issues in dispute between Great Britain and Egypt. Labor had declared its readiness to withdraw British forces from Egypt, as desired by the Egyptian government, but had refused to let the Sudan come under Egyptian rule against the wishes of the Sudanese people. Egypt's pride had been further hurt by the failure of its army to crush the state of Israel, which had arisen after the British mandate ended in 1948. The United States and Soviet Russia granted immediate recognition to Israel and after a successful defense against the surrounding Arab states Israel was taken into the United Nations. The withdrawal of British troops from Palestine weakened Britain's military posture in the Near East and this stimulated Egyptian nationalist demands. Nationalist students and an aroused populace engaged in fierce demonstrations against foreigners and put the Egyptian government under pressure to force the withdrawal of British troops from Egypt, the Sudan, and Suez. Clashes between British troops and Egyptian volunteers, the looting and burning of buildings and shops in Cairo by the excited masses, and the power struggle between a discredited government and a luxury-loving king brought Egypt to the brink of chaos. In 1952 a revolution by nationalist army officers deposed the king, ended the rule of the old party politicians, and established an authoritarian republic. The new regime was anxious for a success in foreign relations; the Conservatives now in power in Britain used this opportunity to arrive at a settlement. They agreed to a complete withdrawal of British forces from

Egypt and the Suez Canal, in exchange for guarantees that free passage through the canal and its control through the international Suez Canal Company would be maintained. Moreover, in case of war the British received the right to reenter the canal area with their troops. The Sudan became an independent state. Opposition to this agreement came from Conservative diehards who regarded the treaty as a British defeat. But the government explained that with the growing importance of air transport and air warfare, the Suez Canal had lost its strategic significance.

It is evident, however, that the British policy makers had still other reasons for seeking an understanding with the new Egyptian rulers. No longer burdened with the mandate over Palestine which had poisoned British relations with the Arab states, Britain's Conservative rulers were anxious again to establish Great Britain as the great ally of the Árab nations and the leading power in the Near East. The wealth of this area—notably oil, with pipelines running to the Mediterranean—and its geographical situation as a link between the Mediterranean and India, meant that the power controlling it was an important force in world politics. Gamal Abdel Nasser (born 1918), who had emerged as the leader of the new Egypt, was trying to combine the Arab nations in a unified bloc, and the British regarded their agreement with him as a step toward strengthening their nation's hold in the entire region. But they seem to have been too confident of Arab backing. When in 1955 Britain made a defense pact with Turkey and Iraq, the so-called Baghdad Pact, Egypt reacted sharply against this western interference in Near Eastern policy, particularly in the plans for a common Arab defense league. And Nasser showed his independence from the West by recognizing Communist China and ordering armaments from Czechoslovakia. This Egyptian flirtation with the East was taken amiss by the United States, which on July 19, 1956, withdrew its offer to help finance the building of a dam at Aswan. A week later, on July 26, Nasser declared that Egypt was nationalizing the Suez Canal Company and would use the revenue for the building of the Aswan Dam.

The Suez affair of October, 1956, must be seen against this background. The Conservative government wanted to maintain a strong British position in the Near East and had agreed to a troop withdrawal from Egypt and the Suez area because it expected to gain Arab cooperation. When Nasser showed more independence than had been expected, the British saw in his breach of the agreement on the Suez Canal an opportunity to crush him. Anthony Eden, who had followed Churchill as prime minister in 1955, joined the leaders of Israel and France in secretly preparing a military operation which would begin with a clash between Israel and Egypt and then lead to the intervention of French and British troops, which would occupy the Suez Canal to separate the Egyptian and Israeli forces. Militarily the operation was executed as planned, but diplomatically the plot failed.

The Suez affair. *British transports land equipment in Port Said. The scene is shown through a bullet-shattered window.*

The British miscalculated the American attitude. An explanation of the zigzag course of American policy in the Suez affair, if an explanation is possible, must be left to specialists in the history of American diplomacy. The fact is that the United States and Soviet Russia, cooperating in the United Nations, forced the British and French to accept a cease fire on November 3, 1956, and to evacuate the canal area. The Suez affair meant the end of a chapter in British imperial history.

In 1958 a *coup d'état* overthrew the pro-British regime in Iraq, killing King Faisal II, his heir, and the prime minister, Nuri as-Said. Britain had lost its most reliable ally in the Near East. When the pro-western president of Lebanon felt threatened, his position was upheld by the landing not of British but of American troops. In 1959, Britain conceded independence to Cyprus, thereby abandoning its last important military stronghold in this region. Henceforth, if outside powers played a role in the rivalries and maneuverings of the Arab countries, they were Soviet Russia and the United States; they no longer included Great Britain.

Britain now also accelerated the termination of its responsibilities in Africa. In 1957 Ghana, the former Gold Coast, became independent; at the celebration the duchess of Kent, the queen's cousin, danced the fox-trot with President Kwame Nkrumah under the admiring gaze of the American vice president, Richard Nixon. Nigeria gained independence in 1960; Sierra Leone and Tanganyika, in 1961; Uganda, in 1962: Kenya, in 1963. All these new republics remained members of the Commonwealth. Only British Somaliland, which in 1960 united with Italian Somaliland, became an independent state outside the Commonwealth. The Conservative conversion to anticolonialism was dramatically underlined by a speech made in Cape Town, South Africa, by Harold Macmillan (born 1894), who replaced Anthony Eden as prime minister after the Suez debacle. Macmillan spoke of the "wind of change" sweeping through the African continent, unmistakably dissociating himself from the white man's belief in his superiority over the black.

The refusal to continue bearing the white man's burden brought financial relief to Great Britain. The nation's military role in the Far East had been steadily reduced and plans were made to withdraw British forces completely from all territories east of Suez by 1970.

Although the termination of British colonial rule had positive effects—giving relief from the pressure of Communist anticolonialism, decreasing possible friction with the United States, and simplifying relations with Europe—the decline of the empire did not solve the problems of British domestic and foreign policy. The reduction of political and military commitments has failed to eliminate the basic weaknesses of the British economic situation. It has proved extremely difficult to overcome the unfavorable balance of trade because a relatively high standard of living makes British goods costly and limits the possibilities for selling them on foreign markets. On the other hand, the need for imports—raw materials and foodstuffs—remains constant and high. Both political parties, Conservatives and Labor, have worked with temporary expedients, like currency restrictions, foreign loans, devaluation, export incentives. But the strenuous efforts which must be made to keep the British economy afloat creates no favorable climate for the needed far-reaching changes in the economic structure. They are also unpopular because some of the required measures—industrial concentration, limitation of the right to strike, flexibility in working conditions—impinge upon the power of the trade unions and might appear to be tampering with the achievements of the welfare state. Moreover, economic measures form only one part of the needed reforms; it is recognized that they must extend into the educational area and must include therefore a change in the composition of the British ruling group. The role of Great Britain as an industrial power is dependent on broadening the possibilities of higher education and on shifting, at least to a certain extent, from a broad general education to the training of specialists and technicians. Plans for a great increase in the number of institutions of higher education have been made in the sixties. But it is doubtful whether these plans went deep enough. This is the more serious because even the execution of the existing plans has been slowed down by the need for economies. But it is evident that such fundamental reforms are needed if improvements, which are permanent rather than temporary, are to be obtained.

The precariousness of the British economic situation is obvious abroad but is less noticeable to people in Great Britain where full employment, good wages, and the welfare state guarantee a satisfactory standard of living. This disproportion between the evaluation of the British position by outside powers and by the British people themselves presents a difficulty in achieving the solution which, as it is widely assumed, is best suited to overcome British economic weaknesses: Britain's entry in the European Common Market.

Adjustment to the decline in imperial power represents not only a political and economic but also a psychological problem. The legacy of Britain's imperial era is more than a shell which can be sloughed off. It is a concrete concern of British policy. Britain's policy in the post-war era has been weak not only because of economic difficulties. Despite its loss in imperial strength and its withdrawal from global obligations Britain has remained the center of a commonwealth and its foreign policy has to take the interests of the nations of the Commonwealth into account. Important members of the Commonwealth, particularly the self-governing dominions of Canada, Australia, and New Zealand, now have to look for protection to the United States and consequently Britain has to maintain a special relationship with the United States. Britain is also obligated to keep substantial military forces on the European continent, and it needs close ties with Europe for its own military security as well as for economic reasons. Britain's operations in the field of foreign policy have become increasingly limited because Britain has to chart a difficult course between its global and its European interests.

Postwar France

The dissolution of the French colonial empire created for France an entirely new situation as well as new opportunities. At the end of the war the situation in France was significantly different from that in Great Britain. The successful British resistance to the Nazi onslaught had confirmed the soundness of the nation's political institutions, and the reforms initiated by the Labor government were carried through by means of the existing parliamentary machinery. But the French defeat in 1940 had demonstrated the defective character of the constitution of the Third Republic. Most of the members of the constituent assembly which was elected in 1945 to draft a new constitution agreed that government instability had been the chief weakness of the Third Republic. De Gaulle, who returned to France with immense prestige, emphasized the necessity of strengthening the power and independence of the executive branch. But the left wing—the Communists and Socialists—which dominated the constituent assembly attempted to ensure stability in the government by means of a complete subordination of the executive to the legislative branch; the Chamber of Deputies became all-powerful. De Gaulle saw in this arrangement a disturbing sign that the period of party squabbles was returning, and he resigned as head of the Provisional Government in January, 1946.

He was right, in that government stability turned out to be no greater in the Fourth Republic than it had been in the Third. There were prolonged government crises and an endless succession of ministries. In 1946 the Communists had emerged as the strongest political party. But after they had been eliminated from the government in May, 1947, they never received much more than 25 per cent of the vote. The majority was formed by a left-center coalition of Catholic democrats, the M.R.P., Socialists, and left-liberal groups; almost every French government under the Fourth Republic obtained its support from these parties. Frequent changes in administration were caused less by political conflicts and disagreement over issues than by the maneuverings of ambitious politicians eager to become ministers and inclined to intrigue against one another. In the 1950's French political life found itself in a depressing rut. When the same men or groups remain in power for a very long time opposition tends to increase in strength and shrillness. Majorities for the existing government became increasingly precarious; but no alternative was in sight. Extremists, particularly of the right, were gaining in popular appeal; and the left and right wings of the coalition began to pull in opposite directions in their efforts to pacify the radicals on their fringes.

Yet, the troubles of the Fourth Republic cannot be blamed just on the resentment of the "outs" against the "ins" or on the bickering of the politicians, who in truth did not quite deserve the harsh criticism which they have received. The obvious difficulties of the transition from a wartime to a peacetime economy were augmented by the need to fulfill demands for social change. As we have seen, works committees in all establishments with more than a hundred workers were introduced to give the employees some part in the organization of the work in the factories, and a number of key industries—fuel and power, insurance and large financial concerns, air transport and the merchant marine—were nationalized. But there was also the fundamental question of how to renew the outmoded French industrial apparatus, which with its numerous small family enterprises was resistant to modern technology. The Fourth Republic did handle this matter well. It set up a special office under Jean Monnet (born 1888) to draw up a comprehensive scheme of economic modernization. The Monnet plan established voluntary programs for updating the basic industries, for improving farming methods, and for furthering reconstruction and new building. The government was to provide advice by experts, facilitate the procurement of the necessary labor, and make available the capital needed for investments. Marshall Plan aid, coming at a very opportune moment, was used to help carry out this policy of modernization. Nevertheless, time was needed for the results to become evident, since—as in the Russian Five-Year Plans—the emphasis was placed on heavy industry and the production of machinery. The plan gave priority to coal, electricity, transport, steel, cement, and agricultural machinery. And it would be the Fifth Republic, of Charles de Gaulle, that would harvest much of what the Fourth Republic planted in the field of economic improvement and modernization.

By 1956 French industrial production was 50 per cent higher than it had been in 1929, France's best year during the interwar period, and 87 per cent higher than in 1938, the last year before the war. But this progress in modernizing industry went relatively unnoticed, while the failure of the French government to handle urgent pocketbook issues was all too obvious. The development which hurt the French people most was inflation, produced by the scarcity of goods after the war, by large government loans to industry, and by a series of budgetary deficits. The rapid course of inflation was marked by a steep rise in prices. Wages, although rising, did not keep step, and the purchasing power of both the workers and the middle classes was low; in 1951 the average working-class family spent a third of its weekly budget on meat. Attempts to stem the inflation were futile because the government was unable to get along without a rising deficit. The nationalized industries were unprofitable at this time: the introduction of new forms of management had been costly; the government lacked the courage to brave the indignation which dismissal of superfluous personnel would arouse; and in view of the inflation, the government felt unable to burden the populace further by increases in the costs of railroads and electricity. The social-security system also showed a high deficit because its funds came from a percentage of the workers' wages, but the size of its benefits was determined in relation to prices. In addition the French system of taxation was unsatisfactory, and the left and right wings of the governments were unable to agree on reform.

But even without these many difficulties, it is unlikely that the budget could have been balanced, for funds spent in the effort to preserve French colonial power seemed to pour into a bottomless hole. During the war the French empire had been thrown into confusion. The colonial administrators, possessing a freedom of action which had been lost by the inhabitants of Axis-controlled Europe, were torn between Vichy France and the Free France of De Gaulle. Some segments of the French empire, such as Indochina, were taken by the Japanese; others, such as Madagascar, Syria, and North Africa, were occupied by British and American forces. The loosening of ties with France during the war revealed widespread dissatisfaction with the French colonial system: the chief targets were the authoritarianism with which the colonies were ruled from Paris and the economic exploitation which had cut off the colonies from trade with all countries but France. In all the colonies dissatisfaction was fed by the nationalist movements which had been active since the First World War and received new impetus during the Second World War.

The members of the French constituent assembly realized the necessity of redefining the relationship between France and its overseas possessions. But the arrangements which resulted were a compromise and lacked clarity: the new constitution provided for a French Union, to consist of metropolitan France, its overseas departments (that is, the administrative units of Algeria, which was regarded as part of France proper), protectorates (Tunisia and Morocco), its colonies (primarily in West Africa), and its associate states (Vietnam, Cambodia, Laos—together constituting Indochina). The president of the French republic was also to be the president of this French Union, and he was assisted by an assembly. But the assembly had only advisory functions, and half of its members represented metropolitan France, so real power remained with the Paris government. A promise for elected assemblies in each of the overseas territories was also rather deceptive, since the composition and the powers of these assemblies were to be determined by the French parliament. Certainly the influence of the natives remained carefully hedged in, and the very limited concessions to the desire for self-rule could not stem the colonial movements toward nationalism and independence.

Yet preservation of the empire bore not only upon French financial interests and economic power but upon the most sensitive nerve of the French political body: the army. The French army had never been entirely integrated into the life of the republic. Against the anticlerical and individualistic spirit of the French Revolution it had regarded itself as the guardian of discipline and of national tradition. With the victory in the First World War the contrasts between the army and the republic had receded into the background, and in the 1920's one of France's greatest soldiers, the monarchist Marshal Lyautey, pacified Morocco and accomplished in the service of the Third Republic what has been characterized as "the masterpiece of French colonization." Lyautey, in whose school many of the officers of the two world wars were trained, composed a famous essay "On the Colonial Role of the Army" (1900). If the spirit of the republic was not very favorable toward the ideas of the army, outside the republic—in the colonies—the army could play a great role in the service of France. Moreover, there were a number of elite regiments, with distinguished military records, consisting of Africans.

Postwar developments strengthened the ties between the officer corps and the French colonial empire. In 1940 the military had suffered a crushing loss of prestige, and at the end of the Second World War cadres of the French resistance demanded a place in the army; for the regular officers they were intruders, an alien and unpalatable element. And the entire atmosphere of postwar France was antagonistic to the traditions of the army. The political climate in which socialists were regarded as a moderating force and the intellectual climate in which the value of revolution was accepted by the most prominent intellectual leaders of postwar France whatever their political views might be—by the Communist Jean-Paul Sartre (born 1905) or the anti-Communist Albert Camus (1913–1960)—were contrary to the ideas in which French officers were trained. The close military collaboration in Europe with officers of other nationalities, particularly with Americans, resulted in an emphasis on new weapons and the technological aspects of warfare and a tendency to overlook the values of the past; and the joint European military organization did not grant French officers that prominent place to which they felt entitled by the great military history of France. But in the colonies the army could be what it had always been; it could maintain—or regain—its identity.

Consequently, when at the end of the war in Germany, a French force was sent to the Far East to assert France's claims to its former possessions and to a voice in the affairs of Asia, the army accepted its new role with enthusiasm. The French officers were convinced that in the guerilla war in Indochina, in which modern technology was of limited usefulness, France would be able to prove that it was still the leading military power of the world. The end of the conflict, the debacle at Dien Bien Phu, was a terrible blow for the army, and was followed by recriminations in which civilian leaders characterized the military as strategically inept, and military leaders blamed the civilians for having refused to provide needed reinforcements.

In November, 1954, only four months after the settlement of the hostilities in Indochina, negotiated by Prime Minister Pierre Mendès-France (born 1907) in Geneva, an outbreak of terrorism in Algeria opened a new theater for colonial warfare. The army was sure that now it had the opportunity of revenging its defeat in the Far East and of proving its value for France. Moslem nationalists had become increasingly active in French North Africa: Morocco, Tunisia, and Algeria. In Morocco and Tunisia the French government decided to yield to the movements for independence. Arrangements were initiated by Mendès-France immediately after the settlement in Indochina, and although French rightists, with the support of the army, succeeded in overthrowing Mendès-France and delaying the conclusion of the necessary agreements, Morocco received independence on March 2, 1956, and Tunisia on March 20, 1956. The defenders of French colonial interests found some justification for the abandonment of Morocco and Tunisia in the expectation that these two countries would now refrain from supporting the Algerian nationalists.

There was no intention of giving up Algeria, where the situation was judged to be fundamentally different from that in Tunisia and Morocco. Algeria had been a French possession for more than a hundred years. Many

Frenchmen had settled there, and administratively Algeria, which was divided into the departments of Algiers, Oran, and Constantine, formed part of continental France. Dissatisfaction with French rule arose from the fact that the role of the Moslems was subordinate to that of the *colons,* or European settlers. There were two electoral colleges, each choosing the same number of deputies, but the electorate of one consisted of 1.2 million settlers, that of the other of 8.5 million Moslems. Because Algeria essentially formed part of France, the granting of independence was vehemently opposed not only by the army and the extreme right but also by many adherents of the government parties. The government therefore jogged a weary course. Together with Israel and Great Britain, France engineered the action against Egypt after the nationalization of the Suez Canal, hoping that this blow to Arab nationalism would discourage the Moslems in Algeria. However, when the Suez affair ended in a fiasco, the movement for Algerian independence grew in strength. Guerilla warfare, which the Moslems conducted with great skill, absorbed more than 400,000 French soldiers, who were unable to put an end to terroristic acts or to restore safety in the hinterland. The mounting costs of the war increased the French budgetary deficit and accelerated inflation.

The barbaric cruelty with which the war was pursued aroused sharp criticism among French intellectuals and men of the church. A left-wing opposition to the war began to develop. The various governments tried to restore peace by offering the Moslems increased political influence but fearing the strength of the French opposition to surrender, they did not go very far in their concessions; and the Frenchmen in Algiers, with the full backing of the officers in command there, were adamant in refusing to accept any diminution of their power. Orders of the French government which ran against the wishes of the *colons* and the army were barely obeyed.

In the spring of 1958 the crisis came to a head. Weak and frequently changing governments slowly moved in the direction of further concessions to the nationalists. On May 13, 1958, during a government crisis in Paris, in the course of a demonstration by the *colons* against the vacillations of Paris the government building in Algiers was occupied, and the army agreed to spearhead the move against further concessions. A new government quickly established in Paris proved unable to assert its authority over the military in Algiers. On the contrary, the Algiers rebels were in direct contact with officers and deputies in metropolitan France; to show the helplessness of the government, troops under order of the generals in Algiers occupied Corsica. Without means to suppress the rebellion the parliamentary politicians gave in, and on May 29, 1958, Charles de Gaulle was installed as prime minister.

Those who brought De Gaulle into power—army officers in Algiers and metropolitan France, *colons* in North Africa, politicians of the right and center such as Jacques Soustelle and Georges Bidault—later had reason to regret what they had done. But in 1958, De Gaulle, who was both an officer and the leader of a popular movement, seemed the only person who might be able to inspire the French people to the efforts required to bring the Algerian war to a victorious end. Much psychological insight would have been needed to realize that he was not the man to serve a movement, that he was accustomed to stand for himself and to chart his own course.

De Gaulle had a remarkable record of independence. During the interwar years he had differed from the overwhelming majority of his military colleagues in advocating a highly motorized professional army. In the dark days of the spring of 1940 he had been stamped as a traitor by his comrades because he refused to accept Marshal Pétain's verdict of the necessity for surrender. During the war—photographs showing De Gaulle with Churchill and Roosevelt notwithstanding—the Anglo-Saxon leaders had found cooperation with him extremely difficult. Even when De Gaulle had no real power he had insisted on the inviolability of every right that France possessed, and he could not be deflected from what he regarded as the appropriate course. When he was deliriously received in the liberated Paris and unanimously elected president of the provisional government by the constituent assembly, this general approval had little effect. He did not become more pliable, and resigned four months later, in January, 1946.

This inflexible independence was deeply rooted in De Gaulle's nature. He came from a noble family that traced its origins back to the thirteenth century but in the twentieth century had no clearly defined position in French social life. Because the De Gaulles had suffered financial losses and had only limited means, they could not take their place in the upper ranks of society. Charles de Gaulle's father was not able to follow the usual career of a French aristocrat—as an officer or a landowner—but had to earn his living as a professor of philosophy, history, and literature. Despite these intellectual activities Henri de Gaulle never became a member of the ruling group of the Third Republic. The De Gaulles were Catholics and Henri de Gaulle taught at a Jesuit college. The Dreyfus Affair and the separation of church and state must have widened the gap between the Third Republic and this family of Catholic monarchical aristocrats. Nevertheless, Henri de Gaulle was too much of an intellectual to share the primitive prejudices of his class; he was no anti-Semite, nor did he believe Dreyfus guilty. Clearly, the De Gaulles were more or less outsiders in the French Third Republic, and their position apart seems to have given them a remarkable independence.

It was natural for a member of this family to chart his own course and to look for the principles behind every action. Charles de Gaulle's entire career shows his disinclination to accept any compromise—because in a compromise immediate practical usefulness is placed above principle. As was demonstrated by his attitude in 1940 when he separated from his fellow officers, or again in 1946 when he cut himself off from his comrades in the resistance, De Gaulle was a man acting on principles and inclined to radical "yes" or "no" decisions.

This attitude was not only inborn in Charles de Gaulle but reinforced by education. One of the most important intellectual influences on him was Henri Bergson (1859–1941), the philosopher of creative evolution. For De Gaulle history does not progress slowly and gradually in a steady stream, but must be directed by great decisions taken at critical moments. De Gaulle came to believe that the turmoil of a crisis is the best moment for giving a new impetus to events; the greater the crisis, the more propitious the time for the intervention of a creative statesman. This was the fitting approach for a man who despite his awareness of his right to rule felt distant from the political reality of his day. What De Gaulle writes in his memoirs about another French general appears to be almost a self-portrait: "Too proud for intrigue, too forceful for mediocrity, too ambitious to be a time-server, he nourished in his solitude a passion for domination, which had long been hardened by his consciousness of his own value, the setbacks he had encountered, and the contempt he had for others."[2]

De Gaulle's conviction of superiority, his self-righteousness, his egotism were kept under control and made bearable by his love for France. In his memoirs he writes that he imagines France, "like the princess in the fairy stories or the Madonna in the frescoes, as dedicated to an exalted and exceptional destiny. . . . Providence had created her either for complete successes or for exemplary misfortunes. If, in spite of this, mediocrity shows in her acts," this is "an absurd anomaly. . . . France is not really herself unless in the front rank. . . . In short, to my mind, France cannot be France without greatness."[3]

Despite his high estimate of his own value, De Gaulle's actions have never been inspired by concern for his own fame; he has always had as his criterion the greatness of France; in ruling, he serves. The religious fervor of his patriotism has brought him into conflict with the internationalist tendencies—both ideological and institutional—of the twentieth century. But it would be quite erroneous to see him as dominated by the aggressive nationalism of the nineteenth century, which aimed to elevate one nation at the cost of all others. De Gaulle's concern has been with preserving the integrity of France—the inviolability of its territory, the uniqueness of its spirit. He is aware that this presupposes a strength which can be acquired only through using the means of modern technology. The integrity of

[2] *The Complete War Memoirs of Charles de Gaulle*, Vol. 1, *The Call to Honour*, trans. by Jonathan Griffin (New York, 1955), p. 72.
[3] *Ibid.*, p. 3.

France must be maintained within the twentieth century. While rejecting a united Europe which would submerge individual nations, he has favored a closer alliance among all the nations of the continent, so that "Europe" would mean "the Europe of the fatherlands."

In his first measures as prime minister in 1958 De Gaulle acted according to expectations. He accepted office on condition that he be permitted to rule by decree for the next six months and to draft a new constitution, which would be submitted to the people for approval in a referendum. As could be foreseen, the constitution, which was adopted by a clear majority in September, 1958, strengthened the executive branch of the government. The president was to be elected for seven years by the members of the parliament (consisting of a Senate and a National Assembly) and by representatives of the local and regional councils. But a few years later, in 1962, this law was changed, and by a referendum, popular election was introduced. The president was a powerful figure. He had the right to appoint the prime minister and to dissolve the National Assembly. The powers of parliament were weakened in that a vote to overthrow the government required a majority of the total membership of the National Assembly, not just of the members present. Moreover, with the approval of the Assembly the government could, for a limited time, rule by decree; only after this period had ended, which would frequently be after the decrees had fulfilled their purpose, did they have to be ratified by parliament. Assured of being able to carry out what he had in mind, De Gaulle, in January, 1959, assumed the presidency of the Fifth Republic, to which he had been elected late in December.

THE DISSOLUTION OF THE EMPIRE

De Gaulle's constitution also provided a settlement of the colonial question. And this aspect of his constitution showed an unexpected adventurousness. It envisaged a French community in which the various colonies would be autonomous, although in matters of defense, foreign affairs, and overall economic policy, they would act jointly. Actually, this plan for a French community never fully materialized. De Gaulle permitted the colonies to vote on whether they wanted to become members of the community or to enjoy complete independence. In 1960 the French colonies (Dahomey, Cameroun, Ubangi-Shari, Chad, Gabon, Ivory Coast, Mali, Niger, Senegal, Upper Volta) achieved full independence; but cultural and economic ties with France remained close. Algeria, however, was excluded from these arrangements, and the war there dragged on. While De Gaulle continued to insist that Algeria had to remain French, he cautiously and gradually moved into a more flexible position, and on September 16, 1959, announced that self-determination for Algeria was the only dignified method by which France could discharge its obligations

Charles de Gaulle in a characteristic pose during a campaign rally.

toward North Africa. In a referendum, the Algerians were to be given the choice of assimilation, full independence, or—as a middle way—close association with France. De Gaulle tried to placate the opposition by stating that such a referendum could be held only after the area had been pacified. Nevertheless, his acceptance of self-determination opened the floodgates. The movement toward the separation of Algeria from France became irresistible. On July 8, 1961, the French people approved in a referendum the principle of self-determination for Algeria. The army officers there, in a last desperate move, tried to repeat the game which they had played in 1958. But now they received no support from France, and their own soldiers began to refuse to obey them. The insurrection collapsed; prominent generals, among them Raoul Salan and Maurice Challe, who had led the rebellion, and politicians such as Jacques Soustelle and George Bidault, who were passionate protagonists of a French Algeria, fled and were condemned *in absentia*. Negotiations with Algerian nationalist leaders now began, and although they were interrupted by recurrent crises, a settlement was reached in March, 1962. Algeria was officially named independent on July 3, 1962.

In terminating the Algerian war De Gaulle succeeded in doing what no other French government had been able to do. He had made people aware that the burdens of the war were too heavy and the price to be paid was too high; at the same time, he proclaimed that the real opportunities for French greatness were in Europe. For this reason the break with the leadership of the army was less dangerous than it might appear; in a France oriented exclusively toward Europe an army based on the traditions of colonial warfare was of little relevance. A modernized force equipped with atomic weapons was appropriate to the goals which De Gaulle had set and De Gaulle spared no expense to make France a nuclear power. For France, the abandonment of the colonies made possible full concentration on Europe. The loss of the empire was a definite end and a new beginning.

The End of Belgium's Rule in the Congo

The movements for emancipation in the various colonial territories of Africa affected one another. Ghana's achievement of sovereignty in 1957 gave impetus to the drives for autonomy and independence in the French colonies, and their success in turn strengthened and accelerated nationalism all over central Africa. In this political climate Belgium, the last of the powers with a large colonial empire, felt unable to keep control over its colonies; in 1960, in a precipitate move, Belgium granted independence to the Congo, and in the same year the Republic of the Congo was admitted to the United Nations. During their rule in the Congo, the Belgians were frequently criticized for exploiting the people, and indeed they cared little about educating or giving rights to their colonial subjects. When the Belgian administration withdrew, the Congolese were insufficiently prepared to take over. The country had rich mineral resources; its mines yielded copper, diamonds, and 90 per cent of the world's supply of uranium. Coffee and cotton were the major products of its agriculture. But the people of this economically important and wealthy region still lived in a tribal society. The sudden relinquishment of power by the Belgian rulers led to outbreaks against the whites, to turmoil and internal war. The central government in Leopoldville was opposed by separatist movements, backed by white businessmen who wanted to protect their lives, their properties, and their investments and were assisted in their struggle by white mercenaries. The central government appealed to Soviet Russia for help against the white capitalists, and the Congo conflict threatened to cause a serious crisis between East and West. Its course was punctuated by bitter debates in the United Nations. By 1963 the struggle had died down, and with the help of the United Nations a settled state was obtained. The Russians had lost their most prominent adherent, Patrice Lumumba, who in 1961 had been murdered by his enemies, but the United States also abandoned support of the prowhite separatist regime in Katanga. Moreover, by then the Cold War had lost its sharp edge.

The Congo crisis strikingly illustrated the fact that in central Africa, the struggle was not just between colonials and their foreign rulers but between black men and white. The conflict had a strongly racial element. The racial issue became decisive in the most southern regions of Africa—South Africa and Rhodesia—where the whites, although their number is not inconsiderable, form a small minority within the total population. Here the white inhabitants vehemently refuse constitutional concessions or changes which might gradually lead to some black participation in the government. Instead they separate blacks and whites completely, preserve the monopoly of power for the whites, and keep the blacks in a state of subjugation.

CHAPTER 12

The New Europe
in the Global System

THE WANING OF THE COLD WAR

Just as the rise of the Cold War tension resulted in the formation of a solid Eastern and solid Western bloc, the ending of the Cold War led to a weakening of the Russian and American alliance systems.

We have said that it is impossible to connect the beginning of the Cold War with a definite event. It is equally difficult to set a definite date for its ending; the decrease in tension occurred gradually, almost unnoticeably.

If seen in wide perspective, the developments which influenced most decisively the relations of the two superpowers and created a new climate in international relations were those in the field of nuclear weapons. From 1953 on both the United States and Russia were in possession of hydrogen bombs, and the leaders of both states recognized the impossibility of war between powers with strong nuclear armaments. In 1957 Russia's successful launching of *Sputnik*, a satellite directed from the ground, renewed fears that a war might be attempted because devices operating in space might give Russia military superiority; American efforts to overtake the Russian technological advance were hastened. Likewise, the threat of the development of a "missile gap," which some American military leaders pretended to be imminent, led to fears of an attack by Russia and accelerated the American missile program. But the conclusion was inescapable that the nuclear armament of the two superpowers was so strong that attack by one could not so cripple the other that it would be unable to carry out a nuclear counterblow. In a nuclear war the United States and Russia would destroy each other. The prospect of such a war could not rationally be envisaged or defended. Acceptance of the view that the alternative created by nuclear technology was either disarmament or annihilation was reflected in the beginning of negotiations about nuclear disarmament: a nuclear test-ban treaty was concluded in 1963 and a nuclear non-proliferation treaty in 1968.

The establishment of a nuclear balance of power was the crucial reason for the gradual reduction in tension between Russia and the United States. Nevertheless, 1953, as we have seen, marked a turning point in the Cold War: military activities in Korea ended in armistice. In the following years bonds between the superpowers and their satellites or allies began to slacken until developments were accelerated by events in the critical year of 1956 which, with the Hungarian Revolt and the Suez affair changed the situation in East and West.

The Soviet Bloc, 1953–1956

For the Eastern bloc the year 1953 was important not only because of the Korean armistice; it was also the year of Stalin's death. When Stalin died he was hated in the west because he was held responsible for the tense and critical situation in which the world found itself. But only a speech by Nikita Khrushchev (born 1894) before the Twentieth Congress of the Communist Party of the Soviet Union in a closed session on February 24–25, 1956, revealed that in Stalin's last years his rule had become a personal despotism so irrational that no one felt safe, and that even in Russia he had been an object of hatred and fear. Stalin's death was of immediate political importance because the struggle to succeed him affected the entire Russian-controlled part of the globe. The most tyrannical features of Stalin's time disappeared: Lavrenti Beria, the chief of police and Stalin's hangman, was executed, but others defeated in the struggle for power— Malenkov, on whom first Stalin's mantle seemed to have fallen, and Molotov, who insisted on unchanging continuation of Stalin's policy— were only demoted and perhaps removed from Moscow; they were not killed. Georgi Malenkov, who was premier from 1953 to 1955, favored the production of consumer goods in Russia, and even after his fall, this orientation persisted, though somewhat modified. Between 1950 and the middle of the 1960's, production of washing machines increased from 300 to 4.2 million; of television sets, from 11,900 to 4.9 million; and of refrigerators, from 1,200 to 2.8 million. Malenkov's promotion of the production of consumer goods was accompanied by a decision to permit a new economic course in the eastern European countries. A change in investment policy was to modify the emphasis on heavy industry; prices and wages were to be kept down; and in compliance with the requests of the rural population, the collectivization of agriculture was to be slowed. However, the introduction of the new wage policy led to a revolt of workers in East Berlin in the summer of 1953, and this was taken as a sign that tension had become more dangerous than had been assumed and that a change of course in economic policy was urgent and had to be undertaken as quickly as possible. The state which embarked on the changes with greatest energy was Hungary; Mátyás Rákosi, who had risen to the prime ministership of Hungary as a loyal Stalinist, remained general secretary of the party but lost the prime ministership to Imre Nagy, an advocate of the new course. In other eastern European countries the shift in direction was more moderate. In Poland the all-powerful Stalinist Boleslarv Bierut prevented any radical change.

Obviously, the establishment of a new leadership and a new political line could proceed more easily in an atmosphere of lowered international tension. Accordingly, at the Geneva Conference in 1954, the Russians helped negotiate the settlement which ended warfare in Indochina. And in the spring of 1955, to almost everyone's surprise, they agreed to a treaty which terminated the occupation of Austria and restored Austrian sovereignty, thus removing one of the sources of friction along the line where American and Russian spheres of interest touched. The various facets of the new Russian policy were clearly indicated by Khrushchev in his speech to the Twentieth Congress of the Communist party. He admitted the possibility of different "forms of transition of various countries to socialism" and he revised the traditional Marxist thesis that "war is inevitable so long as imperialism exists." This speech showed clearly that Khrushchev, the first secretary of the Central Committee of the Russian Communist party, had become the acknowledged leader of Russian policy.

The Russian leaders were not unaware that the relaxation of tensions between East and West, combined with an economic policy which permitted the eastern European states considerable variation within the prescribed general framework, might endanger Russian domination. The Warsaw Pact of 1955 was primarily intended as a countermeasure to the military strengthening of the West indicated by the formation of NATO and by West Germany's rearmament and admission to NATO. But it served also to counterbalance the economic autonomy which the satellites had gained, by tightening their military and political bonds with one another and with Russia. Thus, while the Warsaw Pact was still partly conceived as an instrument of the Cold War, it was also a measure intended to minimize the dangers of a lessening of tensions. At the same time, the Russians were anxious to counteract the centrifugal consequences of greater economic autonomy in the satellite countries. Correspondingly, the Council for Mutual Assistance, established in 1949 in answer to the Marshall Plan, began to work out plans for a division of labor and specialization in industrial production so that while complete identity of the economic policy of each country with that of Russia was no longer demanded, the economic interdependence of the entire area would be maintained. The formation early in 1956 of a Joint Nuclear Research Institute including all the Communist states reflected the same trend. There can be little doubt that the uniformity which Stalin had pressed upon the European Communist world had brought things almost to a breaking point; the attempt of the new Russian leaders to modify his policy was almost unavoidable, but because of the explosive tensions which had accumulated under Stalin, "controlled transition" proved to be a complicated process full of dangers for the coherence of the Russian alliance system.

The Western Bloc, 1953–1956

The Korean War had strengthened the bonds between the United States and its chief European allies, Great Britain and France. Although there had been some friction between the United States and its European allies about how this war was to be pursued—how far the campaign should be extended into the neighborhood of the Chinese borders, and whether the use of the atomic bomb should be considered—both France and Great Britain were anxious to stem the Russian advance into areas of the Far East in which they had interests, and they shared with the Americans the erroneous belief that the attack by the North Koreans was part of a great Russian design; repulsed in Europe, the Russians—it appeared—were now concentrating on Asia. With the end of the Korean War in a stalemate, a divergence appeared between the Far Eastern policies of the United States on the one hand and of Great Britain and France on the other. Great Britain believed that with the armistice in Korea, and the emergence of new independent states in this area, a stable political situation would develop. The British did not regard Communist China as strong enough to pursue a policy of expansion, and gave it diplomatic recognition. The French had favored the action in Korea because they expected it to relieve the pressure exerted on them in Indochina. With the ending of the Korean War, followed by their defeat a year later in Vietnam, the French were anxious to move out of the Far East and devote their military forces to the preservation of their threatened possessions in North Africa. The United States, however, regarded Communist China as a dangerous, aggressive power controlled by Soviet Russia; containment of China therefore became one of the primary concerns of American foreign policy. The United States refused to give diplomatic recognition to China and prevented its admission to the United Nations; it held its protective shield over Formosa, where Chiang Kai-shek was established, and promised to support him if the Communist Chinese should attack Quemoy and Matsu, islands a few miles off the mainland in the Formosa Straits. America's European allies did not share these deep feelings of hostility toward Communist China. They had no particular interest in Chinese affairs and they feared that America's Far Eastern policy might lead to a war in which Europe, and the whole world, would become involved.

There were two other reasons why American ties with western Europe weakened at this time. The military aspects of the NATO alliance acquired primary importance in the American mind. And the United States was increasingly inclined to align itself with any power able to strengthen the

American military posture, whatever its system of government might be. The American attitude toward Spain was typical. During the Second World War, Spanish volunteers had fought on the side of the Axis against Russia, although Franco, emphasizing the poverty of his country, avoided direct participation; after the war the victorious governments seriously considered taking steps to overthrow the Franco regime. But in 1953, after vainly trying to overcome the resistance of its European allies to the admission of Spain to NATO, the United States made agreements with Spain by which in return for assistance to the Spanish army, navy, and air force it obtained military bases in Spain. If at the beginning of the Cold War the notion of defending the traditions and values of western civilization had helped to cement the western alliance system, the ideological bond was now losing significance. When in 1955 after a visit to Spain the American secretary of state, John Foster Dulles, joined Franco to issue a communiqué stating that they "found themselves in mutual understanding" with regard to "the principal problems that affected the peace and security of free nations," the term "free world," which western statesmen liked to apply to the American alliance system, acquired a somewhat hollow sound.

American policy makers courted Franco because United States military strength was needed in Asia, and they were anxious to increase the share of the European nations in the defense of western Europe against Russia. After the Marshall Plan had ended in 1952, further American assistance was given chiefly for military purposes and was channeled through the Mutual Security Agency, which was concerned with military needs.

With the United States giving increased attention to the Far East and centering its effort on reinforcing the military position against Russia, the European nations realized that they had to take more initiative of their own. The Organization of European Economic Cooperation (OEEC), which had been formed by the nations participating in the European Recovery Program to draft plans for the use of Marshall Plan funds, remained in existence after the expiration of the Marshall Plan. Its purpose was to facilitate the transfer of currency and the exchange of goods among its members and to coordinate their efforts in fields like atomic research; in 1958 a European Nuclear Energy Agency came into existence.

Thus, the overall result of the American involvement in the Far East was that the European policy makers became convinced that they could not rely on American support, but must act on their own if they wanted to preserve their interests in other parts of the world.

THE CRISIS OF 1956 IN EAST AND WEST

The centrifugal forces working in the American and Russian alliance systems came out into the open in two dramatic events of October, 1956: the Suez affair and the Hungarian revolt. The British and French acted in

The Hungarian revolution. *The Stalin statue is pulled down and destroyed.*

the Suez affair because they were convinced that American policy took little account of their interests and that only an independent initiative could safeguard their position in the Near East and Africa.

The reasons for the Hungarian revolt were more complicated. The possibility of a revolt arose from a struggle between Stalinists and the adherents of the new Communist line. When Nagy became prime minister, his Stalinist predecessor Rákosi, remained party secretary. In the first year of Nagy's regime, 51 per cent of the collective-farm members left the collective system, and 12 per cent of the collective farms had to be dissolved; Nagy intended to continue the policy of abandoning concentration on heavy industry and instead strengthening the development of the other sectors of the economy. Since the war, the working classes in Hungary had increased by almost 50 per cent, and a thorough training of these masses in Communist doctrine had not been possible. With the slowing down of collectivization in agriculture, Communist control of the rural population also became weakened. Accordingly, the Communist party regarded the measures introduced by Nagy with suspicion and feared that it might be losing its grip over the workers and peasants. When Khrushchev succeeded Malenkov, and accused Malenkov of mistakes in the direction of industrial and agricultural policy, Rákosi, who controlled the Central Committee of the Hungarian Communist party, incriminated Nagy as a follower of Malenkov. Taking advantage of Nagy's temporary illness, he succeeded in deposing him as prime minister and expelling him from the party. Rákosi returned to power as prime minister in the spring of 1955. But the clock could not be turned back. In the meetings of clubs named for the poet Sandor Petöfi, which had been set up by the government for intellectual improvement, students and intellectuals debated political issues; both industrial workers and the rural population remained critical and suspicious of the Rákosi government. When in the summer of 1956 Rákosi moved to arrest Nagy and four hundred of his associates, he encountered opposition in the Central Committee, and some members of this opposition turned to the Soviet embassy for help. Perturbed by the revolutionary ferment in Hungary, the Russians decided to drop Rákosi and install a new prime minister, Ernö Gerö, who was expected to steer a middle line between Rákosi's Stalinism and Nagy's new course.

That this attempt at "controlled transition" failed was to a large extent the result of external events. Just at this time, Khrushchev moved to improve relations with Yugoslavia. The rejection of Stalin's policy, which early in 1956 had been publicly proclaimed at the Twentieth Congress of the Communist party, included a condemnation of Stalin's treatment of Tito, and in consequence meetings between the Russian and Yugoslav leaders took place, which resulted on June 20, 1956, in a communiqué declaring "that the ways of socialist development vary in different countries and conditions," and "that the wealth of the forms of socialist development contributes to its strength." Naturally, the Russian satellites in eastern Europe asked why they also should not have that freedom of choice in the form of socialist development which had been granted to Yugoslavia. The first country in which demands for autonomy in domestic affairs were raised was Poland. There, the changed Russian attitude after Stalin's death had not result in any great shift in leadership or any dramatic reversal in economic policy; it had largely meant a general relaxation which curtailed the power of the secret police and permitted greater freedom in intellectual expression. In March, 1956, the sudden death of Bierut, who had dominated the Polish Communist party since the war, gave new impetus to the liberalizing trend. In April, amnesty was granted to thirty thousand prisoners, among them nine thousand political offenders. And it became evident that demands for a change had spread widely among the workers. In June, a strike in Poznán had to be suppressed by military forces. Impressed by the amount of dissatisfaction which had come to the fore in the Poznán strike, the majority of the government, including Bierut's successor as party secretary, accepted the need to accelerate liberalization. Wladyslaw Gomulka (born 1905), who had been released from prison, was permitted to participate in the deliberations of the Central Committee and became a member of the Polish Politburo, while Marshal Konstantin Rokossovski, the commander of the Russian troops in Poland, was relieved of his membership in the Polish Politburo. The great question was whether the Soviet leaders would regard these actions as provocative. However, in negotiations with the Russians, Gomulka was able to overcome their

distrust. Though he had always been critical of the precipitate collectivization of agriculture which the Russians had imposed on the satellites, he was
a loyal Marxist-Leninist, convinced of the need for the Communist party to
keep control and exert leadership, and persuaded that Russia and Poland
had to stand together. Briefly, he assured the Russians that Poland would
remain a reliable member of the Warsaw Pact. Assured of Polish loyalty in
foreign policy, the Russian leaders were willing to permit Poland autonomy
in seeking its "ways of socialist development." On October 21, 1956,
Gomulka was elected general secretary of the Polish Communist party.

The Russian concessions to Yugoslavia and Poland provided the spark for
events in Hungary. When the Hungarians heard of the success of the Polish
move, they felt that they too should try to gain greater independence. At
the universities of Budapest, Pécs, and Szeged, in the Budapest technical
college, and in other public buildings, heated debates took place about the
means to force the government into greater activity; it was agreed to hold a
"silent sympathy demonstration" before the Polish embassy on October 23.
It is estimated that more than fifty thousand people participated in this
demonstration. In the evening Prime Minister Gerö made a broadcast. He
had been expected to accept the need for a more independent and liberal
policy, but instead, surprisingly, Gerö took a hard Stalinist line in his
speech. In response, the public demonstrations assumed a sharply antigov-
ernment character. The gigantic statue of Stalin in the city park was
demolished, and students attempted to take over the radio station, in order
to broadcast the demands of the opposition. To protect the building, the
police began to shoot. Troops were sent against the crowds surrounding the
station, but instead of dispersing the demonstrators they fraternized with
them. The government proved powerless to control the opposition.

The distinguishing feature of the Hungarian revolution was that, in
contrast to the Polish events of the same month, it did not remain limited
to a struggle within the party between the Stalinists and the adherents of a
new course, but developed into a movement against Communist rule in
general. Encouraging broadcasts from the West, which seemed to promise
outside support, played their role in transforming the intraparty conflict
into an anti-Communist revolt. But the reasons for the broadening impact
of the revolt were manifold. On the night of October 23 the government, in
panicky desperation, appealed to the Russian troops for help and announced
at the same time that Imre Nagy had become prime minister. Nagy's
appointment was expected to appease the demonstrators, but he was also
expected to share the powers of government with Gerö and other Stalinists.
The Russian military forces in Hungary were weak and their advance into
Budapest resulted in bitter, indecisive fighting, while in the countryside,
now free of troops, revolutionary committees were formed. The frontier
between Hungary and Austria was opened.

Nagy, whose appointment had been announced without his own approval, was in a thoroughly untenable position. Because of the government appeal for help to Russian troops, and his presumed cooperation with Gerö, the opposition leaders regarded Nagy with the greatest distrust. They believed that his assumption of office could not be considered a guarantee of the beginning of a new course, and that therefore this was not the time to relax pressure on the government. Complying with the demands of the anti-Stalinists, Nagy got rid of Gerö and formed a government composed chiefly of members of the Communist opposition; György Lukács, the famous Marxist scholar, became minister of education. But by then many non-Communists had joined the opposition movement, and they were not content to abandon the struggle without further liberation measures. For instance, Cardinal Mindszenty, who was freed from prison and whose courageous stand against the government gave him great authority, demanded the formation of a Christian Democratic party similar to Adenauer's party in Germany. He stated that he "rejected *en bloc* everything Hungary had done since 1945, not only since 1949, and the establishment of dictatorship." And he came out in favor of "private ownership."

Nagy was rightly afraid that the Russians might interfere if order were not quickly reestablished. He tried to appease the non-Communist opposition by taking into the government leaders of the former Social Democratic, Small Holder, and National Peasant parties. But they were willing to cooperate with him and the Communists only if he made further concessions. On October 30 Nagy announced the restoration of a multiparty system, and on October 31 he declared that Hungary proposed to withdraw from the Warsaw Pact.

It is evident that the Russians could not permit a break in their bloc. They had been waiting and vacillating in their attitude to the events in Hungary. Probably they would have followed the kind of policy they adopted toward Poland, permitting Nagy freedom to undertake economic and cultural changes, if there had been no doubt of Hungary's adherence to the basic principles of Communism and of its loyalty to the Warsaw Pact. The Russians agreed to withdraw their troops from Hungary on October 30, but at the same time they began to assemble strong forces along the Hungarian frontier, preparing for any eventuality. When Nagy announced Hungary's secession from the Warsaw Pact, they decided to intervene. In the early morning of November 4, Russian troops entered Budapest, and by nightfall the revolt had ended. Mindszenty found asylum in the American embassy. Nagy sought refuge in the Yugoslav embassy, but was handed over to the Hungarians, and he and other leaders of the revolt were executed. Some of the participants managed to escape over the Austrian frontier, and there, as along the Franco-Spanish border seventeen years before, camps were established to house the disillusioned and impoverished refugees whose desperate stand for freedom had been crushed by the pitilessly functioning machines of totalitarian dictatorship.

It has frequently been said that the Suez affair, which began on October 30 and therefore coincided with the events in Hungary, caused the failure of the Hungarian revolt. Perhaps the developments in the Near East did hasten the Russians' decision to intervene, for surely they did not want to have an exposed flank in southeastern Europe in the event of a serious international crisis; without Suez there might have been a chance for the Hungarians to negotiate a less brutal surrender. But there can be no doubt that as soon as the opposition movement had developed into an anti-Communist revolt, the Russians were forced to reestablish their authority over Hungary. And it is certainly nonsense to maintain that if the West had been united, the uprising might have succeeded. Neither the United States nor any western European power was willing at this moment to undertake war with Russia, and since the Russians could not tolerate Hungary's defection to the West, active support of the revolt by the West would have meant war. Actually, the American government owed a certain amount of gratitude to the British and French because the Suez affair provided a justification for America's inactivity in Hungary. The Suez affair concealed the fact that the Russians had called the bluff of the American liberation policy.

The events of October–November, 1956, despite the upheaval which they caused in international relations, ultimately had the effect of reducing tension between the United States and Russia. The unwillingness of the western powers to give more than vocal support to the Hungarian revolt could be taken by Russia as a sign that although they had refused officially to acknowledge that eastern Europe was a Soviet sphere of interest, they did actually recognize Russia's control over this area. In the handling of the Suez affair—in forcing the British and French to evacuate the area which they had occupied—the United States cooperated with the Soviet Union, and although an underlying American motive may have been to prevent the Arab nations from throwing themselves into Russia's arms, the Russians must have regarded the American attitude as a sign of the weakening of imperialist aggression. Most of all, however, both superpowers had to concentrate on restoring order in their badly disorganized camps. Reestablishment of common purpose and common action within these spheres was difficult and was fully achieved by neither Russia nor the United States.

THE TRANSFORMATION IN THE ALLIANCE SYSTEMS

The Soviet Bloc Since 1956

The fact that Gomulka remained in power in Poland demonstrated that there was no return to the policy of forcing uniformity upon the states in

The end of the Czech liberalization movement. *Russian tanks entering Prague.*

the eastern bloc. In many respects each country followed its own economic and cultural course. Thus by 1960, when Gomulka's policy of restraining the collectivization of agriculture had been in force for three years, there was a wide difference among the various eastern countries in the proportion of collectivized arable land. East Germany with 96 per cent and Czechoslovakia with 85.2 per cent were in the lead; while Poland with 13.2 per cent brought up the rear. In general, East Germany and Czechoslovakia still adhered closely to Stalinist policies, and in Ulbricht and Gottwald and then in Gottwald's successor Antonin Novotny, they had leaders who had been personally close to Stalin. But in both countries the rigidity of the political and economic policy resulted in accumulated discontent, and in 1968 this brought about a change of course in Czechoslovakia. The movement toward democratization in Czechoslovakia was not dissimilar to that which had exploded in Hungary twelve years before, although particular emphasis on political and economic decentralization and insistence on the importance of intellectual freedom gave the Czech events their special coloring. The Russians reacted toward the change in Czechoslovakia more slowly than in the case of Hungary. After some hesitation they moved troops in, partly because Czechoslovakia seemed to be sliding out of the eastern camp into a neutralist position, partly because the closeness of Czechoslovakia to the West made its control strategically crucial. Nevertheless, in the Communist parties of the West—in France and Italy—indignation about the Russian invasion was great. However, the Russians took their own counsel; slowly but unalterably, they eased the Czech leaders of the reform movement out of power. The strategic position of Czechoslovakia, and concern for the stability of their own regimes, prompted leaders of several Soviet satellites—Hungary, Poland, East Germany—to support the Russian invasion of Czechoslovakia. Ulbricht in particular was a driving force in the suppression of the Czech reform movement. He has since emerged as one of the most important figures in the eastern bloc.

Ulbricht's position in East Germany had been firmer than that of other Communist leaders of the Stalinist brand because, after 1956, he gradually allowed a larger production of consumer goods, and the economic situation in East Germany did improve remarkably. Of the other satellites, in economic policy it was Poland under Gomulka that went furthest in following its own particular line of socialist development. In Hungary after the suppression of the revolt the government which the Russians established tried to follow a middle course.

Why did these satellite countries, despite the variety of their "ways of socialist development," retain their bonds with one another and with Russia? A chief reason was economic. Overall economic planning for the entire area, while it did not force the establishment of any industries, did help to organize the distribution of the goods which were being produced. For instance, East Germany, building on Germany's prewar accomplishments, became the chief center of the chemical industry for Russia and eastern Europe. Moreover, in purchasing goods from the satellites Russia, after 1956, paid not arbitrarily fixed low prices but world market prices. And while just after the war Russia had moved economic assets from eastern Europe into its own territory, it subsequently made sizable investments in this area. Economic interdependence was deliberately accelerated.

The absence of friction between some satellite countries and Russia was due also to the realization by the Communist leaders of eastern Europe that without Russian support their rule might become precarious. Once the settlement of their frontiers had been imposed by Russia the eastern European states felt that their territorial integrity was safe only as long as they remained within the Russian orbit; for instance, the placing of the Polish-German frontier along the Oder-Neisse line bound the Poles closely to Russia. Thus, although these countries developed somewhat divergent economic policies they retained a uniform ideological outlook and common political-military interests which forged strong bonds among them and with Russia. The fruits of industrialization have begun to appear, and all of the countries have shared in an economic upswing. Exact figures are difficult to obtain but the annual rate of postwar growth in eastern Europe seems to have been at least 6 per cent. The masses of the people have gained considerable advantages from the government policies. Consequently there has been less discontent, and a relaxation of police controls and cultural supervision has been possible. Thus, although these countries are still tied together by strong bonds, their situation has changed since the first decade after the Second World War, when Russia was clearly the head of the alliance and gave orders which everyone obeyed. Now there are frequent meetings of the leaders of all these states; although Russia's voice remains very powerful, the decisions are presented as the results of common deliberations.

There is still another reason why Russia proceeded with careful regard for the views and interests of the eastern European nations, why they have become allies rather than satellites. In the 1960's the Communist world was agitated by the antagonism of the two most powerful Communist nations—Russia and China. The Sino-Soviet conflict was hardly a part of European history, yet it had an important bearing on the European states. It provided the Communist nations of Europe with an alternative, and although probably none of the rest was inclined to follow the example of small Albania, which, separated from the Russian bloc by neutralist Yugoslavia, could afford to side with the Chinese, their bargaining strength was increased. The unity of the eastern European bloc is now maintained by a complicated system of pressures and counterpressures.

The Western Alliance Since 1956

Despite the absence of violent conflicts, signs of disintegration became clearly noticeable in the alliance between the United States and the nations of western Europe. Assuming a role like that of China in the Communist camp, France under De Gaulle, without repudiating friendship with the United States, took an openly anti-American course. De Gaulle declared that the United States had become too powerful and that a counterweight had to be created, that Europe ought to stop following American direction and stand by itself. And he saw to it that France took steps to carry out this program. For example, American troops were forced to leave French soil, and the headquarters of NATO had to be moved from Paris to Belgium.

The independent stance taken by De Gaulle presupposed the liberation of France from the burdens of colonial warfare. But it was made possible only by economic developments in Europe which had been initiated before he seized power. The European Coal and Steel Community, established in 1951, had proved a success; after a shaky beginning, production rose impressively from 1954 on. West German steel production between 1954 and 1957 increased from 17 million to 24 million tons; French steel production, from 10 million to 14 million tons. In view of this success the six countries of the European Coal and Steel Community—France, West Germany, Belgium, Luxemburg, the Netherlands, and Italy—decided to embark on a policy of European unification. In treaties concluded in Rome on March 25, 1957, they founded a European Atomic Energy Community (EURATOM), which would make the uses of atomic energy available to all the participating countries. More important, they agreed on the establishment of a Common Market (European Economic Community). Its aims were to abolish all trade barriers among the six, to establish a common external tariff, to permit the free movement of labor and capital among the member states, and—by equalizing wage rates and social-security systems—to bring about uniform working conditions in the Common Market area without creating unemployment. Clearly, these goals could not be achieved in a single stroke; for instance, in some of the participating countries agriculture was highly protected and would collapse if customs barriers were removed suddenly. The Rome agreement therefore envisaged a development in stages, to be completed within fifteen years. A European Commission with headquarters in Brussels, acting under the instructions of a regularly meeting council of ministers, was entrusted with the administration of the Common Market and the guidance of its development. On January 1, 1959, the Common Market began to function by lowering tariffs 10 per cent among the member countries, and thereafter, despite difficult negotiations and crises, steady progress was made in realizing its program.

The effect of the Common Market on the economy of the six participants was most beneficial. Between 1959 and 1962 production rose 35 per cent in West Germany, 29 per cent in France, 58 per cent in Italy. The increase in French production was particularly significant, for while Germany had shown a steady and marked economic growth since 1950, the French growth rate had been low. A special advantage for the Italian economy was the added mobility given to labor. Large numbers of Italian workers were able to obtain temporary employment in Germany and France, and between 1959 and 1963 unemployment in Italy fell from 1,500,000 to 500,000. The wage level rose correspondingly, and the improving economic and budgetary situation made it possible for the Christian Democrats to undertake a reform program to eliminate the economic disparity between northern and southern Italy. Politically, the adoption of this policy meant a turn to the left and a willingness to cooperate with the left-wing socialists, led by Pietro Nenni.

One of the most significant effects of the Common Market, however, was the impetus that it gave to trade among the six participants. Between 1958 and 1962 intracommunity trade rose by 97 per cent; by contrast, imports from outside the Common Market grew only 38 per cent, and exports to non-Market countries increased by 29 per cent. This "little Europe" began to form a vital and stable basis for the economic life of its six members.

Great Britain did not participate in the Common Market. Its response was to initiate the creation of the European Free Trade Association, with Sweden, Norway, Denmark, Switzerland, Austria, and Portugal. This organization was purely a customs union and did not envisage any further integration of economic life, for taken as a group the participating states were too diverse in their economic interests. However, the connection of the Scandinavian countries with Great Britain did have some geographical, economic, and political justification. Great Britain was one of the most important customers of the Scandinavian countries, and their currencies were tied to the value of the pound. Moreover, they had developed into welfare states with features similar to those of Great Britain. But the chief purpose of the foundation of the Free Trade Association was to strengthen Britain's bargaining position in its attempt to join the European Economic Community without relinquishing her role in the British Commonwealth of Nations.

De Gaulle was opposed to Britain's entry into the European Economic

Community, which he regarded as an independent organization which might serve to remove the American influence from European affairs. Great Britain had close economic and political ties with the United States, and this dependence had been increased by the Suez affair, with its damaging consequences for the British position in Asia, and by Britain's precarious economic situation. And some of the members of the British Commonwealth—notably Australia and New Zealand—looked to the United States for military protection.

De Gaulle's veto of Britain's entry into the Common Market (1963) was opposed by some of the other members, who expected economic advantages from the enlargement of the Common Market. But their resistance to De Gaulle exhausted itself in efforts to keep the door open for further negotiations. Adenauer probably supported De Gaulle because he feared that the widening of the Common Market might delay or prevent the further political integration of Europe, which was his particular interest; moreover, De Gaulle guaranteed him French support for the West German position in the question of Berlin. The other member countries were probably not without reservations about the British application; they had misgivings about getting involved in affairs of the world outside Europe. For while the question of Britain's entry into the Common Market was under discussion, the United States was becoming more and more deeply involved in a war in Vietnam, where it considered itself to be holding the line against Communism. Although Europeans regarded the Cold War as a thing of the past, it was still very real to Americans. Most Europeans were unable to share the view, widespread in America, that the activities of the Vietcong formed part of a great Communist offensive against the "free world." To them, social and nationalist discontent and the division of the country seemed adequately to explain the conflict between the north and the south in Vietnam. Moreover, Europeans believed that the Americans were exaggerating the threat of China, as they had ten years earlier in the Korean conflict. Hence, the United States action in Vietnam had no support from America's European allies, and the strains which the war placed on American financial resources weakened the influence that the United States could exert by economic means; at least temporarily the United States was no longer extending favors, but asking them. It wanted higher payments for the expenses involved in keeping troops stationed in Europe, so that the deficit in the American balance of payments would be decreased, and it was anxious to forestall any autarkic tendency in the Common Market which might place obstacles in the way of American investments in Europe.

The developments in the Russian alliance system and in the American alliance system were strikingly similar insofar as closer economic integration took place in both eastern and western Europe. However, the effect in each area was different. In the East it created a firmer tie with the leading power; in the West it resulted in more independence from the leading power.

The Superpowers in a Multinational System

In the years immediately after the Second World War the United States and Russia appeared to be the only powers able to make decisions and to influence the course of world affairs, but by the 1960's a number of other states could throw some weight on the scales. Perhaps there was no more striking indication of this change from bipolarization to a multinational system than the increase in membership of the United Nations. Between 1946 and 1967 the number of states in the United Nations more than doubled (from 55 to 115), largely as a result of the entrance of the newly independent nations of Asia and Africa and the powers defeated in the Second World War. In the years just after the war the great majority of the members of the United Nations almost automatically voted for the American position, and the Russians replied with frequent recourse to the veto, but now the outcome of voting often cannot be foreseen.

Nevertheless, a world divided into two hostile power blocs has not suddenly turned into a society made up of numerous equal members. Both the United States and Russia are far superior in strength to the entire rest of the world. In resources and technology the United States and Russia are so much ahead that the distance between the superpowers and the other states is likely to increase rather than diminish. The other states—particularly the European nations, which because of their own advanced technological stage can recognize the gap between themselves and the superpowers—are well aware that their influence and their freedom of action are limited. They cannot survive a serious crisis. In a clash between the two superpowers each European nation would be forced to take sides in one camp or the other. Thus, although the various nations in eastern and western Europe have made great, almost unexpected, strides toward autonomy and independence, they nevertheless remain within the gravitational fields of Russian and American power. Leaders in Russia and America are not unaware of this fact, and in the recurrent crises in the relations between these two states it is sometimes difficult to tell whether the policies of the superpowers are primarily directed against each other or are intended mainly to enhance the coherence of their respective blocs. As long as oil remains the most precious and most important raw material of modern industrial society, the oil-rich Near East will be a critical area, and a direct clash between Russia and the United States over its control must remain to be considered a possibility. When the two superpowers oppose each other in other parts of the world—in Cuba, in the Far East, in Berlin—an important reason for confrontation is to demonstrate the vitality of their alliance systems. The policy of the superpowers is mainly directed toward maintaining the established balance of power, not changing it. The continued existence of a balance of power in a state system which is not multinational, but polarized between two superpowers is a novelty and disproves the frequently expressed view that international relations never change.

EPILOGUE

The Outlook

WHEN THE TWENTIETH CENTURY began, Europeans felt that they had reason to be proud. They dominated the globe, and the achievements of their science and technology provided steady proof of continuing progress. One great problem, however, darkened this bright picture. Would the intricate fabric of European civilization be destroyed in a revolution caused by the deep gap which separated the rulers from the ruled?

In our description of the political developments in Europe during the first two thirds of the twentieth century, we have given particular attention to the three areas which constituted the source of European pride and fears: the impact of technology on the conduct of politics; the relations between Europe and the non-European world; and the evolution of the social conflict. Probably nobody at the beginning of the twentieth century foresaw the course which these developments were to take. Science and technology have not only justified the expectations of further progress but revolutionized the external and the internal world of man. Their spread from Europe to the various corners of the globe has even been decisive in what might be regarded as the most unexpected and at the same time the most significant event in Europe's political history during the twentieth century: the ending of European hegemony over the rest of the globe; the restriction of the rule of the European nations to their own continent. As we have seen, the loss of control over Africa and Asia was a complicated and painful process. But it might be said that after industrialization had spread over the world, and Europe no longer possessed a monopoly of advanced technology, the end of the domination of 450 million Europeans over three billion non-Europeans became unavoidable. But while developments in the field of technology and in the relations between Europe and the rest of the world during the first sixty years of the twentieth century had clearly definable results, it is much more difficult to say whether and to what extent the accompanying social changes modified the division into two antagonistic classes which characterized European society at the beginning of the twentieth century.

THE NEW SOCIAL STRUCTURE OF EUROPE

Certainly, the sharpness of the contrast between the classes has been mitigated. Both the composition of the ruling group and the economic situation of the working people have been significantly altered. The role of the landed aristocracy in the European nations has largely ended. In Spain and perhaps in certain parts of Italy the aristocracy still represents an element of power and influence, but even in these countries industrialization and technological progress are loosening the grip of the landowning nobility.

It is perhaps a sign of the vanishing role of the aristocracy that a new expression replacing the notion of the ruling group is now frequently used: the "establishment." This vague and hardly scientific term points to a significant feature determining the character of the policy making group in the present age of industrialization and technology: to the domination of economic and political activity by large organizations of an institutional nature, and to the interlocking relationships of these established institutions. Their leaders are forced to cooperate and support one another because the weakness of one might lead to the collapse of all. The ideals of the liberal age which demanded that the economy be free of government interference, that the relations between employer and employee be regulated by demand and supply, and that scientists do their research disinterestedly on problems of their own choice, have long passed. In the twentieth century the trend has been in the opposite direction, toward coordination and systematic, organized planning.

The experiences of two world wars made planning in modern industrial Europe acceptable; and the interdependence of the military and industry has remained the central justification for planning on a nationwide basis. Because of the complicated nature of modern weapons and the size of the installations they require, defense preparations have become a key factor in the economic and social life of a nation; they involve far-reaching decisions concerning the distribution of manpower and of financial and scientific resources. Of course, economy and war have always been closely connected. The novelty in the twentieth century is the impact of defense requirements on the entire economic structure of a country and their influence on the field of science, through government support of research that is militarily useful—in preference to all other lines of research.

Next to the pressures of military requirements, the most important reason for the extension of planning has been the general acceptance of the view that the modern state should take an active role in determining social policy. Whether the aim of the welfare state is seen as full employment, the establishment of insurance systems covering health and old age, the protection of the workers from capitalist exploitation through nationalization of key enterprises, or all of these, the achievement of its goals requires direction of the economic process, i.e., planning. A result of this widening of the state's functions has been the creation of new government departments. Almost all European nations now have ministries or committees for planning, ministries of social security or social insurance, of technology or scientific research.

Certainly, there is a difference between the centralized planning in eastern Europe, which includes every detail of economic life, and the much less direct guidance and control of economic processes in western Europe by means of public works and government purchases, state-owned enterprises, control of the money market, schemes for regional development, and economic guidelines and production quotas. But though the form of organization and planning is less rigid in the West, the manageability of the economic process as a result of the interdependence of the forces involved in it is clearly recognized and used.

As a integral part of the working of the planned economy, the workers have become an acknowledged power within the existing system. If the vanishing influence of the landed aristocracy may be regarded as inherent in the rise of industrialized society, the acquisition of a share in power by labor is the most evident sign of the decreasing significance in Europe of the concept of the class struggle.

European workers in the second half of the twentieth century no longer constitute a proletariat; they are no longer looked down on as they were at the beginning of the century. In accordance with the revolution in economic theory which Keynes triggered in his books, particularly his *General Theory of Employment, Interest and Money* (1936), the workers are now regarded as consumers. Entrepreneurs recognize that as long as a margin is left for profit, high wages are useful. Increased income for the workers means an increased demand for mass produced goods. The economic situation of the workers also has improved because modern industrial technology requires a large number of skilled workers who receive high wages. Under the conditions of modern technology the skilled worker has the added advantage that his skills can be utilized in more than one kind of job. He can find employment in a number of industries producing different goods.

The living conditions of European workers have been improved by the progressive limitation of working hours and the introduction of guaranteed paid vacations, and above all, by benefits of the welfare state. Unskilled workers with few resources and little bargaining power have not disappeared; in all the European states there are still masses of the semiskilled and unskilled eking out marginal livings. But most workers now have a stake in the existing society. They are no longer convinced that their only chance lies in collective action, but see possibilities of advancing their positions individually. Thus, they do not hesitate to cooperate with the existing political and social system, and—it might be added—such cooperation seems the best way to obtain job security. Job security remains a serious concern. Although many former reasons for unemployment have disappeared, there is no assurance that it may not again become a problem in the future: the situation which will be created by automation cannot yet be clearly appraised.

In contrast to the situation in the early twentieth century, in which a member of the ruling group was expected to adapt to an aristocratic feudal pattern, the "establishment" of modern postwar society has no uniform style of life. In composition, it includes the leaders of all the enterprises, organizations, and activities which must be linked together in a systematically organized economic structure: heads of industrial and financial concerns; trade-union officials; directors of institutes of scientific research; specialists in economics, education and administration; military experts. Inherited wealth is probably still an advantage in reaching the top in business, but in general membership in the ruling group is no longer hereditary.

Because the new ruling group is composed of men active in the most varied fields, the opportunities for entering the policy-making upper stratum of society have been much enlarged. Education—the acquisition of special knowledge and techniques—is the surest way to advancement. But the foreman in a factory, the minor civil servant, the clerk in an office, can all hope to reach the top through their work or through activities in their professional organization.

The upper group is now largely recruited from the middle class, but—like today's working class—the middle stratum of society in Europe differs markedly from what it was at the beginning of the century. Before the First World War the middle class constituted a mixture of different elements with the independent businessman and farmer as the backbone, although the new element of professional men and white-collar workers was increasing in numbers and importance. In the 1960's men who are independent in the sense that they own their own shop, farm, or business are no longer a significant component of the middle class, which is now primarily formed by the employees of large, usually impersonal organizations.

This new middle class has appropriately been called the service class. While the small independent businessman represented a remnant of an earlier economic situation and was in danger of being crushed by industrial giants, the service class is well ensconced in modern industrialized society. Within the general social structure, it forms a link or bridge between the new upper stratum and the workers. Some statistical figures about the German developments provide a striking illustration. In the first decade of the twentieth century 37.6 per cent of the gainfully employed were still independent. By 1967 this figure was halved (18.8 per cent). The percentage of industrial workers among the gainfully employed has remained rather constant, somewhat below 50 per cent, but the number of white-collar workers has increased from 7.5 per cent to 33 per cent. On the other hand the differences in income between workers and employees has steadily diminished; in 1966 the average wage of an industrial worker was only six per cent less than the average salary of a member of the service class. For a large part of the working class the move into the service class is not very difficult and can be achieved in one generation.

Thus, society has not been split into antagonistic groups; instead, under the direction of a broadened and more easily accessible ruling group, the trend has been toward cooperation. However, increased social mobility and easier entrance into the ruling group must be regarded as an underlying tendency rather than an accomplished fact. The degree of realization in a particular western European state depends on the traditions of that state and on the nature of its political and economic problems. For instance, Great Britain is accustomed to gradual reforms along constitutional channels, and factors which determined the composition of its ruling group in the past are still alive. Despite a system which tries to restrict to gifted children attendance at schools preparing for the university, and despite the foundation of many universities intended to widen the availability of academic training, an easy start in business or politics is still facilitated by inherited titles and wealth, education in the public schools, and attendance at Oxford or Cambridge. In Italy the conditions in the south, which has only begun to be drawn into the age of industrialization, promote an alliance of poor peasants and unskilled workers for the purpose of an anticapitalist revolution. Class struggle has remained a reality although the Italian Communist party, because of the improved circumstances of workers in other parts of Italy, walks a tightrope between revolutionary Marxism and revisionism. In France the nationalism and authoritarianism of De Gaulle with its emphasis on subordinating economic measures to a policy of prestige and power kept the workers less well paid and more discontent than in other countries and accordingly less willing to accept compromises. Insofar as class conflicts between workers and the middle classes still exist (as in Italy and France), they can be attributed to circumstances created by history or by a particular political situation. Yet the rigid social stratification which existed in Europe at the beginning of the twentieth century has become almost incomprehensible from the present point of view.

POLITICAL AND SOCIAL DISCORD

The readiness to accept the need for economic cooperation and social integration does not mean, however, that after decades of upheaval and war

Europe has reached a state of contentment and stability. The political temper of a country or a continent is almost impossible to measure, but it is certainly true that western Europe has remained restless and tense.

Dissatisfaction and a sense of uncertainty have remained widespread among many sectors of the European population. The developments which have placed economic life in a new setting have repercussions on every aspect of life and demand a reorientation of the goals and procedures of many established institutions. But because such readjustments sometimes mean a loss of power or a conflict with traditional aims, rights, and customs, the adaptation of these institutions to a planned and organized world has been difficult and incomplete. This has been particularly true in France where De Gaulle's ambition and energy promoted a rapid tempo of modernization. Tall buildings with all modern comforts were erected for the population drawn into the towns but they were constructed around urban centers in which people still lived and worked under the conditions of pre-industrial times. It is rather typical for the entire French situation that after some stretches of broad modern highways roads suddenly narrow down to two lanes. In France, it has been said, there are two economies that uneasily co-exist: a modern one, most of it implanted since the war by the technocrats and a few big state and private firms; and below it, an old creaking infrastructure, based on artisanship, low turnover with high profits, and the ideal of the small family business. The contrasts which this industrializing and modernizing activity created were certainly a factor in bringing about the end of the disquieting regime of De Gaulle in 1969. But all over Europe planning and modernization has created friction and has raised doubts and criticisms. In the center of questioning are the functions of parliament and of political parties and the forms and aims of education. Because the alterations in society have come about under the pressure of external needs rather than in consequence of an evolution or a change in ideas a wide gap has opened between the political and social reality and the ideology which is appealed to in justification of this reality. The result has been the emergence of a radically critical attitude among intellectuals.

After two world wars against authoritarianism and despotism it has become a dogma in the West that democracy is the only justifiable political order. Indeed, the political rights which the individual citizen possesses in most of western Europe go far beyond the most radical demands raised at the beginning of the century. The voting age has been steadily lowered. It is nowhere higher than twenty-five; in Germany and Italy it is twenty-one, and in Great Britain eighteen. Women have received the right to vote. Inequalities in voting, whether of a financial or an educational character, have been eliminated. The parliaments of the various states can be regarded as fully representative. One might have expected that in these circumstances the people of a nation would feel that by means of their parliament they could control their own fate. But one of Europe's problems is that the belief of the people in their capacity to determine the course of events has been shaken. The reputation and the influence of the parliaments has decreased. This phenomenon has its source in various factors, one of which is closely connected with the invention of new and expensive weapons, such as airplanes, rockets, and nuclear bombs. Since their construction is a costly and lengthy process, orders must be given years ahead, and the research necessary for developing these weapons requires steady financial support. Together with outlays for war pensions, military expenses represent a large fixed amount in each year's budget. Parliamentary command of the purse, originally the basis of parliamentary power, exists only to a very limited extent. Connected with the decline of parliament's control over the budget is the rise of the expert at the expense of the elected representative. The scientific problems involved in the maintenance of military preparedness and in the evaluation of the effectiveness and usefulness of weapons and weapons systems have become so complicated that they can be solved only by experts. In many disputes, the voice of the scientist carries more weight than the view of the elected representative. Economic planning too has come into the hands of experts. The members of parliaments frequently lack both the authority to reject the judgment of experts and the will to obstruct projects on which agreement has been reached among the experts and the representatives of business and labor. As long as there is antagonism and conflict in economic life, the holders of political power can choose among alternatives. But when interlocking economic interests establish a consensus, the task of the politicians becomes limited to ratifying the decisions made in other spheres.

The participation of almost all social groups in decision making has been accompanied by the disappearance of radical political forces. There seems to be no basis for parties working for fundamental changes because no groups are excluded from power. Differences between parties have become blurred. In elections choice is frequently determined by the personality and the appeal of the party leader rather than by the voters' preference for a particular policy. The leadership principle has penetrated the politics of democratic countries. This change has resulted partly from a shift in constitutional thinking. During the interwar years the executive was weak and the legislative was strong; at the end of the Second World War it was hoped that a reversal of this situation might help to bring about a less unfortunate political course. But primarily the diminished influence of parliament is due to advances in communication technology. Modern communication techniques focus attention on the leading statesmen. The head of the government appears on television to outline the program of his government or present his country's case during a crisis. He is viewed almost daily welcoming foreign visitors or inaugurating a new power station or a new hospital. His face and figure become familiar to the majority of the citizens. While the leaders of France, Germany, and Italy in the postwar years—De Gaulle, Adenauer, De Gasperi—have certainly been remarkable men, their extended tenure of office in countries inclined toward quick government changes has been to some extent due to the availability of technical devices permitting them to establish direct contact with the people; with the help of radio and television each acquired a definite "image"—selfless, paternalistic, unflappable—which inspired confidence. The concentration of power in the executive has the consequence that the far-reaching democratic rights which the individual has gained no longer assure him that he has real control over the course of events.

Questions and doubts about the functioning of the democratic system have emerged very slowly. In the first decades after the Second World War the reconstruction of economic life and the rebuilding of a new political order went hand in hand; realization of the rigidity of the system which had been established came later, coinciding with the rise of a new generation, which feels it stands outside.

THE NEW GENERATION

The problem of the new generation has been especially important because of the striking developments which, after the Second World War, transformed the demographic structure of Europe. Until 1940 the influence of population changes on political events was limited. To be sure, a steady increase in the German population heightened French fears of German rearmament, since France, with 41 million inhabitants, had only two thirds as many people as Germany, and the French population was almost stagnant. The French were also overtaken by the Italians, spurred by Mussolini to produce large families even though Italy was unable to feed its own people. But on the whole, population growth in Europe was slow, particularly in the 1920's. After the Second World War the entire picture changed; all over the continent a remarkable increase took place. It is true that the European rate of growth has remained moderate in comparison with that of other areas of the globe, but it is now considerably higher than it was in the first quarter of the century and double what it was in the 1920's. Italy, which before the Second World War had 42 million inhabitants, in the 1960's has 53 million; West Germany has about 60 million—not much less than East and West Germany combined before the Second World War—although it must be said that refugees from the east form part of the recent German population increase. The most astounding population rise has occurred in France: from 40 million after the Second

The events of May 1968 in Paris. *Students throwing pavement stones at the police on the Boulevard St. Michel.*

World War, to over 50 million. Certainly, some percentage of the increase in population is due to medical advances which have prolonged life. But the principal reason for the European population growth is a rise in the birthrate. For instance, in France the increase of births over deaths has been between 300,000 and 350,000 in every year since the Second World War. The result is a significant change in the age structure of the population. This shift in the age structure has occurred also in the other nations of western Europe and given a focal point to the discontent which exists despite full employment and economic well-being. The problems of education, particularly those of the universities, have become the testing ground for the viability of postwar western democracy. The crisis in education has revealed the contrast between the requirements of Europe's modernized society and its system of education.

In the early decades of the century, the educational system reflected the class structure, with primary schools for the great bulk of the people, and higher education for only a small group. Higher education was expensive, and in its form and content was calculated to impress upon the students the ideas and behavior standards of the ruling group. Since the end of the Second World War there have been efforts to make higher education accessible to a greater number of young people, by government grants and by facilitating the transition from the primary schools to those preparing for the universities. Before the First World War in the most developed European countries not more than eleven of 10,000 people attended the universities. In 1934 this number had tripled. At the beginning of the 1960's fifty of 10,000 were students and the number has steadily grown since then. Despite this remarkable increase, however, these figures demonstrate that the percentage of the population attending higher schools and universities is still very small. Since a university training provides the means for social improvement, educational institutions form an obstacle to making use of the opportunities for social and economic ascent which modern industrial society could offer.

The universities in their present form do not come up to the requirements of the times. They have not been able to handle the increase in the number of the student population which although insufficient in relation to the growth in overall population has been staggering. The most startling increase has occurred in France where the number of students has risen from 122,000 in 1939 to 247,000 in 1960 and to 514,000 in 1967; similar, although less startling figures can be given for all European nations. The extension of staff and facilities has not kept up with the needs of these masses; the students do not receive the training which they deserve. Difficulties are caused, however, not only by technical problems of adjustments to greater numbers. Because of their traditions the universities find it difficult to respond to the needs of modern industrial society. Because industry requires a scientifically and technically trained personnel, and because such specialized knowledge provides the best possibilities for advancement into the decision-making group, the universities will have to concentrate on professional training for practical life. But this pressure for a professional mass education runs counter to the assumptions which, consciously or unconsciously, have determined the character of the European universities. Among them is the view that the well-educated person can fulfill almost any task; it was only in 1968 that the report of a British civil-service committee admitted that in preparation for the civil service, the acquisition of specialized knowledge may be more useful than a classical education. Another assumption, one which, it must be conceded, has played its part in establishing the reputation of the European universities, is that the university is a place for scientific research and scholarly discoveries and that only a small elite can be taught to accomplish these tasks. Admittedly, the resistance customary to innovations in any academic community has complicated the solution of these problems. But the lack of adjustment of higher education to social changes raises doubts about whether the revolutionary alterations which Europe has undergone since the Second World War have penetrated far below the surface and modified basic traditions and attitudes.

The significance of the educational problem in postwar Europe—the maintenance of an elitist structure in a democratic society—lies in the fact that it has provided the large generation of postwar youth with a practical experience which has focussed attention on the striking contrast between the world as it is and the claims which are made for it, between the claim that the people rule in a democracy and the powerlessness of parliaments to enforce their will against the "establishment"; between the appeal of workers' parties to revolution and their pursuit of advantages for the workers within the existing system. One of the main objections of the new generation to life in Europe—it has been said—is that it is "an institution-alization of hypocrisy."

But these issues and questions concern not only the young generation but most European intellectuals. Although Europe in the 1960's is well func-tioning and relatively prosperous, it does not provide the leisure, the freedom, and the cultural values of which intellectuals have dreamt. But because all elements of society are drawn as active partners into the economic and social order, there is no group, no class, no progressive political force, with which the intellectuals can easily identify. Thus, behind the smooth façade of a prosperous western Europe there is an intense intellectual crisis. The leading writers of the first decade after the Second World War—Brecht, who became almost more popular in the West than in the East, where he directed his theater; and Sartre, whose voice carried great weight in the political discussions of the postwar world—had been deeply concerned with social and political issues. They were committed to action in the political arena. For the following generation of writers, the en-tire structure of society makes no sense. The expectation aroused by pros-pects of reform or revolution is seen as an illusion—like Godot, for whom people wait in Samuel Beckett's play, but who doesn't exist. The task of art has become to demonstrate the absurdity of the world. The argument by reason comes to be replaced by appeals to emotion and imagination and traditional morals are rejected. Thus, there has been a breakdown in com-munication. Those who are established in the existing world no longer have anything to say to those who reject this world in its entirety and find in it nothing with which they can identify. One might see in this rejection, how-ever, not only a withdrawal but also a new beginning—the dawn of an awareness that we cannot chart a course for the future unless we take a probing look at the conditions of existence created by the revolution of our time.

SUGGESTIONS
FOR FURTHER READING

(Books marked * are available in paperback.)

The printed material on the history of the twentieth century—documentary publications, memoirs, comprehensive histories, historical monographs—would fill a library; the following bibliography is severely selective. It is limited to works published in English, with the emphasis on titles of recent date. Included are books providing a general orientation, as well as those describing in detail events which were treated only briefly in the text, because of limitations of space. Special attention has been given to books which permit insight into the conditions of life and to writings which contain interpretations different from those presented in the text.

Printed collections of documentary sources are not listed, but most of the works mentioned contain detailed bibliographies which indicate source material and may serve as guides for further reading.

GENERAL

Contemporary history poses particular problems for both research and presentation. These are well outlined in *Geoffrey Barraclough, *An Introduction to Contemporary History* (New York, 1964) (Penguin). There are few comprehensive treatments of the entire period from 1890 to the present or to the end of the Second World War; one of those is found in the *New Cambridge Modern History*, but the relevant Vol. XII exists in both an original and a revised version—*The Era of Violence*, ed. by David Thomson (Cambridge, Eng., 1960) and *The Shifting Balance of World Forces, 1898–1945*, ed. by C. L. Mowat (Cambridge, Eng., 1968)—and since these versions are not identical both of them must be considered. Illuminating essays on the outstanding problems of international politics are to be found in *Ludwig Dehio, *Germany and World Politics in the Twentieth Century* (New York, 1959) (Norton). For a broad treatment of social developments see *Peter N. Stearns, *European Society in Upheaval* (New York and London, 1967) (Macmillan) and for a brief outline of economic developments see Paul Alpert, *Twentieth Century Economic History of Europe* (New York, 1951). The basic factors determining the economic developments are analyzed in the *Cambridge Economic History of Europe*, Vol. VI, *The Industrial Revolutions and After*, ed. by M. M. Postan and H. J. Habakkuk (Cambridge, Eng., 1965).

418

FROM 1890 TO THE BEGINNING OF THE FIRST WORLD WAR

A lively description of the political scene in Europe before the First World War is given in *Barbara W. Tuchman, *The Proud Tower* (New York, 1966) (Bantam); the reader should be aware, however, that although the general picture stands up well, details are not always correct and the author has an anti-German bias. Much discussion has been aroused by the question of the extent to which intellectual developments in this period prepared the way for the new intellectual trends in the postwar world; for perceptive descriptions of the intellectual climate of this period see *H. Stuart Hughes, *Consciousness and Society* (New York, 1958) (Vintage) and *Gerhard Masur, *Prophets of Yesterday* (New York, 1961) (Harper Colophon); Christopher Caudwell, *Studies in a Dying Culture* (New York, 1938) is also pertinent, although it is concerned exclusively with the literary scene. A brilliant analysis, limited to the intellectual antecedents of later developments, is *Hannah Arendt, *The Origins of Totalitarianism* (New York, 1951) (Meridian). The facts concerning the economic influence of Europe in the non-European parts of the world can be learned from *Herbert Feis, *Europe: The World's Banker, 1870–1914* (New Haven, 1930) (Norton). The two most important works concerning the development of the concept of imperialism are *John A. Hobson, *Imperialism: A Study* (London, 1902) (Ann Arbor) and *V. I. Lenin, *Imperialism, the Highest Stage of Capitalism* (written 1916) (China Books; also International Publishers); for the crisis in Marxism brought about by the economic progress of this period, see Peter Gay, *The Dilemma of Democratic Socialism: Eduard Bernstein's Challenge to Marx* (New York, 1952) (Collier).

For all the great European powers there exist national histories covering this period, some of them reaching up to the Second World War or to the present. For Great Britain, see R. C. K. Ensor, *England, 1817–1914* (Oxford, 1936) and *Robert K. Webb, *Modern England: From the Eighteenth Century to the Present* (New York, 1968) (Dodd, Mead); for France, *D. W. Brogan, *France Under the Republic, 1870–1939* (New York, 1940) (Harper Torchbook, in two volumes), also published under the title *The Development of Modern France*, and *Modern France: Problems of the Third and Fourth Republics*, ed. by Edward Mead Earle (Princeton, N.J., 1951); for Spain, Raymond Carr, *Spain, 1808–1939* (Oxford, 1966); for Italy, Christopher Seton-Watson, *Italy from Liberalism to Fascism, 1870–1925* (London, 1967); for Germany, Hajo Holborn, *A History of Modern Germany*, Vol. III (New York, 1969), on the years 1840–1945; for Austria, *A. J. P. Taylor, *The Habsburg Monarchy, 1809–1918* (London, 1948) (Harper Torchbook); for Russia, *Sir Bernard Pares, *A History of Russia*, revised ed. (New York, 1953) (Vintage).

In addition, for an understanding of particular aspects of British history during this period one may turn to a number of illuminating biographies and autobiographies. *Roy Jenkins, *Asquith: Portrait of a Man and an Era* (New York, 1965) (Dutton), is the biography of the leading British statesman of the period by a prominent member of the Labor party who describes the problem of political leadership in a parliamentary system with deep understanding. The first two volumes of *Winston S. Churchill*, by Randolph S. Churchill—

Youth, 1874–1900 (Boston, 1966) and *Young Statesman, 1901–1914* (Boston, 1967)—deserve attention not only because of their significance in explaining Churchill's early development but also because of the light which they shed on the English ruling group. The power of the British monarch was limited, but Sir Harold Nicolson, in *King George the Fifth: His Life and Reign* (London, 1952), contributes to the analysis of important political developments in his account of the crisis over the House of Lords. Samuel Hynes, *The Edwardian Turn of Mind* (Princeton, 1968) is full of interesting details throwing light on unknown or forgotten aspects of the world before the First World War. The contrast between the autobiographies of two women prominent in politics, Margot Asquith, *Autobiography*, ed. by Mark Bonham Carter (Boston, 1962) and Beatrice Webb, *Our Partnership* (New York, London, and Toronto, 1948), is highly amusing. Among the many good British autobiographies the best is the five-volume series by Leonard Sidney Woolf, consisting of *Sowing* (New York, 1960), covering the years 1880–1904; *Growing* (New York, 1961), on 1904–1911; *Beginning Again* (New York, 1963, 1964), on 1911–1918; *Downhill All the Way* (New York, 1967), on 1919–1939; and *The Journey Not the Arrival Matters* (New York, 1969). It reaches from the beginning of the twentieth century to the present and is a moving commentary on the decline of the English liberal tradition.

For the two leading French statesmen we have good biographical treatments, Geoffrey Bruun, *Clemenceau* (Cambridge, Mass., 1943) and Gordon Wright, *Raymond Poincaré and the French Presidency* (Stanford, 1942). On the details of the Dreyfus case and the present evaluation of the importance of this affair, see Douglas Johnson, *France and the Dreyfus Affair* (London, 1966) and Guy Chapman, *The Dreyfus Case: A Reassessment* (London, 1955). For the background of the affair and some of its consequences see David B. Ralston, *The Army of the Republic: The Place of the Military in the Political Evolution of France, 1871–1914* (Cambridge, Mass., and London, 1967) and Eugen Joseph Weber, *The Nationalist Revival in France, 1905–1914* (Berkeley, Calif., 1959). Roger Henry Soltau, *French Political Thought in the Nineteenth Century* (New Haven, 1931), although not a recent book, is distinguished by its understanding of the tension which led to the separation of church and state.

For Spain, see Joan Connelly Ullman, *The Tragic Week: A Study of Anticlericalism in Spain, 1875–1912* (Cambridge, Mass., 1968), which describes in detail the crisis which frustrated attempts at reform.

The particular character of the Italian parliamentary system is well presented in A. William Salomone, *Italy in the Giolittian Era: Italian Democracy in the Making* (Philadelphia, 1960). For the concrete issues involved in the problem of the Italian south, see Denis Mack Smith, *A History of Sicily: Modern Sicily after 1713* (New York, 1968).

Considering the crucial importance of Germany before 1914, the available historical treatments are meager. Michael Balfour, *The Kaiser and His Times* (London, 1964) is probably the best biography of William II. Norman Rich, *Friedrich von Holstein: Politics and Diplomacy in the Era of Bismarck and Wilhelm II* (Cambridge, Eng., 1965) gives an interesting picture of the German ruling group; for an understanding of the mentality of the German bourgeoisie in this period one turns best to a novel, Heinrich Mann, *Little Superman* (*Der Untertan*, 1918; originally trans. as *The Patrioteer*). For the impact of German industrial development on attitudes in the social democracy, see *Carl E. Schorske, *German Social Democracy, 1905–1917: The Development of the Great Schism* (Cambridge, Mass., 1955) (Wiley).

On Austria-Hungary, see Robert A. Kann, *The Habsburg Empire: A Study in Integration and Disintegration* (New York, 1957) and C. A. Macartney, *Hungary: A Short History* (Chicago, 1962), which provide details on the complex structure of the Habsburg monarchy.

In Russia, personal factors played a decisive role in the fall of tsarism. For a picture of the relevant political personalities of this period, see *Sir Bernard Pares, *The Fall of the Russian Monarchy* (London, 1939) (Vintage), and for the origin of the ideas dominating the rulers, see Robert F. Byrnes, *Pobedonostsev: His Life and Thought* (Bloomington, Ind., and London, 1968). The description of industrial life given in the first chapters of *I. Deutscher, *Stalin: A Political Biography* (New York and London, 1949) (Oxford Galaxy) and the discussion of *Theodore H. von Laue, *Why Lenin? Why Stalin? A Reappraisal of the Russian Revolution, 1900–1930* (Philadelphia and New York, 1964) (Lippincott) rightly stress the immense difficulties in the way of solving Russian economic and social problems.

DIPLOMATIC EVENTS AND THE FIRST WORLD WAR

The diplomatic history of the thirty-five years before the First World War has been examined in minute detail because archives of the foreign offices became accessible soon after 1918. The decisive years for the formation of new constellations among the powers are treated in William L. Langer, *The Diplomacy of Imperialism, 1890–1902*, 2 vols. (New York, 1935), which contains a discussion of the literature and concept of imperialism; articles by the same author collected in *Explorations in Crisis: Papers on International History* (Cambridge, Mass., 1969) study main events in the following decade. The methods and techniques of prewar diplomacy emerge clearly from Sir Harold Nicolson, *Portrait of a Diplomatist* (Boston and New York, 1930). The most comprehensive description of the events leading to the outbreak of the First World War will be found in Luigi Albertini, *The Origins of the War of 1914*, 3 vols. (London, New York, and Toronto, 1952–1957). For those who find these three volumes heavy going, *Laurence Lafore, *The Long Fuse* (Philadelphia and New York, 1965) (Lippincott) can be recommended as a brief and reliable account which also reviews previous literature. Vladimir Dedijer, *The Road to Sarajevo* (New York, 1966) has interest as a very detailed investigation of a special problem, that of responsibility for the events in Sarajevo. *Fritz Fischer, *Germany's Aims in the First World War* (New York, 1967) (Norton) is a study of German war aims but also throws much light on German responsibility for the outbreak of the war. The history of the war itself has been treated in many memoirs, among them those of Lloyd George and Churchill, and also in studies of military history. A valuable analysis of the connection between military planning and political necessities is Paul Guinn, *British Strategy and Politics, 1914–1918* (London, 1965), and the relationship between war and economic developments is investigated in Gerald D. Feldman, *Army Industry and Labor in Germany, 1914–1918* (Princeton, N.J., 1966), which deals with Germany but is of general interest because similar situations existed in other countries. The First World War is placed in a wider historical context in Hajo Holborn, *The Political Collapse of Europe* (New York, 1951).

THE INTERWAR PERIOD

A number of works supply good general views of important aspects of these decades. The connections which linked the two world wars are emphasized in *Raymond Aron, *The Century of Total War* (New York, 1954) (Beacon). The great divide in the interwar years affecting the role of Europe was the depression which began in 1929; for a review of its effects see *Survey of International Affairs, 1931*, ed. by Arnold J. Toynbee (London, 1932), and for a more detailed analysis of its impact in the various European countries see "The Great Depression," *Journal of Contemporary History*, Vol. IV, No. 4 (1969). Fascism is examined as a general European phenomenon in *European Fascism*, ed. by S. J. Woolf (New York, 1968) (Vintage). *E. H. Carr, *The Twenty Years' Crisis, 1919–1939* (London, 1939) (Harper Torchbook) is noteworthy as a document of the time rather than as a valid statement of the significance of these years. Those novels of André Malraux which have the crucial political events of this period as background suggest something of the revolutionary radicalism which the hesitating and wavering policy of the ruling groups produced.

The ideas and interests which influenced and determined the peace settlement have been thoroughly discussed and analyzed by Arno J. Mayer in *Political Origins of the New Diplomacy, 1917–1918* (New Haven, 1959) (Meridian) and *Politics and Diplomacy of Peacemaking. Containment and Counterrevolution at Versailles, 1918–1919* (New York, 1967) (Vintage). *Sir Harold Nicolson, *Peacemaking, 1919* (New York, 1939) (Universal Library) gives a report of the peace conference from a human angle. The results of all the peace negotiations are succinctly summarized in Arnold J. Toynbee, *The World after the Peace Conference* (London, 1925), and throughout the entire following period the yearly volumes of the *Survey of International Affairs*, to which the preceding Toynbee book is a prologue, are a helpful guide. The role of the Russian problem in the politics of the postwar years is clarified in Richard H. Ullman, *Britain and the Russian Civil War* (Princeton, N.J., 1968), at least insofar as Great Britain is concerned.

For a comprehensive treatment of the conduct of foreign affairs during the interwar years see *The Diplomats, 1919–1939*, ed. by Gordon Craig and Felix Gilbert (Princeton, N.J., 1953) (Atheneum). Sir Harold Nicolson, *Curzon: The Last Phase, 1919–1925* (New York, 1939) demonstrates the possibilities and advantages of traditional diplomacy in the settlement of the postwar world. *Louis Fischer, *The Soviets in World Affairs: A History of*

Relations Between the Soviet Union and the Rest of the World, 1917–1929 (Princeton, N.J., 1951) (Vintage) and James Barros, *The Corfu Incident of 1923: Mussolini and the League of Nations* (Princeton, N.J., 1965) show the techniques used by Communist and Fascist diplomacy in the 1920's. For a brilliant summarization of the failure of diplomacy in the 1930's see *Winston S. Churchill, *The Second World War*, Vol. I, *The Gathering Storm* (Boston, 1948) (Bantam). In general, the events of foreign policy in the 1930's cannot be separated from the internal history of the various European countries, extensively treated in books listed in the following paragraphs.

The two states on which we have an overabundance of historical literature are Germany and Great Britain. This is natural because their policies were crucial for the development of the interwar years.

For a survey of the history of the Weimar Republic, see *S. William Halperin, *Germany Tried Democracy* (New York, 1946) (Norton). Two leading statesmen of the Weimar Republic are treated in Klaus Epstein, *Matthias Erzberger and the Dilemma of Germany Democracy* (Princeton, N.J., 1959) and *Henry Ashby Turner, Jr., *Stresemann and the Politics of the Weimar Republic* (Princeton, N.J., 1963) (Princeton); these books indicate how precarious the hold of the democratic forces was. The strength of the opponents of the republic is delineated in *Gordon Craig, *The Politics of the Prussian Army, 1640–1945* (New York, 1955) (Oxford Galaxy) and also in Andreas Dorpalen, *Hindenburg and the Weimar Republic* (Princeton, N.J., 1964), which portrays the surrender of power to the Nazis. For intellectual trends which contributed to the rise of the Nazis see *George L. Mosse. *The Crisis of German Ideology* (New York, 1964) (Universal Library). On Germany under the Nazis only a few books will be mentioned, works which throw light on the diverse aspects of the regime. *Alan Bullock, *Hitler: A Study in Tyranny* (London, 1952) (Harper Torchbook) is the best biography of Hitler, and Hermann Rauschning, *The Voice of Destruction* (New York, 1940) the best report about Hitler by a former adherent. An example of the establishment and functioning of Nazi control is presented in Oron J. Hale, *The Captive Press in the Third Reich* (Princeton, N.J., 1964). For the cultural policy of the Nazis see Barbara Miller Lane, *Architecture and Politics in Germany, 1918–1945* (Cambridge, Mass., 1968). The impact of the Nazi regime on the German social structure is carefully analyzed in *David Schoenbaum, *Hitler's Social Revolution: Class and Status in Nazi Germany, 1933–1939* (New York, 1966) (Doubleday Anchor). A colorful but rather simplified account of the Nazi years, with a very full bibliography, is *William L. Shirer, *The Rise and Fall of the Third Reich: A History of Nazi Germany* (New York, 1960) (Fawcett Crest also Simon and Schuster, in two volumes).

On Great Britain, a lively, amusingly prejudiced history of the interwar years is A. J. P. Taylor, *English History, 1914–1945* (New York and Oxford, 1965); the social problems of this period are well presented in *Robert Graves and Alan Hodge, *The Long Week-End: A Social History of Great Britain, 1918–1939* (New York, 1941) (Norton), and for a discussion of British policy from the point of view of Labor see Alan Bullock, *The Life and Times of Ernest Bevin*, Vol. I, *Trade Union Leader, 1881–1940* (London, Melbourne, and Toronto, 1960). A central issue of historical discussion is the appeasement policy of the 1930's. For the problems of decision making in British policy, see D. C. Watt, *Personalities and Policies: Studies in the Formulation of British Foreign Policy in the Twentieth Century* (Notre Dame, Ind., 1965). The attitude of the entire group of appeasers emerges brilliantly from *A. L. Rowse, *Appeasement: A Study in Political Decline, 1933–1939* (New York, 1961) (Norton). For biographies of two of the main appeasers see Andrew Boyle, *Montagu Norman: A Biography* (London, 1967) and William R. Rock, *Neville Chamberlain* (New York, 1969). The latter book discusses the entire dispute about the appeasement policy and tries hard to be fair to the appeasers —too hard, in my opinion. The desperation among the young produced by the policy of the ruling group is movingly evoked in *Peter Stansky and William Abrahams, *Journey to the Frontier: Two Roads to the Spanish Civil War* (Boston, 1966) (Norton). Hugh Dalton, *The Fateful Years: Memoirs, 1931–1945* (London, 1957) must be mentioned as the best book of political memoirs on this period.

To gain an understanding of the policy of France in the interwar years, see the reports of one of the best-informed journalists of the time, collected in Alexander Werth, *The Twilight of France, 1933–1940* (New York, 1942). Joel G. Colton, *Léon Blum: Humanist in Politics* (New York, 1966) gives a good picture of the most interesting French statesman of this period. Geoffrey Warner, *Pierre Laval and the Eclipse of France* (New York, 1968) represents a very substantial contribution to our understanding of the evolution of French appeasement and defeatism.

On Russia, for an understanding of the situation which existed before Stalin's rise to power see *Adam B. Ulam, *The Bolsheviks: The Intellectual and Political History of the Triumph of Communism in Russia* (New York and London, 1965) (Collier). Because of Stalin's predominance in this period the previously mentioned, detailed biography by *I. Deutscher, *Stalin: A Political Biography* (New York and London, 1949) (Oxford Galaxy), is useful. *Ilya Ehrenburg, *Memoirs, 1921–1941* (Cleveland and New York, 1964) (Universal Library) shows the conditions of intellectual work in Stalin's time.

On Italy, for the rise of Fascism see the book, previously mentioned, by Christopher Seton-Watson, *Italy from Liberalism to Fascism, 1870–1925* (London, 1967). *H. Stuart Hughes, *The United States and Italy* (Cambridge, Mass., 1953) (Norton) places this development in a broader context, and Charles F. Delzell, *Mussolini's Enemies: The Italian Anti-Fascist Resistance* (Princeton, N.J., 1961) shows the oppressive nature of the regime— even before Mussolini came under Nazi influence.

The Spanish Civil War was an international event, but also the climax of the internal developments in Spain during the 1920's and 1930's; as such it is presented in *Gabriel Jackson, *The Spanish Republic and the Civil War, 1931–1939* (Princeton, N.J., 1965) (Princeton) and in *Stanley Payne, *The Spanish Revolution* (New York, 1970) (Norton). A clear, general account of the war will be found in *Hugh Thomas, *The Spanish Civil War* (New York, 1961) (Harper Colophon).

For an exposition of developments in the Balkan countries and their dependence on the policy of the great European powers, see *Hugh Seton-Watson, *Eastern Europe Between the Wars, 1918–1941* (Cambridge, Eng., 1945) (Harper Torchbook). This dependence emerged clearly in the Czech crisis. *John W. Wheeler-Bennett, *Munich: Prologue to Tragedy* (London, 1948) (Viking Compass), although no longer quite up-to-date, remains valuable as a testimony of the emotional atmosphere surrounding the Czech crisis and Munich.

THE SECOND WORLD WAR

The events of the Second World War are fully described in *Gordon Wright, *The Ordeal of Total War, 1939–1945* (New York, Evanston, Ill., and London, 1968) (Harper Torchbook); this book has an excellent bibliography. It should be mentioned that two of the main actors in the Second World War have written memoirs that not only have great historical interest but are also remarkable literary achievements: *Winston S. Churchill, *The Second World War,* 6 vols. (Boston, 1948–1953) (Bantam) and *Charles de Gaulle, *The Complete War Memoirs of Charles de Gaulle, 1940–1946,* 3 vols. in one, Vol. I trans. by Jonathan Griffin, Vols. II–III trans. by Richard Howard (New York, 1955–1960) (Simon and Schuster). Sir Llewellyn Woodward, *British Foreign Policy in the Second World War* (London, 1962) provides an illustration of the interaction of political and military events. The psychological attitude of the British people to the war emerges from Isaiah Berlin, *Mr. Churchill in 1940* (Boston and Cambridge, n.d.), and of the Russian people from *Alexander Werth, *Russia at War, 1941–1945* (New York, 1964) (Avon). An outstanding story of intelligence operations is presented in F. W. Deakin and G. R. Storry, *The Case of Richard Sorge* (New York, 1966). For the German side of the war see Harold C. Deutsch, *The Conspiracy Against Hitler in the Twilight War* (Minneapolis, 1968); F. H. Hinsley, *Hitler's Strategy* (Cambridge, Eng., 1951); and *Hugh R. Trevor-Roper, *The Last Days of Hitler* (New York, 1947) (Collier).

AFTER THE SECOND WORLD WAR

Developments in Europe since the Second World War have been so closely interconnected that a separation into different chronological periods is not feasible. From the point of view of foreign policy, Germany represented the most crucial issue; the international aspects of the German problem are well presented in John L. Snell, *Dilemma over Germany* (New Orleans, 1959). Clear, connected accounts of the Cold War are to be found in Louis J. Halle, *The Cold War as History* (New York and Evanston, Ill., 1967) and *John Lukacs, *A History of the Cold War* (New York, 1961) (Doubleday Anchor). The reasons for the Cold War are now hotly debated. The official American point of view that the war was a defense against Communist aggression has recently been strongly restated by Dean Acheson, *Present at the Creation* (New York, 1969). This view is no longer as generally accepted as it was at that time; many are convinced that American foreign policy was not free from aggressive and imperialist elements. See *Gar Alperovitz, *Atomic Diplomacy:*

Hiroshima and Potsdam (New York, 1965) (Vintage), and for a more balanced statement Gabriel Kolko, *The Politics of War: The World and United States Foreign Policy, 1943–1945* (New York, 1968). For a general survey of Russian foreign policy in this period, see *Adam B. Ulam, *Expansion and Coexistence: The History of Soviet Foreign Policy, 1917–1967* (New York and Washington, D.C., 1968) (Praeger). The manner in which the Bolsheviks established control in eastern Europe has been described in Hugh Seton-Watson, *The Pattern of Communist Revolution* (London, 1953). For a more detailed discussion of the events in the Balkans see *Robert Lee Wolff, *The Balkans in Our Time* (Cambridge, Mass., 1967) (Norton). A most informative description of the situation within the eastern bloc is Zbigniew K. Brzezinski, *The Soviet Bloc: Unity and Conflict* (Cambridge, Mass., 1960).

Regarding western Europe, the most striking development, the emergence of cooperation between Germany and France, is described in *F. Roy Willis, *France, Germany, and the New Europe, 1945–1967* (Stanford and London, 1968) (Oxford Galaxy). The changes in France since the Second World War have been startling. A novel by *Simone de Beauvoir, *The Mandarins* (1954) (Popular Library; also Meridian), is an interesting reproduction of the intellectual atmosphere in France at the time of the end of the war; the principal figures of the novel, although under disguised names, are Sartre and Camus. For a general survey of the economic and political developments in France after the war, see Donald C. McKay, *The United States and France* (Cambridge, Mass., 1951). A special study of the problems created by the colonial wars and the military opposition to the Fourth Republic is George Armstrong Kelly, *Lost Soldiers: The French Army and Empire in Crisis, 1947–1962* (Cambridge, Mass., 1965). An outstanding analysis of the entire French situation is *John Ardagh, *The New French Revolution* (New York, 1968) (Harper Colophon).

Writings in English on postwar Germany are less satisfactory. For German foreign policy in the postwar period see *Gordon Craig, *From Bismarck to Adenauer: Aspects of German Statecraft* (Baltimore, 1958) (Harper Torchbook). Lewis J. Edinger, *Kurt Schumacher: A Study in Personality and Political Behavior* (Stanford, 1965) provides a good introduction to the party struggles of the years immediately after the war, although since then a somewhat new situation has developed. The astounding Italian recovery has been carefully studied; see *H. Stuart Hughes, *The United States and Italy* (Cambridge, Mass, 1953) (Norton) and *Muriel Grindrod, *The Rebuilding of Italy: Politics and Economics, 1945–1955* (London and New York, 1955) (Oxford).

For Great Britain it might be well to refer to the above-mentioned book by *Robert K. Webb, *Modern England: From the Eighteenth Century to the Present* (New York, 1968) (Dodd, Mead), which uses the somewhat dispersed literature in a critical way. As an amusing and enlightening, although not always quite reliable, analysis of the British social structure, *Anthony Sampson, *Anatomy of Britain* (London, 1962) (Harper Colophon) deserves to be read. For the issues which may dominate British and European policy in the coming years see Robert L. Pfaltzgraff, Jr., *Britain Faces Europe* (Philadelphia, 1969).

Index